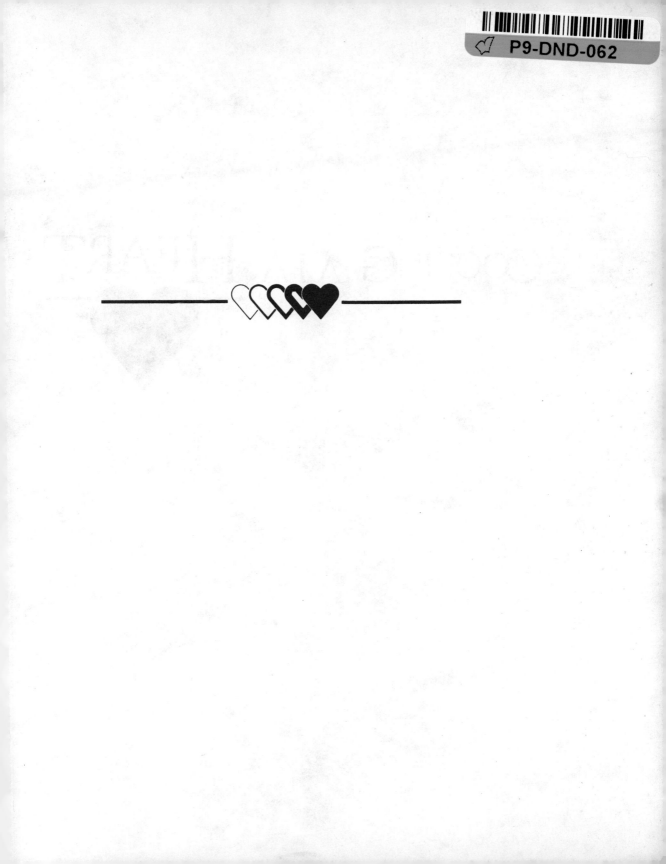

COOKING À LA HEART

COOKING À LA HEART

Delicious Heart Healthy Recipes
to Reduce the Risk of Heart Disease
and Stroke

written by:
Linda Hachfeld, M.P.H., R.D.
Betsy Eykyn, M.S.

SECOND EDITION

APPLETREE PRESS, INC.
Mankato, Minnesota

Published by Appletree Press, Inc.
151 Good Counsel Drive   Suite 125   Mankato, Minnesota 56001

Designed by Harlan Bloomer, M.F.A.
Illustrations by Barry Travis and Larry Eppard

First edition, first through fourth printings: 35,000 copies
Second edition, first printing: 10,000 copies

Library of Congress Cataloging-in-Publication Data

Hachfeld, Linda Jane, 1952-
    Cooking à la Heart.
    Delicious Heart Healthy Recipes to Reduce the Risk
    of Heart Disease and Stroke.

    Bibliography: p. [433]-438
    Includes Index.
    1. Low-fat diet—Recipes   2. Low-cholesterol diet—Recipes
    3. Salt-free diet—Recipes   4. Cookery, Minnesota.   5. Nutrition   6. Health.
    I. Eykyn, Betsy.   II. Appletree Press, Inc.   III. Mankato Heart Health Program Foundation
    IV. Title.

RM 237.H33 1992   641.53
ISBN 0-9620471-2-0 hardcover
ISBN 0-9620471-3-9 softcover

Printed in the United States of America

COOKING À LA HEART is recommended by experts...

"This is a terrific book! It has everything you want from a cookbook for your patients, including nutrient analysis, fiber content and good background information."

Nadine Braunstein, R.D., Boston, Massachusetts

"This may become the 'bible' for heart healthy eating. It has lots of practical advice with a wide array of community tested recipes."

Jane Andrews, R.D., Rochester, New York

"Eating good food does make a difference to health and quality of life! This book teaches preventive nutrition—not just for heart disease. I highly recommend it!"

Kathy King Helm, R.D., Lake Dallas, Texas

"**Cooking à la Heart** offers a practical, hands-on guide to healthy eating. Up-to-date nutrition information and a wide variety of recipes with nutrient breakdown will surely help the reader translate scientific information into day-to-day menus for the family."

Liz Weiss, M.S., R.D., Producer
CNN Nutrition News   Atlanta, Georgia

"If you're determined to make more than a half-hearted attempt this year to be kind to your health, this should be your first resolution: Get a copy of **Cooking à la Heart**."

Eleanor Ostman, Food & Nutrition Editor
St. Paul Pioneer Press Dispatch   St. Paul, Minnesota

"**Cooking à la Heart** is a wonderful investment for heart-healthy eating and cooking. The first chapter is terrific! It explains healthy dietary recommendations and shows how to make substitutes for rich foods without compromising flavor. This book is very complete!"

Angela Allen, Health Editor
The Columbian Newspaper   Van Couver, Washington

6

Reviewers and Readers highly recommend COOKING À LA HEART...

"The recipes are simple and inventive, proof that eating healthily does not have to mean giving up favorite foods... the cookbook begins with a primer that is one of the best sources of nutritional information we've run across... Practical & functional at a very fair price."

Harrowsmith Magazine

"**Cooking à la Heart** presents unified dietary guidelines that are clearly explained in an eye-catching format. The recipes are carefully written with complete directions and many interesting serving ideas. The broad range of enticing recipes will appeal to a variety of clients. It is visually attractive and presents scientifically accurate material in an enthusiastic, positive manner that motivates and supports heart healthy food selection and preparation behaviors.

Journal of Nutrition Education

"Last fall I received your book, **Cooking à la Heart**, for my birthday. I fell in love with it. Not only does it have wonderful recipes, but it is also very informative. I've learned so much from your book."

Pat Sahli, Colorado Springs, Colorado

"Your book is just what I needed after my bypass surgery! It is a wonderful resource book for healthy eating."

Jenelda Moore, Valdez, Alaska

"My husband and I are both on a low-cholesterol diet and sometimes it's difficult to know just what I can substitute in my regular recipes. Your book is so very helpful."

Mrs. Darlene Richmond, Bear Lake, Michigan

DEDICATION

Mankato, Minnesota, set in a wooded river valley, is a typical midwestern small city. What makes it unique are the people whose wide interests were focused in 1980 on their personal wellness by the Minnesota Heart Health Program. Mankato task forces pioneered numerous activities to develop an educational process to determine if a community could change its habits and customs to reduce the risk of cardiovascular disease.

Mankato's citizens have given a resounding "yes!" to this question.

Today, when we glance out the windows of the Program's office, located on the main intersection of town, we can see joggers and others walking briskly on the sidewalks. These same people, in the winter, enjoy walking in the nearby enclosed shopping mall or running on indoor tracks at the state university, up on the hill, or at the YMCA. Many also record their time spent in physical activity for their businesses' part in the "Shape-Up Challenge".

A restaurant in the same downtown mall is one of thirteen in town with hearts on the menu highlighting selections which meet the low-fat, low-sodium criteria of "Dining à la Heart". This program began with restaurateurs and local citizens sitting around a table brainstorming ways to help diners make healthy choices and feel good about them.

Grocery stores all over town have labels on their food shelves and in the meat and dairy cases designating foods which are low in sodium and fat and qualify for "Shopping Smart".

Down the street from the office a billboard proclaims "Check your blood pressure", offering free Blood Pressure Council measurements. Another, farther out, asks "Do you know your cholesterol level?".

Changes in school lunches went along with the "Hearty Heart" curriculum on diet and exercise; the children "Jog and Log" for 10 minutes a day in class; and they compete with their favorite recipes in the "Heart's Delight" recipe contest.

"Quit and Win" campaigns have helped to clean the air by motivating smokers to put out their cigarettes.

Early results from the study indicate that Mankatoans truly have benefitted from the variety of changes they've made and there is interest in continuing to move ahead into even healthier life-styles. In answer to the numerous requests from those who sincerely want to know how to prepare meals at home which are heart healthy, we have written this book.

We dedicate "Cooking à la Heart" to all those who have so enthusiastically supported the Mankato Heart Health Program.

Nadine Sugden
Contributing Editor

CONTENTS

PREFACE

In the quarter century during which I have been writing about medicine and health, it has become increasingly clear that we live—and that we die—as we eat. Our twentieth century habits—particularly our current penchant for high-fat, high-sugar and high-calorie foods along with inadequate physical exercise—dramatically increase our chances of developing heart disease, cancer, obesity, high blood pressure, diabetes, osteoporosis and other ailments that unnecessarily tarnish the Golden Years of so many millions of Americans.

Through reasonable modifications in how we choose, prepare and serve our foods we can go a long way towards reducing the toll of premature and preventable illness and increase our chances for a long, happy, healthy life.

Eating healthfully is neither difficult nor boring. Nor is it a life of deprivation and self denial. Rather, as diners who follow the guidelines, recipes and menu plans of *Cooking à la Heart* are destined to discover, healthful eating is a stimulating trip into new and familiar taste sensations that can help to keep you enjoying good food for many more years than you otherwise might.

Jane Brody
Personal Health Columnist
The New York Times

INTRODUCTION

A long Minnesota tradition, exploring the causes of heart attack and stroke, has resulted in the finding that there are sick (and well) populations just as there are sick (and well) individuals! This central idea led to the Mankato Heart Health Program and one of its many exciting community outcomes, *Cooking à la Heart.*

We and our colleagues overseas found people (e.g., Eastern Finland), having far more heart attacks than we, and others (e.g., the Greek islands and southern Japan) with almost none at all. We also demonstrated that the most consistent and powerful influence on the community-wide risk of heart attacks is the average blood cholesterol level. Where it is high, there are many heart attacks. Where it is low, there are virtually none. Where it goes up or down over time, so, after a few years, do the deaths from heart attack.

These findings in populations, combined with clinical and laboratory research, indicated to us some years ago that blood cholesterol level is the central factor in a community's risk of cardiovascular disease. Mass elevated cholesterol level is, in turn, most strongly influenced by the habitual eating customs of a community. Living then in a country where heart attack risk overall is relatively high, your and my individual risk depends importantly on other factors, especially our heredity, but also smoking habits and blood pressure.

Studies in Minnesota also established clearly that we can substantially modify our blood cholesterol level, that of our family and even whole communities. The cholesterol-lowering eating pattern is easy, palatable, attractive and economic. Preventive experiments indicate that heart attack risk is reduced in groups by about 2% for every 1% average cholesterol-lowering. Moreover, in Minnesota over the past 20 years more healthy eating and exercise patterns, decreasing smoking and control of high blood pressure have contributed to the recent 30% fall in coronary death rates.

But the background for *Cooking à la Heart* goes even farther back in time, to when all people on earth were either hunters or gatherers. Today we remain fundamentally adapted to that eating and lifestyle because it is only about 500 generations since agriculture and civilization began. It has been only 10 generations since the Industrial Revolution began and only a couple of generations since automation and automotion and affluence have affected most of us.

Few would choose to return to hunter-gatherer times, or even to the lifestyle of heart attack-free Mediterranean and Asian farmers. But to the extent we understand those earlier lifestyles, the better we can adapt our ways to modern abundant eating and sedentary living.

As best we can piece it together, the hunter-gatherer lifestyle, to which our bodies adapted through the centuries, was characterized by regular physical activity to secure food and subsistence, up to 30 hours a week. This alternated with rest and socialization, in a harmonious cycle. It is likely that our major foods were plants, rich in starches, fiber, vegetable protein, minerals and vitamins. These plant foods were the staples that allowed humankind to survive and thrive throughout the ages. Hunting for more concentrated food was an early and major adaptation. Humans have sought out and eaten meat opportunistically, probably for all time. But "the opportunity" did not arrive all that often, and the wild game that we humans ate earlier was extremely lean compared to the meat of modern domesticated animals.

In addition, the diet to which we are metabolically adapted contained far more potassium than sodium, in legumes, fruits and vegetables, just the opposite of now. The heavy use of salt started only "recently" in history, with trade and the need to preserve food. Our body requirements for salt are quite low, as colleagues have found in South American Indians who work effectively near the equator with no added salt intake.

Most modern ethnic cuisines derive from the peasant dishes and traditional eating patterns of agriculturalists and pasturalists over the last 10,000 years. By trial and error, word of mouth, and example, healthy eating patterns were passed down, varied, attractive, and healthful, among Mediterranean, Middle Eastern and Asian cultures. They evolved with appropriate combinations of vegetable protein, such as beans and rice, tortillas and beans and the delightful combinations in couscous and other classic staples. This healthful eating pattern is punctuated, on occasion by small servings of meat and fowl, varying amounts of fishes and seafoods, and dominated by lots of legumes, starches, fruits and vegetables.

But all of a sudden, in a very few generations, industrial society produced the opportunity and economic capacity to eat more and fatter, sweeter and saltier foods, and new "staples" of Western countries. For example, as a colleague once explained, "Americans are the only people that were never weaned"; in other words, adults continue to drink whole milk all their lives as a beverage, rather than as elsewhere in the world, milk products as an occasional, rich food. Remarkable changes in animal husbandry and feeding came with the availability of cheap, surplus grains after World War II. This led to practices that produced obese beef, with much of the fat hidden in the fibers of the muscle. To this, combined with increased use of salt in processed foods, we have added easily accessible and concentrated calories of sucrose and alcohol. The crowning blow was disappearance of physical activity in our occupations, along with the automobile and "enforced" sedentation of mass television. On top of that came the mass addiction to American-style cigarettes.

There is a paradox in all this. Efficient American farms and agribusiness have eliminated deficiency disease for most of our society. This, along with better sanitation and medical care, has resulted in many more of us surviving to older ages. But the down side is the arrival of the insidious, mass, middle-age diseases related to modern lifestyles, i.e., fatty artery disease, heart attack, stroke, obesity, diabetes, chronic lung disease from smoking, and the increased rates of cancer related to smoking and to fatty eating patterns.

The Minnesota Heart Health Program brings good news. Heart attack rates are coming down. People are finding that healthier lifestyles open new and attractive benefits. The food industry and agriculture are moving rapidly to offer us more healthy choices. In *Cooking à la Heart,* the innovative volunteers of the Mankato Heart Health Program have found an American way to make our eating pattern more healthy, while at the same time, attractive and convenient. In *Cooking à la Heart* you will find that something good happened in a Minnesota town, and you can apply it to your family's healthier lifestyle.

Henry Blackburn, M.D.
Principal Investigator,
Minnesota Heart Health Program

ACKNOWLEDGEMENTS

We are grateful to the following for the time and the effort they have devoted to this project:

Cookbook Steering Committee

Linda Hachfeld, M.P.H., R.D.
Principal Author and Cookbook
  Coordinator

Betsy Eykyn, M.S.
Contributing Author and Recipe
  Editor

Nadine Sugden, B.A.
Taste-testing Coordinator and
  Editor

Shirley Durfee, B.S.
Associate Editor

Marion Lutes, B.S.
Assistant Editor

Harlan Bloomer, M.F.A.
Book Design

Richard Swanson, M.S.
Mankato Heart Health Program
  Director

Joyce Nettleton, D. Sc., R.D.
Special Advisor

Special Support:

Ogden Confer, Sr.
Business and Financial Advisor,
  without whose support there
  would be no cookbook

George Peterson
Publications Advisor

Jane Confer
Marketing Committee Chair

Dorothy Radichel
Assistant Taste-testing
  Coordinator

Barry Travis
Original Illustrations

Tim Desley
Graphic Arts Assistance

Herb Mocol
Chairman of the Board of
  Directors

Jane Brody,
Personal Health Columnist
The New York Times
New York, NY

Henry Blackburn, M.D.
Minnesota Heart Health Pro-
  gram Director
University of Minnesota
Minneapolis, MN

Joanne DeVore, R.D.
Nutrient Analysis Assistance
Sturdy Memorial Hospital
Attleboro, MA

Reviewers:

Henry Blackburn, M.D.
Principal Investigator and
   Director of the Minnesota
   Heart Health Program
University of Minnesota
Minneapolis, MN

Rebecca Mullis, Ph.D., R.D.
Director of Nutrition
Minnesota Heart Health
   Program
University of Minnesota
Minneapolis, MN

Mary Winston, Ed.D., R.D.
Senior Science Consultant
American Heart Association
Dallas, TX

Liz Weiss, M.S., R.D.
Producer Nutrition News
Cable News Network,
   Atlanta, GA

Kathy King Helm, R.D.
Nutrition Entrepreneur and
   author
Lake Dallas, TX

Joyce Nettleton, D.Sc., R.D.
Nutrition Consultant and
   Lecturer, Tufts University
Lexington, MA

*Current and Former
Mankato Heart
Health Program
Advisory Board
members:*

Jane Confer
Jerry Crest
Mayor David Dehen, D.C.
John Eustermann, M.D.
Virgil "Hap" Halligan
Vera Kvamme, R.N.
Mary Lofy
Fred Lutz, Jr.
William Manahan, M.D.
Rich Meyer
Mayor Herb Mocol
Betty Nelson
C.R. Nelson
Margaret Preska, Ph.D.
Joe Richter
Jim Schindle
Roger Schoeb
Rolf Storvick, M.D.
Nadine Sugden
John Votca

Ogden Confer, Sr.
Rev. Stephanie Frey
Mary Hall
Richard Helgesen, Ph.D.
Jared How
Starr Kirklin
Mike Kluck
John Linder
Delwin Ohrt, M.D.
R.J. Rehwaldt, Ph.D.
Steward Siebens
Paul Stevens
Don Stordahl
Ken Snyder
Brett Taylor, Jr.
Tommy Thompson
Rev. Jack Weston

A WORD ABOUT THE
MANKATO HEART HEALTH PROGRAM

In 1980, the Minnesota Heart Health Program, a pioneering effort in heart disease prevention, was begun by the Division of Epidemiology, School of Public Health at the University of Minnesota and funded by the National Heart, Lung and Blood Institute. This research and demonstration project is based on the premise that a community, by working to change habits and customs that had led to a high rate of heart attack and stroke, can reduce its risk of cardiovascular disease and improve its quality of life.

The Mankato Heart Health Program was the first of three field sites in the Minnesota Program and focuses on the whole community with emphasis on those still healthy. Over the life of the project, a Mankato-University partnership has tested educational strategies and evaluated community-wide changes in:

- eating patterns which contribute to high blood cholesterol, high blood pressure and overweight;

- smoking habits;

- physical activity and fitness;

- incidence and severity of heart disease.

Messages to encourage more healthy choices were started during public screening followed by mass media communication promoting programs for education of adults, youth and family and health professionals.

A Community Advisory Board was formed to insure community input, promote general awareness and give acceptance and understanding of the program.

Interest in continuing the many successful programs following termination of the research project led the Board to form the Mankato Heart Health Program Foundation, Inc., and to incorporate some of its activities into existing agencies and organizations. The non-profit Foundation has supported the ongoing efforts in health promotion and launched new initiatives of its own, of which *Cooking à la Heart* is a major example. Its attractive format and contents were developed, tested and written by Mankato volunteers and published locally. Proceeds from book sales return to the community through health promotion programs.

Read, eat and enjoy!

1

Cooking à la Heart
DIETARY RECOMMENDATIONS

Our goal in preparing **Cooking à la Heart** was to create a book that is as meaningful and useful as possible. This included, among other things, addressing the conflicts arising from the plethora of current dietary recommendations.

In **Cooking à la Heart,** we have unified the nutritional recommendations of the eight leading agencies which study the connections between lifestyle and health. Our guidelines and recipes are consistent with the recommendations of the following agencies:

- The United States Department of Health and Human Services
- The United States Department of Agriculture
- The American Heart Association
- The American Cancer Society
- The American Dietetic Association
- The National Institutes of Health
- The National Academy of Sciences
- The National Cholesterol Education Program (NCEP)

We need over 50 nutrients to stay healthy.

1. Eat a Variety of Foods.

Good nutrition is the result of long-term eating patterns. Nutritionists recognize that we need over 50 different nutrients to stay healthy. These include fats, proteins, carbohydrates, vitamins, minerals and water, all of which are found in foods in varying amounts. No single food or food group supplies all the essential nutrients in the amounts we need. When planning, shopping, and preparing meals for yourself and others, use the following guide for a varied and nutritious diet.

Food Group	Suggested Daily Servings*	Serving Examples
Breads, Cereals and other Grain products	6 to 11 (include several whole-grain products)	1/2 cup rice, 1 slice bread, 1 ounce of ready-to-eat breakfast cereal
Fruits	2 to 4	A piece of whole fruit such as an apple, orange, kiwi, 1/2 cup fruit juice, a melon wedge

continued

Eat a Variety of Foods, continued

Food Group	Suggested Daily Servings*	Serving Examples
Vegetables	3 to 5 (include all types regularly: dark-green leafy, yellow-orange and starchy vegetables)	1/2 cup cooked or chopped raw vegetables, 1 cup leafy raw vegetable such as lettuce or spinach
Legumes, Fish, Poultry, Lean Meat, Nuts, Seeds and Eggs	2 to 3 (limit meat to 6 ounces a day; egg yolks to 4 a week)	1/2 cup cooked dry beans 2 tablespoons peanut butter
Low-fat dairy	2 to 4 (3 for teens and women who are pregnant or breast-feeding)	1 cup low-fat milk, 1-1/2 ounces low-fat cheese, 8 ounces low-fat yogurt

* Note: The pattern for daily food choices described above was developed for those who regularly select foods of all types. Vegetarians and others who do not eat all types of foods may wish to contact a registered dietitian (R.D.) in their community for help in planning food choices.

Excess body weight is hazardous to our health.

2. Maintain Healthy Weight.

Excess body weight raises the risk of four major lifestyle-related diseases: heart disease, high blood pressure, diabetes and cancer. Approximately 40% of our population is overweight. Results of the Framingham Study indicate that even mild degrees of overweight endanger your health. The risk of high blood pressure among overweight people is nearly three times that for those who are not overweight. In addition, blood cholesterol levels are twice as high among those who are overweight and almost three times as high in people who are both overweight and have adult-onset diabetes.[1] Cancer mortality also climbs as weight increases, especially for those who are 40% or more overweight.

[1]National Institutes of Health. **National Institutes of Health Concensus Development Conference Statement on Health Implication of Obesity.** Volume 5, Number 9, 1985.

Recent findings indicate that the site of fat accumulation influences the risk of coronary heart disease. People who carry their extra body fat in their abdominal regions are more likely to suffer a heart attack and have a tenfold greater risk of stroke than those whose fat is stored elsewhere throughout the body.

Waist-to-hip ratio (waist in inches divided by hips in inches) is important in determining whether you are at a high risk for coronary heart disease. Values greater than 1.0 for men and greater than 0.8 for women show an increased risk of heart disease.[2] For instance, a woman whose hips measure 40 inches should have a waist measurement no larger than 32 inches; a man whose hips measure 40 inches should have a waist measurement no larger than 40 inches.

Research suggests that a good method for losing weight and maintaining weight loss is a low-fat, high-carbohydrate diet plan divided into more than three meals a day, with the last meal of the day being the lightest. Converting carbohydrate calories to body fat uses about 25 percent of the calories as fuel, whereas, in converting fat calories to body fat, only 3 percent of fat calories are used in the fueling process. Thus, dietary fat is much more readily stored as body fat than are dietary carbohydrates.

Regular physical activity plays a major role in maintaining a desirable body weight. Our bodies were designed for exercise. Studies have shown that regular physical activity is associated with an increase in lean body mass, aerobic (lung) capacity, high-density lipoprotein levels, bone mass, physical strength and coordination. In fact, if you do not exercise regularly, you will be short-changing yourself and your body will grow old before its time.[3] Even if you are not overweight your body needs regular physical exercise. You may not feel much differently when you first begin to exercise, but there's a good chance that in six months you will:

Benefits of regular exercise

- ♥ Have improved your physical appearance.
- ♥ Look and feel more alert.
- ♥ Feel more energetic, agile and in control of your body.

continued

---

[2]Per Bjorntorp. "Differences Between Male and Female Obesity." **Nutrition & the M.D.** Volume 10, Number 1, 1984.

[3]Stanford Heart Disease Prevention Program. **The Exercise Book: For People Who Don't Exercise.** California: Stanford University, 1981.

♥ Be better able to cope with stress, tension, and depression.

♥ Have reduced your percentage of body fat. (The recommended percentage of body fat is 15-18% for men and 20-25% for women.)

♥ Have a better regulated appetite.

♥ Have stronger bones, thus, reducing the risk of osteoporosis.

♥ Have improved circulation.

♥ Have a better blood pressure reading.

♥ Have an improved blood chemistry.

♥ Have a more efficient heart capable of accomplishing the same amount of work with less effort.

These benefits can be achieved with exercise that is:

Brisk	raising heart and breathing rates
Sustained	done at least 15 to 30 minutes without interruption
Regular	repeated at least three times a week

Some examples of aerobic exercise are walking, running, jogging, bicycling (both stationary and regular), rowing, cross-country skiing, dancing, jumping rope, roller and ice skating and swimming. Examples of non-aerobic exercise are bowling, weight lifting and softball.

Body weight is not always an accurate measure of excess body fat. Answering "yes" to any of the following questions indicates you are carrying excess body fat:

Are you carrying excess body fat?

• Is your waist measurement close to or larger than your chest measurement?

• Is a fold of skin pinched from the back of your upper arm more than an inch thick?

• Does your middle interfere with the sight of your toes?

• Do you see ridges or bulges where there shouldn't be any when you are undressed?

Applying the "10-Calorie Rule"

A gradual but guaranteed way to lose excess body fat is to decrease the number of calories you now consume and increase the number of calories you burn. We recommend following the 10-Calorie Rule proposed by Dr. C. Wayne Callaway, M.D., Director of the Center for Clinical Nutrition at George Washington University. Allow yourself 10 calories a day for each *current* pound of body weight. Weight loss will be a safe 1 to 2 pounds a week, and if you stick with this formula, those extra pounds will *stay* lost.

Avoid weight cycling or the "yo-yo" effect, which results from repeated weight loss followed by weight gain. The lose-regain syndrome is most apt to occur with fad diets that promote rapid weight loss. Dieters lose weight only to gain it all back when they return to their former eating patterns. Indeed, they may even gain back more weight than they lost.

Evidence suggests that the cycle dieter loses weight primarily from lean muscle mass, while the weight re-gained is usually in the form of fat. Losing weight by reducing calories becomes increasingly difficult for repeat dieters. Dr. Kelly Brownell, a psychologist and obesity researcher at the University of Pennsylvania, found that dieters on a second cycle of dieting took twice as long to lose the same amount of weight they lost on the first cycle, and they gained it back three times as fast!

Promise yourself to keep the weight off.

When losing weight, make a serious commitment to maintain that loss. Look carefully at your overall eating pattern to see where you can cut unwanted calories. Here are some places to start.

General Calorie-Cutting Tips:

- Regulate total meat consumption to 6 ounces a day. Select the leanest cuts and remove all visible fat before eating (see *Meat Selection*). Do not eat the skin of poultry or game birds.
- Bake, broil, roast, grill, steam or microwave foods without adding fat. Avoid all frying. Skim the fat from broths and soups.
- Season with spices and herbs in place of butter, margarine, or fat-laden sauces (see *Seasoning Section*).
- Use low-fat dairy products.
- Avoid second helpings and gradually decrease serving sizes.

continued

- Reduce the amount of sugar in baked goods. In most recipes the amount of sugar can be reduced by one-third to one-half without affecting texture or taste.
- Substitute fruits and vegetables for fat- and sugar-laden snacks and desserts.

Calorie-Cutting Tips for the Holidays[4]

Enjoy parties and celebrations without gaining weight.

The five weeks between Thanksgiving and New Year's Day can be expansive times for many people. During the holidays there are office parties, potlucks, tree-trimming buffets, open houses and celebrations at which you are encouraged to eat and drink excessively. These spreads and your own body's "spread" can contribute to a post-holiday letdown. Here are eight ways to help you enjoy parties and celebrations without gaining weight:

- Taste tempting goodies but be satisfied with small portions. The second piece of fudge tastes no better than the first.

- Limit your alcohol consumption. For instance, if you're having wine with dinner, skip the cocktail. Alcohol provides only nutritionally empty calories and undermines discretion and determination to eat wisely.

- Since you will be tempted to overeat at a party or dinner, eat somewhat less for breakfast and lunch. However, do not skip meals or go to a party famished.

- Position yourself away from the hors d'oeuvres and find interesting people to occupy your attention. Stimulating conversation will keep your mind off eating.

- If you're bringing food to a party, make it low-calorie. Then you always have a wise choice available to you.

- If you're hosting a holiday event, plan a nutritionally balanced menu.

- Don't make more candies, cookies and cakes than you expect to serve and store them out of sight or the chances are, you'll eat more of them than either your guests or family members.

- Don't neglect daily exercise. No matter how busy you are, make exercise a part of your daily routine.

[4]Jane Brody. **Jane Brody's Good Food Book.** New York: W.W. Norton & Co., 1985.

Remind yourself how terrific you'll feel the next day after you've refrained from stuffing yourself or drinking too much. If you overindulge one day, don't punish yourself by repeating the performance. Just get back on schedule. One lapse is only that—it does not defeat you or your promise.

3. Choose a Diet Low in Fat, Saturated Fat and Cholesterol.

A diet high in fat raises blood cholesterol levels.

Currently, the average daily fat intake in the United States is approximately 37% or more of total calories,[5] the equivalent of a whole stick of butter![6] A diet high in fat, especially saturated fat, and cholesterol causes elevated blood cholesterol levels in many people. (For adults, blood cholesterol is considered to be high if it measures more than 200 milligrams of cholesterol per deciliter.)

According to the current statements of the National Cholesterol Education Program, the blood cholesterol level of most Americans is undesirably high. Reducing your fat and cholesterol intake will help reduce your blood cholesterol and lower your risk of heart disease and stroke. It also will reduce risk of diabetes and possibly some cancers (see Appendix: Guide to Healthier Eating).

How much fat should we eat?

On average, we should reduce that stick of "butter" to half that amount. For most of us this means consuming no more than 13-16 teaspoons of fat from all foods we eat each day. Determine your average caloric intake from the table below and stay within the recommended amount of fat. (Approximately 4.4 grams of fat is equivalent to 1 teaspoon of fat.)

Table 1: Recommended Daily Fat Intake

Average Calorie Intake	Recommended Grams of Fat	Equivalent Teaspoons of Fat
1200 Calories	33-40 grams	7-9 teaspoons
1500 Calories	42-50 grams	9.5-11 teaspoons
1800 Calories	50-60 grams	11-13 teaspoons
2100 Calories	58-70 grams	13-16 teaspoons
2400 Calories	66-80 grams	15-18 teaspoons
2700 Calories	75-90 grams	17-20 teaspoons
3000 Calories	83-100 grams	19-22 teaspoons

[5]R. Johnson. "Can You Alter Your Heart Disease Risk?" **Journal of the American Medical Association.** 245:19, 1981.

[6]Minnesota Heart Health Program. **Heartbeat: Fat Facts.** Minneapolis: University of Minnesota, September 1987.

Table 2: Trim the Fat

LOWER FAT	CALORIES	FAT (grams)
Meats, Poultry, Fish		
Grilled extra-lean hamburger, 3 ounces	180	7
Broiled tenderloin steak, 3 ounces	174	8
Broiled chicken breast, without skin, 3 ounces	90	3
Broiled cod, 3 ounces	90	<1
Roast lean pork loin, 3 ounces	196	9
Lean ham, 3 ounces	170	7
Milk and Milk Products		
Lowfat milk, 1% fat, 1 cup	100	2
Part skim mozzarella cheese, 1 ounce	70	5
Vanilla ice milk, 1/2 cup	90	3
Nonfat yogurt, 6 ounces	150	0
"Light" cream cheese, 1 ounce	60	5
Grain Products		
Bagel, 1 plain	120	2
Ry Krisp, original, 4 crackers/ounce	80	<1
English muffin, ½ plain	70	0
Pasta with tomato sauce, 1 cup	180	4
Angel food cake, 1 slice	140	0
Other Foods		
Pretzels, 1 ounce	110	1
Mustard, 1 tablespoon	10	<1
Vinegar or lemon juice, 2 tablespoons	5	0
Fresh fruit, apple, 1 medium	80	<1
continued		

Ounce for ounce, fat has more than twice as many calories as carbohydrates or protein.

How To Reduce The Fat In Your Diet

Awareness of the number of calories and grams of fat in foods will help you reduce the percentage of fat in your diet. Fat contains 9 calories per gram or 45 calories for every teaspoon while protein and carbohydrates contain only 4 calories per gram or 16 calories a teaspoon. In many cases, a simple substitution of a lower fat version of the same product, such as lean hamburger for regular or a change in preparation method such as broiled instead of deep-fried, makes a substantial reduction in the number of calories and amount of fat. Switching to low-fat dairy products reduces both the amount of total fat and saturated fat in your diet. Compare the calories and grams of fat in the foods listed in Table 2 to discover where you can "trim the fat."

Table 2: Trim the Fat, continued

HIGHER FAT	CALORIES	FAT (grams)
Meats, Poultry, Fish		
Grilled regular hamburger, 3 ounces	270	19
Broiled porterhouse steak, untrimmed, 3 ounces	254	18
Fried chicken breast, with skin, 3 ounces	221	11
Batter-dipped fish sticks, 3 ounces	250	18
Hot dogs, 2 average	320	30
Salami, 3 ounces	200	16
Milk and Milk Products		
Whole milk, 3.3% fat, 1 cup	150	8
Cheddar cheese, 1 ounce	110	9
Premium vanilla ice cream, 1/2 cup	170	12
Regular yogurt, 3.25% fat, 6 ounces	190	4
Cream cheese, 1 ounce	100	10
Grain Products		
Doughnut, 1 plain	180	9
Ritz crackers, 9 crackers/ounce	160	9
Croissant, 1 plain	170	9
Pasta with cream sauce, 1 cup	400	26
Layer cake, frosted, 2" x 2" x 1", 1 slice	280	10
Other Foods		
Potato chips, 1 ounce	150	10
Mayonnaise, 1 tablespoon	100	11
Salad dressing, Italian, 2 tablespoons	170	18
Cookies, chocolate chip, 2 medium	180	11

Sources: Jean Pennington and Helen Church, **Food Values of Portions Commonly Used**. 14th ed. 1985.
USDA HNIS, **Composition of Foods**: Handbooks 8-1, 8-4, 8-5, 8-13, revised 1976-86.
Personal communication with Eric Hentges, Ph.D., Assistant Director of Nutrition, National Livestock and Meat Board. April, 1988.

Much of the fat we eat is "hidden" or invisible. You must count both visible and invisible fat. Remember, it is the total amount of fat that is important; therefore, you have some latitude to allow for your personal taste. For example, if you prefer to drink whole milk rather than skim you can moderate your fat intake by omitting 2 teaspoons of fat elsewhere in your day's meals. You can exchange the fat in a cup of whole milk for the sour cream on your baked potato, or the margarine on your bread.

Table 3: Fat Equivalents

1 cup whole milk	=	1 cup skim milk + 2 teaspoons fat
1 cup 2% milk	=	1 cup skim milk + 1 teaspoon fat
8 ounces plain low-fat yogurt	=	1 cup skim milk + 1 teaspoon fat
1.5 ounces natural cheese	=	1 cup skim milk + 3 teaspoons fat
2 ounces processed American cheese	=	1 cup skim milk + 4 teaspoons fat
1/2 cup ice cream	=	1/3 cup skim milk + 2 teaspoons fat + 3 teaspoons sugar
2 ounces bologna	=	1 ounce lean meat + 3 teaspoons fat
2 tablespoons peanut butter	=	1 ounce lean meat + 3 teaspoons fat
1/4 cup seeds	=	1 ounce lean meat + 4 teaspoons fat
1/3 cup nuts	=	1 ounce lean meat + 5 teaspoons fat

The fats in food are of three different types.

The fats in foods are of three different types: saturated, polyunsaturated and monounsaturated. Research shows that saturated fats (those fats that are naturally solid at room temperature), raise blood cholesterol levels. Lard, butter, and hydrogenated shortenings are high in saturated fats.

Tropical oils such as coconut oil, palm (or palm kernel) oil and cocoa butter, whole-milk dairy products and meat contribute saturated fat to our diet. *Saturated fats* are often used in baked goods, mixes, prepared desserts and sauces. You can identify the presence of saturated fats in the foods you select from the grocery shelf by reading the label.

Table 4: Sources of Saturated Fat[7]

animal fat	hydrogenated vegetable oil
bacon fat	lamb fat
beef fat	lard
butter	meat fat
chicken fat	milk chocolate
cocoa butter	palm or palm kernel oil
coconut	pork fat
coconut oil	tallow
cream	turkey fat
egg and egg-yolk solids	vegetable shortening
hardened fat	whole-milk solids

[7]U.S. Dept. of Health and Human Services. **Eating to Lower Your High Blood Cholesterol.** Bethesda, M.D.: National Cholesterol Education Program. NIH Publication #87-2920, September 1987.

Polyunsaturated fats are liquid at room temperature.

Polyunsaturated fats, provided primarily by plants and seafood, are liquid at room temperature. Corn, sunflower, walnut and soybean oils are examples of polyunsaturated fats.

The last type of fat is monounsaturated. This fat is also liquid at room temperature. Recent studies indicate that *monounsaturated fats* may decrease blood cholesterol. Olive and canola oil, peanuts and fish are rich in monounsaturated fats. We are advised to replace saturated fats with poly and monounsaturated fats as well as reduce the total amounts of fat in our diet.

Fats vary in degree of saturation because of their differing fatty-acid composition. No fat is 100% saturated or polyunsaturated. Margarine for instance, contains saturated and unsaturated fats. Reading labels will help you choose a margarine, low in saturated fat. Here's how to tell from the label.

If the first ingredient on the label states:

"hydrogenated"	the margarine is primarily saturated fat.
"partially hydrogenated"	the margarine has more saturated fat than unsaturated fat.
"liquid"	the margarine is primarily polyunsaturated fat.

What does "P:S ratio" mean?

The relative fat composition of margarine can also be expressed as a P:S ratio. This ratio compares the amount of polyunsaturated fat (P) to the amount of saturated fat (S).

Fats with equal amounts of each type of fat would have a P:S ratio of 1:1 or 1. Select the margarine with the greatest amount of polyunsaturated fat. A P:S ratio of 2:1 or greater is desirable.

Unfortunately, the P:S ratios currently available understate the relative amount of unsaturated fats. Monounsaturated fats are not included and their beneficial effects on blood cholesterol levels overlooked. Table 5 gives a corrected ratio of poly and monounsaturated fats to saturated fats. (P:S ratios are determined by dividing total unsaturated fat by saturated fat.)

Table 5: P:S Ratios of Selected Fats[8]

	TYPE OF FAT			UNSATURATED: SATURATED
	Polyunsaturated	Monounsaturated	Saturated	Ratio
Canola	32	62	6	15.7:1
Safflower	75	12	9	9.6:1
Sunflower	66	20	10	8.6:1
Corn	59	24	13	6.4:1
Soybean	59	23	14	5.9:1
Olive	9	72	14	5.8:1
Peanut	32	46	17	4.6:1
Sesame seed	40	40	18	4.4:1
Cottonseed	52	18	26	2.7:1
Palm kernel	2	10	80	0.2:1
Coconut	2	6	87	0.1:1
Partially hydrogenated Margarine	19	58	23	3:1
Liquid Margarine	45	35	16	5:1
Mayonnaise	60	20	20	4:1
Hydrogenated Shortening	25	50	25	3.0:1
Lard	8	50	42	1.4:1
Chicken Fat	26	45	29	2.5:1
Beef Fat	4	48	48	1:1
Butter	trace	40	60	0.7:1

Source: USDA, HNIS. **Composition of Foods: Fats and oils,** Handbook Number 8-4., revised 1979.
Note: Other substances, such as water and vitamins, make up the total composition (100%).

[8]USDA, HNIS. **Composition of Foods - Fats and Oils: Raw, Processed, Prepared.** U.S.D.A. Human Nutrition Information Service, Agriculture Handbook 8-4, revised 1979.

*Fish provides a
protective benefit
against heart
disease.*

A Word About Omega-3 Fatty Acids

Several studies of various population groups show that as few as two fish meals a week may reduce the risk of heart disease. Japanese fishermen and Greenland Eskimos who eat liberal amounts of fish (from one fourth to three fourths of a pound each day) have a far lower incidence of heart disease than people in Western countries. In 1985, Dutch researchers provided more evidence for the link between fish and healthy hearts when they reported on a 20-year study of the diets of over 800 middle-aged men. Men who ate an average of just **one ounce of fish each day** had half the incidence of heart disease of those who ate little or no fish.

These results may be due to the fact that fish is low in fat, saturated fat and contain as a bonus, a highly polyunsaturated fat, *Omega-3 fatty acids.*

Omega-3 fatty acid research is highly controversial. Some experts believe that Omega-3 fatty acids make artery walls less inviting to blood clot formation. The platelets (cells involved in clotting) become less "sticky", thus preventing the clumping of blood cells and blockage of blood vessels.

Currently, the National Cholesterol Education Program believes there is little evidence that Omega-3 fatty acids *alone* are useful in reducing blood cholesterol. It appears that by eating fish on a regular basis, which can help reduce total fat and saturated fat intake, is an important factor in lowering risk of heart disease.

One fact that most researchers do agree on is that fish oil supplements are *no* substitute for fish. The American Heart Association does not recommend their use because their long-term effectiveness and safety have not been established. The AHA advises us to make fish a regular part of our diets (two or more times a week) because fish is relatively low in fat, saturated fat and cholesterol.

*Fish is good
food.*

Nutritional Benefits of Fish and Seafood

Long before researchers were aware of omega-3 benefits, fish and seafood were high on the list of recommended foods. A 4-ounce serving of sole, halibut or cod provides nearly one-third of an adult's daily requirement for protein while contributing only 110-130 calories.

Fish and seafood have other pluses, too. They are good sources of niacin, riboflavin and vitamins B_6 and B_{12}. Canned sardines, salmon and mackerel, eaten with the bones, provide calcium. Oysters, clams and mussels are good sources of iron, copper and zinc. And finally, marine foods are a rich source of iodine and selenium, important trace elements.

Where to Get Omega-3 Fatty Acids

Fatty acids in seafood differ from those found in plants and animals.

All fish and seafood contain omega-3 fatty acids. Generally, the higher the fat content of the fish, the higher its omega-3 content. Table 6 lists commonly marketed fish with their fat, omega-3 fatty acid and calorie content.

Table 6: Approximate Total Fat, Omega-3 Fatty Acid and Calorie Content of Fish

Fish:	Fat content (%)	Omega-3 fatty acids (mg)	Calories
	(3.5 ounces raw fillet)		
Atlantic Mackerel	13.9	2600 mg	175
Albacore Tuna	7.2	2100 mg	170
Sockeye Salmon	8.6	2300 mg	160
Pacific Herring	13.9	1800 mg	160
Sardines	6.8	1200 mg	135
Rainbow Trout	3.4	1100 mg	130
Smelt	2.6	800 mg	100
Brook Trout	2.7	600 mg	110
Pollock	1.0	500 mg	80
Tuna, unspecified	2.7	500 mg	110
Atlantic Cod	<1.0	300 mg	75
Ocean Perch	2.8	200 mg	105
Northern Pike	<1.0	100 mg	85
Crustaceans:			
Crab, Alaska King	<1.0	300 mg	86
Shrimp, unspecified	1.1	300 mg	91
Lobster, Northern	<1.0	200 mg	113
Mollusks:			
Oysters, Pacific	2.3	600 mg	90
Scallops, Atlantic	<1.0	200 mg	80
Clams, hardshell	<1.0	trace	80

Sources: Joyce Nettleton. *Seafood Nutrition.* Huntington, NY: Osprey Books, 1985 and *Seafood and Health.* Osprey Books, 1987.

Frank Hepburn, Jacob Exler, and John Weihrauch "Provisional tables on the content of omega-13 fatty acids and other fat components of selected foods." *Journal of the American Dietetic Association.* 86:6 June, 1986.

What about Cholesterol?

The term, "cholesterol", is used in two different senses. There is blood or serum cholesterol and there is dietary cholesterol. Although chemically the same, it is important to recognize that the recommendations for each are different.

*Blood
Cholesterol*

The amount of cholesterol circulating in our blood is a major factor determining our vulnerability to heart disease. The National Cholesterol Education Program of the National Heart Lung and Blood Institute set the following guidelines for adults:

Desirable Blood Cholesterol   below 200 mg/dl

Borderline-High Blood   200-239 mg/dl
Cholesterol

High Blood Cholesterol   240 or greater gm/dl

Since cholesterol is not soluble in water, it cannot travel through blood unaided. Instead, it is carried in envelopes known as lipoproteins. Three types of lipoproteins are important in cholesterol transport.

High Density Lipoproteins (HDL) act as "scavengers" by removing cholesterol from the artery walls and taking it to the liver for excretion. HDL is commonly referred to as the "good" cholesterol.

*Important to
Reduce Total
Blood Cholesterol*

Low Density Lipoproteins (LDL) are the main carriers of cholesterol, keeping cholesterol circulating in the blood and embedding it in the artery walls. This embedded cholesterol or plaque leads to atherosclerosis. Thus, LDL is commonly referred to as "bad" cholesterol.

Very Low Density Lipoproteins (VLDL) are fat carriers that can convert to LDL cholesterol.

Although improving the HDL cholesterol to LDL cholesterol ratio seems to reduce the risk of developing heart disease, it is also important to reduce total blood cholesterol.

To Enhance HDL Cholesterol

To increase HDL cholesterol:
- reduce excess body weight
- reduce total fat intake
- exercise regularly
- stop smoking

To Decrease LDL Cholesterol

To decrease LDL cholesterol:
- replace saturated fat with unsaturated fat in your diet
- eat a low-fat, low-cholesterol and high-fiber diet
- reduce excess body weight

Dietary cholesterol

Dietary cholesterol occurs *only* in foods of animal origin. Organ meats, egg yolk, lobster, and shrimp are high in cholesterol. High-fat dairy products, red meats, poultry and fish also contain cholesterol. Vegetables, grains, fruits and all vegetable oils are cholesterol-free. Table 7 gives the cholesterol content of selected foods.

Total daily intake of dietary cholesterol should not exceed 300 milligrams.

Table 7: Cholesterol Content of Selected Foods

(3-ounce portions)

Food Item:	Cholesterol (mg):
Beef Liver	370
Egg, 1 large	213
Shrimp, northern pink	125-135
Lobster, northern	70-95
Walleye Pike	85
Pork, lean	79
Beef, lean	76
Poultry, white meat without skin	72
Haddock	65
Butter, 1 tablespoon	35
Whole Milk, 1 cup	35
Scallops, Clams	30
1% Milk, 1 cup	10

Source: USDA, HNIS. *Composition of Foods.* Handbooks 8-1, 8-5, 8-10 and 8-13, 1976-1986. and Joyce Nettleton. *Seafood and Health* Huntington, NY: Osprey Books, 1987.

Eating pattern to reduce total blood cholesterol.

To lower blood cholesterol:[9]

♥ Use *half* the amount of fat or oil you presently use: *half* the margarine, *half* the salad dressing, *half* the mayonnaise, and *half* the cooking oil.

♥ Choose fish, chicken, turkey and *lean* red meats, keeping the amount to six ounces or less, cooked, a day. Three ounces is about the size of a deck of cards.

♥ Choose *low-fat* dairy products, including skim and 1% low-fat yogurt and low-fat cheese.

♥ Eat no more than four egg *yolks* a week.

Plus . . .

♥ Eat at least one fruit or vegetable at every meal.

♥ Eat at least one serving of whole-grain bread, cereal, rice, pasta or potatoes at every meal.

The health implications of decreasing your blood cholesterol are impressive. Prevention studies indicate that in people with high blood cholesterol, each *1% reduction in blood cholesterol translate to a 2% reduction in risk of heart disease!*

4. Choose a Diet With Plenty of Vegetables, Fruits and Grain Products.

The National Cancer Institute recommends a daily fiber intake of 20-30 grams, not to exceed 35 grams. By increasing fiber in our diet we can reduce the risk of several digestive diseases, possibly including colon and rectal cancer. Certain types of fiber can also reduce blood cholesterol levels.

Increasing fiber intake can help reduce total blood cholesterol.

When we talk about fiber, we are referring to the part of whole grains, vegetables, legumes, fruits and nuts that resists digestion in the gastrointestinal tract. Because fiber is not digested and absorbed, it is excreted from the body. Fiber helps move food through the intestines and out of the body, thus reducing the time that potentially damaging substances are in contact with intestinal surfaces. Fiber also delays stomach emptying which helps you retain a feeling of fullness longer. Finally, fiber binds with bile acids, forcing excess cholesterol to convert to bile acids and eliminates them from the body. Different types of fiber act differently in our bodies. Fiber is categorized as either water insoluble or water soluble. Wheat and corn bran, fruits, vegetables and nuts are high

[9]Minnesota Heart Health Program. *Fat Facts*. University of Minnesota, September 1987.

in insoluble fiber. They promote bowel regularity and may help reduce the risk of colon cancer.

Oat and barley products, some fruits such as apples and oranges and beans and legumes contain soluble fiber. Studies performed at Northwestern University Medical School indicate that an increase in water-soluble fiber from oat products lowered serum cholesterol by 5-10%. See table below for more information about specific types of fiber.

Table 8: Fiber At A Glance

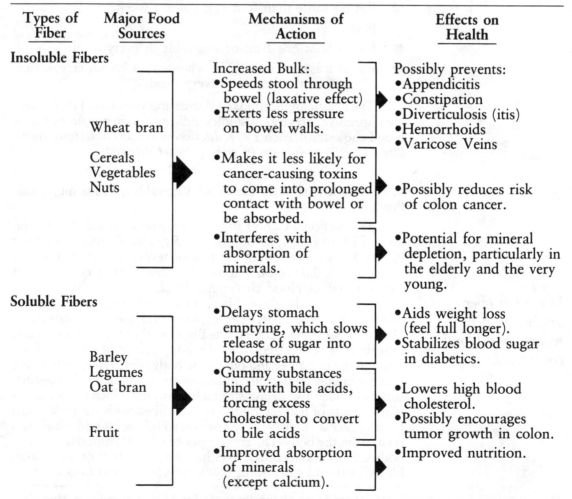

Types of Fiber	Major Food Sources	Mechanisms of Action	Effects on Health
Insoluble Fibers	Wheat bran Cereals Vegetables Nuts	Increased Bulk: •Speeds stool through bowel (laxative effect) •Exerts less pressure on bowel walls.	Possibly prevents: •Appendicitis •Constipation •Diverticulosis (itis) •Hemorrhoids •Varicose Veins
		•Makes it less likely for cancer-causing toxins to come into prolonged contact with bowel or be absorbed.	•Possibly reduces risk of colon cancer.
		•Interferes with absorption of minerals.	•Potential for mineral depletion, particularly in the elderly and the very young.
Soluble Fibers	Barley Legumes Oat bran Fruit	•Delays stomach emptying, which slows release of sugar into bloodstream	•Aids weight loss (feel full longer). •Stabilizes blood sugar in diabetics.
		•Gummy substances bind with bile acids, forcing excess cholesterol to convert to bile acids	•Lowers high blood cholesterol. •Possibly encourages tumor growth in colon.
		•Improved absorption of minerals (except calcium).	•Improved nutrition.

Reprinted with permission from Environmental Nutrition, 2112 Broadway, Room 200, New York, NY 10023.

Caution!
Increase fiber
gradually.

While the National Cancer Institute (NCI) recommends a daily consumption of 20-30 grams of *mixed* dietary fiber, most of us average only about 11 grams a day. Along with this recommendation comes the advice that increasing dietary fiber intake should be done *gradually*. Digestive discomfort (bloating and gas) may occur when fiber intake is increased too suddenly. Give yourself six to eight weeks to methodically increase your fiber intake to allow the body time to adjust. Drink at least a quart of fluids daily to avoid constipation.

Cereal brans are the most concentrated sources of dietary fiber. Whole-grain cereals and breads, fruits, vegetables and legumes are other good sources. Meat, milk and oil products do not contain fiber.

Increase your intake by including fiber from all sources. Foods that are good sources of fiber are typically low in fat, cholesterol and calories. Table 9 gives the dietary fiber content in average serving sizes of selected foods.

Table 9: Fiber Content of Foods

Food Item:	Serving Size:	Grams of Dietary Fiber
Bread & Cereals:		
Whole Wheat Bread	1 slice	1.4 grams
White Bread	1 slice	0.4 grams
Bran Muffin	1 muffin	2.5 grams
Bagel	1 bagel	0.6 grams
Raisin Bread	1 slice	0.6 grams
All-Bran Cereal	1 ounce (⅓ cup)	8.5 grams
Corn Bran Cereal	1 ounce (⅔ cup)	5.4 grams
Cheerios-type Cereal	1 ounce (1¼ cup)	1.1 grams
40% Bran-type Cereal	1 ounce (¾ cup)	4.0 grams
Grape Nuts Cereal	1 ounce (¼ cup)	1.4 grams
Raisin Bran-type Cereal	1 ounce (¾ cup)	4.0 grams
Shredded Wheat Cereal	1 ounce (⅔ cup)	2.6 grams
Oatmeal-regular, quick, and instant, cooked	1 ounce (¾ cup)	1.6 grams
Rice Krispies Cereal	1 ounce (1 cup)	0.1 grams
Legumes:		
Kidney Beans, cooked	½ cup	7.3 grams
Navy Beans, cooked	½ cup	6.0 grams
Lentils, cooked	½ cup	3.7 grams
Baked Beans, tomato sauce	½ cup	8.8 grams

continued

Table 9: Fiber Content of Foods, continued

Food Item:	Serving Size:	Grams of Dietary Fiber
Pasta & Rice:		
Macaroni, cooked	1 cup	1.0 grams
Rice, brown	½ cup	1.0 grams
Rice, white	½ cup	0.2 grams
Spaghetti, whole wheat	1 cup	3.9 grams
Spaghetti, regular	1 cup	1.1 grams
Nuts:		
Almonds	10 nuts	1.1 grams
Peanuts	10 nuts	1.4 grams
Filberts	10 nuts	0.8 grams
Fruits:		
Apple (with skin)	1 medium	3.5 grams
Apple (w/o skin)	1 medium	2.7 grams
Banana	1 medium	2.4 grams
Cantaloupe	¼ melon	1.0 grams
Grapefruit	½ one	1.6 grams
Orange	1 medium	2.6 grams
Pear (with skin)	½ large	3.1 grams
Pear (w/o skin)	½ large	2.5 grams
Prunes	3	3.0 grams
Raspberries	½ cup	3.1 grams
Strawberries	1 cup	3.0 grams
Juices:		
Apple	½ cup	0.4 grams
Grape	½ cup	0.6 grams
Orange	½ cup	0.5 grams
Vegetables:		
Broccoli, cooked	½ cup	2.2 grams
Brussel Sprouts	½ cup	2.3 grams
Corn, plain, cooked	½ cup	2.9 grams
Peas, cooked	½ cup	3.6 grams
Potato (with skin)	1 medium	2.5 grams
Potato (w/o skin)	1 medium	1.4 grams

Source: Elaine Lanza and Ritva Butrum. "Critical Review of Food Fiber Analysis and Data," *The Journal of the American Dietetics Association.* 86:6. June, 1986.

*Sugar provides
no nutritional
benefit to
our diet.*

5. Use Sugars Only in Moderation.

Besides the obvious adverse effect on weight, tooth decay is another major problem related to eating too much sugar. Tooth decay is more than a matter of *how much* sugar you eat; both the form of and the frequency with which you eat it are significant. Sticky or chewy sugary foods stay on the teeth longer and cause more problems than other sweets. Sugary foods eaten between meals are more likely to cause tooth decay than those eaten at mealtime.

The average person consumes 128 pounds of sugar a year or ¾ cup a day! Sugar provides only simple carbohydrates which do not have the nutritional benefits of complex carbohydrates and fiber and provides nutritionally-empty calories. A diet high in sugar also tends to be a diet high in fat (pastries, frozen desserts, candies, cookies, and cakes). Strive to reduce your daily sugar intake by at least half.

*Contrary to popular
belief, honey does
not provide useful
amounts of vitamins
or minerals.*

Since sugar is our most popular food additive, most everything on the grocery shelf contains sugar. You may not recognize sugar even if you read ingredient labels because sugar is known by several different names. Look for: maltose, dextrose, sucrose, fructose, lactose, invert sugar, brown sugar, turbinado, raw sugar, confectioners sugar, honey, corn sweeteners, corn syrup, and molasses. Molasses is the only sugar that has *some* redeeming nutritional value. The darker the molasses, the higher the amount of calcium, iron, potassium and B vitamins content. Blackstrap molasses contains the highest amount of vitamins and minerals.

The two tables below identify the amount of sugar in some of the foods we eat.

Table 10: Sugar Equivalents

Food Item:	Sugar Equivalent:
1 teaspoon jam or jelly	1 teaspoon sugar, syrup or molasses
1 ounce chocolate candy bar	2 teaspoons fat + 5 teaspoons sugar
½ cup frozen sweetened fruit	½ cup unsweetened fruit + 6 teaspoons sugar
½ cup fruit, canned in heavy syrup	½ cup unsweetened fruit + 4 teaspoons sugar
½ cup fruit, canned in light syrup	½ cup unsweetened fruit + 2 teaspoons sugar
8 ounces lowfat vanilla yogurt	8 ounces lowfat milk + 4 teaspoons sugar
8 ounces lowfat fruit yogurt	8 ounces lowfat milk + 7 teaspoons sugar
½ cup ice cream	⅓ cup skim milk + 2 teaspoons fat + 3 teaspoons sugar

continued

Table 10: Sugar Equivalents, continued

Food Item:	Sugar Equivalent:
½ cup ice milk	⅓ cup skim milk + 1 teaspoon fat + 3 teaspoons sugar
½ cup lowfat frozen yogurt	⅓ cup skim milk + 4 teaspoons sugar
2 oatmeal cookies	1 slice bread + 1 teaspoon fat + 1 teaspoon sugar
⅙ of a 9-inch apple pie	2 slices bread + ⅓ med apple + 3 teaspoons fat + 6 teaspoons sugar

Source: USDA, HNIS. *Nutrition and Your Health, Dietary Guidelines for Americans: Avoid Too Much Sugar.* Home and Garden Bulletin, #232-5, April 1986.

Table 11: Sugar Content in Common Foods

Food:	Serving Size:	Teaspoons of Sugar:
Chewing Gum	1 stick	½ teaspoon
Chocolate Cake, iced	1/12 cake	15 teaspoons
Angel Food Cake	1/12 cake	6 teaspoons
Cream Puff, iced	1 average	5 teaspoons
Doughnut, plain	3-inch diameter	4 teaspoons
Gingersnaps, homemade	3 medium	1 teaspoon
Brownies	2" x 2" x 3/4" piece	3 teaspoons
Soft Drinks	12 ounces	9 teaspoons
Kool-Aid	8 ounces	6 teaspoons
Peaches, canned in syrup	2 halves, 1 tablespoon syrup	3 1/2 teaspoons
Honey	1 tablespoon	3 teaspoons

Source: Jane Brody. *Jane Brody's Nutrition Book.* New York: W.W. Norton & Co, 1981.

Artificial sweeteners are not recommended as a substitute for sugar.

Artificial Sweeteners

While recognizing the widespread popularity and increasing consumption of artificial sweeteners, the authors of *Cooking a`la Heart* have not included them in the recipes because their health benefits are unproven and there is some recent evidence of detrimental side effects.

Retail sales of diet foods and beverages are estimated close to $26 billion a year. You will find artificial sweeteners in many foods on the grocery shelf such as gelatins, puddings, desserts, toppings, cereals, powdered beverages, soft drinks, chewing gum, breath mints, dietetic candies, cookies, cakes, jams and jellies.

Use no more than ¼ cup of sweetener to one cup of flour.

Instead of using artificial sweeteners, we encourage simply reducing the amount of sugar in traditional recipes. The sugar in many recipes can be reduced by ⅓ to ½ without affecting the taste or texture of the product. A helpful guideline for baked goods is to use no more than ¼ cup of sweetener (sugar, honey, molasses, etc.) to one cup of flour.

Artificial (non-caloric) sweeteners are popular because people are trying to avoid calories. Interestingly enough, no study has ever shown that the use of artificial sweeteners helps people lose weight and keep it off.

Tips to reduce sugar intake.

We suggest the following tips to curb your sweet tooth:

- Don't keep soft drinks, candy, cookies and cakes on hand. Instead, have a plentiful supply of teas, decaffeinated coffees, fresh fruits, vegetables and popcorn.
- Serve a variety of fruits for desserts *(see FRUIT DESSERT Section)*. Fresh fruits and fruits frozen without sugar are available year 'round in all parts of the country.
- To add flavor without adding calories, use sweet spices such as cinnamon, nutmeg, allspice, and ginger. Vanilla, almond and chocolate extracts also add a touch of sweetness.
- Use juices such as orange juice or apple juice concentrate in place of sugar. Making your own sweets allows you to reduce the amount of sugar, fat and sodium. In most recipes the quality of your product will *not* be affected if you reduce the sugar to one-half the original amounts.
- Don't buy either diet or regular soft drinks. Both perpetuate our desire to have sweet foods and beverages. Try drinking water with ice or lemon, or the many bottled waters flavored without added sweeteners or sugar.
- Buy fresh fruit or fruit packed in water or natural juices.

Avoid rewarding children with food, especially sweets. Use your ingenuity to devise enjoyable alternatives which could include extra time or special attention from you.

6. Use Salt and Sodium Only in Moderation.

One out of every five persons has high blood pressure.

About one in five people has elevated blood pressure (hypertension). Because hypertension often *produces no symptoms,* blood pressure should be checked regularly. High blood pressure greatly increases the risk of heart attack, stroke and kidney disease.

You are more likely to develop high blood pressure if you have:

- a family history of the disease
- excess body weight
- high alcohol consumption
- a high fat diet
- high sodium intake

Studies show weight loss reduces high blood pressure.

Many studies show positive results when people with high blood pressure reduce their body weight, increase their physical activity, reduce alcohol consumption and restrict their sodium intake. Approximately one-third of people with high blood pressure are sodium-sensitive and would benefit from a reduction in sodium intake. Unfortunately, it's very hard to tell if a person is truly sodium-sensitive; so, as a general rule, sodium restriction is recommended for *all* people with high blood pressure. Some research suggests that increases in dietary calcium and potassium may also help to lower high blood pressure. Studies of various populations show that those with low-fat and low-sodium diets seldom develop high blood pressure. Your food choices can make a difference!

The difference between salt and sodium.

Sodium and salt are often confused. Salt contains 40% sodium and 60% chloride. Sodium occurs naturally in foods in small amounts. Most is added to foods in processing, mainly as salt. An estimated two-thirds of our sodium intake comes from processed foods such as packaged dinners, cheese, canned soups and vegetables, packaged and prepared desserts, processed and cured meats and fast foods. One-third of our sodium intake comes from adding salt during food preparation or at the table. We currently eat anywhere from 2,300-10,000 milligrams of sodium a day.

The National Research Council of the National Academy of Sciences suggests that a "safe and adequate" range of daily sodium intake is between 1100-3300 milligrams. This is equivalent to the amount of sodium in 1 to 1½ teaspoons of salt.

Sodium is needed to regulate water balance and maintain proper fluid volume in and around our body's cells. Sodium acts like a sponge to hold water. When too much sodium is present, excess water may be retained and this can lead to high blood pressure.

Look for sodium on the label.

It is essential to read product labels when regulating your sodium intake. Two out of every three teaspoons of salt in the average diet comes from packaged food. Once there, it cannot be removed. In July, 1986, the Food and Drug Administration established guidelines for foods that make claims about sodium. A food label stating:

"sodium-free"   must contain less than 5 milligrams of sodium a serving.

"very-low-sodium"   must contain 35 milligrams or less a serving.

"low-sodium"   must have 140 milligrams or less a serving.

"reduced-sodium"   must have its sodium content reduced to 25% or less of that in the original product.

Furthermore, a product labled "unsalted", "no-salt-added" or "without added salt", has had no salt added during processing.

If you use processed foods, look for the products that have reduced salt or no salt added to them. Several food manufacturers are responding to consumer demand for less sodium and have made entire product lines available to meet this demand. There are many sodium-reduced canned vegetables, tomato products, canned fish, crackers, breads, soups and cereals.

Tips to reduce sodium intake.

We suggest the following tips to reduce sodium in your diet:

• Give yourself time to adjust to less salt. Salt is an acquired taste that often takes several weeks to modify.
• Use salt-free seasonings for cooking. See the **Seasonings Section** for herb blends that will enhance the flavor of foods without adding salt and fat. Remember, flavored salts such as onion salt or celery salt are still salt and contain 2000 milligrams of sodium in each teaspoon.
• Replace high-sodium ingredients in recipes with low-sodium products. For example, substitute low-sodium soy sauce for regular and low-sodium tomato products for high-sodium sauces, juices or canned tomato solids.
• Buy and use cookbooks that are geared to a healthier lifestyle. There are several good low-fat and low-sodium cookbooks available today which replace the "standards" which call for much more fat, salt and sugar than is necessary or desirable.
• Buy unsalted snacks. There is a variety, including nuts, crackers, pretzels and corn chips available without added salt. Freshly popped popcorn, too, is a good

snack if prepared and served without adding fat or salt. Our **Appetizer Section** has several tasty low-sodium recipes.

- When dining out, order your food unsalted and dressings on the side. This will allow you to control the amounts of both salt and fat.

The following tables will help you identify sodium amounts and sources.

Table 12: Salt To Sodium Conversions

1/8 teaspoon salt = 300 milligrams sodium
1/4 teaspoon salt = 600 milligrams sodium
1/2 teaspoon salt = 1,150 milligrams sodium
3/4 teaspoon salt = 1,700 milligrams sodium
1 teaspoon salt = 2,300 milligrams sodium

Table 13: Sodium-Containing Ingredients and Their Uses in Foods:

Baking soda	leavening agent and alkalizer
Baking powder	leavening agent
Brine	preservative
Disodium phosphate	emulsifier, stabilizer, buffer, used in quick cooking cereals and processed cheese
Monosodium glutamate (MSG)	flavor enhancer
Sodium acetate	pH control
Sodium aluminum sulfate	leavening
Sodium benzoate	preservative (used in condiments)
Sodium calcium alginate	thickener and smooth texture
Sodium caseinate	thickener and binder
Sodium citrate	pH control and buffer, used to control acidity in fruit drinks and soft drinks
Sodium diacetate	preservative
Sodium erythrobate	preservative
Sodium hydroxide	pH control, buffer
Sodium nitrite	preservative
Sodium nitrate	preservative
Sodium proprionate	preservative, mold inhibitor
Sodium phosphate	emulsifier, stabilizer, buffer
Sodium saccharin	artificial sweetener
Sodium sorbate	preservative
Sodium stearyl fumarate	bleaching agent, dough conditioner, maturing agent
Sodium sulfite	preservative for dried fruits, bleaching agent for some fresh fruits

Table 14: Sodium Content of Selected Foods

Food Item:	Serving Size:	Sodium (mg.)
Fruits & Vegetables:		
Fresh Green Beans	½ cup cooked	5 mg
Canned Green Beans	½ cup cooked	250 mg
Canned Baked Beans	1 cup	810 mg
Any Fresh Fruit	1 piece	0-5 mg
Any canned Fruit (water-pack to syrup)	½ cup	0-5 mg
Canned Orange Juice	1 cup	6 mg
Canned Tomato Juice	1 cup	676 mg
Canned V-8 Juice Cocktail	1 cup	715 mg
Low-Sodium V-8 Vegetable Juice	1 cup	47 mg
Prepared Main Courses:		
Swanson Turkey Dinner	1 meal	1,735 mg
Chef Boyardee Frozen Cheese Pizza	6½ ounces	925 mg
LaChoy canned chop suey	1 cup	1,339 mg
Kraft macaroni & cheese (as prepared from mix)	1 cup	700 mg
Hunt's Manwich Sloppy Joe Sauce as prepared served on hamburger roll	5.8 ounces	640 mg
Campbell's New England Clam Chowder	8 ounces	930 mg
Starkist Tuna in spring water	2 ounces	310 mg
Mrs. Smith's pancakes plain, from batter	3 medium	660 mg
Bread and Cereals:		
Wonder Enriched Bread	2 slices	355 mg
Pepperidge Farm Whole Wheat Bread	2 slices	214 mg
Cheerios	1 ounce (1¼ cups)	290 mg
Rice Chex	1 ounce (1⅛ cups)	280 mg
Shredded Wheat	1 ounce (⅔ cup)	0 mg
Nature Wheat Granola	1 ounce (⅓ cup)	58 mg
Puffed Rice	1 ounce (2 cups)	0 mg
Oatmeal, cooked (no salt added)	¾ cup	1 mg
Cream of Rice, cooked (no salt added)	¾ cup	1 mg
Maypo (no salt added)	¾ cup	6 mg

continued

Table 14: Sodium Content of Select Foods, continued

Food Item:	Serving Size:	Sodium (mg.)
Cheese and Processed Meats:		
Cheddar Cheese	1 ounce	176 mg
Colby Cheese	1 ounce	171 mg
Cottage Cheese, creamed	½ cup	457 mg
Cottage Cheese, low fat, 1% fat	½ cup	459 mg
Cream Cheese	1 ounce (2 Tbsp.)	84 mg
Mozzarella, part skim	1 ounce	132 mg
Swiss Cheese	1 ounce	74 mg
American Process Cheese	1 ounce	406 mg
American Cheese Spread	2 Tablespoons	436 mg
Crab, canned	½ cup	850 mg
Bacon	2 slices	228 mg
Ham, cured, canned	3 ounces	837 mg
Frankfurter, Beef	1 frank	461 mg
Frankfurter, Chicken	1 frank	617 mg
Frankfurter, Turkey	1 frank	472 mg
Spam, canned	1 ounce	336 mg
Chips, Crackers & Snacks:		
Fritos Corn Chips	1 ounce	218 mg
Ruffles Potato Chips	1 ounce	213 mg
Popcorn, no added salt	1 cup	trace
Pretzels	1 ounce	451 mg
Nabisco Ritz Crackers	3 crackers	104 mg
Saltines	3 crackers	120 mg
Nabisco Low Salt Wheat Thin Crackers	8 crackers	60 mg
Green Olives	2 medium	312 mg
Dill Pickles	1 large	1,428 mg
Bouillon Cube	1 cube	930 mg
Fast Foods:		
Burger King Ham & Cheese	1 sandwich	1,550 mg
Burger King Double Beef	1 sandwich	1,015 mg
Dairy Queen Double Hamburger	1 sandwich	660 mg
Dairy Queen Hog Dog	1 sandwich	830 mg
Dairy Queen Fish w/Cheese	1 sandwich	1,035 mg

continued

Table 14: Sodium Content of Select Foods, continued

Food Items:	Serving Size:	Sodium (mg.)
Fast Foods, continued:		
Domino Pepperoni Pizza	2 slices of a 16" pie	1,080 mg
Hardee's Cheeseburger	1 sandwich	789 mg
Hardee's Big Roast Beef	1 sandwich	1,770 mg
Hardee's Biscuit	1 biscuit	650 mg
Kentucky Fried Chicken	1 thigh (original recipe)	566 mg
Kentucky Fried Chicken (2 pieces chicken, mashed potatoes, gravy, coleslaw, roll, wing & side breast)	1 dinner	1,528 mg
Long John Silver's Fish & Fries	3 fish & 3 ounces fries	2,025 mg
Long John Silver's Chilled Seafood Combo	1 order & 4 crackers	1,009 mg
McDonald's Hamburger	1 sandwich	506 mg
McDonald's Big Mac	1 sandwich	979 mg
McDonald's Chicken McNuggets	1 order (6 pieces)	512 mg
McDonald's Reg. Fries	2.4 ounces	109 mg
Taco Bell's Bean Burrito	1 (5.8 ounces)	272 mg
Taco Bell's Taco	1 (3 ounces)	79 mg
Taco Bell's Enchirito	1 (7 ounce)	1,175 mg
Wendy's Chicken Sandwich	1 sandwich	500 mg
Wendy's Chili	9 ounces	1,070 mg
Wendy's Taco Salad	1 (12.6 ounces)	1,100 mg
Wendy's Broccoli & Cheese Baked Potato	1 (12.9 ounces)	430 mg

Sources: Jean Pennington and Helen Church. *Food Values of Portions Commonly Used*. 14th ed. 1985.
Marion Franz. *Fast Food Facts*. 1987.
and manufacturer's data on specific brands

*Your drinking
water can also be a
source of sodium.*

While the food sources of sodium are generally recognized, the contribution of sodium from drinking water may be overlooked. Drinking water may account for up to 10% of an individual's daily sodium consumption. The American Heart Association recommends a limit of 20 mg of sodium a liter or quart of water as a standard for persons suffering from heart or kidney ailments who require a low-sodium diet. The Environmental Protection Agency (EPA) does not regulate the maximum level of sodium in water, though it also considers the optimal level of sodium in drinking water to be 20 milligrams of sodium a liter or less.

Drinking water can contribute a significant amount of sodium if your water is softened. The amount of sodium added by a water softener can be as high as 100 mg a liter. Check with your local Department of Public Health to find out about your water supply.

7. If You Drink Alcoholic Beverages, Do So in Moderation.

*Alcohol is high
in calories and
robs the body
of vital nutrients.*

Alcohol is a source of "empty calories" or calories without other nutrients. It robs the body by using vital nutrients in the metabolism process. Alcohol is high in calories containing 7 calories a gram as compared to 4 calories a gram in protein or carbohydrate. A simple formula for calculating caloric content of alcoholic beverage is:

$$0.8 \times proof \times ounces = Calories$$

"Proof" tells you the alcoholic content of distilled spirits or hard liquor. In the United States the proof value is equal to twice the percentage of alcohol by volume. One ounce of pure alcohol is 200 proof. Liqueurs vary greatly and their alcohol content is expressed as a "proof". The alcohol content of wine and beer is given as a percent by volume; white wines are about 12 percent; red wines, 14 percent; beer between 3 and 8 percent. Alcohol is metabolized in the body to yield seven calories per gram of energy. When taken in excess of energy need, it is converted to body fat and stored. When consumed in moderate amounts, it can stimulate the appetite, thus causing weight gain. When alcohol contributes a substantial portion of the calories in a person's diet, its effects are harmful.

Chronic consumption of alcoholic beverages in large amounts damage the heart and cardiovascular system. Current evidence suggests that heavy drinkers—six or more drinks a day—have a high risk of a heart attack or stroke. Some studies show that moderate drinkers—one or two drinks a day—are less likely to suffer a heart attack than either abstainers or heavy drinkers. However, not enough is known about this effect in moderate drinkers to justify the intake of alcohol as a protection against heart attack.

There is no doubt that heavy consumption of alcohol significantly increases the risk of cancers of the mouth, throat, esophagus, and liver. Cancer risk is especially high for heavy drinkers who smoke.

Pregnant women should abstain from drinking alcohol-containing beverages.

Women who drink heavily risk giving birth to children with birth defects. The defects, collectively called Fetal Alcohol Syndrome (FAS), affect two infants in every 1,000 births. Symptoms include a varying degree of mental deficiency, facial abnormalities and defects of the heart, lungs, joints and sex organs. Pregnant women are advised not to drink beverages containing alcohol.

The American Heart Association and the National Cancer Institute recommend discriminate use of alcohol, in moderate amounts not to exceed 1½ ounces of ethanol a day.

To stay within those guidelines, daily intake should not exceed one drink a day for women and two drinks a day for men.

Count the following as *a* drink:

- 1½ ounces of hard liquor, 100 proof
        or
- 5 ounces of wine
        or
- 12 ounces of regular beer
        or
- 16 ounces of 3.2 beer

2

COOKING A' LA HEART

Reshaping eating patterns

Understanding the guidelines for a healthier heart is one thing, but implementing them can be quite another. Changing our eating habits requires motivation and commitment over time. We suggest starting with small, manageable changes and gradually, you will reach an eating pattern that will fit you for life.

Begin by taking inventory of the kinds and amounts of food you presently eat. In order to make changes, you must know what needs to be changed. By identifying your present eating habits, you will be able to spot areas in which you can make more healthful choices. A *food diary* can reveal habits that keep you from your best health such as meal skipping, unplanned snacking or dining on quick, high-calorie foods and drinks, constant nibbling through meal preparation or uncontrolled snacking during leisure time.

Identify only one or two problems that you'd like to work on. *Be realistic* in your expectations and set attainable goals. For example, it may take three months before the family accepts the change from 2% milk to skim milk. *Choose* the *area* of *least resistance*. Reducing fat and sodium in recipes, replacing ice cream with ice milk or offering fruit instead of high-calorie chips, cookies and candies are possible places to start.

Be flexible. Experiment. Try different brands and make compromises with your family to allow for individual tastes. Remember, it *takes time* to make changes which are accepted and adopted as a regular part of the family's lifestyle. Mark Twain said that a habit cannot simply be tossed out the window. It should be escorted like an old friend, down the stairs, one step at a time and out the door.

You will find numerous suggestions in this chapter to help you get started. The *Shopping a'la Heart* Section guides you in grocery selection. The *Recipe Modification Guidelines Table* highlights changes you can make in traditional recipes. The *Meal Planning* Section provides sample menus and shows you how to plan your own tasty, wholesome meals using *Cooking a'la Heart* recipes and explains the nutrient analyses.

Shopping a'la Heart
Heart-healthy choices can be found in almost every grocery aisle.

Produce

All fresh fruits and vegetables, except avocados and coconuts, are low in fat and sodium. Our recommendations: serve a fruit at every meal, a vegetable or two for lunch and dinner and use both fruits and vegetables for between-meal snacks.

Canned Goods   Select sodium-reduced vegetables and soups. Select only water-packed fish and water or juice-packed fruits.

Fats & Oils   Buy unsaturated oils such as safflower, sunflower, canola, corn, soybean, sesame, olive, peanut or vegetable-oil blends. Do not buy shortenings or "partially hydrogenated" oils.

Cereals   Select whole-grain cereals without added sweeteners. Cereals, always popular breakfast fare, also make excellent snacks.

Frozen Foods   Beware! Read the labels. Buy plain, frozen vegetables and fruits. Steer clear of vegetables with cream sauces or fruit packed in sugar. Select convenience foods carefully. Many TV dinners, frozen main dishes, french fries, pot pies, pizzas and fish sticks are high in fat and sodium. Choose frozen dinners that contain 10 or fewer grams of fat and contain no more than 1000 milligrams of sodium. High-sugar and high-fat desserts abound in the frozen food section as well. Replace ice cream with ice milk, sherbet or frozen yogurt. However, while these replacements are low in fat, they are still high in sugar.

Spices   Select "powder" instead of "salt" forms, such as garlic powder instead of garlic salt. Try new spices, checking the label to make sure they do not contain sodium. Refer to the *Seasoning Section* of *Cooking a'la Heart* to make your own blends.

Dairy   Buy skim or 1% milk. Purchase part-skim cheeses such as farmer, feta, mozzarella and ricotta; and low-fat yogurt, cottage and cream cheese. Buy margarine that lists *"liquid"* oil as the first ingredient. Purchase fresh eggs. Use unlimited egg whites but restrict each person to four egg yolks a week.

Refrigerated Case   Choose fruit juices instead of fruit drinks. Select whole-grain pocket breads, tortillas, English muffins and bagels.

Fish, Poultry and Meat   Choose fish, chicken, turkey, veal and lean red meats. When purchasing beef, buy these cuts: sirloin tip, round steak, rump roasts, ground round and ground chuck. When selecting pork cuts, choose: lean loin roasts, center-cut fresh ham, loin chops and tenderloin.

Bakery   Buy whole-grain breads and buns, checking the label for whole-grain ingredients. Make your own heart-healthy baked goods from *Cooking a'la Heart* recipes.

Beverages and Snacks

Choose unsalted and unsweetened bottled waters. Select sodium-reduced crackers made from high-fiber, whole grains. Choose unsalted nuts, popcorn and corn chips.

Dry Goods

Select brown or wild rice, whole wheat pasta, bulgur and legumes.

Table 15: Recipe Modification Guidelines

When your recipe calls for:	Use these Heart-Healthy Alternatives:
1 whole egg	2 egg whites or ¼ cup egg substitute or 1 egg white and 1 teaspoon oil*
1 cup butter	1 cup margarine* or ⅔ cup oil
1 cup shortening or lard	1 cup margarine or ⅔ cup oil
½ cup shortening or lard	½ cup margarine or ⅓ cup oil
1 cup whole milk	1 cup skim milk
1 cup light cream	1 cup evaporated skim milk or 3 Tablespoons oil and skim milk to equal 1 cup
1 cup heavy cream	1 cup evaporated skim milk or ⅔ cup skim milk and ⅓ cup oil
1 cup sour cream	1 cup plain low-fat yogurt or **Mock Sour Cream,** *(see APPETIZER & DIPS section)*
1 tablespoon salad dressing	1 tablespoon calorie-reduced salad dressing
1 ounce (a square) baking chocolate	3 tablespoons powdered cocoa and 1 tablespoon oil
Cream Cheese	Use the "light" commercial cream cheese or **Mock Cream Cheese,** *(see APPETIZER & DIPS section)*
2 strips bacon	1 ounce lean Canadian bacon or 1 ounce lean ham
Regular ground beef	Extra-lean ground beef
Chicken with skin	Remove skin from chicken before cooking
Deep-fried meats, poultry & fish	Broiled, baked, braised or grilled lean meats, poultry and fish
Fat for sauteing or broiling	Use ½ the amount of fat or saute in stock or water
Cheddar, colby & American cheese	Choose a cheese with 5 or fewer grams of fat an ounce

continued

Table 15: Recipe Modification Guidelines, continued

When your recipe calls for:	Use these Heart-Healthy Alternatives:
Creamed cottage cheese	Low-fat cottage cheese
1 can Condensed cream soup	**Condensed Cream Soup Mix** or **Medium White Sauce,** *(see SOUP section).*
Cream of celery soup	Medium White Sauce + ¼ cup chopped celery
Cream of chicken soup	Medium White Sauce + 2 sodium-reduced chicken bouillon cubes
Cream of mushroom soup	Medium White Sauce +1 cup chopped fresh mushrooms
1 cup all-purpose white flour	¾ cup all-purpose white flour + ¼ cup bran or ½ cup all-purpose white flour + ½ cup whole-wheat flour or 1 cup whole-wheat flour minus 2 Tablespoons, decreasing the oil by 1 Tablespoon and increasing the liquid by 1-2 Tablespoons
White rice	Brown or wild rice
Sugar	Reduce amount. Reduction can be up to ½ of the original amount. Use no more than ¼ cup of sweetener to each cup of flour.
Salt	Reduce amount or leave out. You may increase other spices and herbs.
Tomato juice	Use no-salt-added tomato juice or dilute one 6-ounce can of no-salt-added tomato paste with 3 cans water.
Tomato paste	Use no-salt-added tomato paste.
Tomato sauce	Use no-salt-added tomato sauce or one 6-ounce can no-salt-added tomato paste with 1 can water.
1 bouillon cube	Use 2 sodium-reduced bouillon cubes or 2 teaspoons sodium-reduced bouillon granules.
1 tablespoon fresh herbs	Use ½ teaspoon powdered or 1 teaspoon dry herbs for every tablespoon of chopped fresh herbs.

*margarine refers to margarine made with *"liquid"* vegetable oil, oil refers to vegetable oil.

Sources: Minnesota Heart Health Program, *Eat to Your Heart's Content: A Guide to Healthier Eating.* Minneapolis: University of Minnesota, 1983. and Marion Franz, *et al.,* A Guide to Healthy Eating. St. Louis Park, Mn: International Diabetes Center, 1986.

Successful Meal Planning

Where to Begin

Menu planning becomes more rewarding as you discover the many ways to achieve a healthful good-tasting diet. In this section, we provide several menu combinations adaptable to your family's needs and tastes. You will find family menus for a week, suggestions for summer and winter entertaining, picnic fare and special occasions.

No one should expect every meal to be perfectly balanced; strive to balance your diet over the course of a week. Try to include on a daily basis a minimum of:

- 6 servings of whole-grain bread, cereal, pasta or rice;
- 4 servings of fruits and vegetables, including good Vitamin A and Vitamin C-source foods;
- 2 servings of a high-protein food (combination of complementary vegetable proteins, fish, poultry or lean red meats);
- 2-4 servings of calcium-rich dairy foods such as low-fat milk, cottage cheese or yogurt.

Advantages of meal planning

Planning meals in advance saves time, money and reduces hassle. With a week's plan in hand you'll:

- save shopping time
- avoid impulse buying
- make better use of leftovers
- have an answer to the perennial question: "What's for dinner?"

More importantly, a plan allows you to review the nutritional content of the foods you choose. Start by planning a day's menu. For each meal select a "theme" or type of main dish and build around it.

SALAD MEAL

Large Bowl of Mixed Greens
  — Suggested Accompaniments

- slivered lean meats
- low-fat cottage cheese, low-fat cheese
- onions and other raw vegetables

continued

- tomatoes and sprouts
- homemade croutons and salad dressings
- nuts and seeds
- breads, muffins, quick bread
- soup

CASSEROLE MEAL

Any Baked Main Dish
— Suggested Accompaniments
- soup
- vegetables
- salads
- breads
- fruit

VEGETABLE MEAL

Vegetable Main Dish such as: Cauliflower Walnut Casserole
Curried Rice Stuffed Tomato
Tofu Italiano

— Suggested Accompaniments
- breads, muffins, rolls
- soups
- fruits
- salads

LEGUME OR GRAIN MEAL

Legume or Grain Dish such as: Savory Black Beans
Rice with Pine Nuts
Barley Pilaf

— Suggested Accompaniments
- bits of meat and lots of vegetables, stir-fried, curried or steamed
- nuts and seeds
- breads
- salad

SOUP MEAL

A Hearty Soup such as Cream of Morel
Creole-Style Lentil Stew
Curried Squash-Apple Bisque

— Suggested Accompaniments

- raw vegetable platter with dips
- homemade breads, dinner rolls, muffins
- fruits
- baked low-fat dessert

BREAD MEAL

Loaves of Freshly-Made Bread served on boards, pocketbread, muffins

— Suggested Accompaniments

- low fat cheeses
- sandwich filling such as:
  Veggie-Cheese Pockets
  Grilled Zucchini-Parmesan
  Tofu Salad
- leafy greens
- tomatoes, sprouts, onions and other raw vegetables
- hot or cold drinks, nogs

Meal planning

Keep menus simple by making fewer dishes and serving adequate portions. Make double or triple amounts of main dishes and baked goods and freeze for later use. Planning menus for a week in advance allows you to organize your meal preparation time most efficiently. Most importantly, everyone can share meal planning, cooking and clean-up tasks within the household. Shared responsibility provides children with valuable learning experiences.

A Week's Worth of Family Fare *(menu selections are recipes in Cooking a' la Heart)*

	Sunday	Monday	Tuesday
Breakfast	**Brunch**	Citrus Juice or Orange	Energy
	Hot Citrus Fruit Compote	Oat Bran Cereal	Breakfast Nog
	Apple Cinnamon	Blueberry Muffin w/	Whole-Grain Cold Cereal
	Pancakes w/ Spicy	Tub Margarine	Whole Wheat Toast w/
	Yogurt Topping	Skim Milk	Tub Margarine
			Skim Milk
	or		
Lunch	Vegetables Quiche	Italian Pasta Salad	Fish Salad Verde
	Cranberry Coffee Cake	Sour Milk Rolls w/	Hearty Wheat Buns w/
		Tub Margarine	Tub Margarine
	Fruit Preserves	Fresh Fruit	Berries 'n Cannoli Cream
	Tub Margarine	Pecan Meringues	Beverage
	Beverage	Beverage	
Supper	Cucumber &	Antipasto (Spinach-	Chicken Almond Stir-Fry
	Tomato Salad	Stuffed Cherry Tomatoes,	on Bed of Brown Rice
		Stuffed Celery and	Orange Cauliflower Salad
	Sole Rolls on a bed	Marinated Vegetables)	w/
	of Green Rice	Tofu Italiano	Surprise Dressing
		Tossed Mixed Greens w/	Whole Wheat French
	Asparagus Oriental	Dilled Vinaigrette	Bread
		Dressing	Sparkling Fruit
	Carrot Cake	Hearty Wheat Buns	Beverage
	Beverage	Apples w/Caramel Sauce	
	(freeze leftover	Beverage	
	carrot cake)		
Snacks	Berry Milk Shake	Bread Sticks	Fruit
	Pretzels	Grapes	Chewy Oatmeal Cookie
	Air-Popped Popcorn	Skim Milk	

continued

A Week's Worth of Family Fare, continued

Wednesday	Thursday	Friday	Saturday
Fresh/Frozen Peaches or Banana Soft Boiled Egg Scrapple Reduced-Calorie Syrup Hot Cocoa	Cantaloupe Hot or Cold Cereal Pecan Oat Muffin w/ Tub Margarine Skim Milk	Citrus Juice Wellness Granola Toasted English Muffin Fruit Preserves Skim Milk	Apple Juice Whole-Wheat Waffles w/Fruit Topping Cottage Cheese and peaches w/cinnamon Beverage
Health Salad w/ Surprise Dressing Cranberry Bread Vanilla Pudding w/ Sliced Strawberries Beverage	Baked Beans Grilled Zucchini Parmesan Sandwiches Fresh Apple Beverage	Gazpacho Hot Chicken Pockets Rice Pudding Beverage	Turkey Vegetable Soup Date Sandwich Spread on Whole-grain Bread Fresh Pear Beverage
Charcoal Herbed Burgers Potato Salad Vinaigrette Coleslaw Broccoli-Corn Salad Watermelon Beverage	Baked Salmon Steaks w/Lemon Steamed New Potatoes Citrus Spinach Salad w/ Mazatlan Dressing Raspberry Chiffon Pie w/Nut Crust Beverage	Veggie-Nut Pizza on Yeast Crust Apple Spinach Salad Ice Milk w/Honey Fudge Sauce Beverage	Garden-Green Salad Pork Chop w/Garlic Sauce on Caraway Rice Carrots Elegante Four-Grain Bread Cranberry Steamed Pudding Beverage
Mulled Cider Whole-Wheat Soft Pretzel	Skim Milk Carrot Cake (leftover)	Sparkling Water Banana	Orange-Yogurt Popsicles Popcorn

Summer Buffet

Raspberry Punch
Assorted Raw Vegetables
Herbed Cheese Dip
Salmon Yogurt Dip
Spinach Crepe Wheels
Julian's Fish Appetizer
Wild Rice Chicken Salad
Baked Garlic Tomatoes
Honey Whole-Wheat Bread
Fruit Pizza
Beverage

Winter Buffet

Mulled Cider
Vegetable Platter
Baked Eggplant Dip
Salsa
Cocktail Meatballs
Savory Stuffed Mushrooms
Chicken Waikiki
Rice and Pine Nuts
Sweet Potatoes and Apples
24-Hour Layered Salad
Old Fashioned Potato Rye Bread
New Zealand Pavlova
Beverage

Picnic Menu

Marinated Vegetables
Curry Glazed Chicken on the Grill
Tabouleh Salad
Confetti Apple Slaw
Rhubarb Cake
Bread Sticks
Beverages

Lunch for Bridge Club

Fish Florentine
Sour Milk Rolls w/Preserves
Pear & Grapefruit Toss w/Mint
Chocolate Mousse

Super Bowl Sunday Supper

Salsa
Homemade Tortilla Chips
Black Bean Chili
Rice
Green Salad w/Creamy Salad Dressing
Corn Zephyrs
Butterscotch Pudding
Applesauce Spice Cookies

Summer Porch Lunch

Chilled Pea Soup
Thai Style Fried Fish
Rice
Strawberry Rhubarb Gelatin Salad
Blueberry Muffin

Trim the Tree

Wassail
Spicy Popcorn to Eat
Plain Popcorn to String
Fresh Fruit to Dip in Banana Yogurt Dressing
Lentil Soup
Confetti Appleslaw
Date Bars
Coffee

Soup & Salad for Saturday Lunch

Potato and Leek Soup
Citrus Beet Salad

Sunday Night Supper

Mulligatawny Soup
Cauliflower Salad
Rolls
Dessert

Casseroles for Potluck Suppers

Wild Rice Chicken Casserole
Crockpot Stroganoff
Cabbage Casserole
Busy Day Pork Stew

Salads to Go

24-Hour Layered Salad
Layered Chicken Salad
Italian Salad

Desserts for Potluck

Sugarless Fruit Bars
Apricot Spice Bars
Baked Fruit Compote

Initiation for the Beginner
"I Can't Believe it's Heart-Healthy"

Marinated Flank Steak, Grilled
Potato Salad Vinaigrette
Ratatouille
Coleslaw
Baked Glazed Pears
or
Peach Yogurt Pie

A Word About The Nutrition Information in the Recipes

Nutrient analysis can guide you in choosing and preparing good food.

The recipes in **Cooking à la Heart** were designed to help you limit your intake of fat, cholesterol and sodium and include nutrient analysis for the following nutrients:

— calories
— fat
— cholesterol
— sodium

Where relevant, these additional nutrients are provided in the analysis:

— calcium
— fiber
— Omega-3 fatty acids, when fish or seafood is a major ingredient

This format is designed to guide you in your choice and preparation of good food while limiting fat calories to 30% or less of your daily total, cholesterol to 300 or fewer milligrams, and sodium to no more than 3300 milligrams a day.

The following computer programs were used to determine the nutritional merit of the **Cooking a' la Heart** recipes:

— Computrition
  21049 Devonshire Street
  Chatsworth, Ca 91311
  Analysis provided by:
   Sturdy Memorial Hospital
   211 Park Street
   Attleboro, Ma 02703

— National Nutrition Coding Center (NCC)
  University of Minnesota
  Minneapolis, Mn. 55455

— Dietary Analysis and Assessment System (DAS)
  Health Management Systems Associates
  1409 Willow, Suite 200
  Minneapolis, Mn. 55403
  Analysis provided by:
   Wellness Center of Minnesota
   Mankato, Mn. 56001

In addition to these systems, the following resources were used:

-USDA, HNIS. *Composition of Foods,* Agriculture Handbook Series 8-1 through 8-14. revised 1976-1986.

-USDA. "Provisional Table on the Fatty Acid and Cholesterol Content of Selected Foods." *Journal of the American Dietetic Association,* 86:6, June 1986.

-Elaine Lanza and Ritva Butrum. "A Critical Review of Food Fiber Analysis and Data." *Journal of the American Dietetic Association.* 86:6, June 1986.

-Joyce Nettleton. *Seafood Nutrition* and *Seafood and Health* New York: Osprey Books, 1985 and 1987.

-Jean Pennington and Helen Church. *Food Values of Portions Commonly Used,* 14th edition. New York: Harper & Row Publishers, Inc., 1985.

As A
Reminder . . .

Keep in mind a teaspoon of fat is equivalent to 4.4 grams of fat and a teaspoon of salt contains 2300 milligrams of sodium. To make the nutrition information meaningful, let's assume an active woman consumes 2000 calories daily. Of those calories, she should consume a maximum of 600 calories as fat. At 9 calories a gram, the 600 calories translates to 66 grams of fat or 15 teaspoons daily. An active man who consumes 3000 calories daily, should consume no more than 900 calories or 100 grams of fat or 20 teaspoons daily.

The following guidelines are provided to assist you in determining how the recipes can fit into your daily meal plan.

Fat: Limit to 30% or less of total calories

Cholesterol: Consume less than 300 milligrams a day

Sodium: Control intake to between 1100-3300 milligrams

Fiber: Strive to consume between 20-30 grams a day

Calcium: Women should consume between 800-1000 milligrams a day; postmenopausal women taking estrogen, 1200 milligrams a day; postmenopausal women not taking estrogen, 1500 milligrams a day; and children and men 800-1200 milligrams a day.

Appetizers, Dips, & Beverages

No man in the world has more courage than the man who can stop after eating one peanut.

Channing Pollock

COLD APPETIZERS

HOT APPETIZERS

HOT BEVERAGES

HOT OR COLD BEVERAGES

DIPS

COLD BEVERAGES

APPETIZERS & DIPS

Often known as canapes or hors d'oeuvres, appetizers can either whet your appetite for the next course or they can help fill you, thus curbing your appetite and preventing you from overeating.

Appetizers need not be calorie-laden bits of greasy food. They can be crunched, dipped, spread, speared, filled or picked up and eaten with fingers and still make a worthwhile nutritional contribution.

Our appetizers are imaginative and festive while low in fat, cholesterol, sodium and calories. We have handpicked this section of appetizers to offer you a variety of flavors and textures.

Appetizer Tips

- Add garnishes to make hor d'oeuvres visually appealing. Fresh vegetables, cut decoratively, make beautiful edible garnishes. Hollowed-out bell peppers, large mushrooms or cucumbers make wonderful dip containers.

- When serving more than one appetizer, select a variety of colors, shapes, tastes and textures.

- For appetizers preceding dinner, allow two or three large appetizers or four to six bite-sized appetizers a person.

- Avoid repetition; don't serve steak sticks with a beef meal or stuffed tomatoes with a tomato-based entree.

- For a party that doesn't include dinner, prepare a variety of hors d'oeuvres. For 8 to 12 people, serve four types of hors d'oeuvres; for 14 to 18 people, five to six types, allowing three to four pieces for each person.

- Appetizers are well worth the effort. Many of our selections can be made several days ahead and stored in either the freezer or refrigerator. An hour or so before serving time, arrange, cover and leave at room temperature. Remember that small serving plates are more easily replenished than large ones.

Whatever your tastes, you can present an attractive and nutritious array of appetizers sure to please your guests.

BEVERAGES

*Don't ignore
calories
beverages
can provide*

There are as many ways to serve beverages as there are recipes. Beverages can be tasty eye-openers in the morning, an interesting accompaniment to a meal, a soothing snack for children or simply refreshments to be enjoyed by themselves.

Because beverages are so easy to sip or drink, we tend to ignore their calories and can consume large numbers of calories in very small quantities. Check some of your favorite beverages in the chart below. Keep in mind, calories are not the only standard by which to judge. Beverages can be valuable sources of vitamins and minerals but often drinks such as sodas, fruit drinks, ades, punches and shakes are high in calories and are hidden sources of fat and sodium while making little or no other nutritional contribution.

Table 16: Calorie, Fat and Sodium Comparison of Select Beverages

Beverage:	Calories:	Fat: (grams)	Sodium: mg
Beer, 4.5% by volume, 12 fl. oz.	150	0.0	18
Beer, light, 12 fl. oz.	70-134	0.0	23
Fruit Juice:			
Orange, 8 fl. oz.	110	<1.0	2
Tomato, 8 fl. oz.	41	<1.0	676
Coconut Milk, 4 fl. oz.	307	30.0	64
Fruit Drink or Ade, 8 fl. oz.	95	0.0	4
Coffee, brewed, 6 fl. oz.	3	trace	2
Tea, brewed, 6 fl. oz.	0	trace	14
Soda, carbonated, 12 fl. oz.	156	0.0	9
Soda, carbonated, diet, 12 fl. oz.	1	0.0	42
Milk:			
Whole (3.5%), 8 fl. oz.	150	8.0	122
2%, 8 fl. oz.	121	5.0	122
1%, 8 fl. oz.	100	2.0	123
Skim, 8 fl. oz.	86	<1.0	126
Milkshake, homemade, 8 fl. oz.	421	18.0	330
Cooking a\la Heart Berry Shake, 8 fl. oz.	240	<4.0	91
Hot Cocoa, whole milk, 8 fl. oz.	218	9.0	123
Cooking a\la Heart Hot Cocoa, 8 fl. oz.	140	<1.0	147

Source: Pennington and Church. *Food Values of Portions Commonly Used,* 14th ed. New York: Harper & Row Publishers, 1985.

We hope you enjoy exploring the tasty, nutrient-rich beverages offered in this section.

VEGETABLE PLATTER

Colorful, tasty and nutritious—the vegetable platter is the center of attraction on the simple as well as on the elaborate appetizer table.

asparagus spears, steamed
beet slices or cubes, cooked
broccoli florets
cauliflower florets
carrot wheels or strips
celery sticks
cherry tomatoes
cucumber slices or spears
green beans, whole and
   steamed
green onions
green or sweet red pepper strips
   or rings
mushrooms, whole or sliced
pea pods, raw or steamed

Wash and cut vegetables into bite-sized portions.

Steam vegetables such as asparagus or green beans until crisp-tender. Plunge into cold water. Drain.

Chill all vegetables. Arrange on platter and serve with a tasty, heart-healthy dip.

STUFFED SNOW PEAS

30 appetizers

30 fresh snow peas
¼ cup light cream cheese
⅛ teaspoon dill weed
2 green onions with some tops,
   finely chopped

Blanch peas for 10 seconds. Dip in cold water and drain. Mix cream cheese, dill weed and green onion.

Open pea along one edge and stuff with about ½ teaspoon of cheese mixture.

Nutrient Analysis: 1 pea pod

Calories: 10   *Fat: 0.4 g*   *Cholesterol: 1 mg*

Sodium: 3 mg   *Dietary Fiber: 0.3 g*

Calcium: 7 mg

Diabetic Exchange: 3 appetizers = 1 vegetable

SAVORY STUFFED MUSHROOMS

12 appetizers

12 large, 2" diameter mushrooms
2 tablespoons finely chopped onion
2 tablespoons finely chopped celery or green pepper
2 tablespoons margarine
1 cup fine, soft, whole-wheat bread crumbs
1 teaspoon lemon juice
1 tablespoon sherry
¼ teaspoon garlic powder
⅛ teaspoon pepper
¼ teaspoon dried basil, crushed
1 teaspoon parsley flakes
½ cup grated part-skim mozzarella or ¼ cup Parmesan cheese

Wipe mushrooms with damp cloth and remove stems. Chop stems finely.

In a small skillet, sauté mushroom stems, onion and celery or green pepper in margarine.

In a bowl, combine bread crumbs, lemon juice, sherry, garlic powder, pepper, basil, parsley and mozzarella or Parmesan. Add sautéd mixture and mix well.

Stuff mushrooms caps and place on non-stick sprayed baking sheet. Bake 15 minutes, then broil until nicely browned. Serve warm.

Oven: 350° Broil
Time: 15 minutes, 2 to 3 minutes

Nutrient Analysis: 1 mushroom

Calories: 50   Fat: 2.9 g   Cholesterol: 3 mg

Sodium: 77 mg   Dietary Fiber: 0.4 g

Calcium: 42 mg

Diabetic Exchange: 1 vegetable
½ fat

TOMATOES STUFFED WITH SPINACH

Filling will stuff 6 medium tomatoes to serve as a luncheon entrée or vegetable side dish. Increase baking time about 10 minutes.

About 2 cups; stuffing for 40 cherry tomatoes or large mushrooms

½ cup sodium-reduced, defatted chicken broth
1 10-ounce package frozen chopped spinach
1 small onion, finely chopped
3 tablespoons calorie-reduced mayonnaise
   cherry tomatoes or large mushrooms

Place broth and frozen spinach block in a small saucepan. Cover and heat on low for 5 minutes, turning block after 2 minutes. When spinach is JUST thawed, stir in chopped onion and mayonnaise. Simmer uncovered, stirring frequently until liquid and mixture is consistency of creamed spinach.

Stuff cherry tomatoes or large mushroom caps and bake. Serve hot or cold.

Oven 350°
Time: 10 to 15 minutes

Nutrient Analysis: 1 tomato or mushroom

Calories: 9	Fat: 0.4 g	Cholesterol: 0
Sodium: 13 mg	Dietary Fiber: 0.4 g	
Calcium: 10 mg		

Diabetic Exchange: 3 appetizers = 1 vegetable

MARINATED VEGETABLES

12 portions

1 8-ounce can button
   mushrooms, drained
1 green pepper, cut in strips
1 carrot, sliced in rounds
1 head cauliflower, broken into
   florets
1 16-ounce can or 2 10-ounce
   packages frozen artichoke
   hearts, cut into fourths
12 small white onions or 6 to 8
   green onions with 1" of their
   tops
1½ cups wine vinegar
1 teaspoon sugar
1 teaspoon salt
½ teaspoon pepper
2 teaspoons dried oregano,
   crushed
2 teaspoons dried tarragon,
   crushed
½ cup vegetable oil
½ cup olive oil
   cherry tomatoes
   chopped fresh parsley

In a large bowl, combine mushrooms, green pepper, carrot, cauliflower, artichokes and onions.

In a saucepan, heat vinegar and stir in sugar, salt, pepper, oregano and tarragon. Cool slightly and add oils. Mix well.

Pour dressing over vegetables, stir, cover and refrigerate for 24 hours before serving. Stir occasionally while vegetables are marinating.

To serve, drain and arrange in a lettuce-lined bowl. Garnish with cherry tomatoes and sprinkle with parsley. Provide cocktail forks or toothpicks for spearing vegetables.

Nutrient Analysis: 1 portion

Calories: 74	Fat: 2.6 g	Cholesterol: 0
Sodium: 165 mg	Dietary Fiber: 1.5 g	
Calcium: 49 mg		

Diabetic Exchange: 2 vegetable, ½ fat

CHICKEN APPETIZERS

3 whole chicken breasts, boned and skinned
¾ cup melted margarine
¼ teaspoon garlic powder
¼ teaspoon dry mustard
½ teaspoon dried basil, crushed
¾ cup fine dry bread crumbs
½ cup grated Parmesan cheese
½ cup chopped fresh parsley

50 appetizer pieces

Cut chicken into bite-sized pieces.

In a large bowl, combine margarine, garlic powder, mustard and basil. Stir chicken pieces in margarine mixture.

In a separate bowl, mix bread crumbs, Parmesan and parsley. Remove chicken from margarine and add to crumb mixture. Toss until chicken pieces are well coated with crumbs.

Spread on baking sheet or broiler pan and bake, turning once. Serve with ORIENTAL SWEET-SOUR SAUCE, *(see page 167).*

Oven: 400°
Time: 12 to 15 minutes

Nutrient Analysis: 1 piece

Calories: 40   Fat: 2.2 g   Cholesterol: 5 mg

Sodium: 70 mg   Calcium: 20 mg

Diabetic Exchange: 2 appetizers = 1 medium-fat meat

SPICY FISH BITES

Quick and easy to prepare in your microwave.

16 appetizer pieces

⅓ cup plain low-fat yogurt
½ teaspoon grated lime peel
2 tablespoons fresh lime juice
½ teaspoon ground cumin
¼ teaspoon ground coriander
¼ teaspoon paprika
⅛ teaspoon pepper
1 pound frozen cod or other
    white fish
4 lime wedges

Mix yogurt, lime peel, lime juice, cumin, coriander, paprika and pepper. Cut fish into 16 appetizer-sized cubes and add to marinade.

Chill fish in marinade 2 to 3 hours. Microwave on high 5 to 7 minutes or until fish is flaky. Let stand 3 minutes.

Serve sprinkled with paprika and garnished with lime wedges.

Nutrient Analysis: 1 piece

Calories: 47	Fat: 2.3 g	Cholesterol: 16 mg
Sodium: 18 mg	Calcium: 17 mg	

Diabetic Exchange: 1 lean meat

JULIAN'S FISH APPETIZER

Or serve as a summer entrée for four accompanied by a crisp green salad and crunchy French bread.

16 appetizer pieces

1 pound white fish fillets
   (walleye, roughy or cod)
½ cup water
¼ cup lemon juice or ⅓ cup dry
   white wine
1 tablespoon grated onion

SAUCE
¼ teaspoon prepared mustard
4 tablespoons calorie-reduced
   mayonnaise
3 drops Tabasco sauce
½ teaspoon sodium-reduced
   Worcestershire sauce
½ tablespoon lemon juice
   paprika
   fresh parsley sprigs

Heat the poaching liquid of water, lemon juice or wine and onion in electric skillet to 280° (stove top skillet, medium-high heat until bubbling). Place whole fillets in liquid and poach gently for 5 to 8 minutes. Remove fish and place in a flat glass casserole dish. Cool poaching liquid and pour over fish. Refrigerate until ready to serve.

Mix together mustard, mayonnaise, Tabasco, Worcestershire and lemon juice.

Remove fish from poaching liquid and cut into 16 appetizer-sized pieces. Top with sauce, sprinkle with paprika and garnish with parsley. Serve chilled.

Nutrient Analysis: 1 portion

Calories: 34	Fat: 1.2 g	Cholesterol: 19 mg
Sodium: 42 mg	Calcium: 8 mg	

Diabetic Exchange: 2 appetizers = 1 lean meat

STEAK STICKS

A versatile marinade. Chicken or pheasant—boned, cubed, marinated and grilled on wooden skewers and served with a variety of spicy mustards—is also outstanding.

10 skewers

  1 garlic clove, minced
½ medium onion, minced
  2 teaspoons sugar
¼ cup sodium-reduced soy sauce
¼ cup dry wine
  1 teaspoon grated fresh ginger
¾ pound lean round steak, ½" to ¾" thick
10 wooden skewers (available at Oriental markets)

In medium bowl, combine garlic, onion, sugar, soy sauce, wine and ginger.

Cut steak into thin slices and place in marinade. Marinate for at least 2 hours, stirring occasionally. Thread steak strips ribbon fashion on 6" wooden skewers.

Broil, turning once, to desired degree of doneness. Serve hot.

Nutrient Analysis: 1 skewer

Calories: 69   Fat: 1.8 g   Cholesterol: 22 mg
Sodium: 112 mg

Diabetic Exchange: 1 lean meat

COCKTAIL MEAT BALLS

The secret to these zesty meat balls is the allspice. After meat balls are baked, they can be frozen until ready to use. Serve in YOGURT SAUCE (below) or your own particular favorite. ORIENTAL SWEET-SOUR and SALSA are popular variations.

About 60 meat balls

1 pound lean ground beef,
    double grind if possible
⅓ cup dry bread crumbs
¼ cup ground onion
⅓ cup skim milk
1 egg white, beaten
¼ teaspoon salt
¼ teaspoon ground allspice
⅛ teaspoon pepper

In a medium bowl, mix beef, bread crumbs, onion, milk, egg white, salt, allspice and pepper. Shape into tiny balls and place on jelly roll pan or baking sheets with sides. Bake until brown.

YOGURT SAUCE
3 teaspoons low-sodium, beef-
    flavored bouillon granules
1½ cups water
1 tablespoon cornstarch
½ cup plain low-fat yogurt

Shortly before serving, dissolve bouillon granules in water. Mix cornstarch with one tablespoon yogurt and stir into remaining yogurt. Add yogurt to bouillon. Add meat balls and heat gently. (The yogurt mixture may look curdled at first, but it will become creamy as it simmers.)

Serve in a chafing dish with the YOGURT SAUCE to keep meat balls warm and moist.

Oven: 400°
Time: 12 to 15 minutes

Nutrient Analysis: 1 meat ball

Calories: 20	Fat: 0.8 g	Cholesterol: 5 mg
Sodium: 24 mg		

Diabetic Exchange: 3 meat balls = 1 lean meat

PIZZA BITES

32 appetizer pieces

8   medium tomatoes; peeled,
      seeded and chopped
1   cup chopped onion
2-4 tablespoons chopped green chili
      peppers
¼   cup chopped green pepper
1   teaspoon ground cumin
1   teaspoon dried oregano,
      crushed
1   teaspoon dried basil, crushed
      dash cayenne pepper
8   slices firm-textured bread
2   cups shredded part-skim farmer
      cheese

In a medium saucepan, combine
tomatoes, onion, chili peppers and green
pepper. Cook over medium heat, stirring
occasionally, until tomatoes are tender.
Drain juice and stir in cumin, oregano,
basil and cayenne pepper.

Remove crusts from bread and toast
slices. Arrange toasted slices on large
baking sheet. Divide the tomato mixture
among the bread slices. Top with
shredded cheese.

Place under broiler and broil until the
cheese melts, 1 to 2 minutes. Cut
diagonally into quarters to serve.

Nutrient Analysis: 1 piece

Calories: 45   Fat: 1.8 g   Cholesterol: 8 mg
Sodium: 60 mg   Calcium: 48 mg

Diabetic Exchange: 2 vegetable

SPINACH CRÊPE WHEELS

CRÊPES
3 eggs
1½ cup skim milk
1 cup all-purpose flour
½ teaspoon freshly ground pepper
⅓ cup chopped cooked spinach
    (½ pound fresh spinach or ½
    package frozen spinach)
1 cup finely chopped green
    onions
1 tablespoon vegetable oil

FILLING
2 8-ounce containers light cream
    cheese at room temperature
1 teaspoon freshly ground pepper
½ cup finely chopped fresh basil
    or 2 tablespoons dried basil
1 tablespoon vodka
2 teaspoons grated lemon rind
4 garlic cloves, minced
1½ ounces dehydrated sun-dried
    tomatoes, finely chopped
½ cup pine nuts, toasted

72 appetizer pieces

In a blender or food processor, combine the eggs, milk, flour and pepper. Process until well blended, about 1½ minutes. Pour into a large bowl and whisk in the spinach and green onions.

Warm a 10" skillet over moderate heat and brush lightly with oil. Pour about ¼ cup batter into hot pan, tilting to coat evenly. Cook until lightly browned (about 2 minutes). Flip the crêpe and cook until brown spots begin to appear on the second side, 15 to 20 seconds longer. Remove the crêpe from the pan and let cool. Repeat with remaining batter and oil to make 12 crêpes. Crêpes can be made ahead and refrigerated for 3 days or frozen for 2 weeks. Return to room temperature before filling.

In a medium bowl, stir together the cream cheese, pepper, basil, vodka, lemon rind and garlic.

Lay the crêpes, spotted side up, on a flat surface and spread each with about 2 tablespoons of the cheese mixture. Sprinkle each crêpe with 1 to 1½ teaspoons each sun-dried tomatoes and pine nuts.

Roll crêpes tightly and wrap in plastic wrap. Refrigerate for at least 1 hour. (Can be prepared up to one day in advance and refrigerated until ready to slice.)

Trim the ends of each crêpe roll. Cut on the diagonal into 6 slices. Serve at room temperature.

Nutrient Analysis: 1 piece

Calories: 37   Fat: 2.5 g   Cholesterol: 13 mg

Sodium: 16 mg   Dietary Fiber: 0.2 g

Calcium: 17 mg

Diabetic Exchange: ½ lean meat

SHRIMP APPLE SLICES

4 dozen

2-3 red Delicious apples
2½ tablespoons lemon juice
2 tablespoons minced red onion
1 tablespoon minced fresh parsley
1 tablespoon minced fresh dill or
    1 teaspoon dried dill weed
4 teaspoons prepared white
    horseradish, drained
⅛ teaspoon freshly ground pepper
2 tablespoons calorie-reduced
    mayonnaise
48 tiny frozen shrimp, thawed
    sprigs of fresh dill

Core and mince half of 1 apple; toss with ½ tablespoon lemon juice. Core and cut enough of the remaining apple to make 48 ¼" slices. Toss with remaining 2 tablespoons lemon juice.

In a medium bowl, combine the minced apple, onion, parsley, dill, horseradish, pepper and mayonnaise.

Pat apple slices dry and top with 1 teaspoon of apple-onion mixture and a shrimp. Garnish with small sprigs of fresh dill.

Nutrient Analysis: 1 piece

Calories: 16	Fat: 0.3 g	Cholesterol: 14 mg
Sodium: 17 mg	Dietary Fiber: 0.3 g	
Calcium: 8 mg		

Diabetic Exchange: 3 appetizers = 1 lean meat

FRUIT AND CHEESE KABOBS

Alternate pieces of fruit and cubes of part-skim farmer or mozzarella cheese on toothpicks. To serve, stick picks into inverted orange or grapefruit halves.

MOCK SOUR CREAM

This can be substituted for sour cream in dips, spreads and dressings. For heated foods such as stroganoff, plain low-fat yogurt is the recommended substitute.

2 cups

2 cups low-fat cottage cheese
2 tablespoons lemon juice
¼ cup skim milk

Process cottage cheese and lemon juice in food processor or blender until creamy.

Add skim milk to desired consistency.

To transform the "sour cream" into tasty dips, add the following ingredients and mix well.

MOCK SOUR CREAM VARIATIONS

HORSERADISH DIP

1 tablespoon prepared
   horseradish

DILL DIP

2 tablespoons fresh dill or 2
   teaspoons dried dill weed
2 tablespoons chopped green
   onion

CREAMY DIP FOR VEGETABLES

¼ cup chopped fresh parsley
2 tablespoons chopped green
   onion
1 tablespoon calorie-reduced
   mayonnaise
1 teaspoon sodium-reduced
   Worcestershire sauce

MUSTARD DIP

½ teaspoon Dijon mustard
3 drops Tabasco sauce
½ small onion
2 tablespoons chopped fresh
   parsley
1 tablespoon minced chives
1-2 tablespoons skim milk if
   necessary

Nutrient Analysis: 1 tablespoon

Calories: 22	Fat: 0.4 g	Cholesterol: 2 mg
Sodium: 93 mg	Calcium: 19 mg	

Diabetic Exchange: 2 tablespoons = ½ skim milk

MOCK CREAM CHEESE

Slightly softer than regular cream cheese, MOCK CREAM CHEESE makes an excellent base for dips and spreads. The addition of a tablespoon or two of powdered sugar to each cup of cream cheese transforms it into a yummy dessert topping.

About 2 cups

½ 15-ounce carton ricotta cheese
½ 14-ounce carton dry curd
　 cottage cheese
¼ cup plain low-fat yogurt

Place ricotta and cottage cheese in blender or food processor bowl. Cover and blend or process at medium speed until smooth. The secret of success is blending long enough so that the ricotta loses its grainy texture.

Blend in yogurt. Cover and chill overnight to set.

Nutrient Analysis: 1 tablespoon

Calories: 16	Fat: 0.7 g	Cholesterol: 3 mg
Sodium: 35 mg	Calcium: 26 mg	

Diabetic Exchange: 2 tablespoons = ½ skim milk

HERBED CHEESE DIP

3 cups

2 cups small curd, low-fat
　 cottage cheese
1 cup calorie-reduced mayonnaise
½ cup grated onion
½ teaspoon garlic powder
1 teaspoon dry mustard
½ teaspoon celery seed
¼ teaspoon pepper
¼ teaspoon Tabasco sauce
½ teaspoon sodium-reduced
　 Worcestershire sauce

Thoroughly blend cottage cheese, mayonnaise, onion, garlic powder, mustard, celery seed, pepper, Tabasco and Worcestershire.

Refrigerate for at least an hour (overnight is better) before serving.

Serve with a medley of raw vegetables, such as carrots, celery, mushrooms, green pepper, broccoli, cauliflower and cherry tomatoes. Or try lightly blanched green beans or snow peas.

Nutrient Analysis: 1 tablespoon

Calories: 23	Fat: 1.5 g	Cholesterol: 0
Sodium: 67 mg	Calcium: 7 mg	

Diabetic Exchange: 2 tablespoons = ½ skim milk

HUMMUS BI TAHINI

A traditional recipe from the Middle East. Chickpeas are also known as garbanzo beans. Tahini is a sesame seed paste available in Oriental and Middle Eastern markets.

About 1¼ cups

¼ cup sesame seed, toasted
1 tablespoon lemon juice
1 garlic clove, halved
1 cup chickpeas (garbanzo beans), cooked and drained
3 tablespoons plain low-fat yogurt
½ teaspoon ground cumin
¼ cup fresh chopped parsley
⅛ cup sliced ripe olives (optional)
whole-wheat pita bread

In food processor or blender, combine sesame seed, lemon juice and garlic. Process or blend until well mixed.

Add chick-peas, yogurt and cumin. Process until smooth. Stir in parsley.

Place dip in a small bowl and garnish with sliced olives if desired. Serve with pita bread cut in triangles.

Nutrient Analysis: 1 tablespoon

Calories: 22   Fat: 1 g   Cholesterol: 0

Sodium: 2 mg   Dietary Fiber: 0.4 g

Calcium: 25 mg

Diabetic Exchange: 2 tablespoons = ½ bread

GARBANZO SPREAD

One tester asked if this was a salmon mold. Flavors will be enhanced by preparing 24 hours in advance.

About 3 cups

½ onion, chopped
2 tablespoons olive oil
½ bunch parsley, finely chopped
1 teaspoon dried basil, crushed
½ teaspoon dried oregano, crushed
¼ teaspoon ground cumin
1 garlic clove, minced or ¼ teaspoon garlic powder
juice of 1 lemon
3 cups cooked garbanzo beans (chickpeas), mashed
⅔ cup sesame seeds, ground (optional)
parsley for garnish

Sauté onion in oil until soft. Add parsley, basil, oregano, cumin and garlic, cooking just long enough to soften parsley. Thoroughly mix onion-herb mixture with lemon juice, garbanzo beans and sesame seeds.

Pack into a bowl and chill overnight. Unmold onto serving plate and garnish with parsley. Serve with crackers or celery sticks.

Nutrient Analysis: 1 tablespoon

Calories: 21	Fat: 0.7 g	Cholesterol: 0
Sodium: 2 mg	Dietary Fiber: 0.4 g	
Calcium: 8 mg		

Diabetic Exchange: 2 tablespoons = ½ bread

SALMON YOGURT DIP

Substitute a can of clams or shrimp for the salmon for a tasty variation.

About 1½ cups

1 15-ounce can salmon, drained
¼ cup finely chopped onions
½ teaspoon prepared mustard
1 teaspoon sodium-reduced Worcestershire sauce
8 ounces plain low-fat yogurt

In blender on low speed, blend salmon, onions, mustard and Worcestershire. Stir in yogurt. Do not overblend or dip may become watery. Serve chilled.

Nutrient Analysis: 1 tablespoon

Calories: 33	Fat: 1 g	Cholesterol: 12.5 mg
Sodium: 75 mg	Calcium: 19.6 mg	

Diabetic Exchange: 2 tablespoons = 1 lean meat

SPINACH DIP

Everybody's favorite dip served in a "bread bowl."

About 4 cups

1 10-ounce package frozen
   chopped spinach
¼ cup finely chopped onion
¼ cup chopped green pepper
¼ teaspoon garlic powder
1 cup plain low-fat yogurt
1 cup small curd cottage cheese
   or 8-ounce package light
   cream cheese
1 8-ounce can sliced water
   chestnuts, drained
1 round loaf of bread, uncut

Thaw and drain spinach well. Combine spinach, onion, green pepper, garlic powder, yogurt, cottage cheese or cream cheese and water chestnuts. Mix well and chill.

Slice off top of bread and scoop out center. Cut bread from center into cubes. Fill center of bread with dip and surround with bread cubes and unsalted crackers.

Nutrient Analysis: 1 tablespoon (dip only)

Calories: 9	*Fat: 0.1 g*	*Cholesterol: 0.5 mg*
Sodium: 20 mg	*Calcium: 14 mg*	

Diabetic Exchange: 3 tablespoons = 1 vegetable

FRUIT WARMER

It makes a good cooler, too!

4½ cups

2 cups unsweetened orange juice
1 cup cranberry juice
½ cup unsweetened pineapple
   juice
1 tablespoon lemon juice
1 cup water
   fresh mint leaves

Combine the orange, cranberry, pineapple, lemon juice and water in a large saucepan. Heat over medium heat until mixture comes to a boil. Reduce heat and simmer 3 to 5 minutes. Serve hot garnished with mint leaves.

Nutrient Analysis: 1 cup

Calories: 98	*Fat: 0*	*Cholesterol: 0*
Sodium: 2 mg	*Calcium: 20 mg*	

Diabetic Exchange: 1½ fruit

BAKED EGGPLANT DIP

Eggplant dip or "Poor Man's Caviar" can be made ahead of serving time. It will keep several days in the refrigerator. Tahini (sesame seed) paste is available in Oriental food stores.

About 2 cups

1 large eggplant
½ garlic clove, minced
¼ cup tahini paste
¼ cup lemon juice
½ tablespoon olive oil
⅛ teaspoon salt
¼ teaspoon white pepper
1 tablespoon finely chopped
   parsley

Wash and dry eggplant. Leave on skin and stem. Pierce with fork several times. Place on baking sheet and bake at 350° for 1 hour. Cool slightly. Under cold running water, remove skin and stem. Drain well.

Mash eggplant with a fork. Add garlic, tahini paste, lemon juice, olive oil, salt and pepper. Mix until well blended.

Place in serving bowl and garnish with chopped parsley.

Nutrient Analysis: 1 tablespoon

Calories: 19	Fat: 1.2 g	Cholesterol: 0
Sodium: 12 mg	Dietary Fiber: 0.4 g	
Calcium: 16 mg		

Diabetic Exchange: 2 tablespoons = 1 vegetable, ½ fat

CHRISTMAS CRANBERRY FLOAT

To trim calories, substitute club soda for ginger ale.

10 cups

6 cups cranberry juice, chilled
1 quart ginger ale or club soda,
   chilled
1 pint lemon, pineapple, orange
   or lime sherbet

In a 4-quart pitcher or punch bowl, combine cranberry juice and ginger ale. Just before serving, add sherbet and ice as desired. For a festive touch, float scoops of sherbet on top. Serve immediately.

Nutrient Analysis: ½ cup with sherbet

Calories: 83	Fat: 0.4 g	Cholesterol: 0
Sodium: 3 mg	Calcium: 16 mg	

Diabetic Exchange: 1½ fruit

MULLED CIDER

Mulled—heated and spiced—drinks are a great warm up!

9 cups

6 cups apple cider
2⅔ cups water
3 tablespoons lemon juice
2 cinnamon sticks
½ teaspoon whole cloves
½ teaspoon whole allspice
    orange or lemon slices for
      garnish; cinnamon sticks for
      stirrers (optional)

Simmer cider, water, lemon juice and spices together in a saucepan for 10 to 15 minutes. Strain and serve hot, garnished with a fruit slice and a cinnamon stick.

WASSAIL

Wassail is a beverage used to toast health and good will to festival participants. Traditionally, it was made with wine or ale spiced with apple and sugar.

9 cups

2¾ cups pineapple juice

Substitute pineapple juice for the water in MULLED CIDER recipe.

Nutrient Analysis: 1 cup

	Mulled Cider	Wassail
Calories:	79	90
Fat:	0.2 g	0.2 g
Cholesterol:	0	0
Sodium:	5 mg	5 mg
Calcium:	12 mg	12 mg
Diabetic Exchange:	1 fruit	½ fruit

ENERGY NOG

Energy packed with vitamins and minerals.

3 cups

1 cup plain low-fat yogurt
⅔ cup orange juice
½ cup cooked pitted prunes, drained
1 tablespoon wheat germ (optional)
8 ice cubes
  nutmeg

In blender, combine yogurt, orange juice, prunes and wheat germ. Blend until smooth.

Add ice cubes and blend again until smooth. Pour into glasses and sprinkle with nutmeg. Serve immediately.

Nutrient Analysis: 1 cup

Calories: 89   Fat: 1.4 g   Cholesterol: 4.7 mg

Sodium: 53 mg   Dietary Fiber: 2 g

Calcium: 98 mg

Diabetic Exchange: 1 skim milk

RASPBERRY PUNCH

Deliciously refreshing! The word "punch" comes from the East Indian word "puny" meaning five, so-called for its five ingredients: spirit, citrus juice, spices, tea and water. Introduced into England from Spain, it was also called "contradiction" because it used spirit to make it strong, water to make it weak, lemon to make it sour and sugar to make it sweet.

3 quarts

2 10-ounce packages frozen raspberries or strawberries
2 cups unsweetened orange juice
1 6-ounce can frozen lemonade
4 cans water
  ice
1 quart club soda

Thaw raspberries or strawberries and mash with a fork or potato masher. Mix berries with orange juice, lemonade and water.

Just before serving, pour fruit mixture over ice and add club soda.

Nutrient Analysis: 1 cup

Calories: 92   Fat: 0.2 g   Cholesterol: 0

Sodium: 31 mg   Dietary Fiber: 1.3 g

Calcium: 18 mg

Diabetic Exchange: 1½ fruit

CITRUS REFRESHER

4 quarts

4 cups fresh orange juice
4 cups pineapple juice
2 cups cranberry juice
2 oranges, sliced and cut into
   quarters
1 lemon, sliced and cut into
   halves
1 lime, sliced
2 cups crushed ice
2 cups club soda

Combine orange, pineapple and cranberry juice. Prepare oranges, lemon and lime; add to juice. Chill. Just before serving, add ice and club soda.

Nutrient Analysis: 1 cup

Calories: 110	Fat: 0	Cholesterol: 0
Sodium: 10 mg	Calcium: 36 mg	

Diabetic Exchange: 2 fruit

TOMATO JUICE COCKTAIL

6 cups

1 46-ounce can low-sodium
   tomato juice
2 teaspoons wine vinegar
¼ teaspoon sugar
1 bay leaf
¼ teaspoon parsley flakes,
   crushed
¼ teaspoon dried basil, crushed
¼ teaspoon dried chervil, crushed
½ teaspoon sodium-reduced
   Worcestershire sauce

In a large sauce pan, combine tomato juice, vinegar, sugar, bay leaf, parsley, basil, chervil and Worcestershire. Bring to a boil. Reduce heat, simmer 10 minutes. Serve hot or cold.

Nutrient Analysis: ¾ cup

Calories: 32	Fat: 0.2 g	Cholesterol: 0
Sodium: 55 mg	Calcium: 14 mg	

Diabetic Exchange: 1 vegetable

INSTANT COCOA MIX

For cocoa-mocha...add hot coffee instead of water to cocoa mix.

17 servings

4 cups non-fat dry milk powder
1 cup powdered sugar
¾ cup cocoa

Mix together milk powder, sugar and cocoa. Place ⅓ cup cocoa mix in a cup and stir in a small amount of warm water to make paste. Fill cup with boiling water. Stir and serve.

Store cocoa mix in airtight container.

Nutrient Analysis: ⅓ cup mix in water

Calories: 140	Fat: 0.3 g	Cholesterol: 7 mg
Sodium: 147 mg	Calcium: 340 mg	

Diabetic Exchange: 1 skim milk, 1 fruit

BERRY MILK SHAKE

5 cups

1 cup frozen unsweetened
  strawberries, thawed
1 10-ounce package frozen
  raspberries, thawed and
  drained
1½ cups cold skim milk
1 cup plain low-fat yogurt
1 whole egg or 2 egg whites
¼ cup honey
½ teaspoon vanilla
  strawberries or raspberries for
  garnish, if desired

Place strawberries, raspberries and ½ cup milk in blender. Blend on high speed 1 minute or until smooth. Add remaining milk, yogurt, egg, honey and vanilla. Blend until frothy.

Serve immediately in tall, chilled glasses. Garnish with berries.

Nutrient Analysis: 1 cup

Calories: 240	Fat: 3.6 g	Cholesterol: 57 mg
Sodium: 91 mg	Dietary Fiber: 2.8 g	
Calcium: 160 mg		

Diabetic Exchange: 1 lowfat milk, 2 fruit

BREADS

Here is bread, which strengthens man's heart, and therefore called the staff of life.

Matthew Henry

BREADS

Recent research indicates that we need to increase our intake of complex carbohydrates and fiber. This section is especially valuable in helping you attain this goal. Choosing whole-grain recipes for making breads, muffins, coffeecakes, waffles and pancakes is a big step toward boosting complex carbohydrates and dietary fiber. A diet high in all types of fiber may reduce the risk of colon-rectal cancers and may also provide a cardiovascular bonus by reducing serum cholesterol levels.

Whole-grain breads and cereals are also recommended in reducing diets. The popular notion that breads are fattening and should be eliminated from a reducing diet has been disproven. In one research study (American J. Clin. Nutr. 32:1703, 1979) overweight college-age men on a restricted calorie diet consumed 12 slices of high-fiber bread each day. These men lost 19 pounds in 8 weeks. A control group ate the same diet except white enriched bread was substituted for the high-fiber bread, and lost only 14 pounds in the same time period. This study is the bearer of good news for two reasons. First, both groups lost weight while eating 12 slices of bread a day. Second, those who ate high-fiber bread also reduced their calorie intake. So, the bottom line is—*don't* omit bread if concerned about weight control.

The availability of new hybrid and high-protein flours has made it almost possible for man to "live by bread alone". As long as we use whole grains and include nuts or seeds and bits of fruit along with egg white and low-fat milk, breads truly are the "staff of life". Whole-grain breads can provide ample protein, complex carbohydrates, many vitamins and minerals and liberal amounts of fiber while adding little fat or sodium.

To substitute whole wheat flour for white flour, follow these guidelines. For each cup of all-purpose flour, use one of the following:

    1 cup whole wheat flour minus 2 tablespoons
    1/2 cup white flour plus 1/2 cup whole wheat flour
    3/4 cup white flour plus 1/4 cup wheat germ and/or bran

These flour combinations are equivalent to 1 cup wheat flour:

    1/2 cup rye flour + 1/3 cup potato flour
    1/3 cup rye flour + 5/8 cup rice flour
    1 cup soy flour + 3/4 cup potato flour
    5/8 cup rice flour + 1/3 cup potato flour
    1/2 cup cornstarch + 1/2 cup rye flour
    1/2 cup cornstarch + 1/2 cup potato flour

Various flours in the following quantities can be substituted for 1 cup of wheat flour:

1 cup corn flour	1-1/3 cups ground rolled oats
3/4 cup coarse cornmeal	1-1/8 cups oat flour
3/4 cup cornstarch	3/4 cup soybean flour or other bean flour
5/8 cup potato flour	
7/8 cup buckwheat	1 cup barley
7/8 cup rice flour	1 cup millet
1-1/4 cup rye flour	1 cup tapioca flour
1/2 cup ground nuts or seed	3/4 cup potato flour

To replace 1 tablespoon wheat flour as a thickener for sauces, gravies and puddings, use one of the following:

1/2 tablespoon cornstarch	2 tablespoons uncooked rice
1/2 tablespoon potato starch	1/2 tablespoon bean flour or nut flour
1/2 tablespoon rice flour	1/2 tablespoon plain gelatin
1/2 tablespoon arrowroot	1 tablespoon tapioca flour
2 teaspoons quick-cooking tapioca	

PECAN OAT MUFFINS

A moist, delicately flavored muffin; that's also sugar-free!

18 muffins

¾ cup finely chopped pecans
1 cup rolled oats
1 cup all-purpose flour
½ cup whole-wheat flour
½ teaspoon baking soda
½ teaspoon baking powder
3 tablespoons margarine
3 tablespoons honey
1 cup *sour skim milk or
   buttermilk
1 egg
¼ teaspoon vanilla

To sour milk, place 1 tablespoon lemon juice or mild vinegar in a 1 cup measure. Add skim milk to make 1 cup.

Mix and dry roast pecans and oats by stirring in heavy skillet over low heat for about 10 minutes or toast on a baking sheet in a 200° *oven for 10 minutes.*

Sift together flours, soda and baking powder. Stir in dry-roasted pecans and oats. Make a well in center of dry ingredients.

Melt margarine and honey together. Beat honey mixture into sour milk or buttermilk, egg, and vanilla until well blended. Pour into well in dry ingredients and mix only until moistened.

Fill non-stick sprayed or paper lined muffin tins two-thirds full. Bake. Remove from tins and cool on wire rack. Serve warm or at room temperature.

Oven: 350°
Time: 20 to 25 minutes

Nutrient Analysis: 1 muffin

Calories: 110   Fat: 5.8 g   Cholesterol: 28 mg

Sodium: 120 mg   Dietary Fiber: 1 g

Calcium: 31 mg

Diabetic Exchange: 1 starch, 1 fat

BANANA BRAN MUFFINS

An excellent source of fiber with no added sugar.

24 muffins

2 cups whole-wheat flour
1¾ cups unprocessed bran
1 tablespoon baking soda
1¾ cups *sour skim milk or
      buttermilk
1 cup mashed ripe bananas
1 egg
¾ cup apple juice concentrate
¼ cup margarine, melted
2 egg whites
¼ cup chopped dates
¼ cup chopped nuts

To sour milk, place 2 tablespoons lemon juice or mild vinegar in a 2 cup measure. Add milk to make 1¾ cups.

Combine flour, bran and baking soda.

Mix together sour skim milk or buttermilk, bananas, egg, apple juice concentrate and melted margarine. Stir into dry ingredients.

Beat egg whites until stiff. Fold beaten egg whites, dates, and nuts into mixture. Fill non-stick sprayed or paper lined muffin tins two-thirds full. Bake. Remove from tins and cool on wire rack. Serve warm or at room temperature.

Oven: 375°
Time: 15 to 20 minutes

Nutrient Analysis: 1 muffin

Calories: 93   Fat: 3.5 g   Cholesterol: 11 mg

Sodium: 145 mg   Dietary Fiber: 10.8 g

Calcium: 37 mg

Diabetic Exchange: 1 starch, ½ fat

BLUEBERRY MUFFINS

12 muffins

1 cup all-purpose flour
1 cup whole-wheat flour
½ cup plus ½ tablespoon sugar
1 tablespoon baking powder
½ teaspoon cinnamon
1½ to 2 cups fresh or unthawed
    frozen blueberries
¼ cup margarine, melted
½ cup skim milk
1 egg
1 egg white
½ teaspoon vanilla

In a medium mixing bowl combine flours, ½ cup sugar, baking powder and cinnamon.

In a separate bowl, toss blueberries with 1 tablespoon of the flour mixture and set aside.

After margarine has cooled slightly, stir in milk, egg, egg white and vanilla. Add mixture to dry ingredients and stir until well-moistened. Stir in berries.

Spoon batter into non-stick sprayed muffin tins. Sprinkle tops with remaining ½ tablespoon sugar. Bake until golden. Let muffins stand for 5 minutes before removing from tins. Serve warm or at room temperature.

Oven: 400°
Time: 20 minutes

Nutrient Analysis: 1 muffin

Calories: 166   Fat: 4.7 g   Cholesterol: 20 mg

Sodium: 129 mg   Dietary Fiber: 2 g

Calcium: 72 mg

Diabetic Exchange: 1½ starch, 1 fat

CARROT BRAN MUFFINS

12 muffins

1 cup 40% bran flakes
¾ cup skim milk
2 cups finely shredded carrots
1 cup whole-wheat flour
1 teaspoon baking powder
½ teaspoon soda
¼ to ½ teaspoon cinnamon
2 tablespoons brown sugar
2 tablespoons vegetable oil
1 tablespoon lemon juice
1 egg, slightly beaten

Combine bran flakes, milk, and carrots; let stand 5 minutes.

Combine flour, baking powder, soda and cinnamon.

Stir sugar, oil, lemon juice and egg into carrot mixture. Add liquid mixture to flour mixture stirring until moistened.

Fill non-stick sprayed or paper-lined muffin tins half full. Bake. Remove from tins and cool on wire rack. Serve warm or at room temperature.

Oven: 400°
Time: 20 to 25 minutes

Nutrient Analysis: 1 muffin

Calories: 95   Fat: 3 g   Cholesterol: 21 mg

Sodium: 120 mg   Dietary Fiber: 2.7 g

Calcium: 42 mg

Diabetic Exchange: 1 starch, ⅓ fat

VEGETABLE CORNMEAL MUFFINS

Stone-ground cornmeal, if you can find it, makes a tastier muffin.

12 muffins

1 cup all-purpose flour
½ cup cornmeal
1 tablespoon sugar
1 tablespoon baking powder
¾ teaspoon Italian seasoning
⅛ teaspoon garlic powder
2 eggs, beaten
1 tablespoon vegetable oil
⅓ cup skim milk
½ cup whole kernel corn, drained
⅓ cup chopped green pepper
¼ cup finely chopped onion

Combine flour, cornmeal, sugar, baking powder, Italian seasoning and garlic powder.

Mix beaten eggs, oil and milk; stir into dry ingredients. Stir in corn, green pepper and onion.

Bake in non-stick sprayed or paper-lined muffin tins. Remove from tins and serve hot.

Oven: 400°
Time: 20 to 25 minutes

Nutrient Analysis: 1 muffin

Calories: 95	Fat: 2.6 g	Cholesterol: 42 mg
Sodium: 137 mg	Calcium: 32 mg	

Diabetic Exchange: 1 starch, ½ fat

ROLLED BISCUITS

This very light, flaky biscuit was a Grand Prize Winner in the Heart's Delight Recipe Contest.

18 biscuits

2 cups all-purpose flour (or 1½ cups all-purpose and ½ cup whole-wheat flour)
1 tablespoon baking powder
⅓ cup vegetable oil
½ cup skim milk
¼ cup buttermilk

Sift together flour and baking powder. Add oil and stir with a fork until mixture looks like coarse crumbs. Add skim milk and buttermilk and stir.

Knead gently on a floured board 6 to 8 times. Roll out to ½" thick. Cut biscuits in 2" rounds. Bake biscuits on ungreased baking sheet. Serve hot with honey.

Oven: 450°
Time: 10 to 12 minutes

Nutrient Analysis: 1 biscuit

Calories: 88	Fat: 4 g	Cholesterol: 0
Sodium: 77 mg	Calcium: 24 mg	

Diabetic Exchange: ½ starch, 1 fat

APPLE CINNAMON PANCAKES

Top pancakes with low-cal, high-taste FRUIT TOPPING, (see page 391) instead of the overly-sweet commercial syrups.

15 3" pancakes

1 cup all-purpose flour ½ cup whole-wheat flour 2 tablespoons sugar 1 tablespoon baking powder 1 teaspoon cinnamon 3 egg whites, beaten ¾ cup skim milk 2 tablespoons margarine, melted 1 cup unsweetened applesauce	Mix together flours, sugar, baking powder and cinnamon. Combine the beaten egg whites, milk, margarine and applesauce and stir into the flour mixture just until moistened. Pour batter from pitcher or large spoon onto hot griddle. When pancakes are puffed and full of bubbles, turn and brown other side. *Griddle: 350°*

Nutrient Analysis: 1 pancake

Calories: 73   Fat: 1.7 g   Cholesterol: 11 mg

Sodium: 120 mg   Calcium: 31 mg

Diabetic Exchange: 1 starch

WHOLE-WHEAT WAFFLES

Tender and light and thoroughly delicious! Top waffles with FRUIT TOPPING (see page 391).

10 waffles

1½ cups whole-wheat flour ¼ cup all-purpose flour 2 teaspoons baking powder 2 eggs, separated 1½ cup skim milk 3 tablespoons vegetable oil 2 tablespoons honey	Heat waffle iron while making batter. Stir together flours and baking powder. Beat egg yolks until they are lemon colored. Add milk, oil and honey. Blend well and stir into the dry ingredients. Beat egg whites until stiff, and fold into batter. Pour batter onto lightly oiled, hot waffle iron. Bake until steaming stops. Lift waffle from iron with a fork.

Nutrient Analysis: 1 waffle

Calories: 150   Fat: 5.6 g   Cholesterol: 51 mg

Sodium: 110 mg   Dietary Fiber: 1.8 g

Calcium: 71 mg

Diabetic Exchange: 1½ starch, 1 fat

CORN BREAD

8 x 8" pan; 16 portions

2 egg whites
¼ cup plain low-fat yogurt
¾ cup skim milk
3 tablespoons honey
1 cup yellow cornmeal
¼ cup all-purpose flour
¾ cup whole-wheat flour
2 teaspoons baking powder
½ teaspoon baking soda
3 tablespoons melted margarine
1 cup shredded carrots (optional)

Beat together egg whites, yogurt, milk and honey.

In a separate bowl mix together cornmeal, flours, baking powder and soda.

Combine liquid ingredients, dry ingredients, melted margarine and carrots (if desired). Stir just enough to blend. Over-stirring will make bread tough. Spread into a non-stick sprayed 8 x 8" pan. Bake. Serve hot.

Oven: 425°
Time: 20 minutes

MEXICORN BREAD VARIATION

1 teaspoon SEASONING BLEND
   #7, *(see page 379)*
1 cup whole kernel corn, frozen
   or sodium-reduced canned
1 tablespoon chopped pimiento
1 tablespoon finely diced sweet
   or hot green pepper

Follow the basic recipe for CORN BREAD, decreasing the honey to 1 tablespoon and omitting the carrots. Add:

Nutrient Analysis: 1 piece

	Corn Bread	Mexicorn
Calories:	100	98
Fat:	2.5 g	2.6 g
Cholesterol:	0	0
Sodium:	100 mg	102 mg
Calcium:	59 mg	54 mg
Diabetic Exchange:	1 starch	1 starch
	½ fat	½ fat

CORN ZEPHYRS

A very light corn puff that's also sugar free!

About 16 corn puffs

1 cup stone-ground white
   cornmeal
1 cup cold water
½ teaspoon salt
3 cups boiling water
1 tablespoon margarine
4 egg whites

Mix corn meal, cold water and salt. Add slowly to boiling water, stirring constantly. Cook over low heat, stirring frequently, for 30 minutes. Remove from heat and lightly oil top with margarine. Let cool.

Whip egg whites until stiff and fold into cooled cornmeal mixture. Spoon onto non-stick sprayed baking sheet. Bake. Remove immediately from baking pan. Serve hot.

Oven: 350°
Time: 25 to 30 minutes

Nutrient Analysis: 1 puff

Calories: 41   *Fat: 1.4 g*   *Cholesterol: 5.1 mg*
Sodium: 87 mg

Diabetic Exchange: ½ starch

SCRAPPLE

There are many varieties of scrapple but our favorite has the addition of cooked pork stripped from neck bones. Scrapple freezes well. Slice when cold and freeze in individual portions.

9 x 5" loaf pan; 16 ½" slices

1-2 pounds pork neck bones
½ large onion, sliced
2 celery ribs with leaves
4-5 whole peppercorns
    water to cover
1 cup cornmeal
1 cup cold water
½ teaspoon salt
½ teaspoon freshly grated nutmeg
4 cups boiling liquid (reserved neck bone liquid plus water)

In a saucepan, cover neck bones with water. Add onion, celery and peppercorns and bring to a boil. Reduce heat and simmer until meat falls from bones (about 2 hours). Strain and refrigerate reserved liquid until fat congeals on top. Remove fat and discard. Pick meat from bones and chop finely.

Mix cornmeal, cold water, salt and nutmeg. Add gradually, stirring constantly, to 4 cups of boiling liquid (reserved meat liquid plus water). Continue stirring and cook over low heat until thickened (about 15 minutes). Cool to lukewarm, add pork and turn into a loaf pan that has been rinsed in cold water. Cover with a sheet of waxed paper and chill well.

Slice cold mush into ½" slices and sauté on both sides very slowly (30 to 45 minutes) in 1 - 2 tablespoons margarine. If you try to rush it, the slices will fall apart. Serve with warm syrup.

Nutrient Analysis: 1 slice

Calories: 53   Fat: 1.2 g   Cholesterol: 9 mg

Sodium: 89 mg   Dietary Fiber: 1 g

Diabetic Exchange: ½ starch

APPLESAUCE NUT BREAD

Very dense and moist. This flavorful loaf is white in color rather than the golden or brown of many of the other quick bread loaves.

9 x 5" loaf pan; 20 slices

½ cup sugar
1 cup unsweetened applesauce
⅓ cup vegetable oil
4 egg whites or egg substitute
    equal to 2 eggs
3 tablespoons skim milk
2 cups sifted all-purpose flour
1 teaspoon baking powder
½ teaspoon cinnamon
½ teaspoon nutmeg
¾ cup chopped pecans

TOPPING
¼ cup brown sugar
½ teaspoon cinnamon
¼ cup chopped pecans

In a large mixing bowl, combine sugar, applesauce, oil, egg whites and milk. Mix together thoroughly.

Sift together the flour, baking powder, cinnamon and nutmeg. Beat dry ingredients into the applesauce mixture until well-combined. Stir in the pecans.

Pour the batter into a non-stick sprayed 9 x 5" loaf pan.

Combine the brown sugar, cinnamon and pecans. Sprinkle evenly over the batter and bake. Cap loosely with foil after the first 30 minutes of baking. When done (a toothpick inserted near the center should come out clean and dry), remove the bread from the pan and cool on a rack.

Oven: 350°
Time: 60 minutes

Nutrient Analysis: 1 slice

Calories: 149	Fat: 7.8 g	Cholesterol: 0
Sodium: 27 mg	Calcium: 27 mg	

Diabetic Exchange: 1 starch, 1½ fat

CRANBERRY BREAD

9 x 5" loaf pan; 20 slices

1 cup all-purpose flour
1 cup whole-wheat flour
½ cup brown sugar
1½ teaspoons baking powder
½ teaspoon baking soda
¼ teaspoon cinnamon
¼ teaspoon ground cloves
   grated rind of 1 orange
¾ cup orange juice
2 egg whites or egg substitute
   equal to 1 egg
¼ cup margarine, melted
1 cup firm, fresh cranberries
½ cup chopped nuts (walnuts,
   pecans)

Sift together flours, sugar, baking powder, baking soda, cinnamon and cloves.

Lightly beat together orange rind, orange juice, egg whites and melted margarine. Stir the liquid ingredients into the dry ingredients.

Coarsely chop the cranberries and add them along with the chopped nuts to the batter. Mix well.

Pour into a non-stick sprayed loaf pan. Bake until a toothpick inserted near the center comes out clean and dry. Cool on wire rack and remove from pan. Wrap tightly to store.

Oven: 350°
Time: 60 minutes

Nutrient Analysis: 1 slice

Calories: 110   Fat: 4.9 g   Cholesterol: 0
Sodium: 58 mg   Dietary Fiber: 1 g
Calcium: 17 mg

Diabetic Exchange: 1 starch, 1 fat

MOLASSES BROWN BREAD

An old-fashioned brown bread with plump raisins. A bonus—no sugar added!

9 x 5" loaf pan or 2 4½" deep x 2¾" diameter round loaf tins; 16 slices

½ cup whole-wheat flour
½ cup all-purpose flour
1 teaspoon baking soda
½ teaspoon cinnamon
1 egg
1 cup 100% bran cereal
½ cup seedless raisins
2 tablespoons vegetable oil
⅓ cup molasses
¾ cup very hot water

Sift together flours, soda and cinnamon. Set aside.

In a large mixing bowl, beat egg until foamy. Mix in cereal, raisins, oil, molasses and water. Add dry ingredients stirring only until combined.

Spread evenly in a non-stick sprayed loaf pan or fill non-stick sprayed round tins two-thirds full. Bake until toothpick inserted near center comes out clean and dry. Remove from pan or tins; slice and serve hot.

Oven: 350°
Time: loaf, 45 minutes; round tins, 35 minutes

Nutrient Analysis: 1 slice

Calories: 87   Fat: 2 g   Cholesterol: 16 mg

Sodium: 120 mg   Dietary Fiber: 2.3 g

Calcium: 28 mg

Diabetic Exchange: 1 starch

LEMON BREAD

Light, tasty and moist!

1 cup all-purpose flour
½ cup whole-wheat flour
2 teaspoons baking powder
2 tablespoons margarine
¾ cup sugar
1 egg
1 egg white
½ cup skim milk
   grated rind of 1 lemon
½ cup chopped nuts

GLAZE
juice of one lemon
1 tablespoon powdered sugar

9 x 5" loaf pan, 20 slices

Sift together flours and baking powder.

Cream together margarine and sugar. Stir in egg, egg white, milk and lemon rind.

Mix thoroughly with dry ingredients. Stir in chopped nuts.

Pour into non-stick sprayed loaf pan and let stand for 20 minutes. Bake until toothpick inserted near center comes out clean and dry.

Brush hot loaf with lemon juice and powdered sugar glaze. Cool on wire rack and remove from pan.

Oven: 350°
Time: 45-50 minutes (Check after 40 minutes. Don't over bake.)

Nutrient Analysis: 1 slice

Calories: 96	*Fat: 3.6 g*	*Cholesterol: 13 mg*
Sodium: 64 mg	*Calcium: 21 mg*	

Diabetic Exchange: 1 starch, ½ fat

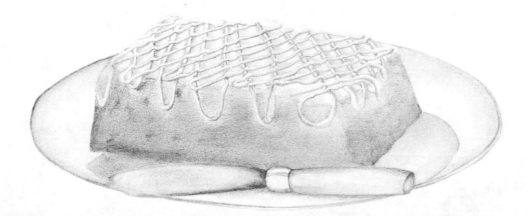

ORANGE BREAD

1½ cups whole-wheat flour
1½ cups all-purpose flour
 ¾ cup sugar
1-2 tablespoons grated orange peel
 2 teaspoons baking powder
 ¾ cup orange juice
 ½ cup skim milk
 ½ cup vegetable oil
 2 egg whites or 1 egg, slightly
     beaten
 ½ cup chopped nuts (optional)

   TOPPING
 1 tablespoon sugar
 ½ teaspoon cinnamon

Nutrient Analysis: 1 slice

Two 8½" x 4½" loaf pans, 36 slices

Mix flours, sugar, orange peel and baking powder.

Stir together juice, milk, oil and egg. Add to dry ingredients and stir. Stir in nuts.

Pour into two 8½ x 4½" non-stick sprayed loaf pans. Sprinkle with sugar and cinnamon mixture. Bake until a toothpick inserted towards the middle comes out clean and dry.

Oven: 350°
Time: 50 minutes

Calories: 97   Fat: 4.4 g   Cholesterol: 7 mg

Sodium: 21 mg   Dietary Fiber: 0.7 g

Calcium: 21 mg

Diabetic Exchange: 1 starch, ½ fat

PUMPKIN BREAD

Puréed squash can be substituted for the pumpkin.

2 9 x 5" loaf pans, 40 slices

2 cups canned or cooked, puréed pumpkin
2 cups sugar
1 cup oil
⅔ cup water
2 eggs
2 egg whites
2 cups whole-wheat flour
1½ cups all-purpose flour
2 teaspoons soda
1½ teaspoons nutmeg
½ teaspoon ginger
1½ teaspoons cinnamon

In a large bowl, blend pumpkin, sugar, oil, water, eggs and egg whites.

Add flours, soda, nutmeg, ginger and cinnamon. Blend at low speed until moistened, then beat 1 minute at medium speed.

Pour batter into two non-stick sprayed and floured (bottom only) loaf pans. Bake until toothpick inserted near center comes out clean. Cool 5 minutes and remove from pan. Cool completely on wire rack.

Oven: 350°
Time: 60 to 75 minutes

Nutrient Analysis: 1 slice

Calories: 126   Fat: 5.8 g   Cholesterol: 13 mg

Sodium: 47 mg   Dietary Fiber: 1.3 g

Calcium: 8 mg

Diabetic Exchange: 1 starch, 1 fat

CRANBERRY COFFEE CAKE

8 x 8" baking pan; 16 pieces

1½ cups all-purpose flour
½ cup whole-wheat flour
1 tablespoon baking powder
½ cup sugar
5 tablespoons margarine
2 egg whites
½ cup skim milk
1 cup fresh cranberries, chopped
     coarsely

TOPPING
¼ cup flour
½ cup sugar
2 tablespoons margarine

Combine flours, baking powder, and sugar. Cut in margarine with a pastry blender until mixture looks like coarse crumbs.

Combine egg whites with milk and stir into dry mixture. Mix well.

Spread batter in a non-stick sprayed 8 x 8" pan. Sprinkle cranberries over top.

Combine flour and sugar for topping. Cut in margarine with pastry blender until crumbly. Sprinkle over cranberries. Bake. Serve warm.

Oven: 375°
Time: 35 to 40 minutes

Nutrient Analysis: 1 piece

Calories: 158	Fat: 5.4 g	Cholesterol: 0
Sodium: 123 mg	Calcium: 26 mg	

Diabetic Exchange: 1½ starch, 1 fat

YOGURT COFFEE CAKE

The good taste of sour-cream coffee cake without the fat.

Angel food or bundt cake pan; 32 slices

½ cup margarine
¼ cup vegetable oil
1 teaspoon vanilla
½ cup plus 2 tablespoons sugar
1 egg
2 egg whites
1 cup plain low-fat yogurt
2 cups flour
1 teaspoon soda
1 teaspoon baking powder

Blend together margarine and oil. Add vanilla and sugar and beat well. Mix in egg and egg whites one at a time. Blend in yogurt.

Sift flour, soda and baking powder together. Add to egg mixture and beat well.

Place half of mixture in bottom of a non-stick sprayed angel food or bundt cake

continued

NUT FILLING
½ cup chopped nuts
2 tablespoons sugar
1 teaspoon cinnamon

pan. Sprinkle with nut mixture. Pour remaining batter over nut mixture. Bake until a toothpick inserted near center comes out clean and dry. Cool and remove from pan.

Oven: 350°
Time: 45 to 50 minutes

Nutrient Analysis: 1 slice

Calories: 103	Fat: 5.9 g	Cholesterol: 8 mg
Sodium: 74 mg	Calcium: 29 mg	

Diabetic Exchange: 1 starch, 1 fat

CASSEROLE BREAD

Lots of flavor with the texture of homemade bread. Delicious!

1½ quart casserole; 12 slices

1½ cups whole-wheat flour
1 cup all-purpose flour
½ cup quick-cooking rolled oats
⅓ cup brown sugar, packed
1 tablespoon finely grated orange peel
2 teaspoons baking powder
½ teaspoon baking soda
1¾ cups sour skim milk* or buttermilk
1 egg white
2 tablespoons sunflower nuts
wheat germ
honey

*To make sour milk, place 2 tablespoons lemon juice or vinegar in a 2 cup measure. Add skim milk to measure 1¾ cups.

In a large bowl combine flours, oats, sugar, orange peel, baking powder and baking soda until well blended. Add milk and egg white. Stir just until ingredients are moistened. Stir in the sunflower nuts.

Sprinkle a non-stick sprayed 1½ quart casserole lightly with wheat germ. Pour batter into casserole. Bake. If necessary, cover loaf with foil during the last 15 minutes of baking to prevent over-browning.

Cool in casserole for 15 minutes; turn out on wire rack. Brush top of loaf with honey and sprinkle with additional sunflower nuts if desired. Serve warm or cool.

Oven: 350°
Time: 50 to 60 minutes

Calories: 120	Fat: 1 g	Cholesterol: 1 mg
Sodium: 128 mg	Dietary Fiber: 2 g	
Calcium: 63 mg		

Diabetic Exchange: 1½ starch

APPLE MUFFIN CAKE

Bake in an 8-cup charlotte pan to create a giant muffin. It could also be baked in an 8-cup soufflé dish or a 9" tube pan.

10 pieces

    2 cups all-purpose flour
    1 tablespoon baking powder
    ½ teaspoon baking soda
    1¼ teaspoons cinnamon
    ½ teaspoon allspice
    ¼ teaspoon cloves
    1 cup sugar
    ¼ cup margarine
    1 cup low-fat vanilla-flavored
      yogurt
    1 egg
    1 egg white
    1 cup finely diced, peeled apple
    fine dry bread crumbs

Combine flour, baking powder, baking soda, cinnamon, allspice, cloves and sugar. Blend well.

Melt margarine and remove from heat. Stir in yogurt and beat in egg and egg white.

Beat the margarine mixture into the dry ingredients and blend until batter is smooth and satiny. Stir in apple.

Sprinkle a non-stick sprayed 8-cup charlotte pan or souffle dish with bread crumbs, tapping out excess. Scrape batter into pan and smooth it level. Bake until a tooth pick inserted near the center comes out clean and dry. Serve warm or at room temperature.

Oven: 350°
Time: 45 to 60 minutes (check at 45 if using tube pan)

Nutrient Analysis: 1 piece

Calories: 248   Fat: 5.3 g   Cholesterol: 24 mg

Sodium: 200 mg   Dietary Fiber: 0.8 g

Calcium: 120 mg

Diabetic Exchange: 1 starch, 2 fruit, 1 fat

UNLEAVENED BREAD

A pleasant change from dinner rolls.

Two round loaves, 12 pieces

1½ cups whole-wheat flour
½ cup all-purpose flour
1 teaspoon baking soda
¼ teaspoon salt
¼ cup vegetable oil
¾ cup water
¼ cup honey

Sift together flours, soda and salt. Add oil, water and honey. Mix thoroughly.

Knead well on floured board. Roll the dough flat, about ½" thick. Shape into two round loaves, score top and place on non-stick sprayed baking sheet. Bake. Serve warm or cold.

Oven: 350°
Time: 20 to 25 minutes

Nutrient Analysis: 1 piece

Calories: 127	Fat: 4.8 g	Cholesterol: 0
Sodium: 113 mg	Dietary Fiber: 1.6	
Calcium: 8 mg		

Diabetic Exchange: 1 starch, 1 fat

A change of heart is the essence of all other change and it is brought about by a re-education of the mind.

Emmeline Pethick-Lawrence

OLD-FASHIONED POTATO RYE BREAD

The day spent making this old fashioned bread is well rewarded—four delicious loaves of bread and they freeze well. To bake bread in stages: Sponge may be refrigerated overnight after adding molasses, sugar, margarine and seeds. Dough may be refrigerated overnight (well-wrapped) after loaves are formed. Final rising time will increase to about three hours.

Four 8 x 4" loaves, 16 slices a loaf

2	medium potatoes
1	quart potato water
1½	cups sugar
2	packages active dry yeast
8	cups all-purpose flour
½	cup molasses
½	cup margarine
1	teaspoon salt
2	tablespoons caraway seed, crushed
1	teaspoon anise seed, crushed
1	teaspoon fennel seed, crushed
4	cups rye flour

Peel and boil two medium-sized potatoes in water. Mash the potatoes and add enough water to make one quart. Cool to lukewarm.

Dissolve the yeast with ½ cup of the sugar in the potato water. Let stand for 10 minutes. Add 4 cups of the all-purpose flour. Let this sponge rise in a warm place for 30 minutes.

Mix the molasses, the remaining cup of sugar, margarine, salt, caraway, anise and fennel together. Add to the sponge. Stir in the remaining 4 cups all-purpose flour and all the rye flour. Knead well. (This is a firm dough and it will take at least 10 minutes of kneading by hand.)

Let rise until double (about 3 hours). Punch down and let rise until double again (about 2 hours).

Form into 4 balls and let them rest for 15 minutes. Shape into loaves. Let rise in non-stick sprayed pans until double (about 1½ hours). Bake. Immediately remove bread from pans and cool on wire racks or across top edges of bread pans.

Oven: 350°
Time: 50 to 60 minutes

Nutrient Analysis: 1 slice

Calories: 93	*Fat: 0.2 g*	*Cholesterol: 0*
Sodium: 39 mg	*Calcium: 12 mg*	

Diabetic Exchange: 1 starch

FOUR GRAIN BREAD

9 x 5" loaf; 16 slices

1	cup whole-wheat flour
½	cup rye flour
½	cup rolled oats
¼	cup cornmeal
3	tablespoons molasses
1	tablespoon vegetable oil
½	teaspoon salt
1	cup boiling water
¼	cup warm water (105-115°)
1	package active dry yeast
1-1¼	cups all-purpose flour

In a large mixing bowl, blend whole-wheat flour, rye flour, oats, cornmeal, molasses, oil, salt and boiling water. Set aside.

Sprinkle yeast over warm water in cup measure. Stir to dissolve. Stir into grain mixture. Gradually stir in all-purpose flour, adding just enough to make a stiff dough.

Turn dough out onto floured surface and knead until smooth and elastic. Lightly oil large bowl and place dough in bowl turning once to coat with oil. Cover with damp cloth and let rise in warm place until double (45 to 90 minutes).

Punch down and shape into loaf. Place in non-stick sprayed pan, cover, and let rise again until double (45 to 75 minutes). Bake. Remove from pan and cool on wire rack or across edges of bread pan.

Oven: 375°
Time: 30 to 35 minutes

Nutrient Analysis: 1 slice

Calories: 83	Fat: 1 g	Cholesterol: 0
Sodium: 90 mg	Dietary Fiber: 1.3 g	
Calcium: 14 mg		

Diabetic Exchange: 1 starch

HONEY WHOLE-WHEAT BREAD

Three 8 x 4" loaves, 16 slices a loaf

4 cups whole-wheat flour
½ teaspoon salt
2 packages active dry yeast
3 cups skim milk
½ cup honey
2 tablespoons oil
1 egg
4½-5 cups all-purpose flour

In a large bowl, combine 3 cups of the whole-wheat flour, salt and yeast.

In a saucepan over low heat, combine milk, honey and oil. Heat until warm. Pour over flour mixture and blend well. Add egg and beat well. Add the remaining cup of whole-wheat flour. Add the all-purpose flour, 1 cup at a time, until mixture forms a stiff dough.

Turn dough out onto floured surface and knead until smooth and elastic (about 7 minutes). Lightly oil a large bowl and place dough in bowl turning once to coat with oil. Cover with damp cloth and let rise in warm place until double (45 to 60 minutes).

Punch down, divide into thirds and shape into loaves. Place in non-stick sprayed 8 x 4" loaf pans, cover and let rise again until double (30 to 45 minutes.)

Place loaves in COLD oven and set at 400°. Bake 10 minutes. Reduce oven temperature to 375° and bake 30 more minutes or until golden. Remove loaves from pans and cool on wire rack or across edges of bread pans.

Oven: COLD set at 400° for 10 minutes; 375° for 30 minutes

Nutrient Analysis: 1 slice

Calories: 101	Fat: 1 g	Cholesterol: 5 mg
Sodium: 34 mg	Dietary Fiber: 1.1 g	
Calcium: 26 mg		

Diabetic Exchange: 1 starch, ½ fat

OATMEAL BREAD

Raisins or cut-up dates make a tasty addition to oatmeal bread.

Two 9 x 5" loaves, 16 slices a loaf

2 packages active dry yeast
1 cup warm water
¼ cup dark molasses
½ teaspoon salt
5½-6 cups all-purpose flour
1¼ cups scalded skim milk,
    cooled to lukewarm
¼ cup honey
1 egg
2 tablespoons softened
    margarine
1 cup quick-cooking rolled oats
1 cup raisins or coarsely cut up
    dates (optional)

In large bowl, combine yeast, warm water, molasses, salt and ½ cup flour. Beat until smooth and let stand in a warm place for 15 minutes.

Add milk, honey, egg, 2 cups flour, margarine and oats. Beat 2 minutes with electric mixer.

Gradually add 3 to 3½ cups flour and raisins or dates if desired. Form into smooth ball, cover with bowl and let stand 10 minutes.

Knead dough for 5 minutes and shape into 2 balls. Cover with bowl and let rest for 10 minutes. Shape into 2 loaves and place in non-stick sprayed loaf pans. Cover with damp cloth and let rise in warm place until double (45 to 60 minutes). Bake.

Oven: 375°
Time: 35-40 minutes

Nutrient Analysis: 1 slice

Calories: 110	Fat: 1.2 g	Cholesterol: 8 mg
Sodium: 57 mg	Calcium: 22 mg	

Diabetic Exchange: 1 starch, ½ fat

FRENCH BREAD

This bread is extra good and crusty if baked on an ungreased, shiny pan (foil) with a pan of hot water on the oven shelf below it.

Two French loaves; 16 slices a loaf

1 **package active dry yeast**
2 **cups lukewarm water, divided**
2 **teaspoons salt**
4 **cups all-purpose flour**
1 **tablespoon sugar**

Dissolve yeast in 1 cup of the water.

In a large bowl, mix salt, flour and sugar. Stir in yeast mixture and just enough of the second cup of water to hold dough together. Cover. Let rise until double.

Punch down and knead until smooth and elastic. Divide in half and shape into two long, thin loaves. Place on ungreased, foil-covered baking sheet. Slash loaves diagonally at 2" intervals. Bake.

Oven: 375°
Time: 45 minutes

Nutrient Analysis: 1 slice

Calories: 48	Fat: 0	Cholesterol: 0
Sodium: 120 mg	Calcium: 3 mg	

Diabetic Exchange: ½ starch

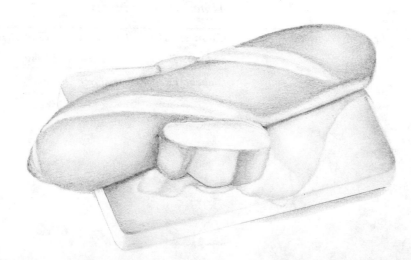

WHOLE-WHEAT FRENCH BREAD

Three loaves; 16 slices a loaf

1 package active dry yeast
1 tablespoon honey
3 cups lukewarm water
5 cups all-purpose flour
1 tablespoon vegetable oil
2½ teaspoons salt
2 cups wheat germ
2 cups whole-wheat flour
⅛ cup corn meal

Dissolve yeast and honey in water. Mix in 3 cups of the all-purpose flour, 1 cup at a time. Stir batter 100 times. Cover and set in warm place for 30 minutes.

Stir in oil and salt. Add wheat germ and whole-wheat flour, 1 cup at a time. Dough should be stiff enough to turn out, but still sticky. Turn onto floured surface and knead 10 minutes, adding as much of the remaining 2 cups of all-purpose flour as necessary to make dough smooth and elastic. Shape into ball.

Lightly oil a large bowl and place dough in bowl turning once to coat with oil. Cover with damp cloth and let rise in warm place until double (45 to 60 minutes). Punch down and let double again.

Turn dough onto floured board (it will be soft). Divide into thirds and shape into 2 x 14" loaves. Place on non-stick sprayed baking sheet sprinkled lightly with cornmeal. Slash loaves diagonally at 3" intervals. Cover and let rise 30 minutes. Place pan of boiling water on bottom shelf of preheated oven. Bake loaves on middle shelf.

Oven: 400°
Time: 40 to 45 minutes

Nutrient Analysis: 1 slice

Calories: 83	Fat: 1 g	Cholesterol: 0
Sodium: 113 mg	Dietary Fiber: 1 g	
Calcium: 7 mg		

Diabetic Exchange: 1 starch

BREAD STICKS

Bread sticks can be made ahead of time and frozen. Reheat just before serving.

36 dinner sticks; 54 cocktail sticks

2 packages active dry yeast
2¼ cups warm water
3 cups all-purpose flour
3 cups whole-wheat flour

COATING
1 egg white, beaten
⅓-½ cup sesame or poppy seeds

Sprinkle yeast over water, dissolve and let stand for 5 minutes.

Mix flours together. Measure 4½ cups of mixed flour into a large bowl. Gradually pour in yeast mixture and mix well with a spoon and then with hands. Add flour as needed from remaining 1½ cups to form stiff dough. Place dough on floured board. Knead 3 to 5 minutes.

Lightly oil a large bowl and place dough in bowl turning once to coat with oil. Cover with damp cloth and let rise in warm place until double (about 2 hours). Punch down. Place on unfloured board and knead lightly. Divide into 36 (54 for cocktail sticks) equal parts and shape into balls. Let dough rest 15 minutes.

Stretch each ball into a ½ x 2½" stick. Place on non-stick sprayed baking sheets. Brush sticks with egg white and sprinkle with sesame or poppy seeds. Bake.

Oven: 425°
Time: 10 minutes

Nutrient Analysis:

	dinner stick	cocktail stick
Calories:	80	54
Fat:	1.2 g	0.8 g
Cholesterol:	0	0
Sodium:	2 mg	1 mg
Calcium:	34 mg	23 mg
Diabetic Exchange:	1 starch	½ starch

SOFT PRETZELS

Children love to help make these!

16 pretzels

1 loaf frozen bread dough
poppy or sesame seeds

Cover dough and thaw overnight in refrigerator or for several hours at room temperature until soft enough to shape.

On a floured surface, cut dough the long way into 8 strips. Cover and let rise 10 minutes.

Roll each strip on floured surface until ½" thick and 18-20" long. Cut each strip in half and twist into pretzel shape. Place on a non-stick sprayed baking sheet. Brush with lukewarm water. Sprinkle with poppy or sesame seeds.

Let rise, uncovered, for 15 to 20 minutes. Place a shallow pan of hot water on bottom shelf of preheated oven. Bake pretzels on middle shelf.

Oven: 425°
Time: 10 to 15 minutes

Nutrient Analysis: 1 pretzel

Calories: 117	*Fat: 2 g*	*Cholesterol: 0*
Sodium: 200 mg	*Calcium: 36 mg*	

Diabetic Exchange: 1 starch, ½ fat

SOUR MILK ROLLS

24 rolls

3 cups whole-wheat flour
2 packages active dry yeast
3 tablespoons sugar
1 teaspoon salt
½ teaspoon soda
1¼ cups sour skim milk* or
    buttermilk
½ cup water
2 tablespoons vegetable oil
1-1½ cups all-purpose flour

To sour milk, place 1 tablespoon lemon juice or vinegar in a 2 cup measure. Add skim milk to measure 1¼ cups.

In a large mixing bowl, combine 1½ cups of the whole-wheat flour, yeast, sugar, salt and soda.

In a saucepan, combine sour milk, water and oil and heat until warm (120 to 130°). Add to flour mixture and beat with electric mixer for 3 minutes at medium speed. Stir in remaining 1½ cups whole-wheat flour plus enough all-purpose flour (1-1½ cups) to make a soft dough.

Knead on floured board for 5 minutes or until dough is smooth and elastic. Lightly oil large bowl and place dough in bowl turning once to coat with oil. Cover with damp cloth and let rise in warm place until double (30 to 45 minutes). Punch down, divide into 24 pieces. Shape into balls and place on non-stick sprayed baking sheet. Cover. Let rise in warm place until almost double, (20 to 30 minutes). Bake.

Oven: 400°
Time: 15 to 20 minutes

Nutrient Analysis: 1 roll

Calories: 94   Fat: 1.5 g   Cholesterol: 2 mg

Sodium: 106 mg   Dietary Fiber: 0.4 g

Calcium: 23 mg

Diabetic Exchange: 1 starch, ½ fat

HEARTY WHEAT BUNS

36 3" diameter buns

1¼ cups lukewarm water
¼ cup soft margarine
3 tablespoons brown sugar
¾ teaspoon salt
⅓ cup honey
¾ cup skim milk, scalded
½ cup wheat germ
2 packages active dry yeast
⅓ cup warm water
1 teaspoon baking powder
3 cups whole-wheat flour
3 cups all-purpose flour

In a large bowl, combine 1¼ cups water, margarine, sugar, salt and honey. Pour scalded milk over wheat germ and cool to lukewarm. Add milk mixture to ingredients in large bowl. Mix.

Dissolve yeast in ⅓ cup warm water and let stand 5 minutes. Add to liquid ingredients and beat well with a wooden spoon.

Mix baking powder and whole-wheat flour. Alternately add whole-wheat and all-purpose flour (about 1 cup at a time) until dough is stiff enough to handle. Turn out dough onto floured surface and knead until smooth and elastic (about 10 minutes).

Lightly oil a large bowl and place dough in bowl turning once to coat with oil. Cover with damp cloth and let rise in warm place until double. Punch down and shape into 36 buns. Place on non-stick sprayed baking sheet, cover and let rise again until almost double. Bake until nicely browned.

Oven: 350°
Time: 10 to 15 minutes

Nutrient Analysis: 1 bun

Calories: 100	Fat: 1.6 g	Cholesterol: 0
Sodium: 76 mg	Dietary Fiber: 1.3 g	
Calcium: 16 mg		

Diabetic Exchange: 1 starch, ½ fat

HERB SEASONED CROUTONS

This savory salad topping is equally as good as a garnish for soup or as a base for poultry stuffing. Choose your favorite herbs for variation.

About 4 cups; 16 portions

10 slices whole-wheat bread
¼ cup vegetable oil
¼ cup grated Parmesan cheese
½ teaspoon dried herbs (majoram, basil, thyme), crushed

Brush both sides of bread with oil. Sprinkle with cheese and crushed herbs. Cut into ½" cubes.

Bake on 10 x 15" jelly roll pan, stirring occasionally. Store in airtight container.

Oven: 300°
Time: 30 minutes or until dry.

Nutrient Analysis: ¼ cup portion

Calories: 74	Fat: 4.3 g	Cholesterol: 1 mg
Sodium: 106 mg	Dietary Fiber: 0.6 g	
Calcium: 33 mg		

Diabetic Exchange: ½ starch, 1 fat

SALADS

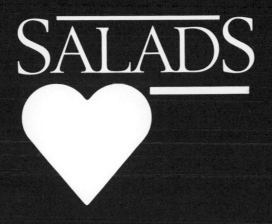

*Salad refreshes without weakening
and comforts without irritating and
I have a habit of saying that it
makes us younger.*

Jean Brillat-Savarin

SALADS

FRUIT SALADS

MAIN DISH SALADS

SALADS

Thanks to modern agriculture, a variety of fresh fruits and vegetables are available year 'round making salad variation limitless.

The keys to making successful salads are fresh ingredients and a willingness to experiment. Salads, whether served as a main dish or as an accompaniment, are foods for health-conscious people. Dark greens used in preparing salads are high in vitamins A and C, fiber, calcium and iron and are low in calories, sodium and fat. However, if iceberg lettuce is the only green you use, you are selecting the one weakling in a family of nutritional champions. Any other lettuce or leafy green vegetable would be a better choice. Here are the "green" facts:

Table 17: Raw Greens Comparison (3.5 Ounces)

Type	Calories	Vitamin A Value (IU)	Vitamin C (mg)	Fiber (g)	Calcium (mg)	Iron (mg)	Comments
Iceberg, or crisphead lettuce	13	330	4	.5	19	.5	The most popular kind of lettuce, but the least nutritious.
Butterhead, Bibb, or Boston lettuce	13	970	8	.5	35	2.0	Sweet and delicate taste.
Romaine, or Cos lettuce	16	2600	24	.7	68	1.4	Strong taste. Used in caesar salads.
Loose-leaf lettuce	18	1900	18	.7	68	1.4	Sweet and delicate taste.
Arugula or roquette	23	7400	91	.9	309	1.2	Strong and peppery. Spices up a salad.
Chicory, or curly emdive	23	400	24	.8	100	.9	Slightly bitter. Mix with milder greens. Radicchio is a red variety.

continued on next page

Table 17: Raw Greens Comparison (3.5 Ounces), continued

Type	Calories	Vitamin A Value (IU)	Vitamin C (mg)	Fiber (g)	Calcium (mg)	Iron (mg)	Comments
Escarole	17	2050	7	.9	52	.8	An endive with broad leaves.
Spinach	22	6700	28	.9	100	2.7	Eat raw or cooked. High in folacin and potassium. Its iron is poorly absorbed by the body.
Watercress	11	4700	43	.7	120	.2	Pungent. In cabbage family. Add to salads or sandwiches.
Dandelion greens	45	14000	35	1.6	187	3.1	Pungent. Very nutritious. Use young leaves in salads; saute tough leaves.
Turnip greens	27	7600	60	.8	190	1.1	Strong flavor. More nutritious than the root vegetable. Eat raw or cooked.
Swiss chard	19	3300	30	.8	51	1.8	Mild flavor. Steam or saute.
Kale	50	8900	120	1.5	135	1.7	Mild, cabbage-like taste. Cook or use in salads. Highly nutritious.
Collards	19	3300	23	.6	117	.6	Strong flavor. In cabbage family; related to kale. Steam or saute.

Reprinted permission of: *University of California, Berkeley Wellness Letter*, P.O. Box 10922, Des Moines, IA 50340, ©Health Letter Associates, 1986.

CHICKEN SALAD HAWAIIAN

8 portions

4 cups diced cooked chicken
1 cup drained, unsweetened
    pineapple chunks
1 8-ounce can water chestnuts,
    drained and thinly sliced
2 green onions, thinly sliced
⅔ cup chopped celery
1 cup HAWAIIAN DRESSING,
    (page 162).
⅓ cup unsalted slivered almonds,
    toasted
    salad greens

In a mixing bowl, combine chicken, pineapple, water chestnuts, green onions and celery. Pour HAWAIIAN DRESSING over chicken mixture and toss lightly.

Chill in refrigerator, covered, at least 1 hour before serving. Serve salad, sprinkled with toasted almonds, on crisp greens.

Nutrient Analysis: 1 portion

Calories: 245   *Fat: 10 g*   *Cholesterol: 65 mg*

Sodium: 163 mg   *Dietary Fiber: 0.7 g*

Calcium: 63 mg

Diabetic Exchange: 3 lean meat, 1 fruit

LAYERED CHICKEN SALAD

Prepared several hours to one day ahead of serving time so flavors blend. Squares cut from a pan make it easy to serve.

9 x 13" pan; 8 portions

1 11-ounce can mandarin orange segments
¾ cup calorie-reduced mayonnaise
¾ cup low-fat plain yogurt
2 teaspoons curry powder
¼ teaspoon ground coriander (optional)
2 tablespoons syrup from orange segments
4 cups fresh spinach, washed and drained
1 10-ounce package frozen peas
1½ cup diced cooked chicken or 2, 5-ounce cans boned chicken, undrained
1 8-ounce can sliced water chestnuts, drained
½ cup chopped red onion
1 medium cucumber, halved lengthwise and sliced

Drain oranges, reserving 2 tablespoons of the syrup and a few orange segments.

Blend together mayonnaise, yogurt, curry powder, coriander and reserved syrup. Set aside.

Tear spinach into bite-sized pieces and place in a 9 x 13" pan. Layer peas, chicken, water chestnuts, onion and cucumber over spinach.

Spread mayonnaise mixture over salad and garnish with reserved orange segments. Cover and refrigerate several hours or overnight. Cut in squares to serve.

Nutrient Analysis: 1 portion

Calories: 188   Fat: 7.5 g   Cholesterol: 30 mg

Sodium: 276 mg   Dietary Fiber: 1.5 g

Calcium: 91 mg

Diabetic Exchange: 2 lean meat, 1 fruit,
1 vegetable

HOT CHICKEN SALAD

1 small green pepper, chopped
1 10-ounce package chopped
    broccoli, thawed and drained
2 cups diced cooked chicken
1 cup sliced fresh mushrooms
½ cup sliced water chestnuts
1 2-ounce jar pimientos, chopped
½ cup calorie-reduced mayonnaise
½ cup HERB SEASONED
    CROUTONS, (page 124).

1½-quart casserole; 4 portions

Combine green pepper, broccoli, chicken, mushrooms, water chestnuts and pimientos. Stir in mayonnaise.

Turn into non-stick sprayed casserole. Sprinkle with croutons. Bake uncovered.

Oven: 350°
Time: 20 to 25 minutes

Nutrient Analysis: 1 portion

Calories: 247	*Fat: 8.4 g*	*Cholesterol: 71 mg*
Sodium: 212 mg	*Dietary Fiber: 2.8 g*	
Calcium: 65 mg		

Diabetic Exchange: 3 lean meat, 3 vegetable

WILD RICE CHICKEN SALAD #1

2 cups cooked wild rice
1 cup diced cooked chicken
½ cup chopped celery
⅓ cup unsalted nuts
¼ cup chopped onions
½ cup cooked garbanzo beans
    (chickpeas)
½ cup sliced fresh mushrooms
½ cup fresh broccoli pieces,
    blanched
¾ cup HERBED VINAIGRETTE
    DRESSING, (page 159).
    lettuce leaves
    tomato wedges

5 portions

In a large bowl, toss together rice, chicken, celery, nuts, onion, chickpeas, mushrooms, broccoli and dressing.

Refrigerate several hours to allow flavors to blend. Serve on lettuce leaves and garnish with tomato wedges.

Nutrient Analysis: 1 portion

Calories: 263	*Fat: 11 g*	*Cholesterol: 25 mg*
Sodium: 70 mg	*Dietary Fiber: .5 g*	
Calcium: 31 mg		

Diabetic Exchange: 2 lean meat, 1 starch,
1 vegetable, 1 fat

WILD RICE CHICKEN SALAD #2

8 portions

  ⅔ cup calorie-reduced mayonnaise
  ⅓ cup skim milk
  2 tablespoons lemon juice
  3 cups diced cooked chicken
  3 cups cooked wild rice
  ⅓ cup finely chopped green
      pepper
  ⅓ cup finely sliced green onion
  1 8-ounce can sliced water
      chestnuts, drained
  ½ teaspoon salt
  ¼ teaspoon white pepper
  ½ pound seedless green grapes,
      halved
  ½ cup unsalted cashews
      salad greens
  8 grape clusters

In a small bowl, blend mayonnaise, milk and lemon juice. Set aside.

In a medium bowl, combine chicken, rice, green pepper, onion, water chestnuts, salt and pepper. Fold in mayonnaise mixture. Cover and refrigerate 2 to 3 hours.

Just before serving, fold in grapes and cashews. Arrange on salad greens on individual salad plates. Garnish with grape clusters.

Nutrient Analysis: 1 portion

Calories: 352	*Fat: 13.7 g*	*Cholesterol: 80 mg*
Sodium: 339 mg	*Dietary Fiber: 1.1 g*	
Calcium: 40 mg		

Diabetic Exchange: 3 lean meat, 1½ starch,
1 vegetable, 1 fat

STRAWBERRY RHUBARB GELATIN SALAD

9 x 13" pan; 12 portions

  3 cups diced rhubarb
  ½ cup water
  1 6-ounce package strawberry-
      flavored gelatin
½-¾ cup sugar
  1 20-ounce can unsweetened
      crushed pineapple

In large saucepan, cook rhubarb in water until tender.

Add gelatin and stir until dissolved. Stir in sugar to taste. Add pineapple and stir.

Pour into 9 x 13" pan and refrigerate until set.

Nutrient Analysis: 1 portion

Calories: 119	*Fat: 0.1 g*	*Cholesterol: 0*
Sodium: 47 mg	*Dietary Fiber: 0.5 g*	
Calcium: 34 mg		

Diabetic Exchange: 2 fruit

CHICKEN LENTIL SALAD

4 portions

⅔ cup lentils
1½ cup water
¼-½ cup calorie-reduced
    mayonnaise
2 tablespoons chopped green
    onion
    dash Tabasco sauce
1 cup diced cooked chicken
½ cup diced celery
½ cup diced cucumber
¼ cup diced green pepper
1 2-ounce jar chopped pimiento
    salad greens
    chopped parsley for garnish

Thoroughly rinse dry lentils in cold water, removing any damaged pieces and foreign material. Drain. Place lentils in a heavy saucepan, add water. Bring to a boil, reduce heat and simmer, covered, for about 20 minutes. Do not overcook; lentils should be tender, with skins intact. Drain immediately and refrigerate until cool.

In a small bowl, stir together mayonnaise, green onion and Tabasco sauce.

In a medium bowl, toss lentils, chicken, celery, cucumber, green pepper, and pimiento with dressing. Cover and refrigerate for an hour or more to allow flavors to blend.

Just before serving, arrange on crisp greens and garnish with chopped parsley.

Nutrient Analysis: 1 portion

Calories: 236   Fat: 7.4 g   Cholesterol: 36 mg

Sodium: 171 mg   Dietary Fiber: 6 g

Calcium: 43 mg

Diabetic Exchange: 1 lean meat, 1½ starch, 1 fat

CHICKEN WALDORF BLOSSOMS

Pretty red "blossoms" filled with crunchy chicken salad.

4 portions

1½ cups diced cooked chicken or
    2, 5-ounce cans boned
    chicken, drained
  1 small apple, chopped
  ½ cup chopped celery
  ⅓ cup calorie-reduced mayonnaise
    dash pepper
  4 tomatoes
    lettuce leaves
  ¼ cup chopped walnuts

Combine chicken, apple, celery, mayonnaise and pepper. Cover and chill to blend flavors.

Cut each tomato into 6 sections almost to stem end and place on a lettuce leaf. Fill each tomato with ½ cup chicken mixture. Sprinkle each with a tablespoon of walnuts.

Nutrient Analysis: 1 portion

Calories:240   Fat: 12.6 g   Cholesterol: 51 mg

Sodium: 177 mg   Dietary Fiber: 2.9 g

Calcium: 33 mg

Diabetic Exchange: 2 lean meat, 3 vegetable, 1 fat

IMAGINATION VEGETABLE SALAD

Begin with the basic vegetables listed and then use your imagination for additions to personalize your salad. Here are a few suggestions to get you started: broccoli, cauliflower, cherry tomatoes, mushrooms, snow peas, red cabbage, yellow squash, zucchini.

10 portions

  4 carrots
  4 stalks celery
  1 large green pepper
  1 large sweet red pepper
  2 cucumbers
  ½ red onion
1¼ cup IMAGINATION
    VINAIGRETTE DRESSING,
    (page 160).

Scrape carrots and cut on diagonal into ¼" pieces. Slice celery into 1" long matchsticks. Cut green pepper into ½" squares. Slice red pepper into strips. Score cucumbers and slice thinly. Chop onion or slice onion thinly and separate into rings.

Add your own "imagination" vegetables.

Toss with dressing. Cover and chill for 1 to 2 hours or longer. Just before serving, toss again.

Nutrient Analysis: 1 portion

Calories: 74   Fat: 4.3 g   Cholesterol: 0

Sodium: 41 mg   Dietary Fiber: 4.3 g

Calcium: 26 mg

Diabetic Exchange: 1 vegetable, 1 fat

CRUNCHY TUNA SALAD

4 portions

¼ cup bulgur
½ cup hot water
½ cup plain low-fat yogurt
2 tablespoons chopped fresh mint
    or 2 teaspoons dried mint,
    crushed
1 tablespoon lemon juice
1 tablespoon Dijon mustard
2 tablespoons thinly sliced green
    onion
1 6½ or 7-ounce can water-
    packed tuna, drained
1 medium tomato, seeded and
    diced
1 cup diced zucchini or cucumber
    lettuce leaves

Nutrient Analysis: 1 portion

In a medium bowl, combine bulgur and water. Let stand 30 minutes. Drain well.

Stir yogurt, mint, lemon juice, mustard and green onion into bulgur.

Add tuna, tomato and zucchini or cucumber. Stir gently to break up tuna and coat with yogurt mixture.

To serve, line small plates with lettuce leaves and top with tuna mixture.

Calories: 132   Fat: 0.9 g   Cholesterol: 1 mg

Sodium: 294 mg   Dietary Fiber: 1.5 g

Calcium: 76 mg   Omega-3: 250 mg

Diabetic Exchange: 1 lean meat, 1 starch

WINTER FRUIT SALAD

6 portions

1 large orange, peeled and
    sectioned
1 medium pear, cubed
2 bananas, sliced
1 cup red or purple grapes
½ cup diced prunes
½ cup walnuts, toasted
1 cup SPICY YOGURT FOR
    FRUIT, *(page 163)*.

Nutrient Analysis: 1 portion

In a medium bowl, combine orange, pear, banana, grapes, prunes and walnuts.

Just before serving, add dressing to fruit and toss well.

Calories: 187   Fat: 3.1 g   Cholesterol: 2

Sodium: 27 mg   Dietary Fiber: 2.6 g

Calcium: 97 mg

Diabetic Exchange: 2 fruit, ½ skim milk, ½ fat

FISH SALAD VERDE

6 portions

1 pound fresh spinach, torn into bite-sized pieces
1½ pounds any white fish fillets
½ cup white wine or lemon juice
1 tablespoon Dijon mustard
¼ cup olive oil
1 teaspoon grated lime rind
¼ cup lime juice
½ teaspoon dried tarragon, crushed
½ to 1 teaspoon sugar
dash pepper
¼ cup plain low-fat yogurt
2 medium tomatoes, cut into wedges

Wash spinach thoroughly and pat dry. Finely chop enough spinach to measure ¼ cup; set aside. Refrigerate remaining spinach leaves.

Place wine or lemon juice in a large skillet. Add water to a depth of 1" and bring to a boil. Place fillets in water; cover and reduce heat to simmer. Poach fish 5 to 10 minutes until translucent white. Remove from poaching liquid and cool.

Place mustard in medium bowl and gradually beat in oil with wire whisk. Add lime peel and juice, chopped spinach, tarragon, sugar and pepper and whisk thoroughly. Stir in yogurt and set aside.

To serve, arrange spinach leaves on large platter. Break fish into pieces and place on top of spinach. Surround with tomato wedges. Spoon dressing over all.

Nutrient Analysis: 1 portion

Calories: 208	*Fat: 10.5 g*	*Cholesterol: 0*
Sodium: 234 mg	*Dietary Fiber: 3.5 g*	
Calcium: 114 mg	*Omega-3: 500 mg*	

Diabetic Exchange: 3 lean meat, 2 vegetable

SEASHORE SALAD OR SPREAD

Serve as a salad or as an appetizer spread on crackers.

6 portions

½ cup ripe olives, halved
1½ cups chopped celery
4 green onions, sliced
1 medium green pepper, chopped
1 8-ounce can sliced water
     chestnuts, drained
2 8-ounce bags frozen Pacific fish
     and crab meat blend, drained
1½ cups CREAMY SALAD
     DRESSING, *(page 161).*

Combine olives, celery, onions, green pepper, water chestnuts and seafood.

Just before serving, toss with dressing. Serve on a bed of lettuce greens.

Nutrient Analysis: 1 portion

Calories: 147	*Fat: 4.5 g*	*Cholesterol: 18 mg*
Sodium: 715 mg	*Dietary Fiber: 1 g*	
Calcium: 571 mg	*Omega-3: 230 mg*	

Diabetic Exchange: 1 medium-fat meat, 2 vegetable

SALAD NIÇOISE

Salade Niçoise—a combination of cooked and raw vegetables, fish and a rich-tasting Provencal dressing—is a luncheon favorite from the Mediterranean.

4 portions

½ pound green beans, trimmed
4 small new potatoes
4 cups romaine lettuce, torn into
     bite-sized pieces
2 tomatoes, quartered
1 small red onion, sliced
½ green pepper, cut into strips
2 3-ounce cans sardines or 1
     7-ounce can tuna or salmon,
     drained and rinsed
1 small bunch radishes, sliced

Blanch or steam green beans until crisp tender. Drain and chill. In small saucepan, cook potatoes until tender (about 15 minutes). Drain and cool; slice ¼" thick and refrigerate.

In a salad bowl, combine beans, potatoes, lettuce, tomatoes, onion and green pepper. Arrange sardines, tuna or salmon neatly over the top. Dress lightly with HERBED VINAIGRETTE DRESSING, *(page 159)* and garnish with radishes.

Nutrient Analysis: 1 portion (without dressing)

Calories: 254	*Fat: 5.4 g*	*Cholesterol: 60*
Sodium: 377 mg	*Dietary Fiber: 3.7 g*	
Calcium: 263 mg	*Omega-3: 2140 mg*	

Diabetic Exchange: 1 lean meat, 2 starch, 1 vegetable

SALMON RICE SALAD, HOT

1 16-ounce can salmon
2 cups cooked brown rice
1 cup thinly sliced celery
½ cup chopped fresh parsley
¼ cup sliced ripe olives
½ cup calorie-reduced mayonnaise
½ cup plain low-fat yogurt
1 tablespoon lemon juice
  pepper to taste
⅓ cup sliced almonds
  grated Parmesan cheese
  paprika

Nutrient Analysis: 1 portion

2-quart casserole; 6 portions

Drain salmon liquid into mixing bowl. Flake salmon and add. Add rice, celery, parsley and olives. Mix well.

Combine mayonnaise, yogurt and lemon juice. Add to salmon mixture and toss lightly. Season to taste with pepper.

Spoon mixture into a non-stick sprayed casserole. Sprinkle with almonds, cheese and paprika. Bake until heated through and golden brown.

Oven: 350°
Time: 30 minutes

Calories: 294	Fat: 11 g	Cholesterol: 34 mg
Sodium: 505 mg	Dietary Fiber: 1.2 g	
Calcium: 239 mg	Omega-3: 760 mg	

Diabetic Exchange: 2 lean meat, 1 starch,
1 vegetable, 1 fat

HOT SEAFOOD SALAD

1 medium green pepper, minced
1 medium onion, minced
1 cup finely chopped celery
6 ounces frozen crab meat or 3
  seafood sticks
8 ounces frozen cooked shrimp
1 teaspoon sodium-reduced
  Worcestershire sauce
½ cup calorie-reduced mayonnaise
½ cup whole-wheat bread crumbs

Nutrient Analysis: 1 portion

2-quart casserole; 6 portions

Combine green pepper, onion, celery, crab meat, shrimp, Worcestershire and mayonnaise.

Place in non-stick sprayed casserole and top with bread crumbs. Bake uncovered.

Oven: 350°
Time: 35 minutes

Calories: 160	Fat: 6 g	Cholesterol: 78 mg
Sodium: 300 mg	Dietary Fiber: 0.6 g	
Calcium: 80 mg	Omega-3: 275 mg	

Diabetic Exchange: 2 lean meat, 2 vegetable

ITALIAN PASTA SALAD

8 portions

1¼ cups rotini or other suitable
    pasta such as shells
1 cup sliced carrots
2 medium zucchini, sliced
1 6-ounce jar marinated artichoke
    hearts
¼ cup sliced ripe olives
4 ounces part-skim mozzarella
    cheese, cubed
¼ cup Parmesan cheese

DRESSING
    reserved marinade from
    artichoke hearts
¼ cup olive oil
2 tablespoons white wine vinegar
1½ teaspoons dry mustard
1 teaspoon dried oregano,
    crushed
1 teaspoon dried basil, crushed
2 garlic cloves, minced

Cook pasta until al dente, about 10 minutes. Drain and rinse in cold water.

Steam carrot slices 15 minutes, add zucchini and steam 5 to 10 more minutes until just crisp-tender. Drain and rinse in cold water.

Drain artichokes, reserving marinade. Quarter.

Place pasta, zucchini, carrots, artichokes, olives, mozzarella and Parmesan in a bowl.

Make dressing from reserved marinade, olive oil, vinegar, mustard, oregano, basil and garlic. Add to pasta-vegetable mixture and mix well.

Chill several hours or overnight.

Nutrient Analysis: 1 portion

Calories: 305   Fat: 15 g   Cholesterol: 15 mg
Sodium: 207 mg   Dietary Fiber: 1.8 g
Calcium: 128 mg

Diabetic Exchange: 2 starch, 1 vegetable, 2½ fat

LENTIL CONFETTI SALAD

5 portions

⅔ cup lentils
1½ cups water
¼ teaspoon salt
1 cup cooked brown rice
½ cup IMAGINATION
    VINAIGRETTE DRESSING,
    (page 160).
½ cup seeded, diced tomato
¼ cup chopped green pepper
3 tablespoons chopped onion
2 tablespoons chopped celery
¼ cup chopped fresh parsley
½ teaspoon dried oregano,
    crushed
    freshly ground pepper
    lettuce leaves

Thoroughly rinse dry lentils in cold water, removing any damaged pieces and foreign material. Drain. Place lentils in a heavy saucepan; add water and salt. Bring to a boil, reduce heat and simmer, covered, for about 20 minutes. Do not overcook; lentils should be tender, with skins intact. Drain immediately.

Combine lentils with cooked rice and pour dressing over mixture. Refrigerate until chilled.

Add tomatoes, green pepper, onion, celery, parsley, oregano and pepper. Mix well. Serve on lettuce leaves.

Nutrient Analysis: 1 portion

Calories: 119	Fat: 3.5 g	Cholesterol: 0
Sodium: 145 mg	Dietary Fiber: 1.3 g	
Calcium: 17 mg		

Diabetic Exchange: 1 starch, ½ fat

TABBOULEH SALAD

Add diced cooked chicken or seafood to tabbouleh for a tasty main dish salad.

About 6 cups; 12 portions

1 cup bulgur
2 cups hot water
¾ cup chopped fresh parsley
¼ cup chopped fresh mint or 2
    teaspoons dried mint, crushed
¼ cup chopped green onion
1 teaspoon dried oregano,
    crushed
6 tablespoons lemon juice
6 tablespoons olive oil

Soak bulgur in hot water for 15 to 30 minutes. Drain off any excess water.

In a large bowl, combine bulgur, parsley, mint, onion and oregano. Add lemon juice, olive oil, salt, pepper and additional spices if desired. Mix well. Refrigerate for 2 to 4 hours.

continued on next page

TABBOULEH SALAD (con't)

¼ teaspoon salt
   freshly ground pepper to taste
½ cup peeled, chopped cucumber
2 tomatoes, peeled, seeded and
   chopped
   romaine lettuce leaves
   plain low-fat yogurt (optional)

For a more spicy mix add:
⅛ teaspoon ground allspice
⅛ teaspoon nutmeg
⅛ teaspoon ground cloves
1 teaspoon cinnamon
5 drops Tabasco sauce

Just before serving, stir in chopped cucumber and tomatoes. Serve on romaine leaves and garnish with a dollop of yogurt if desired.

Nutrient Analysis: 1 portion

Calories: 121	Fat: 7 g	Cholesterol: 0
Sodium: 54 mg	Dietary Fiber: 1.7 g	
Calcium: 14 mg		

Diabetic Exchange: 1 starch, 1 fat

DILLED BEAN SALAD

6 portions

1 16-ounce can small white beans
   (navy), drained
1 large carrot, shredded
1 green onion, finely sliced
2 tablespoons fresh lime juice
1 tablespoon vegetable oil
2 teaspoons chopped fresh dill or
   1 teaspoon dried dill weed
½ teaspoon sugar
   freshly ground pepper
   lettuce leaves, preferably
   red-tipped

In a medium bowl, combine beans, carrot, green onion, lime juice, oil, dill, sugar and pepper. Cover and refrigerate until well chilled.

Line 6 salad plates with lettuce leaves; spoon bean salad on top.

Nutrient Analysis: 1 portion

Calories: 120	Fat: 3.4 g	Cholesterol: 0
Sodium: 260 mg	Dietary Fiber: 1.4 g	
Calcium: 59 mg		

Diabetic Exchange: 1 starch, 1 vegetable, ½ fat

WONDERFUL MISCELLANEOUS SALAD

A real crowd pleaser!

About 12 cups; 24 portions

2 cups chopped fresh broccoli
2 ribs celery, chopped
4 green onions, sliced
1 green pepper, chopped
½ cup green beans, or peas, or carrots or zucchini, raw and sliced
½ cup raisins
2 cups cooked brown rice
1¼ cups cooked or canned garbanzo beans (chickpeas) or kidney beans
¼ cup slivered almonds
½ cup unsalted sunflower nuts
1½ cups grated Parmesan or Romano cheese
1¼ cups IMAGINATION VINAIGRETTE DRESSING, *(page 160).*

CREAMY DRESSING
½ cup calorie-reduced mayonnaise
1 cup plain low-fat yogurt
2 teaspoons curry powder
½ teaspoon ground turmeric
½ teaspoon chili powder
½ teaspoon ground ginger
½ teaspoon paprika

In a large bowl, mix broccoli, celery, onions, green pepper, green beans or peas, or carrots or zucchini, raisins, rice, garbanzo beans, almonds, sunflower nuts, and grated cheese.

Add vinaigrette dressing and toss.

In a small bowl, combine mayonnaise, yogurt, curry powder, turmeric, chili powder, ginger and paprika. Blend well. Add to salad and toss again. Cover and chill salad thoroughly.

Toss salad again just before serving.

Nutrient Analysis: 1 portion

Calories: 130   Fat: 7.2 g   Cholesterol: 6 mg

Sodium: 196 mg   Dietary Fiber: 1.6 g

Calcium: 110 mg

Diabetic Exchange: 1 starch, 1 vegetable, 1 fat

APPLE SPINACH SALAD

4 portions

4 cups spinach leaves
1½ tablespoons vegetable oil
2 tablespoons cider vinegar
¼ teaspoon salt
   pinch sugar
1 medium tart apple, diced
¼ cup chopped red onion
¼ cup dried currants or chopped
   raisins

Wash spinach thoroughly. Pat dry. Tear spinach into bite-sized pieces; set aside in salad bowl.

In a small bowl, mix oil, vinegar, salt and sugar. Add apple, onion and currants to dressing and toss to coat. Cover and let stand at least 10 minutes.

Add dressing to salad bowl and toss with spinach.

Nutrient Analysis: 1 portion

Calories: 95   *Fat: 5 g*   *Cholesterol: 0*

Sodium: 194 mg   *Dietary Fiber: 4.3 g*

Calcium: 27 mg

Diabetic Exchange: 1 fruit, 1 fat

CITRUS SPINACH SALAD

Spinach and citrus fruit are a tasty combination and a healthful one. Citrus aids the absorption of iron from the iron-rich spinach.

6 portions

⅓ cup MAZATLAN LIME
   DRESSING, *(page 157).*
5 cups fresh spinach
1½ cups sliced fresh mushrooms
2 oranges, peeled and sectioned
   or 1 11-ounce can mandarin
   oranges, drained
½ large red onion, sliced and
   separated into rings
½ 8-ounce can sliced water
   chestnuts, drained

Make salad dressing and refrigerate until ready to serve.

In a large bowl, combine spinach, mushrooms, orange sections, onion and water chestnuts. Just before serving, toss with dressing.

Nutrient Analysis: 1 portion

Calories: 107   *Fat: 5 g*   *Cholesterol: 0*

Sodium: 40 mg   *Dietary Fiber: 3.1 g*

Calcium: 69 mg

Diabetic Exchange: 1 vegetable, ½ fruit, 1 fat

ORANGE CAULIFLOWER SALAD

6 portions

2 cups fresh spinach
2 oranges, peeled and sectioned or
    1 11-ounce can mandarin
    oranges, drained
2 cups uncooked cauliflower
    florets
¼ cup chopped green pepper
¾ cup SURPRISE DRESSING,
    (page 156).

Wash and dry spinach. In a large salad bowl, toss spinach, oranges, cauliflower, green pepper and dressing.

Nutrient Analysis: 1 portion

Calories: 80	*Fat: 0.2 g*	*Cholesterol: 0*
Sodium: 35 mg	*Dietary Fiber: 2.1 g*	
Calcium: 92 mg		

Diabetic Exchange: 1 vegetable, 1 fruit

24-HOUR LAYERED SALAD

This make-ahead salad can be made with a variety of vegetables. It is a good recipe for using up small amounts of vegetables on hand.

9 x 13" pan; 12 portions

1 head lettuce, shredded
1 large onion, sliced and separated
    into rings
1 cup diced celery
1 8-ounce can sliced water
    chestnuts, drained
4 hard-cooked egg whites,
    chopped
2 cups frozen peas, uncooked
1 cup plain low-fat yogurt
½ cup calorie-reduced mayonnaise
2 teaspoons sugar
6 ounces part-skim mozzarella
    cheese, shredded

In a 9 x 13" pan, layer vegetables in the order given: lettuce, onion rings, celery, water chestnuts, egg whites and peas.

Mix together yogurt and mayonnaise. Spread over layered vegetables and sprinkle with sugar. Top with shredded cheese.

Refrigerate overnight. Cut in squares to serve.

Nutrient Analysis: 1 portion

Calories: 128	*Fat: 5.2 g*	*Cholesterol: 12 mg*
Sodium: 198 mg	*Dietary Fiber: 0.6 g*	
Calcium: 155 mg		

Diabetic Exchange: 1 medium-fat meat, 2 vegetable

GREEN SALAD

1 small head romaine lettuce
1 small head red leaf lettuce or
   curly endive
6 green onions with tops, thinly
   sliced
6 large fresh mushrooms, thinly
   sliced
¼ cup walnuts, coarsely chopped
1 small bunch fresh parsley,
   finely chopped
¾ cup SURPRISE DRESSING,
   (page 156).

Nutrient analysis: 1 portion

6 portions

Wash and dry lettuce. Tear into bite-sized pieces and place in large salad bowl.

Add onion, mushrooms, walnuts and parsley. Just before serving, toss with dressing.

Calories: 95	Fat: 3.4 g	Cholesterol: 0
Sodium: 22 mg	Dietary Fiber: 1.3 g	
Calcium: 79 mg		

Diabetic Exchange: 2 vegetable, 1 fat

HEALTH SALAD

3-4 cups fresh spinach
1 carrot, shredded
2 ounces chopped cooked
   Canadian bacon
½ cup raisins
3 hard-cooked egg whites,
   chopped
1 cup fresh bean sprouts
¼ cup sunflower nuts
½ cup SURPRISE DRESSING,
   (page 156).

Nutrient analysis: 1 portion

4 luncheon portions

Spinach: wash, dry and tear into bite-size pieces. In a large bowl, combine spinach, carrot, bacon, raisins, egg whites, bean sprouts and sunflower nuts.

Just before serving, toss with dressing.

Calories: 185	Fat: 5.7 g	Cholesterol: 0
Sodium: 100 mg	Dietary Fiber: 4.3 g	
Calcium: 122 mg		

*Diabetic Exchange: 1 medium-fat meat,
                    2 vegetable, 1 fruit*

COLE SLAW

4 cups shredded cabbage
½ green pepper, chopped
1 cup water
1 teaspoon salt
2 stalks celery, finely chopped
shredded carrots, as much as
you like
1½ cups BOILED DRESSING FOR
COLE SLAW, *(page 155)*.

About 7 cups; 14 portions

Soak cabbage and green pepper a minimum of 20 minutes in a brine made of water and salt. Drain.

Add celery, carrots and cooled dressing. Cover and refrigerate overnight. Flavor improves when made a day in advance.

Nutrient Analysis: ½ cup portion

Calories: 77	Fat: 4 g	Cholesterol: 0
Sodium: 48 mg	Dietary Fiber: 0.7 g	
Calcium: 18 mg		

Diabetic Exchange: 1 vegetable, 1 fat

CONFETTI APPLESLAW

2 tablespoons orange or apple
juice concentrate, defrosted
1 unpeeled red apple, cored and
diced
4 cups shredded cabbage
2 small red onions, finely
shredded
1 red or green sweet pepper,
thinly sliced
3 tablespoons raisins
1 tablespoon calorie-reduced
mayonnaise
½ cup plain low-fat yogurt
½ teaspoon dry mustard
paprika to taste
freshly ground pepper to taste

About 7 cups; 14 portions

In a large bowl, stir together juice concentrate and diced apple. Add cabbage, onion, pepper and raisins.

In a small bowl, stir together mayonnaise, yogurt, mustard, paprika and pepper. Add to vegetable mixture. Cover tightly and refrigerate until ready to serve.

Nutrient Analysis: ½ cup portion

Calories: 35	Fat: 0.5 g	Cholesterol: 1 mg
Sodium: 17 mg	Dietary Fiber: 1 g	
Calcium: 34 mg		

Diabetic Exchange: ½ fruit

VEGIE SLAW

1 large carrot, shredded
2 cups shredded cabbage
⅔ cup unsalted sunflower nuts or other chopped nuts such as almonds, walnuts or pecans
½ cup raisins
1 apple, diced
1½ cups BANANA-YOGURT DRESSING, *(page 163)*.

About 5 cups; 10 portions

Toss together carrot, cabbage, sunflower nuts, raisins and apple.

Add dressing and mix lightly.

Nutrient Analysis: ½ cup portion

Calories: 124	Fat: 5 g	Cholesterol: 1 mg
Sodium: 62 mg	Dietary Fiber: 1.8 g	
Calcium: 56 mg		

Diabetic Exchange: 1 vegetable, 1 fruit, 1 fat

BROCCOLI-CORN SALAD

1 bunch (about 1½ pounds) broccoli
2 ears sweet corn
½ cup chopped red onion
¼ cup vegetable oil
5 tablespoons cider vinegar
2 teaspoons dried oregano, crushed
1½ teaspoons ground cumin

8 portions

Trim broccoli. If stalks are thick, peel off tough outer skin. Remove broccoli florets. Cut stalks into ¼" thick slices. Steam florets and stems until crisp-tender but still bright green, about 5 minutes. Cool.

Husk and cook corn in boiling water until tender (about 7 minutes). Cool. Scrape kernels from cob into a large bowl. Add broccoli and onion.

In jar with a tight-fitting lid, combine oil, vinegar, oregano and cumin. Cover and shake well. Pour dressing over vegetables and toss well. Marinate at room temperature about 1 hour and then refrigerate about 1 hour or marinate in refrigerator several hours or overnight.

Nutrient Analysis: 1 portion

Calories: 109	Fat: 7.4 g	Cholesterol: 0
Sodium: 27 mg	Dietary Fiber: 1.2 g	
Calcium: 44 mg		

Diabetic Exchange: ½ starch, 1 vegetable, 1 fat

CARROT RAISIN SALAD

Adding a ¼ cup crushed pineapple makes a tasty variation.

About 2 cups; 4 portions

4 medium carrots, shredded
¼ cup raisins
2 teaspoons sugar
   juice of 1 lemon

In a medium bowl, thoroughly mix carrots, raisins, sugar and lemon. Served chilled.

Nutrient Analysis: ½ cup portion

Calories: 69	Fat: 0.1 g	Cholesterol: 0
Sodium: 28 mg	Dietary Fiber: 2.4 g	
Calcium: 26 mg		

Diabetic Exchange: 1 vegetable, 1 fruit

CAULIFLOWER SALAD

Tempting, even to those who usually shun cauliflower.

6 portions

4 cups thinly sliced cauliflower
   florets
½ cup sliced ripe olives, drained
⅔ cup chopped green pepper
2 tablespoons chopped pimiento
½ cup chopped onion
½-1¼ cups TANGY
     VINAIGRETTE
     DRESSING, *(page 160).*

In a medium bowl, combine cauliflower, olives, green pepper, pimiento and onion.

Pour well-blended dressing over vegetables. Mix well. Cover and refrigerate for 4 hours or overnight.

Toss again and drain thoroughly before serving.

Nutrient Analysis: 1 portion

Calories: 52	Fat: 3.5 g	Cholesterol: 0
Sodium: 95 mg	Dietary Fiber: 1.3 g	
Calcium: 33 mg		

Diabetic Exchange: 1 vegetable, ½ fat

CITRUS BEET SALAD

6 portions

4 medium beets
1 small head escarole
1 large grapefruit, peeled and
   sectioned
2 green onions, sliced
2 tablespoons walnut oil or other
   light salad oil
3 tablespoons red wine vinegar
1 teaspoon dried basil, crushed
¼ teaspoon pepper

Cut off and discard beet tops. In medium saucepan, heat 1" water to boiling. Add beets and cook, covered, until tender (about 40 minutes). Drain and cool; remove skins. Cut beets into julienne strips.

Wash, dry and tear escarole into bite-sized pieces.

Just before serving, place torn escarole in a medium bowl. Arrange beets, grapefruit sections and onions on top of escarole.

In a jar with tight-fitting lid, combine oil, vinegar, basil and pepper. Cover and shake well. Drizzle dressing over salad and toss.

Nutrient Analysis: 1 portion

Calories: 81	*Fat: 4.7 g*	*Cholesterol: 0*
Sodium: 43 mg	*Dietary Fiber: 0.9 g*	
Calcium: 26 mg		

Diabetic Exchange: 1 vegetable, 1 fat

CUCUMBER TOMATO SALAD

6 portions

2 medium cucumbers
2 medium tomatoes
2 tablespoons olive oil
2 tablespoons lemon juice
1 teaspoon dried basil, crushed

Pare, score and cut cucumbers into ¼" slices. Slice tomatoes thinly and cut slices in half. Arrange cucumbers and tomatoes in a shallow dish.

Combine oil, lemon juice and basil and mix well. Pour over cucumbers and tomatoes.

Nutrient Analysis: 1 portion

Calories: 61	*Fat: 4.7 g*	*Cholesterol: 0*
Sodium: 5 mg	*Dietary Fiber: 0.8 g*	
Calcium: 15 mg		

Diabetic Exchange: ½ vegetable, 1 fat

POTATO SALAD VINAIGRETTE

Best when served at room temperature.

About 7 cups; 14 portions

2 pounds small new potatoes,
   scrubbed
¼ cup minced fresh parsley
½ cup diced green pepper
½ cup thinly sliced green onions
½ cup vegetable oil
¼ cup red wine vinegar
1 tablespoon Dijon mustard
1 teaspoon sugar
½ teaspoon salt
½ teaspoon pepper

Boil unpeeled potatoes just until tender (15 to 20 minutes). Do not overcook. Drain.

Cut potatoes in quarters and arrange in a 7x11" glass dish. Sprinkle with parsley, green pepper and onions.

In a jar with a tight fitting lid, combine oil, vinegar, mustard, sugar, salt and pepper. Shake well and pour dressing over vegetables while potatoes are still warm. Toss gently.

Marinate several hours at room temperature before serving.

Nutrient Analysis: ½ cup portion

Calories: 131	*Fat: 6 g*	*Cholesterol: 0*
Sodium: 178 mg	*Dietary Fiber: 0.4 g*	
Calcium: 7 mg		

Diabetic Exchange: 1 starch, 1 fat

DRESSINGS & SAUCES

What is sauce for the goose may be sauce for the gander but it is not necessarily sauce for the chicken, the duck, the turkey or the guinea hen.

Alice B. Toklas

DRESSINGS AND SAUCES

Your nutritious and low-calorie salad needn't be compromised by a salty, high-calorie dressing. Two tablespoons of an oil, sour cream or mayonnaise-based dressing can add as many as 200 calories and 400 milligrams of sodium! Dressings and sauces are meant to "enhance" the flavors of meats, fish, greens and fruit. Never should they cover up the crispness nor freshness of the foods they are served on.

Dressings and sauces can be good sources of unsaturated fats. Both types (monounsaturated and polyunsaturated) help to lower the amount of cholesterol in your blood. The recipes in this section are lower in fat than traditional recipes, have virtually no saturated fat nor cholesterol, and are very low in sodium. When fat is an essential part of the dressing or sauce, only unsaturated fats, the kinds that don't damage blood vessels, were used. Only three of the recipes in this section require salt.

Use the following chart to compare the amount of calories, fat, cholesterol and P:S ratios of various types of bases used in preparing dressings and sauces. For more information on the P:S ratios of various oils, please refer to Table 5 in Chapter 1.

Table 18: Sauces & Dressings Comparison Chart

Type of Base: (Per Tablespoon)	Calories	Total Fat grams	P:S Ratio	Cholesterol mg
Vegetable Oil	126	13.6	4:1	0
Margarine, liquid oil	104	11.4	2:1	0
Margarine, hydrogenated	104	11.4	1:2	0
Tub Margarine	50	6.0	3:1	0
Shortening, vegetable	113	12.8	.5:1	0
Butter	108	12.2	.06:1	33.0
Sour Cream	30	2.5	.06:1	7.0
Land 'O Lakes™ Lean Cream	20	5.0	.03:1	3.5
Cream Cheese	50	5.0	.06:1	16.0
Light Cream Cheese	30	2.5	.02:1	7.5
Mayonnaise	100	12.0	3:1	10.0
Mayonnaise-type salad dressing	65	7.0	3:1	8.0
Light mayonnaise-type salad dressing	40	4.0	2:1	5.0
Yogurt, whole milk, 4 Tablespoons	90	3.5	.08:1	14.0
Yogurt, skim milk, 4 Tablespoons	64	0.2	.05:1	trace
Wine, 4 Tablespoons	88	0	0	0

Sources: USDA, HNIS. *Composition of Foods: Dairy and Egg Products* and *Fats and Oils*. Agriculture Handbooks 8-1 and 8-4, revised 1976 and 1979. Personal communication with Land O' Lakes and Kraft, Inc. March, 1988.

HERBED VINEGAR

1 cup white wine vinegar
½ teaspoon dill weed
¼ cup snipped chives
1 garlic clove
⅓ cup snipped fresh mint or 1
   tablespoon dried mint,
   crushed

TARRAGON VINEGAR

Combine vinegar, dill weed, chives, garlic and mint.

Refrigerate in a covered bottle for at least four days to allow flavors to blend. Strain before using.

Add a sprig of fresh tarragon to a bottle of white wine vinegar.

Nutrient Analysis: 1 tablespoon

Calories: 2.5	Fat: 0	Cholesterol: 0
Sodium: 2 mg		

Diabetic Exchange: free

BOILED DRESSING FOR COLE SLAW

About 1½ cups

½ cup sugar
½ cup water
⅓ cup vinegar
1 teaspoon mustard seed or
   celery seed or ½ teaspoon of
   each
¼ cup vegetable oil

Combine sugar, water, vinegar, seeds and oil in small saucepan. Bring to a boil and boil about 1 minute. Cool.

Nutrient Analysis: 1 tablespoon

Calories: 37	Fat: 2.3 g	Cholesterol: 0
Sodium: 0		

Diabetic Exchange: ½ fat

SURPRISE DRESSING

Surprisingly delicious on greens or on citrus and greens combinations!

About 1¼ cups

½ cup evaporated skim milk
1 6-ounce can frozen orange juice
concentrate, thawed
pinch of ground ginger

Mix milk, orange juice concentrate and ginger. Shake well before using.

Nutrient Analysis: 1 tablespoon

Calories: 20	Fat: 0	Cholesterol: 0
Sodium: 6 mg	Calcium: 20 mg	

Diabetic Exchange: free (2 tablespoons = ½ fruit)

CELERY SEED DRESSING

A thick dressing, excellent on greens and fruit combinations. Keeps for several months in the refrigerator.

About 1½ cups

⅓ cup honey or sugar
1 teaspoon dry mustard
1 teaspoon paprika
1 small onion, minced
¼ cup white wine vinegar
1 tablespoon lemon juice
¾ cup vegetable oil
2 teaspoons celery seed

Place honey, mustard, paprika and onion in blender. Slowly add part of vinegar while blending at medium speed. Add the rest of the vinegar, the lemon juice and the oil, blending until creamy. Add celery seed and mix well. Refrigerate until ready to serve.

Nutrient Analysis: 1 tablespoon

Calories: 78	Fat: 6.9 g	Cholesterol: 0
Sodium: 1 mg		

Diabetic Exchange: ½ fruit, 1 fat

MAZATLAN LIME SALAD DRESSING

Delicious on mixed greens with slices of fresh orange and garnished with toasted almonds. Also excellent on tossed lettuce, tomato and cucumber salad.

About ⅔ cup

¼ cup vegetable oil
¼ cup fresh lime juice
1 teaspoon grated lime rind
2 tablespoons sugar
¼ teaspoon garlic powder
(optional)

In a jar with a tight fitting lid, mix oil, lime juice, lime rind, sugar and garlic powder if desired. Shake well.

Refrigerate until ready to serve.

Nutrient Analysis: 1 tablespoon

Calories: 59	Fat: 5.3 g	Cholesterol: 0
Sodium: 0		

Diabetic Exchange: 1 fat

WESTERN DRESSING

This dressing can also be used as a marinade for meats.

About 1½ cups

½ cup sodium-reduced ketchup
½ cup vegetable oil
⅓ cup sugar
2 tablespoons lemon juice
¼ teaspoon pepper
¼ cup cider vinegar
1 small onion, grated (optional)

In a jar with a tightly-fitting lid, combine ketchup, oil, sugar, lemon juice and pepper. Cover and shake vigorously. Add vinegar, and onion, if desired. Shake again. Refrigerate.

Shake well before each use.

Nutrient Analysis: 1 tablespoon

Calories: 57	Fat: 4.5 g	Cholesterol: 0
Sodium: 2 mg		

Diabetic Exchange: 1 fat

SESAME DRESSING — SWEET

This light, sweet-sour Oriental-style dressing, enhanced by the nutty flavor of toasted sesame, is excellent with chicken or fresh spinach salad.

About ½ cup

4 tablespoons toasted sesame
   seeds
6 tablespoons rice wine vinegar
¼ teaspoon salt
½ teaspoon sugar
½ teaspoon freshly ground black
   pepper

Toast sesame seeds in frying pan over medium heat. Shake or stir and watch carefully! Sesame goes from toasted to burned in the blink of an eye.

Add cooled seeds to vinegar, salt, sugar and pepper. Mix. Refrigerate until ready to use.

Nutrient Analysis: 1 tablespoon

Calories: 26	Fat: 2.2 g	Cholesterol: 0
Sodium: 75 mg		

Diabetic Exchange: ½ fat

VINAIGRETTE DRESSING

Just as the taste preference for certain oils and vinegars is very personal, so are the proportions in which they are combined. Experiment and adjust to suit your taste.

About 1 cup

½ cup oil (olive, vegetable,
   sunflower, etc.)
½ cup vinegar (wine, tarragon,
   cider, etc.)
1 teaspoon dry mustard
½ teaspoon freshly ground pepper
1 teaspoon sugar (optional)
½ teaspoon paprika (optional)

In a jar with a tightly-fitting lid, combine oil, vinegar, mustard, pepper and sugar and paprika, if desired.

Cover and shake vigorously. Refrigerate. Shake again just before using.

Nutrient Analysis: 1 tablespoon

Calories: 62	Fat: 6.9 g	Cholesterol: 0
Sodium: 0		

Diabetic Exchange: 1½ fat

DILLED VINAIGRETTE

About 1¼ cups

½ cup vegetable oil
½ cup red wine vinegar
2 garlic cloves, minced
½ teaspoon dill weed
½ teaspoon dried oregano,
    crushed
¼ teaspoon freshly ground pepper
½ teaspoon lemon juice

In a jar with a tightly-fitting lid, combine oil, vinegar, garlic, dill weed, oregano, pepper and lemon juice. Cover and shake vigorously.

Refrigerate. Shake again just before using.

Nutrient Analysis: 1 tablespoon

Calories: 62	*Fat: 6.9 g*	*Cholesterol: 0*
Sodium: 0		

Diabetic Exchange: 1½ fat

HERBED VINAIGRETTE DRESSING

About 1 cup

½ cup safflower oil
¼ cup red wine vinegar
1-3 tsp. Dijon mustard
2 tablespoons lemon juice
1 teaspoon sugar
½ teaspoon pepper
1 teaspoon dried rosemary,
    crushed
1 teaspoon dried tarragon,
    crushed

In a jar with a tightly-fitting lid, combine oil, vinegar, mustard, lemon juice, sugar, pepper, rosemary and tarragon. Cover and shake vigorously.

Refrigerate. Shake again just before using.

Nutrient Analysis: 1 tablespoon

Calories: 63	*Fat: 6.8 g*	*Cholesterol: 0*
Sodium: 28 mg		

Diabetic Exchange: 1½ fat

TANGY VINAIGRETTE DRESSING

A tart and lively dressing, exactly the right addition to vegetable and pasta salads.

About 1¼ cups

½ cup olive oil
6 tablespoons lemon juice
6 tablespoons wine vinegar
¼ teaspoon pepper
1 teaspoon sugar

In a jar with a tightly-fitting lid, mix oil, lemon juice, vinegar, pepper and sugar. Shake well.

Refrigerate. Shake again before using.

Nutrient Analysis: 1 tablespoon

Calories: 50	Fat: 5.4 g	Cholesterol: 0
Sodium: 0		

Diabetic Exchange: 1 fat

IMAGINATION VINAIGRETTE DRESSING

Good as a marinade too.

About 1¼ cups

3 tablespoons olive oil
5 tablespoons wine vinegar
2 tablespoons lemon juice
6 tablespoons water
1 teaspoon Dijon mustard
1 large garlic clove, crushed
2 tablespoons minced onions
1 tablespoon honey
1 teaspoon dried tarragon, crushed
¼ teaspoon paprika
   freshly ground pepper

In a jar with a tightly-fitting lid, combine oil, vinegar, lemon juice, water, mustard, garlic, onions, honey, tarragon, paprika and pepper. Cover and shake well.

Refrigerate until ready to use.

Nutrient Analysis: 1 tablespoon

Calories: 23	Fat: 2 g	Cholesterol: 0
Sodium: 8 mg		

Diabetic Exchange: ½ fat

AMISH-STYLE SALAD DRESSING

Similar to traditional sour cream dressing. Experiment with different herbs and spices.

About 1 cup

1 cup plain low-fat yogurt
1 tablespoon Dijon mustard
1 teaspoon dill weed
1 teaspoon sugar

Blend together yogurt, mustard, dill weed and sugar.

Refrigerate until ready to use.

Nutrient Analysis: 1 tablespoon

Calories: 10	Fat: 0.1 g	Cholesterol: 0
Sodium: 39 mg	Calcium: 29 mg	

Diabetic Exchange: free

CREAMY SALAD DRESSING

A good basic dressing for greens, vegetable and seafood salads.

About 1½ cups

1 cup plain low-fat yogurt
¼ cup calorie-reduced mayonnaise
½ teaspoon Dijon mustard
2 green onions, sliced
2 tablespoons minced fresh parsley

In blender, combine yogurt, mayonnaise, mustard, onions and parsley. Blend until smooth.

Refrigerate until ready to use.

CREAMY SALAD DRESSING VARIATIONS

CREAMY GARLIC DRESSING

Add 1 teaspoon garlic powder

CREAMY CUCUMBER DRESSING

Add ½ cup chopped cucumber

continued on next page

CREAMY HERB DRESSING

Add 2 to 4 tablespoons mixed fresh or 1 to 2 teaspoons dried herbs such as basil, rosemary, tarragon, chervil, dill.

Nutrient Analysis: 1 tablespoon

Calories: 13.5	Fat: 0.7 g	Cholesterol: 1 mg
Sodium: 25 mg	Calcium: 20 mg	

Diabetic Exchange: free

HAWAIIAN DRESSING

About 1 cup

½ cup plain low-fat yogurt
½ cup calorie-reduced mayonnaise
2 teaspoons lemon juice
1 tablespoon honey
1 teaspoon grated fresh ginger
¼ teaspoon paprika

Blend yogurt, mayonnaise, lemon juice, honey, ginger and paprika.

Refrigerate until ready to use.

Nutrient Analysis: 1 tablespoon

Calories: 28	Fat: 2 g	Cholesterol: 3 mg
Sodium: 48 mg	Calcium: 14 mg	

Diabetic Exchange: ½ fat

FETA CHEESE DRESSING

About 1¼ cups

1 cup plain low-fat yogurt
2 ounces feta cheese, crumbled
1 garlic clove, minced
2 tablespoons chopped fresh
   parsley
¼ teaspoon dried oregano,
   crushed

Combine yogurt, feta cheese, garlic, parsley and oregano.

Cover and refrigerate for at least 30 minutes before using.

Nutrient Analysis: 1 tablespoon

Calories: 14	Fat: 0.6 g	Cholesterol: 3 mg
Sodium: 40 mg	Calcium: 37 mg	

Diabetic Exchange: free

BANANA YOGURT DRESSING

A creamy sweet-sour dressing that is particularly good on cabbage or fresh fruit. It doubles as a tasty dip for fruit.

About 1⅓ cups

½ very ripe banana
½ cup low-fat cottage cheese
2 tablespoons honey
½ cup plain low-fat yogurt

In blender or food processor, mix banana, cottage cheese, honey and yogurt until smooth and creamy.

When used as a dip for fruit, mix banana, cottage cheese and honey in blender. Remove from blender and carefully stir in yogurt.

Refrigerate until ready to use.

Nutrient Analysis: 1 tablespoon

Calories: 17	*Fat: 0.1 g*	*Cholesterol: 1 mg*
Sodium: 26 mg	*Calcium: 15 mg*	

Diabetic Exchange: free (2 tablespoons = ½ fruit)

SPICY YOGURT FOR FRUIT

1 cup low-fat vanilla yogurt
¼ teaspoon ground cinnamon
⅛ teaspoon ground cardamon or nutmeg

In small bowl, combine yogurt, cinnamon and cardamon or nutmeg. Chill.

Just before serving, add dressing to fruit and toss well.

Nutrient Analysis: 1 tablespoon

Calories: 12	*Fat: 0.2 g*	*Cholesterol: 1 mg*
Sodium: 9 mg	*Calcium: 6 mg*	

Diabetic Exchange: free

WHITE (BÉCHAMEL) SAUCE

Use light sauce for creamed vegetables and as a soup base, medium for creamed and scalloped dishes, and heavy for croquettes or soufflés.

About 1 cup

Light
1 tablespoon margarine
1 tablespoon flour
1 cup skim milk
⅛ teaspoon white pepper

Medium
2 tablespoons margarine
2 tablespoons flour
1 cup skim milk
⅛ teaspoon white pepper

Heavy
4 tablespoons margarine
4 tablespoons flour
1 cup skim milk
⅛ teaspoon white pepper

In saucepan, melt margarine. Add flour, stirring constantly, until mixture bubbles. Cook and stir an additional minute. DO NOT ALLOW TO BROWN.

Add skim milk and continue stirring until mixture comes to a boil and thickens. Add pepper.

WHITE SAUCE VARIATIONS

MORNAY SAUCE

Delicious with fish and vegetable dishes.

1 cup medium white sauce
1 tablespoon Parmesan cheese
1 tablespoon shredded part-skim
   brick cheese
⅛ teaspoon nutmeg or ½
   teaspoon Dijon mustard

Cook over moderate heat, stirring until cheeses are melted.

WHITE SAUCE VARIATIONS

VELOUTÉ SAUCE

For fish, veal or poultry. Slightly thinner and not as rich as traditional Velouté which is topped with heavy cream.

Substitute one cup of reduced-sodium chicken broth for the skim milk in the white sauce recipe.

DUGLERE SAUCE

For fish

About 1¾ cups

½ cup chopped tomatoes
¼ cup sliced onions
2 tablespoons white wine
1 tablespoon lemon juice
1 cup medium white sauce

Simmer the tomatoes, onions, wine and lemon juice for 12 to 15 minutes. Add to medium white sauce.

Nutrient Analysis: 1 tablespoon	Medium	Heavy	Mornay	Velouté	Duglere
Calories:	20	37	20	17	15
Fat:	1.4 g	2.8 g	1.6 g	1.4 g	0.9 g
Cholesterol:	0	0	1 mg	0	0
Sodium:	22 mg	36 mg	33 mg	15 mg	14 mg
Calcium:	19 mg	19 mg	26 mg	——	12 mg
Diabetic Exchange:	free	½ fat	free	free	free

PLUM SAUCE

Somewhere between a chutney and a sweet-sour sauce, this sauce is good with meats as well as with Oriental appetizers.

About 2 cups

1	16-ounce can plums, packed in light syrup
¾	cup plum syrup
3	small pears, peeled, cored and diced
6	tablespoons red wine vinegar
3	slices fresh ginger, minced
3	garlic cloves, minced (optional)
1½	teaspoons sodium-reduced soy sauce
¾	teaspoon lemon juice
2	tablespoons cornstarch
6	tablespoons water

Drain plums and reserve syrup. Remove and discard plum pits. In food processor or blender, combine plums with syrup, pears, vinegar, ginger, garlic, soy sauce and lemon juice. Process until smooth.

Pour mixture into small saucepan. Bring to a boil; reduce heat.

Dissolve cornstarch in water. Add to plum mixture. Simmer for about 10 minutes or until mixture thickens, stirring occasionally. Serve warm or at room temperature.

Nutrient Analysis: 1 tablespoon

Calories: 43	Fat: 0.1 g	Cholesterol: 0
Sodium: 0.1 mg	Dietary Fiber: 0.5 g	

Diabetic Exchange: 1½ tablespoons = 1 fruit

ORIENTAL SWEET-SOUR SAUCE

Particularly good with CHICKEN APPETIZERS, (see page 73).

About 1½ cups

2 slices canned unsweetened
  pineapple, diced
1 tablespoon vegetable oil
2½ teaspoons cornstarch
2 tablespoons vinegar*
½ tablespoon tomato sauce
1½ teaspoons brandy (optional)
1½ teaspoons sugar
½ teaspoon sodium-reduced
  soy sauce
1 cup water
2-3 green onions, chopped fine

**Flavored vinegars, such as
raspberry or blueberry, are a
delicious added touch.*

In a non-stick sprayed or teflon pan, sauté pineapple in oil.

Dissolve cornstarch in vinegar. Add tomato sauce, brandy, sugar and soy sauce. Stir mixture into pineapple. Add water. Bring to a boil; reduce heat and simmer 5 minutes. Cool.

Just before serving, stir in chopped onions. Serve with Oriental appetizers. Refrigerate any remaining sauce.

Nutrient Analysis: 1 tablespoon

| Calories: 11 | Fat: 0.6 g | Cholesterol: 2 mg |

Sodium: 14 mg

Diabetic Exchange: free

SWEET-SOUR MUSTARD

About 1¼ cups

½ cup sugar
2 tablespoons all-purpose flour
3 tablespoons dry mustard
¼ cup vinegar
¾ cup water

In small saucepan, combine sugar, flour and dry mustard. Add vinegar and water. Stir and heat over medium heat until mixture comes to a boil. Stir a few more minutes until thickened. Cool and store in refrigerator.

Nutrient Analysis: 1 tablespoon

| Calories: 26 | Fat: 0.3 g | Cholesterol: 0 |

Sodium: 0

Diabetic Exchange: 2 tablespoons = 1 fruit

HOME-STYLE BARBECUE SAUCE

This tangy barbecue sauce is also delicious mixed with lean ground beef for grilled burgers.

About 1½ cups

½ cup plain low-fat yogurt
½ cup sodium-reduced ketchup
¼ cup sodium-reduced
    Worcestershire sauce
¼ cup prepared mustard
¼ cup firmly packed brown sugar
⅛ teaspoon Tabasco sauce
    (optional)
1 teaspoon onion powder
½ teaspoon garlic powder

In a small bowl, combine yogurt, ketchup, Worcestershire, mustard, brown sugar, Tabasco, onion powder and garlic powder. Whisk until smooth.

Brush on chicken or ribs during the last 20 minutes of cooking, on steaks or pork chops for last 5 to 10 minutes of cooking.

Nutrient Analysis: 1 tablespoon

Calories: 16	Fat: 0.2 g	Cholesterol: 0
Sodium: 36 mg	Calcium: 9 mg	

Diabetic Exchange: free (2 tablespoons = ½ fruit)

GARLIC SAUCE FOR CHOPS

A surprisingly mild, faintly sweet sauce similar to onion butter. Excellent served with pork, veal or lamb chops.

About ⅓ cup

10 garlic cloves
3 mushrooms, sliced
    pinch nutmeg
½ cup sodium-reduced chicken
    broth
2 teaspoons chopped fresh
    parsley

In a small saucepan, cover garlic with water. Bring to a boil; drain. Repeat 3 times.

Mash garlic with fork and return to saucepan. Add mushrooms, nutmeg, chicken broth and parsley. Bring to a boil and reduce to desired consistency.

Nutrient Analysis: 1 tablespoon

Calories: 13	Fat: 0.2 g	Cholesterol: 0
Sodium: 3 mg	Dietary Fiber: 0.2 mg	
Calcium: 12 mg		

Diabetic Exchange: free

GRAINS, PASTAS, & LEGUMES

These were the staples that allowed humankind to survive and thrive throughout the ages.

Henry Blackburn

GRAINS, PASTAS AND LEGUMES

Let grains, pasta and legumes play a central role in your diet.

Once thought of only as side dishes, pasta, legumes and grains (such as barley, bulgur and rice) make tasty and filling entrees. These foods provide plenty of protein when combined with low-fat dairy products, bits of lean meat, poultry or fish, or other grains, nuts and seeds.

Learning how to combine vegetable proteins to make complete protein is not difficult. Vegetable proteins have varying strengths and weaknesses in terms of the essential amino acids they contain. The goal is to combine vegetable proteins so that the strengths of one compensate for the weaknesses of the other. See Table 19 for methods and examples of combining vegetable proteins to make complete protein.

Table 19: Combining Vegetable Protein to Make Complete Protein
All examples can be found in the recipe sections of Cooking à la Heart.

Method:	Examples:
Combine legumes such as soybeans, lentils, navy beans, pinto beans, split peas and peanuts with grains, such as barley, corn, rice and wheat.	Baked Beans and Brown Bread Herbed Lentils and Rice Casserole Spanish Red Beans and Rice Hearty Pea Soup served with Corn Bread Lentil Confetti Salad Better Peanut Butter on whole-grain Bread
Combine either grains or legumes with nuts and seeds such as pine nuts, almonds, walnuts, sesame seeds and sunflower seeds.	Hummus Bi Tahini Garbanzo Spread Wellness Granola Crispy Cereal Snacks Rice Almond Bake Rice with Pine Nuts
Combine any grain, legume, nut or seed with egg or low-fat dairy product.	Cauliflower Walnut Casserole Tofu Italiano Black Bean Chili (containing low-fat yogurt and cheese) Rice Pudding Baked Green Rice Vegetable Lasagna

continued on next page

Table 19: Combining Vegetable Protein to Make Complete Protein, continued

Method:	Examples:
Combine any grain, legume, nut or seed with small amounts of seafood, poultry or lean red meats.	Lemon Shrimp on Bed of Rice
	Stir-Fry Beef with Vegetables served on Rice
	Wild Rice Chicken Salad
	Hearty Pea Soup
	Chicken Lentil Salad
	Seafood Pockets

Cooking Yields of Pasta and Grains

To help reduce our intake of fat and cholesterol, we are advised to use complementary vegetable proteins at least once a week. (See how this can be done as illustrated in the one-week menu plan in the *Menu Planning Section* in Chapter 2.)

To determine the amount of pasta and grains you need to purchase to make a meal, we have included two tables giving weights, dry measures and cooking yields of various types of pasta and grains.

Table 20: Determining Yields of Pasta & Grains

Pasta/Grain/Legume:	Dry Measure:	Yield:	Water Needed To Cook:
Pasta-			
Macaroni	1 pound	5 cups uncooked 8-10 cups cooked	5 quarts
Noodles	1 cup	1¾ cups cooked	4 cups
Spaghetti	2 ounces	1 cup cooked	4 cups
Grain - Rice:			
White or Brown	1 pound raw	2½ cups uncooked	5 cups
White	1 cup raw	3 cups cooked	2 cups
Brown	1 cup raw	3 cups cooked	2 cups
Wild	1 cup raw	4 cups cooked	3 cups

continued on next page

Table 20: Determining Yields of Pasta & Grains, continued

Pasta/Grain/ Legume:	Dry Measure:	Yield:	Water Needed To Cook:
Barley:	1 cup	3½ cups cooked	3 cups
Buckwheat Groats (Kasha):	1 cup	2½-3 cups cooked	2 cups
Bulgur (Cracked Wheat):	1 cup	2½-3 cups cooked	2 cups
Millet:	1 cup	3½ cups cooked	3 cups
Oats:	1 pound rolled oats	5 cups uncooked	—
	1 cup	1¾ cups cooked	—

Source: Jane Brody. *Jane Brody's Good Food Book*. New York: W.W. Norton & Co., 1985.

Cooking times for grains vary; brown and wild rice will take forty-five minutes; buckwheat and bulgur, less than half an hour; millet, forty-five minutes and rolled oats less than five minutes.

How to Cook Legumes

Dried beans, split peas and lentils *must be cooked* before they are eaten in order to modify toxins that can cause stomach cramps, nausea and diarrhea.

Soaking Methods

Most legumes, except lentils, split peas and black-eyed peas, should be soaked in cold water for 6-8 hours or overnight at room temperature before cooking. This traditional method of soaking shortens the cooking time and improves the flavor, texture and appearance of the beans.

Another option of soaking legumes is the "quick-soak" method, in which 6-8 cups of hot water is added for each pound of dry beans. The water is heated to boiling and the legumes cooked for 2 minutes. Set them aside, cover and let stand to soak for 1 full hour. Drain and rinse the legumes and you're ready to cook.

Cooking Methods

Legumes can be cooked quickly in the pressure cooker, slowly in the slow cooker (crockpot), or on top the range. Legumes cooked in the pressure cooker will be done in 10-35 minutes at 15 pounds of pressure. In the slow cooker, legumes will take 10-12 hours at low heat or 5-6 hours at high heat.

*Cooking Tips
for Legumes*

Follow the cooking requirements of legumes in the table below when cooking legumes on top the range. Be sure to use a large kettle or Dutch oven because legumes expand greatly when cooked. Adding a teaspoon of vegetable oil to the simmering legumes will help to prevent foaming. Don't add acidic ingredients such as lemon juice, vinegar or tomatoes to the cooking water until the beans are almost done as the acid slows the softening process.

Table 21: Cooking Requirements of and Yields From Legumes
(1 cup dry = ½ pound)

Legume:	Cooking Time (in hours)	Minimum water (cups)	Yield (cups)
Black beans	1½	4	2
Black-eyed peas	1	3	2
Chickpeas (garbanzo)	3	4	4
Great Northern Beans	2	3½	2
Kidney Beans	1½	3	2
Lentils*	1	3	2¼
Lima beans	1½	2	1¼
Navy beans	1½	3	2
Pinto beans	2½	3	2
Red beans	3	3	2
Soybeans	3 or more	3	2
Split peas	1	3	2¼

*Lentils are the one legume you can cook quickly (in fifteen minutes) even without soaking.

Source: Laurel Robertson, Carol Flinders, and Bronwon Godfrey. *Laurel's Kitchen*. New York: Bantam Books, 1982.

WELLNESS GRANOLA*

Granola—honey-sweetened whole grains, nuts and dried fruit—makes a delicious, fiber and protein-packed snack or breakfast.

About 10⅓ cups

½ cup vegetable oil
⅔ cup honey
5 cups rolled oats
1 cup non-fat dry milk powder
1 cup wheat germ
1 cup sesame seeds
1 cup unsalted sunflower nuts
1 cup unsalted nuts (walnuts, almonds, or cashews)
1 cup raisins
½ cup chopped, dried apricots

In a small saucepan, stir oil and honey over low heat until combined thoroughly.

In a large bowl or roaster pan, mix together rolled oats, dry milk powder, wheat germ, sesame seeds, sunflower nuts and unsalted nuts. Add oil and honey mixture and stir well.

Spread mixture on two non-stick sprayed jelly roll pans or a large roaster pan. Bake, stirring occasionally. Remove from oven; stir in raisins and dried apricots. Cool. Store covered in refrigerator.

Oven: 250°
Time: 60 minutes

Nutrient Analysis: ⅓ cup

Calories: 200   Fat: 10.2 g   Cholesterol: 1 mg

Sodium: 110 mg   Dietary Fiber: 3 g

Calcium: 71 mg

Diabetic Exchange: 1 starch, ½ fruit, 2 fat

*Be careful! Granolas are not a low-fat food.

CRUNCHY GRANOLA*

Delicious and hearty as a cereal or a snack. Make a batch and freeze half to keep fresh.

About 11 cups

5 cups rolled oats
1 cup wheat germ
1 cup unsalted sunflower nuts
⅓ cup warm water
½ cup brown sugar
½ cup vegetable oil
2 tablespoons vanilla
1 cup Grape Nuts
1 cup All-Bran
1 cup chopped pecans
1 cup raisins

In a large bowl, mix oats, wheat germ and sunflower nuts.

Mix together water, sugar, oil and vanilla. Add to oat-nut mixture and stir thoroughly. Spread in two 9 x 13" pans and bake at 325° for 20 minutes stirring every 10 mintues.

Add Grape Nuts, All-Bran and chopped pecans. Bake another 18 minutes, stirring after 10 minutes and when finished. Remove from oven. When cool, add raisins.

Oven: 325°
Time: 38 minutes

Nutrient Analysis: ⅓ cup

Calories: 175	Fat: 9.2 g	Cholesterol: 0
Sodium: 56 mg	Dietary Fiber: 3.4 g	
Calcium: 22 mg		

Diabetic Exchange: 1 starch, 2 fat

*Be careful! Granolas are not a low-fat food.

OAT BRAN CEREAL

The soluble fiber in oat products appears to significantly lower blood cholesterol levels. For a tasty variation, cook cereals in apple juice instead of water.

4 portions

4 cups water
¼ teaspoon salt
1 cup rolled oats
1 cup oat bran
4 teaspoons raisins

In a medium saucepan, bring water to a boil. Add salt. Stir in rolled oats and oat bran. Add raisins and cook over medium heat until thick.

Nutrient Analysis: 1 portion

Calories: 175	Fat: 3 g	Cholesterol: 0
Sodium: 149 mg	Dietary Fiber: 2.7 g	
Calcium: 47 mg		

Diabetic Exchange: 1 starch, 1 fruit, ½ fat

CRISPY CEREAL SNACKS

A heart-healthy update of an old favorite.

About 6 cups

4 cups unsalted popped popcorn
2 cups bite-sized shredded wheat biscuits
4 cups puffed rice
1 cup unsalted peanuts
½ cup margarine
½ teaspoon paprika
¼ teaspoon garlic powder
¼ teaspoon curry powder
1 teaspoon sodium-reduced Worcestershire sauce

In a large roasting pan, mix popcorn, shredded wheat, puffed rice and peanuts.

In a small saucepan, melt margarine over low heat. Stir in paprika, garlic powder, curry powder and Worcestershire sauce.

Pour over cereal-nut mixture. Toss until well coated. Bake, uncovered, stirring every 15 minutes. Cool before serving. Store in an airtight container.

Oven: 250°
Time: 45 minutes

Nutrient Analysis: ⅓ cup

Calories: 126	Fat: 9 g	Cholesterol: 0
Sodium: 53 mg	Dietary Fiber: 0.5 g	
Calcium: 10 mg		

Diabetic Exchange: ½ starch, 2 fat

SPICED POPCORN

Popcorn is an inexpensive, easy to make, low-cal snack as long as it isn't drenched with butter. Try sprinkling popcorn with spices such as curry or chili powder or grated Parmesan.

½ cup unpopped corn equals about 6 cups of popped corn.

Nutrient Analysis: 1 cup

Calories: 20	Fat: 0.3 g	Cholesterol: 0
Dietary Fiber: 1 g		

Diabetic Exchange: free

HONEY POPCORN BALLS

10 balls

- 3 quarts popped corn (about 1 cup unpopped)
- ½ cup sugar, brown or white
- ½ cup honey or light corn syrup
- 2 tablespoons margarine
- 1 teaspoon vanilla

Pop corn and set aside in a large bowl.

In a small saucepan, combine sugar and honey. Heat and stir to dissolve sugar. Boil to hard ball stage (260°). Add margarine and vanilla. Stir the syrup slowly into the popped corn until every kernel is covered.

Shape the corn into balls with lightly oiled or floured hands as soon as it is cool enough to handle. Wrap balls in waxed paper or plastic wrap.

Nutrient Analysis: 1 ball

Calories: 180	Fat: 5.5 g	Cholesterol: 24 mg
Sodium: 22 mg	Dietary Fiber: 2 g	
Calcium: 12 mg		

Diabetic Exchange: 1 starch, 1 fruit, 1 fat

BARLEY PILAF

A nice change from potatoes or rice. Serve with meat or fish.

About 3 cups; 6 portions

3 tablespoons margarine
½ cup chopped onion
2 ribs celery, sliced
1 4-ounce can mushroom pieces, drained (or 4 oz. fresh, sliced)
1 cup pearl barley
3 teaspoons low-sodium, chicken-flavored bouillon granules
3¼ cups water
¼ teaspoon pepper
1 bunch fresh spinach

Melt margarine in a large saucepan. Stir in onion, celery and mushrooms; sauté until tender (about 5 minutes).

Stir in barley and cook, stirring frequently, until lightly browned. Add bouillon, water and pepper; heat to boiling. Reduce heat to medium-low; cover and simmer 45 to 55 minutes or until liquid is absorbed and barley is tender. Or place barley mixture in covered casserole and bake at 325° until liquid is absorbed and barley is tender.

Meanwhile, wash spinach thoroughly. Steam 3 to 5 minutes. Remove from heat and stir into cooked barley mixture. Cook until heated through.

Nutrient Analysis: 1 portion

Calories: 189	Fat: 6.4 g	Cholesterol: 0
Sodium: 170 mg	Dietary Fiber: 4.9 g	
Calcium: 43 mg		

Diabetic Exchange: 1 starch, 2 vegetable, 1 fat

FRUITED BARLEY

A versatile dish suitable for brunch, a meat accompaniment or dessert.

About 4 cups; 8 portions

½ cup barley
2½ cups water
½ cup raisins
½ cup prunes
½ cup quartered apricots, dried or canned
½ cup quartered peaches, dried or canned
½ tablespoon brown sugar
1 tablespoon lemon juice

In a medium saucepan, soak barley in 1½ cups of water overnight. When ready to cook barley, add remaining cup of water. Bring to a boil, cover and simmer 45 minutes.

Add fruit and simmer 5 more minutes or until fruit is soft. Just before serving, add brown sugar and lemon juice.

Nutrient Analysis: 1 portion

Calories: 118	Fat: 0.4 g	Cholesterol: 0
Sodium: 9 mg	Dietary Fiber: 2.3 g	
Calcium: 16 mg		

Diabetic Exchange: ½ starch, 2 fruit

BULGUR SAUTÉ

Bulgur, a cracked wheat product, and popular throughout the Middle East, is as versatile as rice or potatoes.

About 3 cups; 6 portions

2 tablespoons margarine
1 cup bulgur wheat
⅓ cup chopped onion
⅓ cup chopped celery
2 cups water
2½ teaspoons low-sodium, beef-flavored bouillon
2 tablespoons chopped fresh parsley

In a medium saucepan, melt margarine. Stir in bulgur, onion and celery. Cook over low heat, 10 to 15 minutes. Stir in water and beef bouillon; bring to a boil. Reduce heat, cover and simmer for about 15 minutes or until bulgur is tender and water is absorbed. Stir in parsley.

Nutrient Analysis: 1 portion

Calories: 129	Fat: 4 g	Cholesterol: 0
Sodium: 59 mg	Dietary Fiber: 2.6 g	
Calcium: 15 mg		

Diabetic Exchange: 1 starch, 1 fat

RICE ALMOND BAKE

Serve as a side dish or use as a stuffing for poultry (enough to stuff one small turkey).

5 cups; 10 portions

2 tablespoons margarine
2 large onions, finely chopped
1 cup celery, finely chopped
2 cups defatted chicken broth
⅔ cup uncooked brown rice
1 cup raisins
2 teaspoons dried sage, crushed
1 teaspoon poultry seasoning
½ teaspoon pepper
1 cup sliced almonds

In a medium-sized saucepan, heat margarine. Add onion and celery and sauté until slightly soft.

Add chicken broth, rice and raisins and bring to a boil. Add seasonings and almonds. Place in a 1½-quart casserole. Cover and bake.

If used as a poultry stuffing, simmer onion, celery, chicken broth, rice and raisins until most of the liquid is absorbed. Add sage, poultry seasoning, pepper and almonds; mix thoroughly. Stuff lightly into turkey cavity.

Oven: 350°
Time: 60 minutes

Nutrient Analysis: 1 portion

Calories: 181	*Fat: 7.6 g*	*Cholesterol: 0*
Sodium: 41 mg	*Dietary Fiber: 2.2 g*	
Calcium: 53 mg		

Diabetic Exchange: 1 starch, ½ fruit, 1½ fat

RICE PILAF

About 3 cups; 6 portions

1 cup chopped onion
½ bay leaf
2 tablespoons margarine
¾ cup long grain rice
¼ cup white wine or vermouth
1⅓ cup water
1 teaspoon low-sodium, chicken-flavored bouillon granules
2 tablespoons chopped fresh parsley or 1 tablespoon dried parsley flakes
freshly ground pepper

In a medium saucepan, sauté the onions and bay leaf in margarine until the onions are softened.

Add the rice and continue to cook over medium heat, stirring constantly, until rice is golden. Add wine, water, bouillon, parsley and pepper.

Bring to a boil. Reduce heat, cover and simmer for 25 minutes or until liquid is absorbed. OR Place in covered casserole dish and bake in oven at 300° for about 40 minutes.

Nutrient Analysis: 1 portion

Calories: 137	*Fat: 4 g*	*Cholesterol: 0*
Sodium: 43 mg	*Dietary Fiber: 0.4 g*	
Calcium: 14 mg		

Diabetic Exchange: 1 starch, 1 fat

RICE WITH PINE NUTS

About 4 cups; 8 portions

¼ cup pine nuts, roasted
2 tablespoons margarine
¼ cup chopped onion
½ teaspoon finely minced garlic
1 cup brown rice
3 cups water

Place pine nuts in skillet. Place over medium heat (300° in electric frying pan), cook and stir until lightly browned (approximately 7 minutes).

continued on next page

RICE WITH PINE NUTS (con't)

In a saucepan, heat 1 tablespoon margarine; add onion and garlic and sauté until onion is wilted. Stir in the rice. Add water and pine nuts.

Bring to a boil. Reduce heat, cover tightly and simmer about 45 to 50 minutes or until water is absorbed and rice is tender.

Fluff the rice with a fork and stir in the remaining tablespoon of margarine.

Nutrient Analysis: 1 portion

Calories: 156	Fat: 7.5 g	Cholesterol: 0
Sodium: 64 mg	Dietary Fiber: 0.5 g	
Calcium: 22 mg		

Diabetic Exchange: 1 starch, 1½ fat

GREEN RICE

1 egg white
1 cup skim milk
½ cup finely chopped fresh parsley
1 garlic clove, minced
1 small onion, minced
2 cups cooked rice
½ cup shredded Cheddar cheese
⅛ teaspoon curry powder
¼ teaspoon salt

Nutrient Analysis: 1 portion

5 portions

Beat egg white. Add milk, parsley, garlic, onion, rice, cheese, curry powder and salt. Stir well.

Place in a non-stick sprayed 7" ring mold and bake.

Oven: 325°
Time: 30 minutes

Calories: 145	Fat: 3.9 g	Cholesterol: 12 mg
Sodium: 202 mg	Dietary Fiber: 0.5 g	
Calcium: 107 mg		

Diabetic Exchange: 1 lean meat, 1 starch

ITALIAN RICE BAKE

6 portions

⅔ cups rice (or 2 cups leftover
    cooked rice)
1⅓ cups water (if using uncooked
    rice)
1 onion, chopped
1 tablespoon margarine
1 6-ounce can tomato paste and
    1 can water (to make tomato
    sauce)
½ teaspoon garlic powder
1 teaspoon sugar
    dash pepper
½ teaspoon whole thyme
½ teaspoon dried oregano,
    crushed
1 teaspoon parsley flakes
1½ cups low-fat cottage cheese
½ cup grated part-skim cheese
    (mozzarella or farmer cheese)

Cook rice in water.

In a skillet, sauté onion in margarine. Add tomato paste, water, garlic powder, sugar, pepper, thyme, oregano and parsley to onion mixture.

Combine cottage cheese and rice.

Put ⅓ of rice mixture in non-stick sprayed casserole dish. Top with ⅓ of tomato sauce. Continue to alternate layers, ending with tomato sauce. Top with grated cheese. Bake until hot and bubbly.

Oven: 325°
Time: 30 minutes

Nutrient Analysis: 1 portion

Calories: 211   Fat: 6.1 g   Cholesterol: 13 mg

Sodium: 356 mg   Dietary Fiber: 0.8 g

Calcium: 180 mg

---

*Diabetic Exchange: 2 lean meat, 1 starch,
    1 vegetable*

WILD RICE

Wild rice, native to the North American continent, is actually the seed of an aquatic grass. It contains almost twice as much protein as white rice.

About 4 cups; 8 portions

1 cup raw wild rice
3 cups water
2 tablespoons low-sodium, chicken-flavored bouillon granules.

Rinse rice and put in a covered baking dish. Add water and bouillon. Cover and bake. Check after 1 hour, fluffing with a fork and adding more water if necessary. Continue to bake until rice is tender but not dry.

OR in the top of a double boiler, bring rice, water and bouillon granules to a boil. Boil 5 minutes, then cover and place over simmering water in bottom of double boiler. Steam, stirring occasionally with a fork, until rice is tender and the water is absorbed (about 1 hour).

Do several batches at one time. Wild rice freezes well and is so handy to have on hand.

Oven: 350°
Time: 75 to 90 minutes

Nutrient Analysis: 1 portion

| Calories: 71 | Fat: 0.1 g | Cholesterol: 0 |
| Sodium: 1 mg | Dietary Fiber: 0.3 g | |

Diabetic Exchange: 1 starch

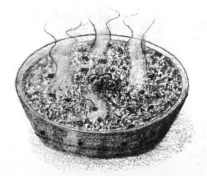

SPINACH LASAGNA

8 lasagna noodles
2 large bunches spinach, washed
   and trimmed
2 tablespoons oil
1 medium onion, chopped
2 garlic cloves, minced
1 8-ounce can no-salt added
   tomato sauce
1 6-ounce can no-salt added
   tomato paste
1 cup water
1 teaspoon honey
¾ teaspoon dried basil, crushed
¾ teaspoon dried oregano,
   crushed
   freshly ground pepper
2 cups low-fat cottage or part-
   skim ricotta cheese
1 cup shredded part-skim
   mozzarella cheese
1 cup freshly grated Parmesan
   cheese

9 x 13" baking pan; 8 portions

Cook lasagna noodles in boiling water until tender. Drain and set aside. Place spinach in steamer over medium heat and cook about 2 minutes. Drain well and set aside.

In a medium skillet, heat oil. Sauté onion until soft. Add garlic and sauté a few minutes more. Stir in tomato sauce, tomato paste, water, honey, basil, oregano and pepper. Reduce heat and simmer 20 minutes, stirring occasionally.

Lay 4 noodles on bottom of non-stick sprayed 9 x 13" baking pan. Layer spinach, cottage or ricotta cheese and mozzarella cheese evenly over noodles. Top with half the sauce mixture. Cover with remaining noodles and sauce. Sprinkle with Parmesan. Cover and bake until lasagna is heated through and the cheeses are melted.

Oven: 350°
Time: 20 to 25 minutes

Nutrient Analysis: 1 portion

Calories: 295	Fat: 10 g	Cholesterol: 24 mg
Sodium: 661	Dietary Fiber: 3.7 g	
Calcium: 430		

Diabetic Exchange: 3 lean meat, 1 starch,
2 vegetable

VEGETABLE LASAGNA

As pretty to look at as it is good to eat!

9 x 13" baking dish; 8 portions

3 cups diced zucchini (about 2 medium)
2 cups coarsely chopped broccoli (about ½ bunch)
1 cup chopped onion
2 garlic cloves, minced
½ teaspoon dried oregano, crushed
5 tablespoons margarine
2 cups firmly packed spinach leaves (about 4 ounces), coarsely chopped
1 15-ounce container part-skim ricotta cheese
2 eggs
8 ounces lasagna noodles (about 9 noodles)
¼ cup all-purpose flour
2½ cups skim milk
¼ cup grated Parmesan cheese
8 ounces part-skim mozzarella cheese, sliced

In a medium skillet over medium heat, sauté zucchini, broccoli, onion, garlic and oregano in 2 tablespoons margarine until crisp-tender (about 5 minutes). Add spinach and toss until wilted. Remove from heat.

In a medium bowl, mix ricotta and eggs; set aside.

Cook lasagna noodles according to package directions. Drain.

In a medium saucepan, melt 3 tablespoons margarine. Stir in flour. Gradually stir in milk and cook, stirring constantly, until sauce boils and thickens. Remove from heat and stir in Parmesan cheese.

In a 9 x 13" baking pan, layer half the lasagna noodles, half the ricotta mixture, half the vegetable mixture, half the mozzarella and half the white sauce. Layer the remaining noodles, ricotta and vegetable mixture. Spoon remaining sauce over vegetables and top with mozzarella. Bake until hot and bubbly. Let lasagna stand 10 minutes before serving.

Oven: 350°
Time: 40 to 45 minutes

Nutrient Analysis: 1 portion

Calories: 355   Fat: 15 g   Cholesterol: 94 mg

Sodium: 358 mg   Dietary Fiber: 1.9 g

Calcium: 427 mg

Diabetic Exchange: 3 medium-fat meat, 1 starch, 2 vegetable

SPINACH LINGUINE WITH SPRING SAUCE

6 portions

3 tablespoons olive oil
1½ cups diced zucchini
1 cup chopped onion
1 cup diced carrots
1 garlic clove, minced
2 cups skinned and chopped fresh tomatoes or 1 16-ounce can sodium-reduced tomatoes
½ teaspoon dried basil, crushed
¼ teaspoon salt
½ teaspoon sugar
1 8-ounce package spinach linguine
¾ cup grated Parmesan cheese

In large, deep skillet, heat oil. Add zucchini, onion, carrots and garlic. Cook, stirring occasionally, until vegetables are crisp-tender. Stir in tomatoes with juice, basil, salt and sugar. Cover and simmer over low heat 10 to 15 minutes, stirring occasionally to break up tomatoes.

Meanwhile, cook linguine in boiling water until al dente (about 8 to 10 minutes). Drain.

Add linguine and Parmesan cheese to tomato mixture. Toss until well coated. Serve.

Nutrient Analysis: 1 portion

Calories: 265   Fat: 11.4 g   Cholesterol: 39 mg

Sodium: 512 mg   Dietary Fiber: 2.1 g

Calcium: 175 mg

Diabetic Exchange: 2 starch, 1 vegetable, 2 fat

PASTA PRIMAVERA

8 portions

1 cup zucchini, sliced
1½ cups broccoli florets
1½ cups snow peas
8 stalks asparagus
1 pound spaghetti or fettucine
16 cherry tomatoes
3 tablespoons olive oil
2 teaspoons minced garlic
   freshly ground pepper
¼ cup chopped fresh parsley
¼ cup pine nuts
10 large mushrooms, sliced
2 tablespoons margarine
1 cup evaporated skim milk
½ cup grated Parmesan cheese
¼ cup chopped fresh basil
⅓ cup sodium-reduced chicken
   broth

Blanch zucchini, broccoli, snow peas and asparagus until crisp-tender. Drain and refresh under cold water.

Cook pasta.

Sauté tomatoes in 1 tablespoon oil with 1 teaspoon garlic, pepper and parsley for a minute or so. Set aside.

In a large pan, heat remaining 2 tablespoons oil and saute pine nuts until golden. Add remaining garlic and all vegetables. Heat thoroughly.

In another large pan, melt margarine. Add evaporated milk, cheese and basil. Stir to blend and melt cheese. Stir in chicken broth. Add pasta and toss to coat. Add a third of the vegetables and toss.

Divide the pasta mixture among 8 plates. Top with remaining vegetables. Serve.

Nutrient Analysis: 1 portion

Calories: 380   Fat: 14.7 g   Cholesterol: 5 mg

Sodium: 170 mg   Dietary Fiber: 3.2 g

Calcium: 243 mg

---

*Diabetic Exchange: 1 medium-fat meat, 2 starch,
                  2 vegetable, 2 fat*

VEGETABLE NOODLE CASSEROLE

Resembles lasagna with a crunchy topping.

7½ x 11" baking pan; 6 portions

2 tablespoons margarine
2 green onions, sliced
2 garlic cloves, minced
3 tablespoons all-purpose flour
2 cups skim milk
¼ cup chopped fresh parsley
¼ teaspoon white pepper
¼ teaspoon whole thyme
   dash nutmeg
1 cup low-fat cottage cheese
1 8-ounce package wide egg
   noodles, cooked
3 cups diced, crisp-tender cooked
   vegetables (carrots, broccoli,
   mushrooms, celery)
1 cup shredded part-skim farmer
   cheese
1 cup whole-grain bread crumbs

In a medium sauce pan, sauté onions and garlic in margarine until soft. Blend in flour and cook over medium heat several minutes, stirring constantly. Slowly add the milk, continuing to stir. Add the parsley, pepper, thyme, nutmeg and cottage cheese. Cook until sauce thickens.

In a 7½ x 11" non-stick sprayed baking dish, layer half the noodles, half the vegetables and half the sauce. Repeat with remaining noodles, vegetables and sauce. Top with cheese and bread crumbs.

Bake until piping hot and bubbly.

Oven: 350°
Time: 20 to 25 minutes

Nutrient Analysis: 1 portion

Calories: 337	Fat: 8.1 g	Cholesterol: 46 mg
Sodium: 316 mg		Dietary Fiber: 3.3 g
Calcium: 190 mg		

Diabetic Exchange: 3 lean meat, 1½ starch,
                    2 vegetable

SPINACH PASTA CASSEROLE

4 portions; 1½ quart casserole

6 ounces spinach noodles
½ cup sliced onion
¼ cup chopped green pepper
2 tablespoons margarine
1 cup low-fat cottage cheese
½ cup plain low-fat yogurt
1 tablespoon sodium-reduced
    Worcestershire sauce
¼ teaspoon pepper
¼ teaspoon garlic powder
1 cup shredded part-skim
    mozzarella cheese

Cook noodles according to package directions. Drain and set aside.

In a small skillet, sauté onion and green pepper in margarine until onion is tender and golden.

In a large bowl, combine noodles, onion, green pepper, cottage cheese, yogurt, Worcestershire sauce, pepper, garlic powder and cheese. Toss to mix. Turn into a non-stick sprayed 1½-quart casserole. Cover and bake 25 minutes. Remove cover and bake an additional 15 minutes.

Oven: 350°
Time: 25 minutes covered, 15 minutes uncovered

Nutrient Analysis: 1 portion

Calories: 252   Fat: 9.3 g   Cholesterol: 23 mg

Sodium: 439 mg   Calcium: 287 mg

Diabetic Exchange: 3 lean meat, 1 starch

SEAFOOD PASTA

6 portions; 2½ quart casserole

1 cup medium WHITE SAUCE,
    (page 164).
½ pound spaghetti
1 green pepper, diced
6 ounces frozen crab or lobster
    meat
8 ounces frozen cooked shrimp
1 cup sliced fresh mushrooms
1 cup frozen peas
¼ cup diced pimiento
½ pound part-skim farmer cheese,
    cubed

Make white sauce.

Cook spaghetti in boiling water for 8 minutes. Drain and rinse with cold water.

Combine spaghetti, green pepper, crab or lobster, shrimp, mushrooms, peas, pimiento and cheese. Turn into a non-stick sprayed casserole and pour white sauce over the mixture. Cover and bake 30 minutes. Remove cover and bake an additional 15 minutes.

Oven: 350°
Time: 30 minutes covered, 15 minutes uncovered

Nutrient Analysis: 1 portion

Calories: 295   Fat: 6.1 g   Cholesterol: 76 mg

Sodium: 218 mg   Dietary Fiber: 2.6 g

Calcium: 126 mg

*Diabetic Exchange: 2 lean meat, 2 starch,
                1 vegetable*

SPAGHETTI SAUCE

About 10 cups

½ cup onion slices
1 cup sliced fresh mushrooms
2 tablespoons olive oil
1 pound lean ground beef
2 garlic cloves, minced
4 cups skinned and chopped fresh
    tomatoes or 2 16-ounce cans
    sodium-reduced tomatoes
2 8-ounce cans sodium-reduced
    tomato sauce
¼ cup chopped fresh parsley
1½ teaspoons dried oregano,
    crushed
    freshly ground pepper
1 bay leaf
1 cup water

In a large sauce pan, sauté onions and mushrooms in oil. Add ground beef and garlic and brown lightly.

Add tomatoes, tomato sauce, parsley, oregano, pepper, bay leaf and water. Bring to a boil. Reduce heat, cover and simmer for 4 hours. Remove bay leaf.

Serve over pasta and sprinkle with grated Parmesan cheese.

Nutrient Analysis: ¾ cup portion

Calories: 105   Fat: 5.7 g   Cholesterol: 23 mg

Sodium: 35 mg   Dietary Fiber: 0.5 mg

Calcium: 11 mg

Diabetic Exchange: 1 medium-fat meat,
*   1 vegetable*

DON'T COOK THE MANICOTTI

This dish can be prepared up to baking point a day ahead and refrigerated. If refrigerated, increase baking time by 15 minutes.

9 x 13" baking pan; 8 portions

1 pound lean bround beef
½ cup chopped onion
¼ teaspoon garlic powder
4 cups sodium-reduced tomato juice
1 6-ounce can no-salt added tomato paste
2 teaspoons dried oregano, crushed
1 teaspoon sugar
⅛ teaspoon pepper
4 cups shredded part-skim mozzarella cheese
1 12-ounce container low-fat cottage cheese
1 10-ounce package frozen chopped spinach, thawed and drained
1 egg
1 egg white
½ cup Parmesan cheese
1 8-ounce package manicotti shells

In a skillet, brown meat with onion and garlic powder. Stir in 2 cups tomato juice, tomato paste, oregano, sugar, and pepper. Simmer 15 minutes.

In a large bowl, combine 2 cups mozzarella cheese, cottage cheese, spinach, egg, egg white and Parmesan cheese. Stuff uncooked manicotti shells with cheese mixture. Arrange in a non-stick sprayed 9 x 13" baking pan. Spread remaining stuffing mixture over the top and spoon meat sauce over shells. Pour remaining 2 cups tomato juice over all. Cover and bake.

Remove from oven and top with remaining 2 cups mozzarella cheese. Cover and let stand 15 minutes.

Oven: 350°
Time: 60 minutes

Nutrient Analysis: 1 portion

Calories: 405   Fat: 13.4 g   Cholesterol: 109 mg

Sodium: 672 mg   Dietary Fiber: 1.4 g

Calcium: 597 mg

Diabetic Exchange: 4 lean meat, 2 starch,
                    1 vegetable

BAKED BEANS #1

Maple syrup adds that "something special" to these beans.

2½-quart casserole; 8 portions

  2 cups dried navy beans
  ½ onion, chopped
  2 cups tomato juice
  ⅔ cup maple syrup
  1 6-ounce can no-salt added
       tomato paste
  1 6-ounce can water
  ¼ teaspoon black pepper

Sort and rinse beans. Cover with water in a 2-quart saucepan and bring to a boil. Turn off heat, cover and let beans sit in their cooking water for 1 hour. Return to heat and simmer the beans, covered, for 1 hour. Drain. Beans should be tender but firm. Do not stir beans.

In a medium saucepan, combine and heat onion, tomato juice, maple syrup, tomato paste, water and pepper. Layer beans and sauce in a non-stick sprayed 2½-quart casserole. Cover and bake.

Oven: 325°
Time: 2½ hours

Nutrient Analysis: 1 portion

Calories: 269	Fat: 0.9 g	Cholesterol: 0
Sodium: 242 mg	Dietary Fiber: 12.7 g	
Calcium: 115 mg		

Diabetic Exchange: 3 starch, 1 vegetable

BAKED BEANS #2

Long, slow cooking for these deep-brown, old-fashioned baked beans.

2½-quart casserole; 8 portions

  2 cups dry navy beans
⅓ pound Canadian bacon
½ cup chili sauce
  1 tablespoon vinegar
  1 medium onion, chopped
½ teaspoon dry mustard
  6 tablespoons molasses
¼ cup brown sugar
  2 cups bean water

Sort and rinse beans. Cover beans with water and soak overnight or, bring beans to a boil, turn off heat, cover and allow beans to sit in their cooking water for one hour. Return beans to heat. Add chunk of Canadian bacon and bring beans to a boil. Simmer, covered, for one hour or until beans are tender.

Remove bacon and dice. Drain beans reserving 2 cups bean water.

Combine chili sauce, vinegar, onion, mustard, molasses, brown sugar and bean water.

Place beans and diced Canadian bacon in a non-stick sprayed 2½-quart casserole and pour sauce over beans. Cover and bake in a slow oven.

Oven: 275°
Time: 4 to 5 hours

Nutrient Analysis: 1 portion

Calories: 264	Fat: 2.2 g	Cholesterol: 0
Sodium: 724 mg	Dietary Fiber: 12.6 g	
Calcium: 132 mg		

Diabetic Exchange: 3 starch, ½ fat

BLACK BEAN CHILI

Spicy-hot, meatless chili. Make a large pot and freeze for another occasion.

8 portions

4 cups dried black beans
2 tablespoons cumin seed
2 tablespoons dried oregano, crushed
2 large yellow onions, finely chopped
1½ cups finely chopped green pepper
2 garlic cloves, minced
¼ cup olive oil
1 teaspoon cayenne pepper
1½ tablespoons paprika
3 cups canned sodium-reduced tomatoes, crushed
½ cup finely chopped jalapeno chilies (fresh or canned)
8 ounces part-skim farmer cheese or Lorraine Swiss, shredded
⅔ cup plain low-fat yogurt
½ cup green onions, finely chopped
8 sprigs fresh cilantro or parsley

Sort and rinse beans well. Place beans in a large pot and cover with water to several inches above top of beans. Cover pot and bring to a boil. Reduce heat and cook until beans are tender (about 1 hour) adding more water if beans begin to show above water level. Drain the beans reserving 1 cup of the bean water. Return beans and water to pot.

Place cumin seed and oregano in a small pan and bake in a 325° oven until the fragrance is toasty (10 - 12 minutes).

Sauté onions, green pepper and garlic in olive oil with cumin, oregano, cayenne pepper and paprika until onions are soft (about 10 minutes). Add onion mixture, tomatoes and chilies to the beans. Stir and heat thoroughly.

To serve: Place one ounce shredded cheese in heated bowl and cover with 1¼ cups hot chili. Top with a spoonful of yogurt and sprinkle with one tablespoon chopped green onion. Garnish with a sprig of cilantro or parsley.

Nutrient Analysis: 1 portion

Calories: 470   Fat: 8.9 g   Cholesterol: 2 mg

Sodium: 60 mg   Dietary Fiber: 26.9 g

Calcium: 229 mg

*Diabetic Exchange: 1 lean meat, 4 starch,
                    2 vegetable, 1 fat*

SPANISH RED BEANS AND RICE

8 portions

1 cup dried kidney beans
3 cups water
1 tablespoon dried basil, crushed
1 tablespoon dried marjoram, crushed
1 tablespoon black pepper
1 tablespoon jalapeno peppers, seeded and chopped
2 cups brown rice
5½ cups water
1 cup chopped green onions
    lemon wedges

Sort and rinse beans. In a saucepan, soak kidney beans in 3 cups water overnight. Add basil, marjoram, pepper and chili peppers. Bring to a boil, reduce heat and simmer, covered until beans are tender (about 3 hours).

In a saucepan, combine rice and 5½ cups water. Bring to a boil. Cover, reduce heat and simmer for 45 minutes. Remove from heat and let stand, covered, for 10 minutes.

To serve, dish rice onto individual serving plates, top with beans and garnish with onions and lemon wedge.

Nutrient Analysis: 1 portion

Calories: 242	Fat: 1.4 g	Cholesterol: 0
Sodium: 11 mg	Dietary Fiber: 6.5 g	
Calcium: 48 mg		

Diabetic Exchange: 3 starch

SAVORY BLACK BEANS

A good crock-pot recipe.

8 portions

1 pound black beans
10 cups water
½ cup olive oil
1 large onion, sliced
1 green pepper, chopped
4 garlic cloves, minced

Sort, rinse and soak beans in water to cover overnight. Next morning, simmer beans, covered, in water for 1 hour.

Add oil, onion, green pepper, garlic, salt, pepper, oregano, bay leaf and sugar. Cook 1 hour.

continued on next page

SAVORY BLACK BEANS (con't)

½ teaspoon salt
½ teaspoon pepper
¼ teaspoon dried oregano,
    crushed
1 bay leaf
2 tablespoons sugar
2 tablespoons vinegar

Add vinegar and cook over low heat or in crock-pot until tender (5 to 6 hours).

Serve with steamed rice.

Nutrient Analysis: 1 portion

Calories: 315	Fat: 13 g	Cholesterol: 0
Sodium: 162 mg	Dietary Fiber: 14.5 g	
Calcium: 86 mg		

Diabetic Exchange: 2 lean meat, 2 starch, 1 fat

GINGERED LENTILS

6 portions

3 cups water
1 cup lentils
½ teaspoon salt
3 tablespoons vegetable oil
1 teaspoon grated fresh ginger
⅓ cup chopped green onions
⅓ cup chopped green pepper
2 tablespoons white wine vinegar

In a medium saucepan, heat water, lentils and salt to boiling. Reduce heat, cover and simmer 20 to 25 minutes or until lentils are tender but not mushy. Drain lentils and set aside.

In medium skillet, heat oil and ginger for 1 minute, stirring often. Add green onion and pepper. Stir-fry for 2 minutes.

Add lentils and vinegar. Heat thoroughly.

Nutrient Analysis: 1 portion

Calories: 153	Fat: 5 g	Cholesterol: 0
Sodium: 206 mg	Dietary Fiber: 5.6 g	
Calcium: 30 mg		

Diabetic Exchange: 1 starch, 1 vegetable, 1 fat

HERBED LENTILS AND RICE CASSEROLE

2½-quart casserole: 6 portions

2⅔ cups sodium-reduced, chicken-
  flavored broth
¾ cup raw lentils
¾ cup chopped onion
½ cup raw brown rice
¼ cup white wine or water
½ teaspoon dried basil, crushed
¼ teaspoon dried oregano,
  crushed
¼ teaspoon whole thyme
¼ teaspoon garlic powder
⅛ teaspoon pepper
½ cup shredded part-skim
  mozzarella cheese

In a 2½-quart casserole, combine broth, lentils, onion, rice, wine, basil, oregano, thyme, garlic powder and ¼ cup of the grated cheese. Cover and bake 2 hours adding more broth if casserole becomes dry.

Top with the remaining cheese and bake another 2 to 3 minutes or until the cheese is melted.

Oven: 350°
Time: 2 hours

Nutrient Analysis: 1 portion

Calories: 212   Fat: 3.6 g   Cholesterol: 11 mg

Sodium: 100 mg   Dietary Fiber: 4.4 g

Calcium: 152 mg

Diabetic Exchange: 1 lean meat, 2 starch

TOFU ITALIANO

No one suspects this dish is made from tofu! Tastes like lasagna.

9 x 13" baking dish; 8 portions

2	1-pound packages tofu, diced
2	eggs
2	egg whites
1½	cups sodium-reduced tomato sauce
1¾	cups sodium-reduced canned tomatoes, crushed
⅓	cup chopped onion
⅓	cup chopped green pepper
4	teaspoons garlic powder
2	tablespoons dried basil, crushed
⅛	teaspoon nutmeg
1½	teaspoons onion powder
¼	cup flour
20	ounces part-skim mozzarella cheese, shredded

In large bowl, mix together the tofu, eggs, egg whites, tomato sauce, tomatoes, onion, green pepper, garlic powder, basil, nutmeg, onion powder and flour.

Spread half the mixture in a non-stick sprayed 9 x 13" baking dish. Top with half the mozzarella. Cover with remaining tofu mixture.

Bake 40 minutes then remove from oven and cover with remaining cheese. Bake another 10 minutes or until the cheese is nicely browned.

Oven: 350°
Time: 50 minutes

Nutrient Analysis: 1 portion

Calories: 331   Fat: 13.5 g   Cholesterol: 91 mg

Sodium: 385 mg   Dietary Fiber: 0.4 g

Calcium: 627 mg

Diabetic Exchange: 4 lean meat, 1 starch, 1 vegetable

We do not succeed in changing things according to our desire, but gradually our desire changes.

Marcel Proust

SUKIYAKI

Sukiyaki (pronounced "ski ya ke") is a great choice for casual entertaining. It is prepared at the table in a large skillet and guests help themselves to their choice of goodies from the simmering pot.

6 portions

1 7-ounce package bean thread noodles
4 medium carrots, shredded
2 medium onions, thinly sliced in rounds
2 bunches green onions, 1" diagonal cuts
6 ribs bok choy or celery, 1" diagonal cuts
4 ounces mushrooms, ¼" slices
1 8-ounce can sliced bamboo shoots
1 8-ounce cake tofu, in ¼-½" cubes (optional)
4 cups spinach leaves
1½ pounds sirloin, sliced 2" x 1" x ¼"
2 cups low-sodium beef broth
¾ cup sodium-reduced soy sauce
¼ cup sugar
3 tablespoons dry sherry
3 tablespoons oil

Soak bean thread in hot water for 20 minutes. Prepare vegetables and meat. In a pitcher, mix broth, soy sauce, sugar and sherry.

Arrange a row of bean thread down the center of a large platter and place meat slices on top. Place carrots in a row on one side, onions on the other.

Arrange the remainder of the vegetables in a similar manner.

Heat an electric skillet to 350°. Add enough oil just to coat skillet and when almost smoking, lay meat slices flat in the pan. Brown quickly on each side, 1 to 2 minutes and remove.

Add about a third of the broth mixture along with a third of the carrots, onions, bok choy, mushrooms and bamboo shoots. Bring to a boil. Add more broth if the pan seems dry.

Place a third of the bean thread, tofu and raw spinach over vegetables and top with a third of the meat.

When everything is boiling, have the guests help themselves. Repeat the above process as the skillet is emptied.

Nutrient Analysis: 1 portion

Calories: 320   Fat: 9 g   Cholesterol: 107 mg

Sodium: 916 mg   Dietary Fiber: 4.7 g

Calcium: 172 mg

Diabetic Exchange: 3 lean meat, 1 starch, 3 vegetable

VEGETABLES

*It is nearly fifty years since I was
assured by a conclave of doctors
that if I did not eat meat I should
die of starvation.*

George Bernard Shaw

VEGETABLES

VEGETABLE SAUCES:

VEGETABLE CASSEROLES

QUICHES

STUFFED TOMATOES

EGG YOLK DILEMMA

VEGETABLES

Vegetables are versatile foods.

Among the most versatile of foods, vegetables make fine side dishes, main dishes and snacks. They are delicious raw or cooked, can be eaten alone or in combination with other foods, and are essential to many classic soups, stews, casseroles, salads, beverages, sandwiches, cakes, pies, and cookies.

Vegetables are good news for anyone changing their eating habits and they meet the following U.S. Dietary Guidelines:

U.S. DIETARY GUIDELINES:	FRESH OR PLAIN, FROZEN VEGETABLES OFFER:
Eat a variety of foods	A wide variety containing many vitamins and minerals
Maintain desirable body weight	Few calories in a serving
Avoid too much fat, saturated fat and cholesterol	Low-fat content (except avocados and coconuts) and are cholesterol-free
Eat foods with adequate starch and fiber	Digestible starch with significant amounts of fiber
Avoid too much sugar	Minimal amounts of sugar
Avoid too much sodium	Low-sodium content

Use fresh vegetables as quickly as possible to retain nutrition and maximize flavor.

Proper storing and preparation preserves the nutrient content of vegetables. Pick or purchase vegetables at peak quality and refrigerate them unwashed and in air-tight containers. It's recommended that vegetables be used as quickly as possible. To maximize their flavor, texture and nutrients, cook vegetables with skins on and only until crisp-tender. Cooking liquid can be saved for soups and stews.

Preparation Methods:

Steam: The preferred method, because vegetables do not come in direct contact with water which leaches nutrients.

Simmer: Add vegetables to a small amount of unsalted water. Simmer until crisp-tender.

Bake: Vegetables such as potatoes, rutabagas, squash and eggplant can be baked in skins with most nutrients retained. Pierce skins before baking to allow steam to escape.

Stir-fry: Add coarsely chopped vegetables to a small amount of hot liquid in a wok or skillet. Cook, stirring often, until vegetables are bright, glossy and crisp-tender.

Microwave: Check your microwave cookbook for specific instructions. Adding salt toughens vegetables. Vegetables with skins should be pierced before cooking. Cover and cook until slightly underdone (they will finish cooking after being removed from the microwave).

> † Recipes marked with this symbol exceed the American Heart Association's and the Minnesota Heart Health Program's fat recommendations for vegetables.

SEASONINGS FOR VEGETABLES*

Discover the world of herbs and spices which add interest and enhance the flavors of cooked and raw vegetables. Try the following suggestions as well as your own personal favorites.

Asparagus: chives, lemon juice, caraway seed

Broccoli: caraway seeds, mustard, lemon, oregano, sesame seed, tarragon

Carrots: cinnamon, curry, dill, ginger, lemon juice, mace, marjoram, mint, nutmeg, rosemary, savory, tarragon, thyme

Cauliflower: nutmeg, oregano, savory, tarragon

Corn: caraway seed, celery seed, curry, dill, mustard, green pepper, chives, parsley, onion

Green beans: basil, dill, lemon juice, nutmeg, marjoram, mustard, onion, oregano, chives, rosemary

Peas: basil, chili powder, dill, chives, marjoram, mint, mustard, nutmeg, orange rind, oregano, parsley, rosemary, sage, chervil, thyme

Potatoes: basil, bay leaves, caraway seed, celery seed, chives, dill, mace, mustard, oregano, parsley, dill, rosemary, savory, sesame seed, thyme

Squash: ginger, mace, onion, basil, chives

Tomatoes: garlic, onion, parsley, basil, sage, Italian seasoning.

*See SEASONINGS section for additional herb and spice blends.

ARTICHOKES

Artichokes are cooked whole and then served hot or cold, whole or cored. The leaves are pulled off one by one, dipped in a sauce and then the lower end is pulled through the teeth to extract the edible portion. When the outer leaves are gone, the light colored cone of immature leaves appears. With a spoon remove and discard the cone and the thistle-like center (the choke). Cut the heart into bite size pieces and dip in sauce.

Select green artichokes with leaves tight together. Discolored ones with loosely spreading leaves will be tough.

To prepare artichokes, cut off stem and one-third of the pointed top. Trim off the prickly points with a scissors. Rinse the trimmed artichokes in water.

Place artichokes upright in steamer basket or in about 2 inches of boiling water. Cook, covered, until tender (about 45 minutes) or pressure cook 15 minutes. Serve one artichoke for each person.

ARTICHOKES SMOTHERED WITH TOMATOES AND HERBS†

Serve one artichoke for each person as a vegetable or an appetizer.

One artichoke.

TOPPING FOR EACH ARTICHOKE
1 green onion, finely minced
1 small onion, thinly sliced
1 teaspoon olive oil
1 medium tomato, peeled, seeded and coarsely chopped
½ teaspoon tiny capers
   freshly ground pepper

GARNISH
chopped fresh basil, oregano or marjoram or 1 teaspoon finely chopped jalapeno pepper (canned or fresh)

Clean and rinse artichokes. Pry apart the center of the artichoke and scoop out the hairy core with a sharp teaspoon (a grapefruit spoon works well. This process takes a little practice but artichokes are very resilient and will take a lot of punishment.) Do be careful not to tear off outer leaves. Stand artichokes upright in a deep, covered casserole, or 9 x 13" pan.

Combine onion, olive oil, tomato, capers and pepper. Spoon some of the mixture into center cavity of artichoke and sprinkle the rest over tops and in between outer leaves.

Add boiling water to cover bottom third of artichokes (or half way up the side of 9 x 13" pan). Cover and simmer gently on stove top or bake in oven until artichokes are tender but not mushy. Garnish and serve hot, warm or at room temperature.

Stove top: Simmer 30 to 45 minutes
Oven: 350°
Time: 60 minutes

Nutrient Analysis: 1 artichoke

Calories: 150   Fat: 5.2 g   Cholesterol: 0
Sodium: 197 mg   Dietary Fiber: 2.1 g
Calcium: 86 mg

Diabetic Exchange: 4 vegetable, 1 fat

ASPARAGUS ORIENTAL†

6 portions

1½	pounds fresh asparagus
1	tablespoon vegetable oil
1½	teaspoons sodium-reduced soy sauce
1	teaspoon sesame oil
1	teaspoon water
1	garlic clove, pressed
¼	teaspoon ground ginger
1	tablespoon sesame seed, toasted

Steam asparagus spears until crisp-tender (8 to 10 minutes).

In small jar with tight fitting lid, combine vegetable oil, soy sauce, sesame oil, water, garlic and ginger. Cover and shake. Pour over asparagus and marinate at room temperature or in refrigerator for at least an hour.

Serve cold or reheat in microwave. Just before serving, sprinkle asparagus with sesame seed.

Nutrient Analysis: 1 portion

Calories: 68	Fat: 4.7 g	Cholesterol: 0
Sodium: 51 mg	Dietary Fiber: 1.2 g	
Calcium: 29 mg		

Diabetic Exchange: 1 vegetable, 1 fat

GREEN BEANS CREOLE†

4 portions

1	cup chopped onion
1	tablespoon olive oil
2	tomatoes, peeled and chopped
1	pound fresh green beans
½	teaspoon dried basil, crushed
½	teaspoon dried tarragon, crushed
¼	teaspoon salt
	freshly ground pepper
3	dashes Tabasco sauce

In medium saucepan, sauté onion lightly in olive oil.

Add tomatoes and cook until juice is released.

Add beans, basil, tarragon, salt, pepper and Tabasco. Cook on low until beans are tender (15 to 20 minutes).

Nutrient Analysis: 1 portion

Calories: 91	Fat: 3.7 g	Cholesterol: 0
Sodium: 164 mg	Dietary Fiber: 2.6 g	
Calcium: 61 mg		

Diabetic Exchange: 2 vegetable, 1 fat

PINEAPPLE BEETS

4 portions

1½ tablespoons cornstarch
⅔ cup unsweetened pineapple
    juice
⅓ cup sugar
2 tablespoons cider vinegar
1 16-ounce can small, whole
    beets, drained
½ cup juice-packed pineapple
    tidbits

Moisten the cornstarch and mix to a smooth paste using 2 tablespoons of the pineapple juice.

In a medium saucepan, mix remaining juice, sugar and vinegar and bring to a boil. Add the cornstarch mixture and cook, stirring to prevent lumping, until clear and thickened.

Add the beets and pineapple and heat thoroughly.

Nutrient Analysis: 1 portion

Calories: 153	*Fat: 0*	*Cholesterol: 0*
Sodium: 202 mg	*Calcium: 25 mg*	

Diabetic Exchange: ½ starch, 2 vegetable, 1 fruit

ITALIAN BROCCOLI WITH TOMATOES†

6 portions

4 cups broccoli florets
1 tablespoon water
½ teaspoon dried oregano,
    crushed
¼ teaspoon pepper
1 tablespoon lemon juice
2 medium ripe tomatoes, cut in
    wedges
½ cup shredded part-skim
    mozzarella cheese

Wash and cut broccoli florets into ½" pieces. Place broccoli and water in a shallow, round microwave-safe dish. Cover with plastic wrap or lid. Microwave on HIGH for 6 to 8 minutes or until tender. Stir several times. Drain.

Stir in oregano, pepper, lemon juice and tomato wedges. Sprinkle cheese on top. Cover. Microwave to melt cheese. Let stand 2 minutes before serving.

Nutrient Analysis: 1 portion

Calories: 80	*Fat: 3.4 g*	*Cholesterol: 11 mg*
Sodium: 111 mg	*Dietary Fiber: 1.6 g*	
Calcium: 191 mg		

Diabetic Exchange: 1 lean meat, 1 vegetable

BRUSSELS SPROUTS†

6 portions

1½ pounds Brussels sprouts
 1 cup low-sodium chicken broth
 1 tablespoon chopped onion
¼ teaspoon fresh ground pepper
 1 tablespoon margarine
 1 tablespoon lemon juice

Remove wilted leaves, cut off stems and cut an X on the bottom of each sprout.

In a medium saucepan, bring chicken broth to a boil. Add sprouts and onions. Return to a boil and cook uncovered 5 minutes. Cover and cook another 5 to 8 minutes or until sprouts are crisp-tender. Drain.

Add pepper, margarine and lemon juice. Toss and serve immediately.

Nutrient Analysis: 1 portion

Calories: 60	*Fat: 2.6 g*	*Cholesterol: 0*
Sodium: 44 mg	*Dietary Fiber: 1.4 g*	
Calcium: 41 mg		

Diabetic Exchange: 1 vegetable, ½ fat

CRISP CABBAGE MEDLEY†

A nice complement to pork.

6 portions

 2 tablespoons margarine
 3 cups shredded cabbage
 1 medium onion, chopped
 1 green pepper, chopped
 1 cup thinly sliced celery
½ cup dry white wine

In a medium saucepan, melt margarine. Add cabbage, onion, green pepper, celery and wine. Cover and steam until vegetables are crisp-tender (about 5 minutes). Serve immediately.

Nutrient Analysis: 1 portion

Calories: 70	*Fat: 4 g*	*Cholesterol: 0*
Sodium: 64 mg	*Dietary Fiber: 0.9 g*	
Calcium: 33 mg		

Diabetic Exchange: 1 vegetable, 1 fat

RED CABBAGE

¼ cup sugar
1 teaspoon whole cloves
½ cup cider vinegar
1 medium onion, chopped
½ cup water
1 medium head red cabbage,
    shredded (about 12 cups)

8 portions

In a small saucepan, combine sugar, vinegar and cloves. Bring to a boil; reduce heat and simmer 6 minutes. Remove cloves.

Add onion and water and simmer 5 more minutes.

Place shredded cabbage in a large saucepan and pour hot vinegar solution over cabbage. Cook until cabbage is hot and crisp-tender (5 to 6 minutes). Serve.

Nutrient Analysis: 1 portion

Calories: 55   Fat: 0.3 g   Cholesterol: 0

Sodium: 12 mg   Dietary Fiber: 1.3 g

Calcium: 59 mg

Diabetic Exchange: 1 vegetable, ½ fruit

CARROTS ÉLÉGANT†

1½ pounds carrots, scrubbed and
    sliced
2 tablespoons margarine
¼ teaspoon cardamom
¼ cup orange juice or 1
    tablespoon frozen concentrate

6 portions

In a waterless cooker or steamer, cook carrots until tender but not soft.

In a small saucepan, melt together margarine, cardamom and orange juice. Pour hot sauce over carrots and serve.

Nutrient Analysis: 1 portion

Calories: 80   Fat: 3.9 g   Cholesterol: 0

Sodium: 57 mg   Dietary Fiber: 2.8 g

Calcium: 32 mg

Diabetic Exchange: 1 vegetable, ½ fruit, ½ fat

GLAZED CARROTS†

6 portions

1½ pounds carrots
1 tablespoon olive oil
¾ teaspoon dried basil or
   oregano, crushed
1 teaspoon brown sugar
½ small garlic clove, minced
½ cup water
   freshly ground pepper

Scrub the carrots and cut on bias into slices ½" thick.

Heat oil in frying pan. Add carrots, cover and cook over medium heat for 10 minutes, stirring occasionally.

Add basil or oregano, sugar, garlic, water and pepper. Cook uncovered, about 20 minutes until carrots are tender and liquid is reduced to a thin syrup.

Nutrient Analysis: 1 portion

Calories: 71	Fat: 2.5 g	Cholesterol: 0
Sodium: 40 mg	Dietary Fiber: 2.8 g	
Calcium: 32 mg		

Diabetic Exchange: 2 vegetable, ½ fat

STEAMED CARROTS WITH APRICOTS

8 portions

1 cup dried apricots
3 cups carrots, cut into ½"
   rounds
3 tablespoons water
1 teaspoon margarine
   pinch of sugar
   chopped fresh parsley or dill
   for garnish

Soak apricots in hot water for 1½ hours. Pat dry and cut in julienne strips.

In a skillet with a tightly fitting lid, combine scraped carrots, water, margarine and sugar. Cover and cook over medium heat for 12 to 15 minutes or until carrots are fork tender. Shake occasionally to prevent sticking.

Stir in apricots and heat through. Serve garnished with parsley or dill.

Nutrient Analysis: 1 portion

Calories: 64	Fat: 0.9 g	Cholesterol: 0
Sodium: 34 mg	Dietary Fiber: 1.4 g	
Calcium: 21 mg		

Diabetic Exchange: 1 vegetable, ½ fruit

CARROTS AND CUCUMBERS†

An unusual but tasty combination.

6 portions

2 large cucumbers (about 1¼ pounds)
2 large carrots (about ½ pound)
1 cup boiling water
2 tablespoons margarine
1 tablespoon finely chopped green onion
¼ teaspoon ground cumin
freshly ground pepper to taste

Peel cucumbers and cut lengthwise in half. Seed and slice thinly crosswise. There should be about 4 cups. Set aside.

Trim and scrub carrots. Cut carrots into 1½" matchsticks. There should be about 2 cups.

Place carrots in a medium saucepan and add enough boiling water to cover. Cook about 4 minutes.

Add cucumber and cook about a minute more. Drain well.

In a skillet, heat margarine and add onion. Cook briefly, stirring.

Add carrots and cucumbers and sprinkle with cumin and pepper. Cook, stirring occasionally, about 2 minutes. Serve.

Nutrient Analysis: 1 portion

Calories: 62	*Fat: 3.9 g*	*Cholesterol: 0*
Sodium: 52 mg	*Dietary Fiber: 1.4 g*	
Calcium: 24 mg		

Diabetic Exchange: 1½ vegetable, ½ fat

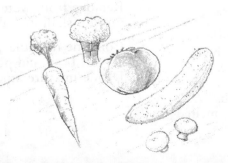

EGGPLANT CASSEROLE†

This hearty vegetable casserole is a satisfying main dish.

1½-quart casserole: 4 entrée portions

1 medium eggplant, peeled and diced
3 tablespoons margarine
3 tablespoons whole-wheat flour
3 large tomatoes, diced
1 small green pepper, chopped
1 small onion, chopped
1 tablespoon brown sugar
½ bay leaf, optional
2 whole cloves
½ cup bread crumbs

In medium saucepan, cook eggplant in boiling water until tender but not mushy. Drain and place in a non-stick sprayed casserole.

In same saucepan, melt margarine and stir in the flour. Add the tomatoes, green pepper, onion, brown sugar, bay leaf and cloves. Cook 15 minutes. Remove bay leaf. Pour over eggplant and top with bread crumbs. Bake.

Oven: 350°
Time: 30 minutes

Nutrient Analysis: 1 portion

Calories: 223	Fat: 9.6 g	Cholesterol: 0
Sodium: 193 mg	Dietary Fiber: 3.8 g	
Calcium: 83 mg		

Diabetic Exchange: 1 starch, 2 vegetable, 2 fat

STUFFED PEPPERS†

4 portions

2 medium green peppers
2 tomatoes, peeled, seeded and chopped
¼ cup chopped onion
¼ cup chopped fresh mushrooms
2 tablespoons chopped chives
⅛ teaspoon dried basil, crushed
¼ teaspoon pepper
½ cup fresh bread crumbs
1 tablespoon margarine, melted

Cut peppers in half lengthwise; remove stems and seeds. Parboil 3 to 5 minutes. Remove from water and place cut side up in a shallow baking dish.

Combine tomatoes, onions, mushrooms, chives, basil and pepper and mix well. Divide mixture among the pepper shells.

continued on next page

STUFFED PEPPERS (con't)

Mix bread crumbs with melted margarine and sprinkle over filled peppers. Pour ½" water into bottom of baking dish and bake uncovered.

Oven: 350°
Time: 25 to 30 minutes

Nutrient Analysis: 1 portion

Calories: 102	Fat: 3.8 g	Cholesterol: 1
Sodium: 124 mg	Dietary Fiber: 0.7 g	
Calcium: 28 mg		

Diabetic Exchange: 3 vegetable, ½ fat

BROCCOLI BAKED POTATOES†

6 medium Idaho potatoes
3 stalks broccoli
¼ cup skim milk
1 cup shredded Cheddar cheese
⅛ teaspoon pepper

1 potato, entrée; half a potato, side dish

Scrub potatoes. Make shallow slits around the middle as if you were cutting the potatoes in half lengthwise. Bake until done, 30 to 60 minutes, depending on size.

Peel broccoli stems. Steam whole stalks just until tender and chop finely.

Carefully slice the potatoes in half and scoop the insides into a bowl with the broccoli. Add the milk, ¾ cup cheese and pepper. Mash together until the mixture is pale green with dark green flecks.

Heap into the potato jackets and sprinkle with remaining cheese. Return to oven to heat through (about 15 minutes).

Oven: 350°
Time: 30 to 60 minutes; 15 minutes to melt cheese or to reheat.

Nutrient Analysis: Half a potato

Calories: 135	Fat: 3.3 g	Cholesterol: 10 mg
Sodium: 77 mg	Dietary Fiber: 0.8 g	
Calcium: 99 mg		

Diabetic Exchange: 1 lean meat, 1 starch

CAULIFLOWER WALNUT CASSEROLE†

Because of the cheese and nuts, this is more appropriately considered a vegetable entrée than a vegetable side dish. Serve with a salad, French bread and a fruit dessert. For variety, substitute broccoli or cabbage for the cauliflower.

10 x 6" baking dish; 4 entrée portions

1 medium head cauliflower, broken into florets
1 cup plain low-fat yogurt
1 cup shredded Cheddar cheese
1 tablespoon flour
2 teaspoons low-sodium, chicken-flavored bouillon granules
1 teaspoon dry mustard
⅓ cup chopped walnuts
1 tablespoon margarine
⅓ cup fine dry bread crumbs
1 teaspoon dried marjoram, crushed

In a medium sauce pan, bring water to a boil. Add cauliflower, reduce heat and simmer 15 minutes. Drain.

Mix yogurt, cheese, flour, bouillon granules and mustard. Place cauliflower in 10 x 6" baking dish and spoon yogurt mixture over cauliflower.

Mix together walnuts, bread crumbs, margarine, marjoram and sprinkle over cauliflower and sauce. Bake until casserole is bubbly.

Oven: 400°
Time: 20 minutes

Nutrient Analysis: 1 portion

Calories: 320	Fat: 19.8 g	Cholesterol: 32 mg
Sodium: 345 mg	Dietary Fiber: 2.3 g	
Calcium: 395 mg		

Diabetic Exchange: 3 medium-fat meat, 2 vegetable, 1 fat

I realized that if what we call human nature can be changed, then absolutely anything is possible.

Shirley MacLaine

BAKED POTATO TOPPINGS

A medium potato has only about 100 calories, but the toppings can be whopping calorie and fat contributors. Try the following low-cal toppings on baked potatoes.

toasted sesame seeds
a spoonful of stewed tomatoes
   and a bit of shredded cheese
melted margarine thinned with
   lemon juice
dried herb mixture: parsley,
   chives, basil, dill
MOCK SOUR CREAM,
   (page 81).
chopped onion with freshly
   ground pepper
chive-spiked yogurt
lemon juice and freshly ground
   pepper
SALSA, *(page 226).*

PARMESAN POTATOES†

6 portions

4 medium potatoes, scrubbed
2 tablespoons flour
2 tablespoons Parmesan cheese
pepper to taste
2 tablespoons margarine

Cut each potato into 4 to 6 chunks.

In a plastic bag, combine flour, Parmesan and pepper. Shake potatoes, a few at a time, in cheese mixture.

Melt the margarine in a 9 x 13" baking pan. Place potatoes in a single layer and bake turning once during baking.

Oven: 350°
Time: 60 minutes

Nutrient Analysis: 1 portion

Calories: 115   Fat: 4.2 g   Cholesterol: 1 mg

Sodium: 66 mg   Dietary Fiber: 0.4 g

Calcium: 50 mg

Diabetic Exchange: 1 starch, 1 fat

SWEET POTATOES AND APPLES

6 portions

1½ pounds sweet potatoes
 3 tart apples, unpeeled, cored and
      sliced
 ¾ cup orange juice
 ¾ teaspoon grated fresh ginger
 ½ teaspoon cinnamon
 ¼ teaspoon allspice
 ¼ teaspoon nutmeg

In a medium saucepan, cook unpeeled potatoes in boiling water for 25 minutes.

In a medium skillet, over high heat, heat apples and orange juice with ginger, cinnamon, allspice and nutmeg. Cover and cook until apples soften, 3 to 5 minutes. Uncover and reduce heat; simmer apples a few minutes longer.

Peel and slice cooked sweet potatoes and add to apple mixture. Mix gently and heat thoroughly.

Nutrient Analysis: 1 portion

Calories: 172	*Fat: 0.6 g*	*Cholesterol: 0*
Sodium: 15 mg	*Dietary Fiber: 5.9 g*	
Calcium: 32 mg		

Diabetic Exchange: 1½ starch, 1 fruit

SPAGHETTI SQUASH SAUTÉ†

6 portions

 1 spaghetti squash (about 2
      pounds)
 2 tablespoons vegetable oil
 ½ cup chopped green onions
 2 garlic cloves, minced
 ½ cup chopped fresh parsley
 1 tablespoon lemon juice
 ¼ cup grated Parmesan cheese

Place whole spaghetti squash in baking dish. Prick all over with fork. Bake in preheated 350° oven 45 to 60 minutes or until tender; cool. Cut squash in half lengthwise; remove seeds. With fork, scoop out flesh into medium bowl, separating into spaghetti-like strands.

In large skillet, heat oil over medium-high heat. Cook green onions and garlic in oil about 3 minutes, stirring constantly. Add squash and stir-fry 3 to 5 minutes more until heated through. Stir in parsley and lemon juice; mix well. Add cheese and toss to coat.

Nutrient Analysis: 1 portion

Calories: 112	*Fat: 6.4 g*	*Cholesterol: 3 mg*
Sodium: 90 mg	*Dietary Fiber: 2.3 g*	
Calcium: 94 mg		

Diabetic Exchange: 1 starch, 1 fat

SQUASH STUFFED WITH RICE†

The RICE ALMOND BAKE, (see page 181) also makes a tasty stuffing for squash.

6 entrée portions

1½ cups cooked rice
½ cup chopped walnuts
¼ cup cracker crumbs
1 medium onion, finely chopped
2 egg whites, slightly beaten
½ teaspoon ground sage
½ teaspoon nutmeg
1 tablespoon chopped fresh
    parsley
2 tablespoons brown sugar
    freshly ground pepper
3 buttercup or acorn squash,
    halved and seeded

Combine rice, walnuts, cracker crumbs, onion, egg whites, sage, nutmeg, parsley, brown sugar and black pepper.

Spoon mixture loosely into squash halves. Bake in foil-covered pan until squash is tender.

Oven: 350°
Time: 60 minutes

Nutrient Analysis: 1 portion

Calories: 252	Fat: 7.2 g	Cholesterol: 0
Sodium: 163 mg	Dietary Fiber: 3.6 g	
Calcium: 107 mg		

Diabetic Exchange: 1 lean meat, 2 starch, 1 fat

BAKED GARLIC TOMATOES†

The baking time is correct!

8 portions

4 ripe tomatoes
¼ cup olive oil
4 garlic cloves, minced
2 tablespoons chopped fresh basil
    or 1 tablespoon chopped
    fresh rosemary
¼ teaspoon salt
    freshly ground pepper

Core tomatoes and slice in half crosswise. Place in baking dish, cut side up.

Mix olive oil, garlic, basil or rosemary, salt and pepper. Pour over tomatoes. Bake.

Oven: 325°
Time: 2 hours

Nutrient Analysis: 1 portion

Calories: 75	Fat: 6.8 g	Cholesterol: 0
Sodium: 79 mg	Dietary Fiber: 0.6 g	
Calcium: 8 mg		

Diabetic Exchange: 1 vegetable, 1 fat

HOW TO PREPARE TOMATOES FOR STUFFING

6 portions: one tomato for each serving

6 tomatoes

Prepare tomatoes by slicing ½" from the stem end of medium to large tomatoes and a thin sliver from the bottom if necessary to make the tomato stand upright. Scoop out the seeds and pulp, leaving a ¼" shell. Drain pulp well and reserve the pulp for stuffing. Invert the tomatoes to drain while preparing stuffing. Stuff shells with filling and arrange in a baking pan. Bake until shells and stuffing are thoroughly heated, usually 20-30 minutes in a moderate oven.

STUFFED TOMATO VARIATIONS

CURRIED RICE STUFFED TOMATOES

6 tomatoes
¼ teaspoon salt
⅛ teaspoon pepper
¼ cup diced green pepper
⅓ cup minced onion
1 teaspoon sodium-reduced
   Worcestershire sauce
1 teaspoon curry powder
2 cups cooked rice
¼ cup fine soft bread crumbs

Prepare tomatoes as in STUFFED TOMATOES, (above).

In a medium sauce pan, mash drained pulp and combine with salt, pepper, green pepper, onion, Worcestershire and curry powder. Cook over low heat for 5 minutes.

Add rice and stir. Stuff tomato shells and sprinkle with bread crumbs. Bake.

MUSHROOM STUFFED TOMATOES†

6 tomatoes
1 tablespoon margarine
½ pound coarsely chopped
    mushrooms
⅓ cup minced onion
1 teaspoon minced garlic
1½ cups HERB SEASONED
    CROUTONS, *(page 124)*.

Prepare tomatoes as in STUFFED
TOMATOES.

In a large, non-stick sprayed skillet, melt
margarine. Sauté mushrooms, onion and
garlic for 5 minutes.

Stir in tomato pulp and croutons. Stuff
tomato shells and bake.

CHEESE STUFFED TOMATOES†

6 tomatoes
1 cup low-fat cottage cheese
1 tablespoon lemon juice
2 tablespoons margarine
½ pound fresh mushrooms, sliced
3 green onions with tops, sliced
    thinly
1 tablespoon minced fresh parsley
1 tablespoon flour
½ cup coarse whole-wheat bread
    crumbs

Prepare tomatoes.

In blender or food processor, whip
cottage cheese with lemon juice.

In a large skillet, melt margarine. Add
mushrooms and onions and sauté 5
minutes.

Blend parsley and flour and stir into
mushroom-onion mixture.

Stir in cottage cheese and cook about 5
minutes. DO NOT BOIL. Stuff tomato
shells and bake.

Oven: 375°
Time: 15 to 20 minutes

Nutrient Analysis: 1 tomato

	Rice	Mushroom	Cheese
Calories:	125	156	136
Fat:	0.6 g	6.3 g	5.3 g
Cholesterol:	0	1 mg	3 mg
Sodium:	142 mg	138 mg	251 mg
Dietary Fiber:	1.4 g	2.1 g	1.8 g
Calcium:	26 mg	50 mg	49 mg
Diabetic Exchange:	1 starch 2 vegetable	1 starch 1 vegetable 1 fat	1 medium- fat meat 2 vegetable

TOMATOES ROCKEFELLER†

6 portions

3 large tomatoes, cut in half
1 tablespoon margarine, melted
3 tablespoons finely chopped
   onion
2 tablespoons finely chopped
   fresh parsley
2 cups chopped fresh spinach
1 tablespoon calorie-reduced
   mayonnaise
   freshly ground pepper
   paprika
3 tablespoons Italian seasoned
   bread crumbs

Place tomatoes cut-side up in a non-stick sprayed baking dish.

In a medium skillet, melt margarine. Sauté onion slowly until tender but not brown.

Add parsley and spinach. Cover pan and "sweat" spinach 1 to 2 minutes until wilted.

Mix in mayonnaise, pepper and paprika.

Top tomato halves with mounds of the spinach mixture. Sprinkle with crumbs and bake.

Oven: 375°
Time: 15 to 20 minutes

Nutrient Analysis: 1 portion

Calories: 56   Fat: 2.9 g   Cholesterol: 1 mg

Sodium: 77 mg   Dietary Fiber: 1.4 g

Calcium: 31 mg

Diabetic Exchange: 1 vegetable, ½ fat

TOMATO SAUCE

Use on any meat, pasta or pizza calling for tomato sauce. This sauce freezes well.

About 2 cups

⅓ cup onion, finely chopped
2 tablespoons olive oil
4 parsley sprigs
1 small bay leaf
¼ teaspoon thyme
2 teaspoons flour
4 cups fresh tomatoes, peeled,
    seeded and chopped
⅛ teaspoon sugar
2 garlic cloves, mashed
⅛ teaspoon fennel
⅛ teaspoon basil
    pinch coriander
½ teaspoon salt

In heavy, 3-quart saucepan over low heat, cook onion in olive oil until tender but not browned.

Make herb bouquet by tying parsley, bay leaf and thyme in cheesecloth or place in a spice infuser.

Stir flour into onion and cook slowly for 3 minutes.

Add herb bouquet, tomatoes, sugar, garlic, fennel, basil, coriander and salt. Cover and cook slowly for 10 minutes.

Uncover and simmer for 30 minutes, stirring often. If sauce becomes too thick, add a small amount of water. When the sauce is thick enough to mound in a spoon, remove the herb bouquet.

Nutrient Analysis: 1 tablespoon

Calories: 17	Fat: 0.9 g	Cholesterol: 0
Sodium: 28 mg	Calcium: 6 mg	

Diabetic Exchange: free
            (2 tablespoons = 1 vegetable)

SALSA

SALSA is an all-purpose topping for everything from rice or tacos to baked potatoes or salad greens. It will keep for two weeks in the refrigerator. It can also be made with fresh tomatoes, although it doesn't keep as long (2 to 3 days). If using fresh tomatoes, add a tablespoon of vinegar or lemon juice.

About 2 cups

4 tablespoons chopped parsley
1 medium onion, finely chopped
2 green chilies or jalapeno
   peppers, finely chopped
1 28-ounce can sodium-reduced
   tomatoes, drained
   freshly ground pepper
¼ teaspoon ground coriander

In a food processor chop parsley, onion, chilies or peppers and tomatoes, one ingredient at a time.

Return all ingredients to food processor, add pepper and coriander and process for a few seconds.

Nutrient Analysis: 1 tablespoon

Calories: 7	Fat: 0.1 g	Cholesterol: 0
Sodium: 41 mg	Calcium: 8 mg	

Diabetic Exchange: free

SWEET-SOUR SAUCE FOR VEGETABLES

A chilled vegetable arranged on plate, garnished with tomato wedges and dressed with SWEET-SOUR SAUCE is a refreshing change from traditional hot vegetables.

About ¼ cup

2 tablespoons vegetable oil
2 tablespoons cider vinegar
   freshly ground pepper
   grated onion (optional)

Combine oil, vinegar, pepper and grated onion, if desired.

Serve hot or cold over asparagus spears, green beans, or broccoli stalks which have been steamed or blanched until crisp-tender.

Nutrient Analysis: 1 tablespoon

Calories: 55	Fat: 6 g	Cholesterol: 0
Sodium: 0		

Diabetic Exchange: 1 fat

STEAMED VEGETABLE MEDLEY†

6 portions

2 cups cauliflower florets
1 cup carrots, sliced diagonally
1 medium red onion, sliced and
    separated into rings
1 cup sliced fresh mushrooms
1½ tablespoons margarine
1 tablespoon lemon juice
¼ teaspoon dried basil, crushed
¼ teaspoon dried marjoram,
    crushed

Place the cauliflower, carrots and onion in steamer basket. Cover and steam over boiling water for 10 minutes.

Add mushrooms and steam 5 minutes more or until vegetables are just tender.

Meanwhile, melt margarine. Add lemon juice, basil and marjoram.

To serve, place vegetables in serving bowl. Pour lemon mixture over vegetables and toss to coat.

Nutrient Analysis: 1 portion

Calories: 51	*Fat: 3 g*	*Cholesterol: 0*
Sodium: 40 mg	*Dietary Fiber: 1 g*	
Calcium: 20 mg		

Diabetic Exchange: 1 vegetable, ½ fat

AUTUMN VEGETABLE STEW†

6 portions

2 tablespoons vegetable oil
1 large onion, sliced
2 carrots or parsnips, peeled and
    sliced
½ pound green beans, trimmed
    and halved
2 cups shredded green cabbage
2 cups low-sodium tomato juice
1 teaspoon ground coriander
1 teaspoon chili powder
1 teaspoon turmeric

In a large skillet or Dutch oven, heat oil. Add onion and sauté 3 minutes, stirring frequently.

Stir in carrots or parsnips, green beans, cabbage, tomato juice, coriander, chili powder and turmeric. Heat to boiling. Reduce heat to medium; cover and simmer 20 to 30 minutes or until vegetables are tender.

Nutrient Analysis: 1 portion

Calories: 91	*Fat: 4.8 g*	*Cholesterol: 0*
Sodium: 23 mg	*Dietary Fiber: 2.1 g*	
Calcium: 46 mg		

Diabetic Exchange: 2 vegetable, 1 fat

TURNIP CASSEROLE†

This colorful vegetable casserole is even better the next day.

4 portions

1 pound fresh white turnips
2 tablespoons margarine, melted
¼ cup chopped onion
1 cup peeled, chopped, fresh tomatoes
½ cup chopped celery
½ teaspoon sugar
¼ teaspoon dried sage, crushed
⅛ teaspoon pepper

Peel and cube the turnips. Place in 1" of boiling water in a medium saucepan and cook, covered, about 5 to 10 minutes or until barely tender.

Mix turnips, margarine, onion, tomatoes, celery, sugar, sage and pepper and turn into a non-stick sprayed 1-quart casserole. Cover and bake until vegetables are hot and tender.

Oven: 350°
Time: 15 to 20 minutes

Nutrient Analysis: 1 portion

Calories: 98	Fat: 5.9 g	Cholesterol: 0
Sodium: 148 mg	Dietary Fiber: 1.1 g	
Calcium: 47 mg		

Diabetic Exchange: 2 vegetable, 1 fat

ZUCCHINI MEDLEY†

As colorful as a Mexican fiesta.

8 portions

3 tablespoons vegetable oil
4 cups thinly sliced zucchini
1 cup coarsely shredded carrot
1 medium onion, chopped
¾ cup chopped celery
½ green pepper, cut in thin strips
½ teaspoon garlic powder
½ teaspoon dried basil, crushed

In a large skillet, heat oil. Add zucchini, carrot, onion, celery, green pepper, garlic powder, basil, pepper, dry mustard and taco sauce. Toss to mix well. Cover and cook over medium heat 4 minutes, stirring occasionally.

continued on next page

ZUCCHINI MEDLEY (con't)

dash of pepper
2 teaspoons dry mustard
⅓ cup taco sauce
2 tomatoes, cut in wedges
   grated Parmesan cheese

Nutrient Analysis: 1 portion

Add tomato wedges and cook, uncovered, 3 to 5 minutes or until tomatoes are heated through. Sprinkle with Parmesan and serve.

Calories: 86	Fat: 6.1 g	Cholesterol: 0
Sodium: 154 mg	Dietary Fiber: 1.7 g	
Calcium: 41 mg		

Diabetic Exchange: 1½ vegetable, 1 fat

RATATOUILLE†

Versatile ratatouille—hot vegetable entrée or side dish, cold salad, condiment, stuffing or seasoning. Make plenty while vegetables are in season and freeze.

1 1-pound eggplant
1 large zucchini
3 tablespoons olive oil
1 green pepper, seeded and cut in squares
1 large onion, cut in squares and separated
2 garlic cloves, minced
2 cups cubed fresh tomatoes
3 tablespoons tomato paste
1 bay leaf
½ teaspoon whole thyme
   pepper to taste
¼ cup Parmesan cheese

8 portions

Trim and peel the eggplant. Cut into ¾" cubes.

Trim the ends of the zucchini but do not peel. Cut into ½" cubes.

In a heavy casserole, heat the oil until it is very hot. Add the eggplant and zucchini and cook, stirring often, for about 2 minutes.

Add the green pepper and onion and cook for 6 minutes, stirring gently.

Add garlic, tomatoes, tomato paste, bay leaf, thyme and pepper. Bring to a boil, stirring.

Pour the mixture into a non-stick sprayed 9 x 13" baking dish. Bake 20 minutes. Sprinkle with Parmesan cheese and bake an additional 10 minutes.

Serve immediately.

Oven: 400°
Time: 20 minutes, 10 minutes

Nutrient Analysis: 1 portion

Calories: 91	Fat: 5.5 g	Cholesterol: 2 mg
Sodium: 58 mg	Dietary Fiber: 1.6 g	
Calcium: 69 mg		

Diabetic Exchange: 2 vegetable, 1 fat

VEGETABLE SHEPHERD'S PIE†

6 portions

4 large potatoes	Cook and drain potatoes. Mash potatoes with yogurt, chives and parsley until fluffy. Set aside.

4 large potatoes
⅓-½ cup plain low-fat yogurt
½ cup chopped fresh or 4
    teaspoons dried chives
½ cup chopped fresh or 4
    teaspoons dried parsley
1½ cups chopped onion
1 large garlic clove, minced
1½ tablespoons margarine
1 stalk celery, chopped
1 eggplant (about 1 pound),
    peeled and cubed
1 green pepper, chopped
¼ teaspoon whole thyme, crushed
1 14-ounce can whole tomatoes,
    drained and cut in pieces
½ teaspoon dried basil, crushed
½ teaspoon dried oregano,
    crushed
½ cup shredded Cheddar cheese
1 tablespoon cider vinegar

Cook and drain potatoes. Mash potatoes with yogurt, chives and parsley until fluffy. Set aside.

In a medium saucepan, sauté onions and garlic in the margarine.

Add celery, eggplant and green pepper. Cook until eggplant is soft, stirring occasionally and covering pan between stirrings.

Add tomato, thyme, basil and oregano. Cook 5 minutes longer. Toss with cheese and vinegar and turn into a non-stick sprayed casserole.

Top with potato mixture to form a crust. Bake.

Oven: 350°
Time: 15 to 20 minutes

Nutrient Analysis: 1 portion

Calories: 230   Fat: 7.6 g   Cholesterol: 12 mg

Sodium: 433 mg   Dietary Fiber: 3.1 g

Calcium: 225 mg

Diabetic Exchange: 1 lean meat, 1 starch,
*   2 vegetable, 1 fat*

STIR-FRY VEGETABLES

The following recipe is basic for most vegetables or combination of vegetables. It works well for asparagus, sliced broccoli, bean sprouts, green beans, carrots or celery.

6 portions

1 pound bok choy
2 tablespoons peanut oil
¼ teaspoon salt
1 thin slice fresh ginger
¼ cup low-sodium chicken broth
¼ teaspoon sugar
   dash pepper

Slice bok choy diagonally (⅛").

Heat wok over high heat. Add oil, salt and ginger. Stir for 30 seconds.

Add bok choy and stir-fry 1 minute.

Add chicken broth, sugar and pepper. Cover for 1½ minutes. Uncover and cook an additional 15 seconds.

Nutrient Analysis: 1 portion

Calories: 64	Fat: 4.8 g	Cholesterol: 0
Sodium: 149 mg	Dietary Fiber: 0.6 g	
Calcium: 83 mg		

Diabetic Exchange: 1 vegetable, 1 fat

SPINACH QUICHE†

9" quiche; 6 portions

CRUST
1½ cups fine bread crumbs
3 tablespoons melted margarine

FILLING
8-10 fresh sliced mushrooms
1 garlic clove, minced
¼ cup chopped onions
1 teaspoon vegetable oil
¾ cup torn fresh spinach or chopped broccoli
½ teaspoon basil
freshly ground pepper
1 cup shredded part-skim farmer cheese
1 cup plain low-fat yogurt
5 egg whites or 3 egg whites and ¼ cup egg substitute *(see page 220)*.

Mix bread crumbs and margarine and pat into pie tin.

Sauté mushrooms, garlic and onion in oil.

Mix together sautéd vegetables, spinach or broccoli, basil and pepper. Place in pie shell.

Sprinkle cheese over vegetables.

Blend together yogurt and egg whites and pour over cheese. Bake.

Oven: 425° for 10 minutes
*   350° for 20 to 25 minutes*

Nutrient Analysis: 1 portion

Calories: 255   Fat: 10 g   Cholesterol: 4 mg

Sodium: 321 mg   Dietary Fiber: 0.6 g

Calcium: 153 mg

Diabetic Exchange: 3 lean meat, ½ starch, 2 vegetable

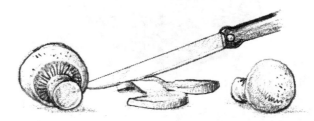

VEGETABLE QUICHE†

Can be sliced very thin and served as an appetizer. Make rice crust at least 8 hours ahead.

RICE CRUST
1 **cup cooked rice, hot**
1 **egg, beaten**
⅔ **cup shredded part-skim farmer cheese**

FILLING
½ **cup chopped onion**
½ **cup sliced fresh mushrooms**
⅔ **cup shredded part-skim farmer cheese**
½ **teaspoon safflower oil**
1 **cup egg substitute** *(see page 234).*
1 **cup evaporated skim milk**
½ **teaspoon salt**
¼ **teaspoon pepper**
1 **large tomato, sliced thin**
1 **tablespoon fresh chopped basil or ½ teaspoon dried basil, crushed**

9" quiche, 6 portions

Mix hot rice, egg and cheese. Press into a deep 9" pie tin. Refrigerate for about 8 hours or overnight.

In a non-stick sprayed pan, sauté onion and mushrooms in oil.

Sprinkle vegetables and cheese evenly on the bottom of the rice crust.

Beat egg substitute, milk, salt and pepper until well blended. Pour into pie shell and top with tomato slices. Sprinkle with basil.

Bake until a knife inserted near the center comes out clean. Let stand for 10 minutes before serving.

Oven: 375°
Time: 50 to 60 minutes

Nutrient Analysis: 1 portion

Calories: 176   Fat: 5.9 g   Cholesterol: 48 mg

Sodium: 333 mg   Dietary Fiber: 0.5 g

Calcium: 196 mg

Diabetic Exchange: 2 lean meat, 1 starch

HOMEMADE EGG SUBSTITUTE

A whole egg contains 213 mg cholesterol while the egg substitute contains only 1 mg. The egg substitute will keep for a week in the refrigerator. It also freezes well.

¾ cup; ¼ cup equals 1 whole egg

6 **egg whites**
¼ **cup non-fat dry milk powder**
1 **tablespoon vegetable oil**
6 **drops yellow food coloring (optional)**

Combine all ingredients in a mixing bowl and blend until smooth. Refrigerate until used.

Nutrient Analysis: ¼ cup or 1 egg equivalent

Calories: 36	Fat: 1.5 g	Cholesterol: 1
Sodium: 50 mg	Calcium: 44 mg	

Diabetic Exchange: ½ skim milk

THE EGG YOLK DILEMMA

While we may be totally convinced that we should reduce cholesterol, we still have difficulty throwing away perfectly good egg yolks. Limiting egg yolks to three a week would be a lot easier if we weren't so concerned about wasting food.

The every-other-yolk rule: In preparing recipes that call for a number of whole eggs, use one whole egg, one white, one whole egg and so on. If the recipe calls for eight eggs, use four whole eggs and four whites. Since egg yolks freeze well, save them in the freezer, and then use them in the recipes on the next page.

continued

THE EGG YOLK DILEMMA, continued

You can feed egg yolks to your dog since dogs are not bothered by cholesterol and clogged arteries. Egg yolk is good for them and promotes a shiny coat.

You can make all-natural cosmetics with egg yolk.

HAIR AND SCALP CONDITIONER #1

1 tablespoon wheat germ oil
1 tablespoon glycerin
1 egg yolk, beaten

In the top of a double boiler, mix the oil, glycerin and egg. Heat until warm over hot water.

Apply to hair and scalp. Leave on for 30 minutes. Rinse well with cool water.

HAIR AND SCALP CONDITIONER #2

½ cup yogurt
1 egg yolk, beaten
1 teaspoon grated lemon rind

Mix together yogurt, egg yolk and lemon rind. Rub into scalp and leave it on for 10 minutes. Rinse and shampoo hair.

HAND LOTION AND SKIN SOFTENER

1 egg yolk
3 tablespoons glycerin
3 tablespoons lemon juice

In a small saucepan, mix together yolk, glycerin and lemon juice. Cook over low heat until thickened. Do not boil. Cool and place in a jar. Use regularly as hand lotion and skin softener.

FISH & SEAFOOD

Buy the best fish you can find, preferably from Byzantium, sprinkle with marjoram. Wrap fish in fig leaves. Bake. Have slaves serve it on silver platters.

Archestratus, 330 B.C.

SEASONINGS

FISH AND SEAFOOD

Fish is a versatile meat.

Fish is as versatile as poultry or red meat. It can be prepared by baking, poaching, steaming, broiling or stir-frying; all without added fat or salt. Fish is appealing because it is so easy and quick to prepare. This section presents a variety of fish and seafood recipes with fresh ideas for preparation and serving. The sea's the limit!

Besides its ease of preparation and good taste, fish makes a healthful addition to our daily diets. Fish is a complete protein containing all the essential amino acids, and is generally low in fat which also makes it less caloric than the same sized portion of meat or poultry. Fish and seafood can help to lower total fat intake while providing other valuable nutrients such as vitamin B_6, niacin, iron, calcium, magnesium, fluorine, iodine and selenium. The belief that seafood should be avoided because of its high cholesterol is not valid. New methods of analyzing the amount of cholesterol show that seafood usually contains less cholesterol than red meat. Table 22 shows the cholesterol content of finfish and shellfish.

Table 22: Cholesterol Content of Fish

Finfish: (3½ ounces, raw)	Approximate	Cholesterol	Content (mg)
Smelt		25	
Pacific Cod		35	
Northern Pike		40	
Ocean Perch		40	
Lake Trout		50	
Sardine		50	
Rainbow Trout		55	
Haddock		65	
Walleye Pike		85	
Shellfish: (3½ ounces, raw)			
Softshell clams		25	
Scallops		35	
Oysters		45	
King Crab		60	
Lobster		70-95	
Northern Pink Shrimp		125-135	
Gulf White Shrimp		140-180	

Source: Joyce Nettleton. *Seafood Nutrition.* Huntington, NY: Osprey Books, 1985.

Preparing Fish

The 10-Minute Rule

Microwave Directions

Timing is all important when it comes to cooking fish and seafood. Perfectly cooked fish is moist and has a delicate flavor; overcooked fish is dry and tasteless. Fish is done when it has just turned opaque and is easily separated with a fork. The *10-Minute Rule* is a good guide to cooking seafood properly. Here's how to use it:

1. Measure the fish at its thickest part. Fold thin parts under to make the fish as evenly thick as possible.
2. Cook thawed or fresh fish 10 minutes per inch of thickness.
3. Cook frozen fish for 20 minutes per inch of thickness.
4. Add 5 minutes to the total cooking time if you are cooking the fish in foil or if fish is cooked in a sauce.

When preparing fish in the microwave, the 10-minute rule does not apply. Place the fish in a shallow dish and cover with plastic wrap leaving one corner turned back for venting. Microwave at high power for 3 minutes per pound of boneless fish. Rotate the dish once during cooking time to ensure even cooking. Remove from microwave when the edges of the fish are firm and opaque and the center is slightly translucent. Let the fish stand, still covered for 3 to 5 minutes. It will continue to cook by retained heat.

Preparing fish in the microwave helps to prevent fishy odors from spreading in the house. To remove the fishy odor from the microwave, combine 2 tablespoons of lemon juice with a cup of water. Place in the microwave and let boil for 1-2 minutes.

The population's growing awareness of the delicious taste and health benefits of fish has resulted in a rapidly growing market for an ever-increasing variety of fish and seafood. Over 500 seafood species of finfish and shellfish are available commercially in the United States. Although many varieties are best known in the region in which they are caught, modern transportation and refrigeration have made a large selection obtainable nationwide.

To educate us about the many varieties now available, the National Marine Fisheries Service developed an "Edibility Profile" which rates fish on such eating characteristics as color of meat, moistness, flavor, flakiness and fat content. The following table groups finfish according to color and flavor which is helpful in substituting one fish for another in your recipe.

Table 23: Edibility Profile of Finfish

Characteristics:	Types of Finfish:		
White Meat,	Cod Cusk	Pacific Halibut Pacific Sanddab	Spotted Cabrilla Summer Flounder
Very Light Delicate Flavor	Dover Sole Haddock Lake Whitefish	Petrale Sole Rex Sole Southern Flounder	Witch Flounder Yellowtail Flounder Yellowtail Snapper
White Meat, Light to Moderate Flavor	American Plaice Arrowtooth Flounder Butterfish Catfish Cobia English Sole Lingcod	Mahi Mahi Pacific Whiting Red Snapper Rock Sole Sauger Snook Spotted Sea Trout	Starry Flounder White King Salmon White Sea Trout Whiting Winter Flounder Wolffish
Light Meat, Very Light Delicate Flavor	Alaska Pollock Brook Trout Giant Sea Bass Grouper	Orange Roughy Pacific Ocean Perch Rainbow Trout Smelt Tautog	Walleye White Crappie White Sea Bass
Light Meat, Light to Moderate Flavor	Atlantic Ocean Perch Atlantic Salmon Black Drum Buffalofish Burbot Carp Chum Salmon Crevalle Jack Croaker Eel Greenland Turbot Swordfish	Jewfish King (Chinook) Salmon Lake Chub Lake Herring Lake Sturgeon Lake Trout Monkfish Mullet Northern Pike Perch Pink Salmon	Pollock Pompano Rockfish Sablefish Sand Shark Sculpin Scup/Porgie Sheepshead Silver (Coho) Salmon Spot Striped Bass Vermillion Snapper
Light Meat, More Pronounced Flavor	Atlantic Mackerel King Mackerel	Spanish Mackerel	
Darker Meat, Light to Moderate Flavor	Black Seabass Bluefish	Ocean Pout Sockeye (Red) Salmon	

Source: U.S. Department of Commerce, National Fisheries Service. *Seafood Selection Guide.* 1982.

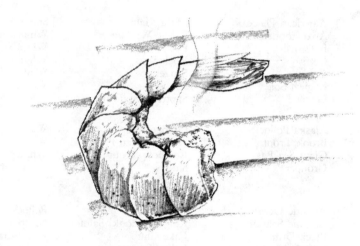

SEASONING FOR FISH

The delicate flavor of fish is enhanced by the addition of the following: bay leaf, curry powder, dry mustard, fennel, green pepper, lemon juice, marjoram, mushrooms, paprika and tarragon.

SPICE BLEND FOR FISH

1 tablespoon dried basil
1 tablespoon dried chervil
1 tablespoon dried marjoram
1 tablespoon parsley flakes
1 tablespoon dried tarragon

Crush dried herbs and blend thoroughly. Sprinkle on fish during cooking or use in shaker on table. Store extra in tightly covered glass container.

See SEASONINGS for additional herb and spice blends.

HERBED LEMON SPREAD

A zesty spread for baked, broiled or poached fish.

About 6 tablespoons

¼ cup margarine
1 tablespoon grated lemon rind
½ teaspoon dried basil, crushed
1 teaspoon parsley flakes
1 teaspoon chopped chives
½ teaspoon chervil

Cream margarine and lemon rind until well mixed. Stir in basil, parsley, chives and chervil. Spread lightly (about 1 teaspoon a serving) on very hot fish.

Nutrient Analysis: 1 teaspoon

Calories: 34   Fat: 3.7 g   Cholesterol: 0

Sodium: 38 mg

Diabetic Exchange: 1½ teaspoons = 1 fat

SOLE ROLLS

An attractive, delicious fish dish suitable for family or guests.

6 portions

3 8-ounce fillets of sole or 6
   4-ounce any white fish fillets

FILLING
1½ tablespoons margarine
1½ tablespoons flour
 ½ cup skim milk
 ½ cup cooked, chopped shrimp
 ½ cup flaked, boned crab
 ¼ cup finely chopped celery
 ¼ cup finely chopped green
    onions
 1 tablespoon chopped fresh
    parsley
 ½ teaspoon salt

SAUCE
1 tablespoon margarine
1 tablespoon flour
1 cup skim milk
1 tablespoon calorie-reduced
   mayonnaise
1 tablespoon fresh lemon juice
1 teaspoon chopped fresh parsley
6 cooked whole shrimp for
   garnish

Defrost fish if frozen. Divide into six equal portions.

In a medium saucepan, melt margarine. Add flour and stir with whisk to combine thoroughly. Add milk and cook, stirring constantly, until sauce is thick. Remove from heat and stir in shrimp, crab, celery, onions, parsley and salt.

Spread filling on fillets. Roll and secure with toothpicks. Place in a non-stick sprayed baking dish. Bake until turns from translucent to opaque flakes. If browning too fast, cover with foil.

Meanwhile, make sauce. Melt margarine and stir in flour. Add milk and cook, stirring constantly, until sauce is thick. Remove from heat and stir in mayonnaise, lemon juice and parsley.

At serving time, carefully transfer sole rolls to serving plate. Remove wooden picks. Pour sauce over sole rolls and garnish with whole shrimp.

Oven: 375°
Time: 20 minutes

Nutrient Analysis: 1 portion with sauce

Calories: 173   Fat: 6.4 g   Cholesterol: 78 mg

Sodium: 400 mg   Calcium: 110 mg

Omega-3: 130

Diabetic Exchange: 2 lean meat, 1 skim milk

FISH FLORENTINE

6 portions

1½ 10-ounce packages frozen
    chopped spinach, thawed and
    drained
 ¾ cups shredded part-skim
    mozzarella cheese
1½ tablespoons grated Parmesan
    cheese
 1 teaspoon lemon juice
 ¾ teaspoon pepper
 ¼ teaspoon salt
 ¼ teaspoon dried oregano,
    crushed
 2 teaspoons dill weed
 3 fresh or frozen sole fillets
    (about 7 ounces each)
 1 tablespoon margarine

In a saucepan, thaw spinach over low heat, then cook on high until liquid is almost evaporated. Drain.

In a medium bowl, stir together spinach, mozzarella, Parmesan, lemon juice, pepper, salt, oregano and dill weed.

Cut fillets into 6 portions. Place in a single layer in a non-stick sprayed baking dish. Spread filling over each portion, dividing equally. Dot each fillet with ½ teaspoon margarine.

Cover pan loosely with aluminum foil. Bake.

With a spatula, carefully transfer fillets to serving plate.

Oven: 425°
Time: 10 minutes

Nutrient Analysis: 1 portion

Calories: 186	*Fat: 7.3 g*	*Cholesterol: 67 mg*
Sodium: 397 mg	*Dietary Fiber: 1.5 g*	
Calcium: 292 mg	*Omega-3: 100 mg*	

Diabetic Exchange: 3 lean meat, 1 vegetable

COD FILLETS WITH CUCUMBER DILL SAUCE

6 portions

1½ pounds cod fillets
2 tablespoons lemon juice

SAUCE
1 medium cucumber, unpared and
   sliced
½ teaspoon dill weed
4 green onions, chopped
1 cup plain low-fat yogurt
   lemon wedges

Place fish in shallow, non-stick sprayed baking pan. Sprinkle with lemon juice. Bake.

Meanwhile, make sauce. In a blender, purée cucumber, dill weed and onions. Combine with yogurt. Pour into a small saucepan and heat over low heat just to simmer. DO NOT BOIL.

When fish is done, drain liquid from pan. Top with sauce and garnish with lemon wedges. Serve.

Oven: 400°
Time: 20 minutes

Nutrient Analysis: 1 portion

Calories: 119	*Fat: 0.3 g*	*Cholesterol: 38 mg*
Sodium: 203 mg	*Dietary Fiber: 0.3 g*	
Calcium: 90 mg	*Omega-3: 250 mg*	

Diabetic Exchange: 2 lean meat

VEGETABLE COD BAKE

4 portions

1 pound frozen cod fillets
3 tablespoons lemon juice
½ teaspoon paprika
½ cup sliced fresh mushrooms
¼ cup chopped tomato
¼ cup chopped green pepper
1 tablespoon chopped fresh parsley
   freshly ground pepper
   lemon wedges

Thaw cod fillets. Cut into 4 portions and place in non-stick sprayed baking dish. Sprinkle with lemon juice and paprika.

Combine mushrooms, tomato, green pepper, parsley and pepper. Spread over fish. Cover and bake. Serve with lemon wedges.

Oven: 350°
Time: 25 minutes

Nutrient Analysis:

Calories: 100	*Fat: 0.3 g*	*Cholesterol: 36 mg*
Sodium: 175 mg	*Dietary Fiber: 0.3 g*	
Calcium: 10 mg	*Omega-3: 250 mg*	

Diabetic Exchange: 2 lean meat

FILLETS AU GRATIN

4 portions

4 4-ounce fish fillets (sole,
    halibut, roughy, flounder)
¼ teaspoon pepper
2 small zucchini, sliced
2 medium tomatoes, sliced
3 tablespoons sliced green onions
½ cup fresh bread crumbs
2 tablespoons melted margarine
2 tablespoons lemon juice
½ cup freshly grated Parmesan
    cheese

Place fillets in non-stick sprayed baking dish. Season with pepper. Cover with zucchini, tomatoes and onions.

In a small bowl, combine bread crumbs, margarine and lemon juice. Toss together and spread over vegetables. Top with cheese and bake.

Oven: 425°
Time: 20 to 30 minutes

Nutrient Analysis: 1 portion

Calories: 260   Fat: 10.5 g   Cholesterol: 65 mg

Sodium: 431 mg   Dietary Fiber: 1 g

Calcium: 183 mg   Omega-3: 100 mg

Diabetic Exchange: 3 lean meat, 1 starch,
*   1 vegetable*

HADDOCK WITH MOCK SOUR CREAM

6 portions

1½ pounds haddock, cod or any
     white fish
     freshly ground pepper
 2 tablespoons margarine
 ¼ teaspoon whole thyme
 1 bay leaf
 1 tablespoon finely chopped
     onion
 1 tablespoon finely chopped fresh
     dill or ½ teaspoon dried dill
     weed
 ¼ teaspoon sugar
 ¼ cup calorie-reduced mayonnaise
 ¼ cup plain low-fat yogurt
     parsley
     lemon wedges

Season haddock with pepper and place in shallow non-stick sprayed baking dish.

Melt margarine in saucepan or in microwave. Add thyme, bay leaf, onion, dill, sugar, mayonnaise and yogurt. Pour over fillets and bake. Remove bay-leaf. Garnish with parsley and lemon wedges. Serve.

Oven: 350°
Time: 25 minutes

Nutrient Analysis: 1 portion

Calories: 155   Fat: 6.4 g   Cholesterol: 71 mg

Sodium: 170 mg   Calcium: 90 mg

Omega-3: 200 mg

Diabetic Exchange: 3 lean meat

SALMON STEAKS

A winner served with steamed new potatoes, fresh peas and a crisp salad.

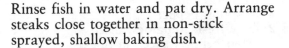

4 portions

4 5-ounce salmon steaks
3 tablespoons lemon juice
1 tablespoon dry vermouth or
    white wine
1 teaspoon onion powder
½ teaspoon dried oregano,
    crushed
    freshly ground pepper
    paprika
    chopped fresh parsley
    lemon wedges

Rinse fish in water and pat dry. Arrange steaks close together in non-stick sprayed, shallow baking dish.

Stir together lemon juice, vermouth, onion powder and oregano. Pour evenly over fish. Sprinkle with pepper and paprika. Bake.

Spoon the juices over fish and garnish with chopped parsley and lemon wedges. Serve.

Oven: 350°
Time: 10 to 15 minutes

Nutrient Analysis: 1 portion

Calories: 191	*Fat: 6.2 g*	*Cholesterol: 85 mg*
Sodium: 106 mg	*Calcium: 113 mg*	
Omega-3: 1400 mg		

Diabetic Exchange: 3½ lean meat

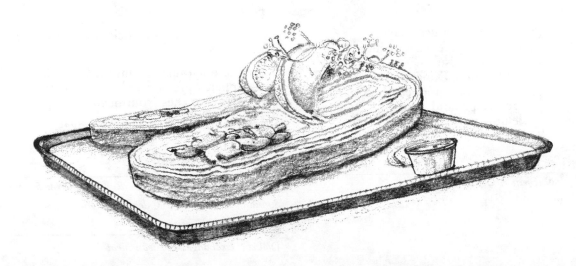

SUMMER LAKE BAKE

6 portions

1½ pounds walleye fillets
 2 teaspoons lemon juice
 ¼ teaspoon salt
 ¼ teaspoon pepper
 2 large fresh tomatoes, sliced
 1 green pepper, sliced in rings
1½ cups fresh or frozen corn
 ¼ cup dry bread crumbs
 2 teaspoons chopped fresh basil or
    ½ teaspoon dried basil,
    crushed
 ½ teaspoon dried oregano, crushed
 1 tablespoon vegetable oil
   chopped fresh parsley
   lemon wedges

Place fillets in non-stick sprayed, shallow baking dish. Sprinkle with lemon juice, salt and pepper. Layer tomato and green pepper slices over fish and cover with corn.

Combine bread crumbs, basil, oregano and oil. Spread bread crumb mixture over corn. Bake.

Serve hot garnished with chopped parsley and lemon wedges.

Oven: 350°
Time: 20 minutes

Nutrient Analysis: 1 portion

Calories: 199	*Fat: 4.4 g*	*Cholesterol: 63 mg*
Sodium: 194 mg	*Dietary Fiber: 1.7 g*	
Calcium: 38 mg	*Omega-3: 400 mg*	

Diabetic Exchange: 2 lean meat, 1 starch

FLOUNDER FILLETS WITH MUSTARD

6 portions

1½ pounds flounder fillets
 2 tablespoons calorie-reduced
    mayonnaise
 1 tablespoon Dijon mustard
 1 tablespoon chopped fresh parsley
   freshly ground pepper
   lemon wedges

Arrange fillets on non-stick sprayed broiler pan.

Combine mayonnaise, mustard, parsley and pepper. Spread evenly over fillets. Broil 3 to 4 inches from heat.

Serve garnished with lemon wedges.

Oven: Broil
Time: 4 to 5 minutes

Nutrient Analysis: 1 portion

Calories: 87	*Fat: 2.1 g*	*Cholesterol: 52 mg*
Sodium: 145 mg	*Calcium: 17 mg*	
Omega-3: 270 mg		

Diabetic Exchange: 1½ lean meat

HADDOCK WITH TOMATO CHEESE SAUCE

6 portions

2 pounds haddock fillets (or sole, pollock, etc.)
1 tablespoon margarine
½ cup no-salt-added tomato paste
½ cup water
1 medium onion, finely chopped
½ cup shredded Cheddar cheese

Place fish in non-stick sprayed broiler pan. Dot with margarine. Broil on middle shelf for about 8 minutes.

Blend tomato paste and water until smooth. Sprinkle fish with chopped onion, and pour tomato sauce over all. Broil another 3 to 4 minutes.

Top with shredded cheese, and broil until bubbly.

Oven: Broil
Time: About 15 minutes

Calories: 189	*Fat: 5.2 g*	*Cholesterol: 10 mg*
Sodium: 175 mg	*Dietary Fiber: 0.3 g*	
Calcium: 112 mg	*Omega-3: 300 mg*	

Diabetic Exchange: 3 lean meat, 1 vegetable

Nutrient Analysis: 1 portion

ROUGHY ALMONDINE

4 portions

4 orange roughy fillets
1 egg white
¼ cup plain low-fat yogurt
¼ cup toasted sliced almonds
1-2 teaspoons grated orange rind

Poach fillets 4 minutes in simmering water. Drain and dry thoroughly on paper toweling.

Whip egg white until stiff. Fold in yogurt, almonds and orange rind. Coat the drained fillets with egg white mixture.

Broil until brown and puffy (about 2 to 3 minutes).

Oven: Broil
Time: 2 to 3 minutes

Calories: 136	*Fat: 5.7 g*	*Cholesterol: 52 mg*
Sodium: 108 mg	*Dietary Fiber: 1.3 g*	
Calcium: 51 mg	*Omega-3: 220 mg*	

Diabetic Exchange: 2 lean meat, ½ skim milk

Nutrient Analysis: 1 portion

BROILED SALMON STEAK

4 portions

4 4-ounce salmon steaks
   freshly ground pepper
2 tablespoons margarine
1 tablespoon finely chopped fresh
      dill or 1 teaspoon dill weed
2 tablespoons lemon juice
   lemon wedges, sprigs of fresh
      dill for garnish

Preheat broiler. Season both sides of salmon with pepper.

In a small saucepan or microwave, melt margarine and mix with dill and lemon juice. Brush steaks with mixture.

Place salmon on broiler pan and broil 3 inches from heat for 3 to 5 minutes. Turn salmon, brush with margarine mixture. Broil an additional 3 to 5 minutes or until fish turns from translucent to opaque.

Garnish steaks with lemon wedges and dill. Serve on heated plates.

Oven: Broil
Time: 3 to 5 minutes a side

Nutrient Analysis: 1 portion

Calories: 220   Fat: 11.7 g   Cholesterol: 68 mg

Sodium: 140 mg   Calcium: 90 mg

Omega-3: 1140 mg

Diabetic Exchange: 4 lean meat

THAI-STYLE FRIED FISH

Some like it hot—a spicy fish dish!

8 portions

2 pounds fish fillets
¼ cup vegetable oil
6 green onions cut into 1" pieces
4 garlic cloves, minced
3 teaspoons finely grated fresh
      ginger

Wash and wipe fish well. Fry in hot oil on both sides until lightly browned and cooked through. Remove fish to serving platter and keep warm.

continued on next page

THAI-STYLE FRIED FISH (con't)

2 tablespoons sodium-reduced soy
    sauce
1 tablespoon sugar
1 tablespoon lemon juice
¼ teaspoon freshly ground pepper
2 tablespoons chopped fresh
    cilantro
1 fresh red chili pepper, seeded
    and sliced

Let oil cool slightly, then fry green onions until soft. Add garlic and ginger and cook on low heat, stirring until soft and golden.

Add soy sauce, sugar, lemon juice and pepper. Simmer the mixture for 1 minute. Pour over fish. Garnish with cilantro and chili. Serve at once with steamed rice.

Nutrient Analysis: 1 portion

Calories: 163	Fat: 7 g	Cholesterol: 0
Sodium: 215 mg	Dietary Fiber: 0.3 g	
Calcium: 32 mg	Omega-3: 300 mg	

Diabetic Exchange: 3 lean meat

CHARCOAL GRILLED TROUT

4 portions

4 whole medium trout with heads
1 lemon, thinly sliced
    olive oil

Wash trout and pat dry. Place several slices of lemon in body cavity. Brush both sides liberally with olive oil.

Grill over high heat 5 to 7 minutes a side. Serve whole trout. The slightly charred skin peels off easily. Run knife along back bone. Open fish. Lift off head and back bone.

Charcoal grill or broil
Time: 5 to 7 minutes a side

Nutrient Analysis: 1 portion

Calories: 61	Fat: 3.3 g	Cholesterol: 16 mg
Sodium: 24 mg	Calcium: 24 mg	
Omega-3: 500 mg		

Diabetic Exchange: 1 lean meat

POACHING FISH

Poach fish in court bouillon, a light stock or water. Lower small or cut pieces of fish into boiling liquid and reduce heat to simmer. Start larger pieces or whole fish in cold liquid. Allow 5 to 8 minutes to the pound, depending on the size of the fish.

MICROWAVE: Place fish and liquid in shallow dish. Cover with plastic wrap. Microwave on high for 2 minutes. Remove wrap, turn fish and return plastic wrap cover. Let sit until cool. Fish turns from translucent to opaque when done. If not done, microwave another minute.

COURT BOUILLON

1 quart water
1 cup dry white wine
1 carrot, chopped
1 rib celery with leaves, chopped
1 small onion, chopped

Bring water, wine, carrot, celery and onion to a boil. (A large shallow pan such as an electric fry pan works well.) Add fish and reduce immediately to simmer.

Time: 5 to 8 minutes to the pound.

SNAPPER WITH TOMATO AND BASIL SAUCE

4 portions

4 red snapper fillets, or any firm white fish without skin
  COURT BOUILLON, *(see preceding page)*

SAUCE
1 cup court bouillon
1 carrot, shredded
1 small onion, shredded
1 teaspoon no-salt-added tomato paste
½ teaspoon dried basil, crushed
2 tablespoons low-fat cottage cheese, puréed

Poach fish in COURT BOUILLON about 5 minutes. Remove to serving platter and keep warm.

Strain bouillon. In small sauce pan combine 1 cup of strained bouillon with carrot and onion. Bring to a boil and reduce to one half. Add tomato paste and basil. Stir in cottage cheese. Serve hot over fillets.

Nutrient Analysis: 1 portion

Calories: 164	Fat: 1.1 g	Cholesterol: 63 mg
Sodium: 66 mg	Dietary Fiber: 0.3 g	
Calcium: 26 mg	Omega-3: 200 mg	

Diabetic Exchange: 3 lean meat

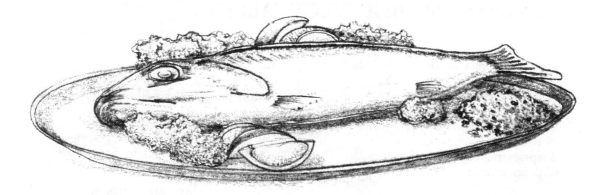

STEAMED HALIBUT STEAKS

4 portions

1 leek or mild onion, thinly sliced
1 tablespoon grated fresh ginger
1 teaspoon dried tarragon, crushed
4 halibut steaks, cut about ½"
    thick
  lemon wedges

In small bowl, combine leek or onion, ginger and tarragon. Spread half the leeks on a large, non-stick sprayed, heat-proof plate. Lay halibut steaks on top. Sprinkle remaining leeks over top.

Fill large saucepan or Dutch oven with 1" water and place steamer rack in water. Place plate with halibut on top of rack and cover pan tightly. Steam over medium-high heat 7 to 10 minutes or until fish turns opaque.

Serve garnished with lemon wedges.

Nutrient Analysis: 1 portion

Calories: 91	Fat: 1 g	Cholesterol: 57 mg
Sodium: 97 mg	Dietary Fiber: 0.5 g	
Calcium: 23 mg	Omega-3: 400 mg	

Diabetic Exchange: 2 lean meat

STEAMED FISH AND VEGETABLES

4 portions

1 pound fillets or steaks, ½" thick
    (salmon, any white fish,
    walleye)
2 tablespoons lemon juice
  freshly ground pepper
  water
2 sprigs parsley
6 peppercorns

Pat the fish dry and cut into serving portions. Sprinkle with 1 tablespoon of the lemon juice and freshly ground pepper.

Combine 1 inch water, remaining tablespoon lemon juice, parsley sprigs, peppercorns and bay leaf in bottom of steamer. Bring to a boil.

Separate onion slices into rings and place half the rings on steamer rack. Place fish

continued on next page

STEAMED FISH AND VEGETABLES (con't)

1 bay leaf
1 small onion, thinly sliced
3 carrots, julienne strips
¼ pound green beans, French cut
2 potatoes, julienne cut

on onions and cover with carrots, beans, potatoes and remaining onion rings.

Reduce heat to simmer. Cover and steam about 10 minutes for each inch of thickness or until fish turns from translucent to opaque. Remove bay leaf. Transfer fish and vegetables to heated serving plate. Serve hot.

Nutrient Analysis: 1 portion

Calories: 253	*Fat: 7.1 g*	*Cholesterol: 62 mg*
Sodium: 84 mg	*Dietary Fiber: 2.4 g*	
Calcium: 66 mg	*Omega-3: 300-1300 mg (depending on fish used)*	

Diabetic Exchange: 3 lean meat, ½ starch, 2 vegetable

SCALLOPS AND MUSHROOMS IN WINE SAUCE

6 portions

1½ pounds scallops
1 cup dry white wine
¼ cup chopped fresh parsley
water
1 cup sliced fresh mushrooms
2 green onions, chopped
5 tablespoons margarine, divided
3 tablespoons flour
½ cup evaporated skim milk
1 cup whole-wheat bread crumbs

Simmer scallops 8 minutes in the wine, parsley and enough water to cover. Remove scallops and reserve 1 cup liquid.

In a saucepan, sauté mushrooms and onions in 1 tablespoon margarine. Remove from pan.

Melt 2 tablespoons margarine, stir in flour. Add reserved water and cook until thickened. Stir in milk, scallops, mushrooms, and onions. Heat until bubbling. Place in a non-stick sprayed casserole.

Melt remaining 2 tablespoons margarine and toss with bread crumbs. Sprinkle over scallop mixture and broil 5 inches from heat until crumbs are toasted (about 3 minutes).

Nutrient Analysis: 1 portion

Calories: 303	*Fat: 10.5 g*	*Cholesterol: 62 mg*
Sodium: 534 mg	*Dietary Fiber: 0.5 g*	
Calcium: 179 mg	*Omega-3: 230 mg*	

Diabetic Exchange: 3 lean meat, 1 starch, 2 vegetable

SALMON LOAF

Don't discard the salmon backbone; mix it in for added calcium.

5 portions

¾ cup bulgur
1½ cups very hot water
½ cup chopped onion
½ cup chopped celery
¼ cup chopped green pepper
   (optional)
1 tablespoon margarine
1 egg or egg substitute
3 tablespoons lemon juice
1 tablespoon Dijon mustard
2 tablespoons fresh chopped
   parsley
¼ teaspoon dried tarragon,
   crushed
1 16-ounce can salmon, drained
   and flaked
½ cup liquid (salmon water plus
   skim milk)

In a large bowl, combine bulgur and hot water. Let stand until water is absorbed and bulgur is tender (about 30 minutes).

Sauté onion, celery and green pepper in margarine. Thoroughly mix sautéd vegetables, lemon juice, mustard, parsley, tarragon and reserved salmon liquid with bulgur.

Add salmon and mix lightly. Place in a non-stick sprayed 9 x 5" loaf pan. Bake.

Serve with lemon wedges and DUGLERE SAUCE *(page 165).*

Oven: 350°
Time: 60 minutes

Nutrient Analysis: 1 portion

Calories: 292	Fat: 10.1 g	Cholesterol: 32 mg
Sodium: 754 mg	Dietary Fiber: 1.1 g	
Calcium: 294 g	Omega-3: 800 mg	

Diabetic Exchange: 3 lean meat, 1 starch,
*   1 vegetable*

SHRIMP CASSEROLE (MICROWAVE)

6 portions

8 ounces fresh mushrooms, sliced
2 tablespoons margarine
1 cup medium WHITE SAUCE,
    (page 164)
2 tablespoons chopped green
    pepper
2 tablespoons chopped onion
2 tablespoons lemon juice
2 cups cooked brown rice
½ teaspoon sodium-reduced
    Worcestershire sauce
½ teaspoon dry mustard
¼ teaspoon pepper
1 pound frozen cooked shrimp,
    thawed
¼ cup bread crumbs
    paprika

Sauté mushrooms in 1 tablespoon margarine.

In a medium saucepan make white sauce. Add mushrooms, green pepper, onion, lemon juice, rice, Worcestershire, mustard, pepper and shrimp to sauce.

Place in non-stick sprayed casserole. Sprinkle with bread crumbs and dot with remaining tablespoon of margarine. Sprinkle with paprika.

Cover and microwave, turning dish around halfway through baking time. Uncover for last 2 minutes.

Microwave: high
Time: 10 minutes

Nutrient Analysis: 1 portion

Calories: 236   Fat: 8.7 g   Cholesterol: 74 mg

Sodium: 200 mg   Fiber: 1.8 g

Calcium: 96 mg   Omega-3: 380 mg

Diabetic Exchange: 2 lean meat, 1 starch, 1 fat

SHRIMP JAMBALAYA

Jambalaya is a Creole dish consisting of rice cooked with fish, poultry or meat and vegetables and spices.

5 portions

4 ounces fresh mushrooms, sliced
1 ounce Canadian bacon, chopped
1½ teaspoons margarine
1 small onion, chopped
½ green pepper, chopped
1 rib celery, chopped
2 garlic cloves, minced
1 large fresh tomato, diced
1 6-ounce can no-salt-added tomato paste
1 can water
¼ teaspoon Tabasco sauce or to taste
½ teaspoon sodium-reduced Worcestershire sauce
1 tablespoon chopped fresh parsley
1 large or 2 small bay leaves
1½-2 cups water
¾ cup brown rice
⅛ teaspoon salt
freshly ground pepper to taste
8 ounces shelled and deveined shrimp
1 tablespoon lemon juice

In 4-quart saucepan, sauté mushrooms and bacon in margarine. Add onion, green pepper, celery and garlic and sauté on low heat for 10 to 12 minutes or until golden brown.

Add tomatoes, tomato paste, water, mushrooms, Tabasco, Worcestershire, parsley, and bay leaves. Bring to a boil, reduce heat, cover and simmer 8 to 10 minutes.

Add 3 cups water and bring to a boil again. Add rice, reduce heat, cover and simmer 15 minutes. When rice begins to swell, add salt, pepper and shrimp. Stir, cover and cook over very low heat until rice is done. Add more water if thinner consistency is desired. Just before serving, remove bay leaf and stir in lemon juice.

Nutrient Analysis: 1 portion

Calories: 214	*Fat: 3 g*	*Cholesterol: 68 mg*
Sodium: 318 mg	*Dietary Fiber: 1.5 g*	
Calcium: 66 mg	*Omega-3: 230 mg*	

Diabetic Exchange: 1 lean meat, 1 starch
3 vegetable

LEMON SHRIMP

6 portions

2 tablespoons cornstarch
1 tablespoon sugar
⅛ teaspoon pepper
1 teaspoon low-sodium, chicken-flavored bouillon granules
1 cup water
½ teaspoon grated lemon rind
3 tablespoons lemon juice
2 tablespoons vegetable oil
1 green pepper, sliced in strips
1½ cups diagonally sliced celery
¼ cup sliced green onion
2 cups sliced mushrooms
6 ounces snow peas
1 pound fresh shrimp, peeled and deveined

Combine cornstarch, sugar, bouillon and pepper. Blend in water, lemon rind and lemon juice. Set aside.

Heat wok on high. Add 1 tablespoon oil. Add green pepper, celery and onion. Stir-fry 3 minutes.

Add mushrooms and pea pods. Stir-fry 3 minutes. Remove vegetables and keep warm.

Heat wok on high and add remaining tablespoon oil. Add shrimp and stir-fry 7 to 8 minutes.

Stir lemon-cornstarch mixture and add to wok. Cook and stir until bubbly. Add vegetables, cover and cook 1 minute.

Serve over steamed rice.

Nutrient Analysis: 1 portion without rice

Calories: 160	*Fat: 5.6 g*	*Cholesterol: 113 mg*
Sodium: 137 mg	*Dietary Fiber: 1.2 g*	
Calcium: 76 mg	*Omega-3: 380 mg*	

Diabetic Exchange: 2 lean meat, 2 vegetable

POULTRY

Health is the thing that makes you feel that now is the best time of the year.

Franklin P. Adams

SEASONINGS

POULTRY

The good taste, versatility and low-fat content of poultry make it an excellent addition to your meal plans. This section contains a wide range of recipes for family fare as well as for elegant entertaining. You won't need a wishbone to bring you exciting ideas for preparing poultry. As shown in the table below, fat and cholesterol content varies between light and dark meat. Skin adds mainly fat.

Table 24: Fat and Cholesterol Content of Poultry

Poultry Item: (3 ounces, cooked)	Total Fat (tsp)	Cholesterol (mg)
Chicken, white meat, with skin	1.5	72
Chicken, white meat, no skin	.7	72
Chicken, dark meat, with skin	2.2	78
Chicken, dark meat, no skin	1.1	78
Kentucky Fried Chicken,		
thigh, Original Recipe	4.1	Not avail.
thigh, Extra Crispy	5.2	Not avail.
Turkey, white meat, no skin	.1	71
Turkey, dark meat, no skin	.7	102
Turkey Roast, commercially prepared	1.1	45
(light and dark meat)		
Turkey Frankfurters	3.4	92
Duck, domesticated, with skin	5.5	72
Duck, domesticated, no skin	2.2	76
Duck, wild, with skin	3.0	69
Duck, wild, no skin	.8	Not avail.
Goose, domesticated, no skin	2.5	82

Source: Marion Franz. *Fast Food Facts.* 1985. and USDA, HNIS. *Composition of Foods: Poultry Products:* Agriculture Handbook 8-5, 1979.

In preparing poultry, always remove the skin prior to cooking and roast, bake or grill to decrease fat intake. Try basting with low-sodium broths, fruit juices and seasoned marinades. Turkey and chicken can be roasted with rice, fruit and vegetables such as carrots, onion and celery in the cavity to add flavor to the bird. Stuffings can be baked separately using fat-free broth to flavor them; roasting poultry with stuffing inside causes it to absorb too much fat. When choosing whole turkeys, avoid self-basters because these are injected with fat, usually saturated fat such as coconut or palm kernel oils.

STIR-FRY

Stir-frying helps you use smaller portions of meat and several vegetables.

Although the wok is the favored cooking utensil for stir-fry, a large, heavy skillet or an electric fry pan will do very well. The wok's advantage is that very little oil is needed as the flaring sides of the wok allow tossing the ingredients and searing them in a single layer.

One of the benefits of stir-fry and wok cookery is that it is fast. The food is cut into bite-sized pieces and tossed in sequence with a small amount of hot liquid (oil, broth, or water). Ingredients are moved rapidly over the hot surface, making the vegetables translucent for a minute or two, and then their natural color intensifies. At that point, they are done and should be removed from the wok. They will finish cooking from their retained heat.

Many stir-fry recipes end with the addition of cornstarch dissolved in broth or water to thicken the pan juices. Remember, the sauce is intended as a glaze, not a gravy.

Cutting the ingredients properly for stir-fry is important. Diagonally cut tubular vegetables such as celery and green beans. Slice meat, poultry, fish, or other vegetables into thin strips 2" long by 1" wide; 1/8" to 1/4" thick. Shred hard vegetables such as carrots or turnips into cuts 1" to 2" long; 1/8" wide, and 1/8" thick. (If you don't have the patience for this, a coarse grater or a food processor works nicely.)

Try any one of the eight stir-fry recipes contained in *Cooking A' La Heart.* You'll find them in the **Vegetable, Grains and Legumes, Fish** and **Meat Sections.** You'll not want to miss the Chicken Almond Stir-Fry recipe in this section located on page 285.

SEASONING

A number of spices and herbs complement poultry and reduce the need for salt. Experiment with the following flavor enhancers: basil, bay leaf, chervil, curry powder, garlic, green pepper, dried ground lemon peel, lemon juice, lemon verbena, marjoram, mushrooms, paprika, parsley, pepper, poultry seasoning, rosemary, sage and thyme.

HERB BLEND FOR POULTRY

1 tablespoon dried basil
1 tablespoon dried chervil
1 tablespoon dried marjoram
1 tablespoon parsley flakes
1 teaspoon whole thyme
1 teaspoon dried lemon verbena

Crush herbs and blend thoroughly. Sprinkle on poultry during cooking or use in a shaker at the table. Store extra in a tightly covered glass container.

See SEASONINGS for additional herb and spice blends.

EASY OVEN-BAKED CHICKEN

Try our easy, tasty SHAKE AND MAKE as an alternative to high sodium commercial preparations.

4 portions

1 broiler chicken, disjointed and
   skinned
⅔ cup SHAKE AND MAKE, *(see
   page 381).*

Shake chicken pieces in SHAKE AND MAKE mixture. Place in non-stick sprayed baking pan and bake until chicken is tender.

Oven: 375°
Time: 45 to 60 minutes

Nutrient Analysis: 1 portion

Calories: 204	Fat: 3.4 g	Cholesterol: 78 mg
Sodium: 194 mg	Calcium: 262 mg	

Diabetic Exchange: 3 lean meat, ½ skim milk

CHICKEN WITH HERBS

8 portions

2 broiler chickens, quartered and
    skinned
    freshly ground pepper
1 garlic clove, crushed
½ cup skim milk
¾ cup fine dry bread crumbs
1 teaspoon dried rosemary,
    crushed
¼ cup fresh chopped parsley
½ teaspoon dry mustard

Sprinkle chicken pieces lightly with
pepper.

In small bowl, combine garlic and milk.

On a piece of waxed paper, combine
bread crumbs, rosemary, parsley and
mustard. Dip chicken in milk, then roll
in bread crumbs to coat well.

Place in a foil-lined baking pan and
bake, uncovered.

Oven: 375°
Time: 60 minutes

Nutrient Analysis: 1 portion

Calories: 182	*Fat: 3.8 g*	*Cholesterol: 75 mg*
Sodium: 185 mg	*Calcium: 48 mg*	

Diabetic Exchange: 3 lean meat

LEMON CHICKEN

4 portions

2½ pound fryer chicken, disjointed
    and skinned
¼ cup vegetable oil
¼ cup lemon juice
2 teaspoons dried oregano or
    tarragon, crushed
⅛ teaspoon garlic powder
2 tablespoons chopped fresh
    parsley
¼ teaspoon paprika

Arrange chicken in single layer in a
baking dish.

Combine oil, lemon juice, oregano or
tarragon and garlic powder and brush on
chicken.

Cover and bake for 35 minutes. Remove
cover and brush again with lemon-oil
mixture. Bake another 20 minutes.
Sprinkle with parsley and paprika. Serve.

Oven: 350°
*Time: 35 minutes covered; 20 minutes
uncovered*

Nutrient Analysis: 1 portion

Calories: 188	*Fat: 9.9 g*	*Cholesterol: 74 mg*
Sodium: 85 mg	*Calcium: 12 mg*	

Diabetic Exchange: 3 lean meat

CURRY-GLAZED CHICKEN

4 portions

2 tablespoons margarine
¼ cup honey
3 tablespoons Dijon mustard
2 teaspoons curry powder
2½ pound fryer chicken, disjointed
and skinned

Place margarine in 9 x 13" baking dish and heat in oven until melted.

Stir in honey, mustard, and curry powder. Add chicken, turning to coat.

Bake, turning after 20 minutes.

Oven: 375°
Time: 40 to 45 minutes

Nutrient Analysis: 1 portion

Calories: 225   Fat: 9.4 g   Cholesterol: 74 mg

Sodium: 477 mg   Calcium: 12 mg

Diabetic Exchange: 3 lean meat, 1 fruit

GINGERED CHICKEN BREASTS

4 portions

GINGER MARINADE
2 teaspoons grated fresh ginger
3 dashes Tabasco sauce or
cayenne pepper
2 large garlic cloves, minced
1 teaspoon dried rosemary,
crushed
¼ cup dry vermouth
½ cup sodium-reduced chicken
stock
1 tablespoon wine vinegar
1 tablespoon vegetable oil
1 tablespoon minced fresh parsley

2 whole chicken breasts, skinned
2 tart green apples, peeled, cored
and finely diced
2 tablespoons minced fresh parsley
1 bay leaf, crushed

In a jar with a tightly-fitting lid, combine ginger, Tabasco or cayenne pepper, garlic, rosemary, vermouth, stock, vinegar, oil and parsley. Shake well to blend.

Rinse the chicken and pat dry. Place in large bowl and pour marinade over chicken, turning to coat. Cover tightly and refrigerate overnight. Remove chicken from refrigerator 1 hour before baking.

Drain chicken, reserving marinade. Pat chicken lightly with paper toweling. Split breast in half. Bone or make a pocket. Stuff half-breasts with apple, parsley and bay leaf. Secure with string or skewer. Bake, basting 4 to 5 times with marinade.

Oven: 350°
Time: 30 to 45 minutes

Nutrient Analysis: 1 portion

Calories: 228   Fat: 4.3 g   Cholesterol: 82 mg

Sodium: 102 mg   Dietary Fiber: 2.7 g

Calcium: 27 mg

Diabetic Exchange: 3 lean meat, 1 fruit

BREADED CHICKEN BREASTS

8 portions

1 cup evaporated skim milk
4 teaspoons lemon juice
1½ tablespoons sodium-reduced
    Worcestershire sauce
1 teaspoon paprika
1½ garlic cloves, minced
¼ teaspoon pepper
4 whole chicken breasts, boned,
    split and skinned
2 cups whole-wheat bread crumbs
¼ cup melted margarine

In a large bowl, combine the milk, lemon juice, Worcestershire, paprika, garlic, pepper. Add the chicken breasts. Cover and refrigerate overnight to marinate.

When ready to bake, roll breasts in crumbs and place on jelly roll pan. Drizzle 2 tablespoons of the margarine over the chicken. Bake 30 minutes, turn and drizzle remaining margarine over chicken. Bake an additional 15 to 20 minutes until brown and tender.

Oven: 350°
Time: 45 to 50 minutes

Nutrient Analysis: 1 portion

Calories: 245	Fat: 9 g	Cholesterol: 85 mg
Sodium: 387 mg	Calcium: 141 mg	

Diabetic Exchange: 3 lean meat, 1 starch

CHICKEN BREASTS IN MUSHROOM SAUCE

4 portions

2 whole chicken breasts, boned, split and skinned
½ cup evaporated skim milk
1 cup fine whole-wheat bread crumbs
2 cups sliced fresh mushrooms
2 tablespoons diced green onions
½ cup dry white wine
1 teaspoon fresh lemon juice
⅛ teaspoon whole thyme
⅛ teaspoon dried marjoram, crushed

Flatten chicken breasts. Dip in milk, then in bread crumbs, coating well. Roll up and arrange, seam down, in non-stick sprayed baking pan. Cover and bake 25 minutes.

While chicken is baking, simmer the mushrooms and onions in wine and lemon juice. Add thyme and marjoram.

Uncover chicken and spoon mushroom mixture over chicken. Bake, uncovered, 10 to 15 minutes longer, or until chicken is tender and brown.

Oven: 350°
Time: 25 minutes, covered; 10 to 15 minutes, uncovered

Nutrient Analysis: 1 portion

Calories: 245   Fat: 3.7 g   Cholesterol: 85 mg

Sodium: 320 mg   Dietary Fiber: 0.4 g

Calcium: 146 mg

Diabetic Exchange: 3 lean meat, 1 starch

ORANGE BAKED CHICKEN BREASTS

5 portions

5 half chicken breasts, skinned
¼ cup onion, chopped
¼ teaspoon dried rosemary, crushed
½ teaspoon paprika
⅛ teaspoon pepper
2 tablespoons flour
2 cups orange juice

Place chicken in shallow pan, meat side up. Sprinkle onion, rosemary, paprika and pepper over chicken.

Blend flour with orange juice and pour over chicken. Bake uncovered until done, basting often with juice.

Oven: 350°
Time: 60 minutes

Nutrient Analysis: 1 portion

Calories: 187   Fat: 2 g   Cholesterol: 66 mg

Sodium: 78 mg   Calcium: 29 mg

Diabetic Exchange: 3 lean meat, ½ fruit

CHICKEN TANDOORI

Grand Prize Winner Heart's Delight Recipe Contest—Senior Division

8 portions

4 whole chicken breasts, split and skinned
½ cup plain low-fat yogurt
1 tablespoon fresh lemon juice
4 garlic cloves, crushed
1 tablespoon grated fresh ginger
1½ teaspoons ground coriander
½ teaspoon ground cumin
1 teaspoon paprika
¼ teaspoon cayenne pepper
¼ teaspoon whole cumin seed or caraway seed
¼ cup margarine, melted
   lettuce leaves
   green chilies
   lime wedges
   radishes

Lightly score breasts.

In a small bowl, combine yogurt, lemon juice, garlic, ginger, coriander, cumin, paprika, cayenne pepper and whole cumin or caraway. Blend thoroughly. Using a pastry brush, brush generously over breasts. Cover and refrigerate 12 hours or overnight.

Place breasts on a non-stick sprayed shallow baking pan and drizzle with melted margarine. Bake at 500° for 8 to 10 minutes then at 350° until breasts are done (20 to 25 minutes).

Arrange breasts on lettuce leaves and garnish with chilies, lime wedges and radishes.

Oven: 500°, 10 minutes
      350°, 20 to 25 minutes

Nutrient Analysis: 1 portion

Calories: 174	*Fat: 7.9 g*	*Cholesterol: 82 mg*
Sodium: 164 mg	*Calcium: 48 mg*	

Diabetic Exchange: 3 lean meat

WAIKIKI CHICKEN

Entertaining a group? Easy, quick and delicious WAIKIKI CHICKEN, steamed rice and a green garden salad is a real crowd pleaser.

25 portions

25 chicken quarters, skinned
2 cups flour
1 tablespoon freshly ground pepper

Wash and dry chicken.

Mix flour and pepper in a paper or plastic bag. Shake chicken in mixture to coat. Arrange in shallow baking pan.

continued on next page

WAIKIKI CHICKEN (con't)

SAUCE
- 2 16-ounce cans mandarin oranges
- 3¼ cups orange syrup plus water
- 1 cup sugar
- 6 tablespoons cornstarch
- ½ cup plus 1 tablespoon cider vinegar
- 3 tablespoons sodium-reduced soy sauce
- ¾ teaspoon ginger
- 3 tablespoons low-sodium, chicken-flavored bouillon granules
- 2 green peppers, seeded and julienne strips

Brown in 425° oven for 10 minutes. Reduce oven to 350°.

In the meantime, drain oranges, reserving syrup. Add water to equal 3¼ cups.

In a medium saucepan, combine sugar and cornstarch. Add mandarin orange syrup, vinegar, soy sauce, ginger and bouillon. Bring to a boil stirring constantly. Boil for 3 minutes.

Pour over chicken. Bake uncovered, 30 minutes.

Arrange mandarin orange slices and green pepper attractively over chicken. Cover. Bake for an additional 20 to 30 minutes or until chicken is tender. Serve with steamed rice.

Oven: 425° for 10 minutes
350° for 50 to 60 minutes

Nutrient Analysis: quarter chicken

Calories: 214	*Fat: 3.3 g*	*Cholesterol: 73 mg*
Sodium: 158 mg	*Calcium: 13 mg*	

Diabetic Exchange: 3 lean meat, 1 fruit

CHICKEN QUICK-FRY

Heart-healthy "Nuggets" are a big favorite with kids.

4 portions

- 2 whole chicken breasts, skinned and boned
- ½ cup crushed bran flakes
- ½ teaspoon dried tarragon, crushed
- ⅓ cup skim milk
- 2 tablespoons safflower oil

Cut chicken in chunks or strips.

Mix bran flakes and tarragon. Dip chicken pieces in milk, then roll in bran flakes.

In a heavy skillet or wok, heat oil. Fry chicken pieces quickly (about 10 to 15 minutes), turning once.

Nutrient Analysis: 1 portion

Calories: 238	*Fat: 9.4 g*	*Cholesterol: 83 mg*
Sodium: 107 mg	*Calcium: 47 mg*	

Diabetic Exchange: 3 lean meat, 1 starch

SESAME CHICKEN

4 portions

8 chicken thighs, skinned
½ cup calorie-reduced Russian
    salad dressing
¼ cup sodium-reduced soy sauce
½ onion, minced
1 tablespoon sesame seeds
2 tablespoons water
½ teaspoon ground ginger
1 garlic clove, minced
⅛ teaspoon red pepper

Place chicken in a large, shallow baking dish.

In a jar with a tightly-fitting lid, combine salad dressing, soy sauce, onion, sesame seeds, water, ginger, garlic and red pepper. Shake well and pour over chicken, turning chicken to coat well. Cover and refrigerate at least 12 hours, turning occasionally.

Remove chicken from marinade and grill over slow coals 45 to 50 minutes or until chicken is tender. Turn and baste with marinade every 15 minutes.

Or broil in oven. Place thighs on non-stick sprayed broiler rack, and broil 8 inches from heat. Turn and baste every 10 minutes until tender.

Nutrient Analysis: 1 portion

Calories: 186   Fat: 9.8 g   Cholesterol: 138 mg
Sodium: 800 mg   Calcium: 30 mg

Diabetic Exchange: 3 lean meat

CHICKEN TERIYAKI

4 portions

MARINADE
2 tablespoons sugar
¼ cup sodium-reduced soy sauce
⅓ cup water
¼ cup sherry
1 teaspoon grated fresh ginger
⅛ teaspoon garlic powder
⅛ teaspoon white pepper

Mix sugar, soy sauce, water, sherry, ginger, garlic powder and pepper for marinade.

continued on next page

CHICKEN TERIYAKI (con't)

2 whole chicken breasts, boned, split and skinned
1 green pepper, seeded and cut in julienne strips
2 cups cooked brown or wild rice

Place chicken in marinade and marinate for 2 hours or longer, turning occasionally.

Over low heat, poach chicken in marinade until tender (about 20 minutes). Add green pepper strips and cook until crisp-tender.

Serve chicken breasts over rice topped with green pepper strips. Serve marinade on the side as a sauce.

Nutrient Analysis: 1 portion

Calories: 270   Fat: 2.2 g   Cholesterol: 67 mg

Sodium: 661 mg   Dietary Fiber: 2.3 g

Calcium: 25 mg

Diabetic Exchange: 3 lean meat, 1 starch, 1 vegetable

CHICKEN CUTLETS

8 portions

Sprinkle cutlets with pepper.

2 pounds chicken cutlets, pounded thin
   freshly ground pepper
1 tablespoon vegetable oil
1 tablespoon margarine
4 tablespoons flour
½ cup skim milk
½ cup unsalted chicken stock, or 1 teaspoon low-sodium, chicken-flavored bouillon granules in ½ cup water
1 cup white wine
½ teaspoon dried tarragon or basil, crushed
1 teaspoon dried parsley flakes
½ cup sliced fresh mushrooms

In a large skillet, melt the oil and margarine and sauté the cutlets over medium heat 5 to 8 minutes on each side. Remove from pan and keep warm.

Blend flour with milk and stock. Add to pan drippings and cook and stir over medium heat until thick. Reduce heat and add wine, tarragon or basil, parsley and mushrooms. Heat thoroughly and serve immediately over cutlets.

Nutrient Analysis: 1 portion

Calories: 215   Fat: 6.1 g   Cholesterol: 66 mg

Sodium: 106 mg   Calcium: 37 mg

Diabetic Exchange: 3 lean meat, ½ starch

ITALIAN CHICKEN

4 portions

2½-3 pound fryer chicken, disjointed and skinned
  1 tablespoon vegetable oil
  ½ cup sliced green onions (with some green tops)
  1 35-ounce can unsalted tomatoes, drained
  ¾ cup buttermilk
  1 tablespoon snipped fresh dill or 1 teaspoon dried dill weed
  ½ teaspoon sugar
⅛-¼ teaspoon freshly ground pepper
    dash Tabasco sauce
  ½ cup plain low-fat yogurt
  ¼ cup grated Parmesan cheese
  ½ cup minced fresh parsley

In a large skillet with a cover, lightly brown the chicken pieces in oil. Add ¼ cup of the green onions and cook the chicken and onions until the onion is wilted. Remove from heat.

In a blender or food processor, combine the tomatoes, buttermilk, dill, sugar, pepper and Tabasco. Blend until the mixture is smooth.

Pour the sauce over the chicken and bring the contents of the skillet to a boil. Reduce the heat, cover pan and simmer the chicken for about 20 minutes or until it is tender.

Stir in the yogurt and the Parmesan and heat thoroughly but do not boil.

To serve, garnish the chicken with the remaining ¼ cup onions and parsley.

Nutrient Analysis: 1 portion

Calories: 240	*Fat: 8.3 g*	*Cholesterol: 76 mg*
Sodium: 262 mg	*Dietary Fiber: 0.4 g*	
Calcium: 243 mg		

Diabetic Exchange: 3 lean meat, 1 skim milk

CHICKEN BROCCOLI CASSEROLE

2-quart casserole; 6 portions

1 10-ounce package cut broccoli
2½ cups diced cooked chicken
3 tablespoons margarine
3 tablespoons flour
¾ cup skim milk
1 tablespoon lemon juice
1 cup sliced fresh mushrooms
½ cup sliced water chestnuts
1 cup plain croutons

Cook broccoli until crisp-tender. In non-stick sprayed baking dish, layer chicken and broccoli.

In saucepan, melt margarine. Stir in flour and add milk. Cook and stir over medium heat until mixture comes to a boil and thickens.

Add lemon juice, mushrooms and water chestnuts. Pour over chicken and broccoli and top with croutons. Bake.

Oven: 350°
Time: 25 minutes

Nutrient Analysis: 1 portion

Calories: 291   Fat: 11.1 g   Cholesterol: 81 mg

Sodium: 256 mg   Dietary Fiber: 1.5 g

Calcium: 86 mg

Diabetic Exchange: 3 lean meat, 1 starch,
*   2 vegetable*

COTTAGE BROCCOLI CASSEROLE

1½-quart casserole; 4 portions

1 10-ounce package broccoli cuts
    or 2 cups fresh broccoli cuts
1 cup diced cooked chicken or
    turkey
1 cup low-fat cottage cheese
½ cup EGG SUBSTITUTE,
    (page 234).
1 teaspoon instant onion flakes
⅛ teaspoon paprika
⅛ teaspoon garlic powder
⅛ teaspoon curry powder
⅛ teaspoon celery seed
¼ teaspoon pepper
¼ teaspoon dried sage or
    marjoram, crushed

TOPPING
2 tablespoons vegetable oil
⅓ cup whole-wheat bread crumbs
2 tablespoons sesame seeds

Cook broccoli until crisp-tender. In a non-stick sprayed casserole, layer broccoli and chicken.

In blender, blend together cottage cheese, egg substitute, onion, paprika, garlic powder, curry powder, celery seed, pepper and sage or marjoram. Pour over broccoli and chicken.

In small bowl, combine oil, bread crumbs and sesame seeds. Sprinkle over top of casserole. Bake.

Oven: 325°
Time: 30 to 40 minutes

Nutrient Analysis: 1 portion

Calories: 286   Fat: 13.9 g   Cholesterol: 50 mg

Sodium: 302 mg   Dietary Fiber: 2.1 g

Calcium: 98 mg

Diabetic Exchange: 2 lean meat, 1 skim milk,
1 vegetable, 1½ fat

ENCHILADA CASSEROLE

9 x 13" baking dish; 8 portions

1 cup heavy WHITE SAUCE,
   (page 164).
2 teaspoons low-sodium chicken-
   flavored bouillon granules
1 cup water
4 ounces fresh mushrooms, sliced
1 medium onion, chopped
2 cups plain low-fat yogurt
1 4-ounce can chopped green
   chilies
8 6" corn tortillas
2-3 cups diced cooked chicken or
   turkey
8 ounces part-skim farmer cheese,
   shredded
6 green onions, chopped

Make white sauce. Add bouillon granules dissolved in water, mushrooms, onion, yogurt and chilies. Heat.

In a non-stick sprayed 9 x 13" baking pan, layer tortillas, chicken, and sauce. Repeat until pan is filled.

Top with grated cheese and onion. Bake until cheese is melted and casserole is heated through.

Oven: 350°
Time: 30 minutes

Nutrient Analysis: 1 portion

Calories: 389   Fat: 16.9 g   Cholesterol: 78 mg

Sodium: 329 mg   Dietary Fiber: 0.5 g

Calcium: 459 mg

Diabetic Exchange: 2 lean meat, 1 skim milk,
*   1 starch, 1 vegetable, 2 fat*

CHICKEN MARENGO

A good buffet dish which can be made a day ahead.

8 portions

1 onion, thinly sliced	In heavy skillet, sauté onion in olive oil until soft and transparent. Remove onion and set aside.
¼ cup olive oil	
2 fryer chickens, skinned and quartered	
½ cup dry white wine	Sauté chicken in same pan, browning well on all sides. Remove chicken and drain. Pour off olive oil from pan and discard.
2 garlic cloves, minced	
½ teaspoon whole thyme	
1 bay leaf	
1 cup low-sodium CHICKEN STOCK, *(page 329)* or 2 teaspoons low-sodium chicken-flavored bouillon granules in 1 cup water	Add wine, garlic, thyme, bay leaf, chicken stock and tomatoes in their juice to the pan. Mix well and return chicken to the sauce. Cover and simmer about 30 minutes or bake 30 minutes at 300°.
2 cups canned Italian tomatoes	
2 tablespoons margarine	In a separate pan, melt margarine and sauté sliced mushrooms. Add whole onions and sauté lightly. Set aside.
1 pound fresh mushrooms, sliced	
16-20 small white onions, whole	
¼ cup sliced black olives	When chicken is tender, remove meat and keep warm. Strain tomato sauce and reduce it by boiling rapidly for 5 minutes.
1 ounce brandy	
chopped fresh parsley	

In heavy skillet, sauté onion in olive oil until soft and transparent. Remove onion and set aside.

Sauté chicken in same pan, browning well on all sides. Remove chicken and drain. Pour off olive oil from pan and discard.

Add wine, garlic, thyme, bay leaf, chicken stock and tomatoes in their juice to the pan. Mix well and return chicken to the sauce. Cover and simmer about 30 minutes or bake 30 minutes at 300°.

In a separate pan, melt margarine and sauté sliced mushrooms. Add whole onions and sauté lightly. Set aside.

When chicken is tender, remove meat and keep warm. Strain tomato sauce and reduce it by boiling rapidly for 5 minutes.

Arrange chicken, onions, mushrooms and olives in a deep earthenware casserole. Sprinkle with brandy. Pour tomato sauce over all and reheat 15 to 20 minutes at 350°.

Sprinkle with chopped parsley and serve with steamed rice or pasta.

Oven: 300°, 30 minutes
Time: 350°, 15 to 20 minutes

Nutrient Analysis: 1 portion

Calories: 260   Fat: 14.2 g   Cholesterol: 78 mg
Sodium: 250 mg   Dietary Fiber: 0.9 g
Calcium: 55 mg

Diabetic Exchange: 3 lean meat, 2 vegetable, 1 fat

WILD RICE CHICKEN CASSEROLE

8 portions

4 tablespoons margarine
5 tablespoons flour
1 cup low-sodium CHICKEN BROTH, *(page 329)* or 2 teaspoons low-sodium, chicken-flavored bouillon granules in 1 cup water
1½ cups evaporated skim milk
¼ teaspoon salt
1 cup raw wild rice
2 cups diced cooked chicken
¾ cup sliced fresh mushrooms
¼ cup diced pimiento
⅓ cup chopped green pepper
½ cup sliced almonds

In a heavy saucepan, melt margarine. Add flour and blend. Add chicken broth, milk and salt. Cook over medium-high heat until thick, stirring constantly.

Mix together raw rice, chicken, mushrooms, pimiento and green pepper. Place in a non-stick sprayed 8 x 10" baking dish. Pour sauce over casserole and top with almonds. Cover and bake until rice is tender, about 1 hour. Add more chicken broth if casserole becomes dry during baking.

Oven: 350°
Time: 1 hour

Nutrient Analysis: 1 portion

Calories: 343   Fat: 12 g   Cholesterol: 7 mg

Sodium: 245 mg   Dietary Fiber: 1 g

Calcium: 172 mg

*Diabetic Exchange: 2 lean meat, 2 starch,
                1 vegetable, 1 fat*

CHICKEN COUSCOUS

Couscous is a North African dish made of crushed grain with various meats, vegetables and spices.

6 portions

¼ cup vegetable oil
3 medium onions, sliced (about 2 cups)
2 garlic cloves, minced
2 teaspoons turmeric
½ teaspoon allspice
⅛-¼ cayenne pepper
2½-3 pound fryer chicken, disjointed and skinned
2 tablespoons low-sodium, chicken-flavored bouillon granules
3 cups warm water
1 cup bulgur
½ cup dried apricots
1 cup dark seedless raisins
3 small zucchini, sliced (about 3 cups)
½ cup slivered almonds, toasted

In Dutch oven or large, deep skillet, heat oil. Add onions and garlic and sauté until limp. Reduce heat. Add turmeric, allspice and pepper. Cook, stirring constantly, for 5 minutes.

Add chicken pieces and cook 5 minutes on each side. Dissolve bouillon granules in water and add to chicken. Heat to boiling, reduce heat to low. Cover and cook 10 minutes. Stir in bulgur, cover and cook 10 minutes.

Add apricots, raisins and zucchini. Cover and cook 10 minutes more or until chicken and bulgur are tender and liquid is absorbed. If some liquid remains, cook uncovered until evaporated but not dry. Stir in almonds and heat through. Serve.

Nutrient Analysis: 1 portion

Calories: 430   Fat: 16.2 g   Cholesterol: 75 mg

Sodium: 196 mg   Dietary Fiber: 7 g

Calcium: 89 mg

Diabetic Exchange: 3 lean meat, 1 starch, 1 vegetable, 2 fruit, 1 fat

CHICKEN ALMOND STIR-FRY

4 portions

2 whole chicken breasts, split, boned and skinned
1 tablespoon cornstarch
2 tablespoons sherry
½ cup diced green pepper
½ cup diced sweet red pepper
4 green onions sliced including some of the tops
¼ cup sliced water chestnuts
2 tablespoons vegetable oil
1 8-ounce can pineapple chunks in natural juices, drain and reserve juice
3 tablespoons slivered almonds

SAUCE
1½ tablespoons sherry
1 teaspoon sesame oil
1 teaspoon sugar
¼ cup low-sodium chicken broth
1½ tablespoons sodium-reduced soy sauce
1 teaspoon cornstarch
1 teaspoon reserved pineapple juice

Cube chicken. Stir with 1 tablespoon cornstarch and 2 tablespoons sherry. Set aside while preparing vegetables and combining sauce ingredients.

Heat oil in wok or heavy skillet. Add chicken and stir-fry until lightly browned.

Add green and red peppers, onions and water chestnuts. Stir-fry 2 minutes.

Add pineapple, slivered almonds and sauce mixture. Cook 2 more minutes or until sauce is thickened and smooth. If sauce is too thick, thin with reserved pineapple juice.

Serve over steamed rice.

Nutrient Analysis: 1 portion without rice

Calories: 326   Fat: 13 g   Cholesterol: 67 mg

Sodium: 299 mg   Dietary Fiber: 1.5 g

Calcium: 50m g

Diabetic Exchange: 3 lean meat, 2 vegetable, 1 fruit, 1 fat

TURKEY THIGHS FLORENTINE

6 portions

½ cup chopped onion
1 garlic clove, minced
½ teaspoon mixed Italian
   seasoning
1 tablespoon margarine
2 egg whites
½ cup chopped cooked spinach
½ cup fine soft bread crumbs
½ cup grated Parmesan cheese
   pepper to taste
2 turkey thighs (about 2 pounds)

In small skillet, sauté onion, garlic and Italian seasoning in margarine until soft, but not browned.

Combine egg whites, spinach, bread crumbs, cheese and pepper. Add onion mixture and mix well. Set aside.

Skin and debone turkey thighs. Pound as flat as possible. Divide filling mixture between two flattened thighs. Bring edges together to enclose filling and skewer or tie with string.

Place in shallow, non-stick sprayed baking pan and cover with foil. Bake. Open foil after 1 hour and bake an additional 30 minutes to brown.

Serve either hot or cold cut into slices.

Oven: 325°
Time: 60 minutes covered; 30 minutes uncovered

Nutrient Analysis: 1 portion

Calories: 275   Fat: 12 g   Cholesterol: 86 mg

Sodium: 290 mg   Dietary Fiber: 1 g

Calcium: 154 mg

---

*Diabetic Exchange: 3 lean meat, ½ skim milk,
              1 vegetable, 1 fat*

TURKEY SCALLOPS À LA ORANGE

Easy but elegant!

5 portions

2 tablespoons margarine
½ teaspoon minced garlic
1¼ pounds boneless turkey breast, skinned and cut into ¼" slices
½ cup orange juice
2 tablespoons lemon juice
white pepper to taste
2 teaspoons cornstarch

In large skillet over medium heat, cook margarine with garlic until foamy.

Add turkey slices and cook until opaque and no longer pink (about 2 minutes a side). Remove to platter and keep warm.

In small bowl, stir orange juice, lemon juice, pepper and cornstarch until smooth. Stir orange mixture into skillet, scraping up browned bits on bottom. Boil 1 minute, stirring constantly, until thickened. Pour over turkey and serve.

Nutrient Analysis: 1 portion

Calories: 184	*Fat: 6.4 g*	*Cholesterol: 66 mg*
Sodium: 123 mg	*Calcium: 16 mg*	

Diabetic Exchange: 3 lean meat, ½ fruit

TURKEY AND FRUIT KABOBS

Four 10" skewers

¾ pound cooked boneless turkey breast, cut in 12, 1" cubes
1 orange, cut in wedges
1 firm pear, cut in wedges
1 green pepper, cut in squares
4 small spiced crab apples
½ cup jellied cranberry sauce
½ cup apricot preserves
¼ cup lemon juice
2 tablespoons margarine
¼ teaspoon ground cinnamon
    dash ground cloves

Thread pieces of turkey, orange, pear, green pepper and a crab apple onto four 10" skewers.

In a saucepan, combine cranberry sauce, apricot preserves, lemon juice, margarine, cinnamon and cloves. Bring to a boil, stirring occasionally. Brush sauce over turkey and fruit.

Grill about 4" above medium-hot coals, turning and basting until meat and fruit are hot and well glazed (about 10 minutes).

Nutrient Analysis: 1 skewer

Calories: 275	*Fat: 7 g*	*Cholesterol: 45 mg*
Sodium: 145 mg	*Dietary Fiber: 4.2 g*	
Calcium: 58 mg		

Diabetic Exchange: 2 lean meat, 2 fruit, 1 fat

ORIENTAL CASSEROLE

Reheats well.

1½-quart casserole; 4 portions

1 cup heavy WHITE SAUCE, *(page 164)*.

2 teaspoons low-sodium, chicken-flavored bouillon granules

½ pound fresh broccoli

1 pound ground turkey

1 tablespoon vegetable oil

1 tablespoon sodium-reduced soy sauce

1 small onion, chopped

1 garlic clove, minced

1 cup sliced celery

½-1 cup bean sprouts

½ cup chow mein noodles

Make heavy WHITE SAUCE and stir in bouillon granules.

Separate the broccoli florets and cut the stems into ⅛" slices.

In a skillet, brown turkey quickly in hot oil, stirring constantly and sprinkling with soy sauce.

Add broccoli, onion, garlic, celery and bean sprouts to the turkey and stir-fry for 2 to 3 minutes.

Mix white sauce, turkey and vegetables and chow mein noodles and pour into non-stick sprayed casserole dish. Bake.

Oven: 350°
Time: 30 minutes

Nutrient Analysis: 1 portion

Calories: 315   Fat: 13 g   Cholesterol: 92 mg

Sodium: 466 mg   Dietary Fiber: 1.4 g

Calcium: 138 mg

Diabetic Exchange: 3 lean meat, 2 vegetable, 2 fat

SWEET AND SOUR TURKEY

6 portions

3 cups cubed turkey breast
   tenderloin
½ cup chopped green onion
1 garlic clove, minced
2 tablespoons vegetable oil
2 14-ounce cans unsweetened
   pineapple chunks
2 tablespoons red wine vinegar
2 tablespoons sodium-reduced soy
   sauce
1 cup water
1 tablespoon brown sugar
2 teaspoons low-sodium, chicken-
   flavored bouillon granules
3 tablespoons cold water
2 tablespoons cornstarch
1 green pepper, cut in strips
⅓ cup toasted slivered almonds
   (optional)

In large skillet, sauté turkey cubes, onion and garlic in hot oil until meat is lightly browned and onion is tender.

Drain pineapple reserving juice. Add reserved juice, vinegar, soy sauce, brown sugar, bouillon granules and 1 cup water to turkey. Simmer, covered, for 15 minutes.

Blend together cold water and cornstarch. Stir into turkey mixture and cook until thick and bubbly, stirring often.

Add pineapple and green pepper, continue cooking 2 to 3 minutes or until pepper is crisp-tender.

Garnish with toasted almonds and serve over steamed rice.

Nutrient Analysis: 1 portion without rice

Calories: 195	*Fat: 6.5 g*	*Cholesterol: 37 mg*
Sodium: 200 mg	*Dietary Fiber: 2.9 g*	
Calcium: 25 mg		

Diabetic Exchange: 2 lean meat, 1 vegetable,
1 fruit

MEAT

We often live as if our habits don't matter. They do.

John Farquhar

MEAT

Lean red meat in modest amounts can be part of a heart healthy eating pattern.

Historically, the meat industry and health groups have different positions regarding the relationship between good health and the consumption of red meat.[10] Health promotion groups have expressed concerns about fat and saturated fat in meat. In response, the meat industry has produced leaner animals to provide consumers with many low-fat meat choices. Recognizing that red meat provides valuable nutrients such as protein, iron, zinc, thiamine, riboflavin, niacin and vitamin B$_{12}$, the authors of **Cooking à la Heart** have emphasized the dietary recommendations of the American Heart Association and the National Cancer Institute which advise selecting low-fat meat cuts, keeping portion sizes modest (at best, 3 ounces of cooked red meat twice a day) and varying red meat meals with those featuring vegetables, grain, chicken and fish.

As shown in the chart below, the fat and cholesterol content of red meat varies with the cut.

Table 25: Fat and Cholesterol Content of Red Meat

Cut of Meat: 3 ounces, cooked	Total Fat (tsp)	Cholesterol (mg)
Round Steak, beef	1.5	70
Extra-Lean Ground Beef, 85% lean	2.8	70
Lean Ground Beef, 80% lean	3.4	76
Regular Ground Beef, 73% lean	4.1	76
Sirloin, pork	2.5	83
Tenderloin, lean, pork	1.0	80
Cured Ham, extra-lean, pork	<1.0	32
Cured Ham, regular, pork	2.5	33
Loin Chop, veal	1.0	138
Loin Chop, lamb	1.8	80

Sources: USDA, HNIS. *Composition of Foods—Pork and Beef:* Agriculture Handbooks 8-10 and 8-13, 1983 and 1986. Personal communication with Eric Hentges, Assistant Director of Nutrition, National Livestock and Meat Board. April, 1988.

When selecting meats, choose the **lean** cuts as listed below:

Beef: Extra-lean ground beef
Round steak, top and bottom round steak, eye round steak, round roast, boneless rump roast, round tip roast and round tip steak

[10]Rebecca Mullis and Phyllis Pirie. "Lean Meats Make the Grade—A Collaborative Nutrition Program." *Journal of the American Dietetic Association.* 88:2, February 1988.

Loin strip steak, tenderloin steak, tenderloin roast and tips, loin and toploin sirloin steak
Flank steak

Pork:

Loin center rib roast, pork loin chop, butterfly chop, pork tenderloin, and top loin roast
Fresh leg (ham) steak and cutlets
Lean and extra-lean cured hams (labeled 93-97% fat-free)
Extra-lean ground pork

Veal:

Loin roast and chop
Loin sirloin roast, leg steak, leg round steak, leg rump roast and veal cutlets
Shoulder arm roast and steak
Loin ground veal

Lamb:

Loin roast and chop
Leg roast, whole leg and leg sirloin
Loin ground lamb

Use low-fat cooking methods.

The following preparation suggestions will help you keep the fat content of your meal low:

- Trim all visible fat from meat prior to cooking.

- Prepare meats by roasting, baking, broiling or braising. When roasting meat, use a rack so fat can be easily drained. Low-temperature roasting (325-350°F.) is recommended because more of the fat will come out of the meat. Higher temperatures will seal the fat in.

- After making soup or stew containing meat, refrigerate until the fat congeals on the surface so that it can be easily removed.

- When using meat drippings for gravy, remove the fat first. This can be done by placing the drippings in the freezer or adding ice cubes. Either way, the fat will harden and be easier to remove.

- Use non-stick pans to brown meat.

- Use vegetable cooking sprays instead of fat to brown meat.

The recipes in this chapter reflect serving sizes no larger than three ounces and low-fat cooking methods. Many recipes include combination dishes using smaller amounts of meat with pasta, vegetables and grains. We know you'll enjoy the adventuresome variety.

SEASONING

Reduce your dependency on salt by discovering the subtleties of herbs and spices. The following additions enhance the flavor of beef: bay leaf, chili powder, dry mustard, garlic, ginger, green pepper, sage, marjoram, mushrooms, nutmeg, onion, oregano, pepper and thyme.

HERB BLEND FOR BEEF

    1 tablespoon dried marjoram
    1 tablespoon dried basil
    1 tablespoon dried parsley
    1 tablespoon dried celery leaves
    ¼ teaspoon dried summer savory
    ¼ teaspoon whole thyme

Crush dried herbs and blend thoroughly. Sprinkle on beef during cooking or use in a shaker at the table. Store extra in a tightly-covered glass container.

See SEASONINGS for additional herb and spice blends.

MARINATED FLANK STEAK

Carve flank steak very thinly diagonally across the grain.

4 portions

    ¼ cup orange juice
    1 teaspoon grated orange peel
    ¼ cup vegetable oil
    1½ tablespoons sodium-reduced soy
       sauce
    2 garlic cloves, minced
    2 tablespoons sodium-reduced
       ketchup
    ⅛ teaspoon Tabasco sauce
    1 pound flank steak
    1 medium orange, sliced

In shallow baking dish, combine orange juice, peel, oil, soy sauce, garlic, ketchup and Tabasco. Mix well.

Add flank steak, turning to coat both sides. Arrange orange slices on top of meat, cover and marinate several hours or overnight in refrigerator.

Prepare charcoal grill or preheat broiler. Remove steak from marinade and set orange slices aside. Grill or broil steak 4 to 6 minutes a side or until desired doneness. During last 2 minutes of cooking, grill or broil orange slices until heated through.

Serve steak thinly sliced and garnished with orange slices.

Nutrient Analysis: 1 portion

Calories: 249   Fat: 13.2 g   Cholesterol: 107 mg

Sodium: 184 mg   Dietary Fiber: 0.7 g

Calcium: 32 mg

Diabetic Exchange: 3 medium-fat meat, ½ fruit

STEAK AND VEGETABLES

4 portions

1 pound boneless beef round
    steak, cut ½" thick
freshly ground pepper
1 tablespoon vegetable oil
2 cups water
1 6-ounce can no-salt-added
    tomato paste
2 teaspoons sodium-reduced
    Worcestershire sauce
¼ teaspoon dried basil, crushed
¼ teaspoon whole thyme
¼ teaspoon dried marjoram,
    crushed
4 medium carrots, cut in ¼"
    strips
1 medium green pepper, cut in
    ¼" strips
2 cups sliced fresh mushrooms

Nutrient Analysis: 1 portion (without rice)

Trim excess fat from steak and cut into 4 portions. Sprinkle with pepper.

In a 3-quart saucepan, brown meat on both sides in oil. Stir in water, tomato paste, Worcestershire, basil, thyme and marjoram. Bring to boil; reduce heat. Cover and simmer 30 minutes.

Add carrots, green pepper and mushrooms. Cover and simmer 15 minutes or until meat and vegetables are tender. Transfer meat and vegetables to a serving dish and pour tomato sauce over all.

Serve with rice or noodles.

Calories: 274   Fat: 10.2 g   Cholesterol: 107 mg

Sodium: 119 mg   Dietary Fiber: 2.3 g

Calcium: 51 mg

Diabetic Exchange: 3 medium-fat meat, 2 vegetable

BEEF SHISH KABOBS

Six 8" skewers

1½ pounds round steak or sirloin
    tip
2 tablespoons vegetable oil
2 tablespoons fresh lemon juice
1 teaspoon dried oregano,
    crushed

continued on next page

Trim excess fat from steak and cut into 1½" cubes.

In a mixing bowl, combine oil, lemon juice, oregano, bay leaf and pepper. Add beef and cover, turning occasionally, for at least 3 hours.

BEEF SHISH KABOBS (con't)

1 bay leaf
freshly ground pepper
1 sweet red pepper cut into 1½"
    chunks
1 green pepper cut into 1½"
    chunks
2 large tomatoes, quartered
1 onion, quartered and separated
12 large fresh mushrooms

Thread beef cubes on skewers alternately with vegetables. Grill kabobs over medium-hot coals, three minutes a side for rare or until desired doneness. Baste with marinade during cooking.

Nutrient Analysis; 1 skewer

Calories: 217	Fat: 9 g	Cholesterol: 107 mg
Sodium: 80 mg	Dietary Fiber: 1.2 g	
Calcium: 28 mg		

Diabetic Exchange: 3 lean meat, 2 vegetable

GROUND BEEF STROGANOFF

8 portions

2 pounds lean ground beef
2 medium onions, chopped
2 garlic cloves, minced
8 ounces fresh mushrooms, sliced
2 teaspoons sodium-reduced,
    beef-flavored bouillon
    granules
1 cup water
1½ cups plain low-fat yogurt
4 tablespoons flour
3 tablespoons tomato paste
½ teaspoon salt
¼ teaspoon pepper

Brown meat in skillet; drain fat.

Add onions, garlic and mushrooms and sauté until onion is golden. Place in crock pot.

Dissolve bouillon granules in water. Mix together yogurt and flour. Add bouillon, yogurt, tomato paste, salt and pepper to crock pot. Cover and cook on low for 6 hours*.

Serve hot over noodles or rice.

Simmer in Dutch oven for about 1 hour or bake at 350° for 1 hour.

Nutrient Analysis: 1 portion (without noodles)

Calories: 310	Fat: 12 g	Cholesterol: 74 mg
Sodium: 250 mg	Dietary Fiber: 2.8 g	
Calcium: 110 mg		

Diabetic Exchange: 3 medium-fat meat, 1 skim milk

BEEF STROGANOFF

4 portions

1 pound lean boneless beef, thinly sliced into strips
3 tablespoons flour
1½ teaspoons paprika
1 tablespoon vegetable oil
1 onion, chopped
1 garlic clove, crushed or ¼ teaspoon garlic powder
¼ teaspoon pepper
8 ounces fresh mushrooms, sliced*
⅓ cup water or wine*
1 teaspoon low-sodium, beef-flavored bouillon granules
1 cup plain low-fat yogurt

May substitute 1 4-ounce can mushrooms with liquid and omit the water or wine.

Shake beef strips in mixture of flour and paprika.

In a large skillet or Dutch oven, heat oil. Over high heat, brown beef, onion, garlic, pepper and mushrooms.

Stir in water or wine, beef bouillon and yogurt. Bring to a boil stirring constantly. Reduce heat, cover and simmer for 12 to 15 minutes.

Serve over rice or noodles.

Nutrient Analysis: 1 portion (without rice)

Calories: 274   Fat: 10.4 g   Cholesterol: 108 mg

Sodium: 123 mg   Dietary Fiber: 0.5 g

Calcium: 140 mg

Diabetic Exchange: 3 medium-fat meat, ½ skim milk

SWEDISH MEAT BALLS

The secret to making Swedish meat balls is: good meat—finely ground, finely chopped onion and thorough mixing of ingredients.

30 meat balls; 10 portions

1 large onion, very finely chopped
1 tablespoon water
1½ pounds lean ground beef
½ pound ground pork
¼ teaspoon ground allspice
⅓ teaspoon ground cloves
½ teaspoon salt
2 cups whole-wheat bread crumbs
3 tablespoons flour
2 cups skim milk
1½ tablespoons low-sodium, beef-flavored bouillon granules

In a covered saucepan, heat onion with water until onion pieces are soft.

Mix onion, beef, pork, allspice, cloves, salt and bread crumbs thoroughly. Form into 30 medium balls.

In skillet (or in oven at 350°), brown meat balls. Remove balls to casserole dish.

Make gravy by mixing together flour, milk, bouillon granules and drippings in the same skillet. Cook until thickened. Pour gravy over meat balls. Bake or simmer.

Oven: 350°
Time: 45 minutes

Nutrient Analysis: 3 meat balls with gravy

Calories: 289	Fat: 10 g	Cholesterol: 63 mg
Sodium: 373 mg	Calcium: 162 mg	

Diabetic Exchange: 3 medium-fat meat, 1 starch

CHARCOAL HERBED HAMBURGERS

8 patties

½ cup finely chopped onion
¼ teaspoon garlic powder
1 tablespoon chopped fresh parsley
½ tablespoon vegetable oil
2 pounds lean ground beef
¼ teaspoon dried marjoram, crushed
¼ teaspoon dried basil, crushed
2 tablespoons lemon juice

In small skillet, sauté onion, garlic and parsley in oil until soft.

Add onion mixture to ground beef along with marjoram, basil and lemon juice. Mix well and form into 8 patties.

Charcoal broil over medium-high heat to desired degree of doneness.

Nutrient Analysis: 1 patty

Calories: 207   Fat: 12.2 g   Cholesterol: 74 mg

Sodium: 74 mg   Calcium: 13 mg

Diabetic Exchange: 3 medium-fat meat

NEVADA ANNIE CHILI

Hot! Hot!

8 portions

1 cup chopped onion
½ cup chopped green pepper
½ cup chopped celery
1 garlic clove, minced
1 tablespoon canned green chilies, diced
1 tablespoon margarine
2 pounds lean ground beef
1 cup no-salt-added tomato sauce
3 tablespoons tomato paste
2 teaspoons chili powder
¾ teaspoon ground cumin
⅛ teaspoon garlic powder
⅛ teaspoon salt
¼ teaspoon pepper
   dash Tabasco sauce
⅓ cup beer
⅓ cup charged water

Sauté onions, green pepper, celery, garlic and green chilies in margarine.

Add ground beef and brown.

Add tomato sauce, tomato paste, chili powder, cumin, garlic powder, salt, pepper, Tabasco, beer and charged water. Simmer about 3 hours.

Nutrient Analysis: 1 portion

Calories: 247   Fat: 12.9 g   Cholesterol: 74 mg

Sodium: 240 mg   Dietary Fiber: 0.6 g

Calcium: 33 mg

Diabetic Exchange: 3 medium-fat meat, 1 vegetable

MINNESOTA CHILI

Make a double batch of meat sauce and freeze. Add beans when ready to use.

About 12 cups

1 pound lean ground beef
3 garlic cloves, minced
2 cups chopped onion
2 cups chopped celery with leaves
2 28-ounce cans whole tomatoes
3 tablespoons chili powder
¼ cup chopped parsley
½ teaspoon pepper
2 16-ounce cans dark red kidney
   beans

In a heavy saucepan or Dutch oven, brown meat.

Add garlic, onion and celery and cook until onion is golden.

Break tomatoes into pieces and add along with juice to meat mixture. Add chili powder, parsley and pepper. Bring to a boil, reduce heat, cover and simmer for 2 hours.

Shortly before serving, add kidney beans with liquid and heat thoroughly.

Nutrient Analysis: 1 cup

Calories: 173	*Fat: 4.1 g*	*Cholesterol: 25 mg*
Sodium: 767 mg	*Dietary Fiber: 8.2 g*	
Calcium: 86 mg		

Diabetic Exchange: 1 lean meat, 1 starch, 2 vegetable

MEAT LOAF

9 x 5" loaf pan, 8 portions

8 ounces sodium reduced tomato
   sauce
2 teaspoons SEASONING BLEND
   #1 or #2, *(page 377)*.
¼ teaspoon pepper
1½ pounds extra lean ground beef
1 large onion, finely chopped
1 egg white
1 cup Wheatena, farina, or bran
   cereal, uncooked
½ cup chopped green pepper
¼ cup chopped fresh parsley

Mix tomato sauce, SEASONING BLEND and pepper.

Combine the ground beef, onion, egg white, uncooked cereal, green pepper, parsley and half the seasoned tomato sauce.

Pat into 9 x 5" loaf pan. Spread remaining tomato sauce on top. Bake.

Oven: 350°
Time: 50 to 60 minutes

Nutrient Analysis: 1 portion

Calories: 230	*Fat: 9.8 g*	*Cholesterol: 50 mg*
Sodium: 81 mg	*Dietary Fiber: 18 g*	
Calcium: 32 mg		

Diabetic Exchange: 3 lean meat, 1 starch

BEEF STEW

A tasty, easy-to-prepare stew.

4 portions

¾ pound lean beef, cubed
1 tablespoon whole-wheat flour
1 quart water
1 onion, coarsely chopped
3 garlic cloves, minced
⅛ teaspoon pepper
3 carrots, diced
3 potatoes, diced
½ cup sliced fresh mushrooms
1 green pepper, cut in 1" squares
1 tomato, peeled and cut in
   eighths
4 sprigs parsley, chopped
½ cup red wine

Trim all visible fat from meat. Shake in flour.

In a teflon or non-stick sprayed pan, brown beef at high heat.

In heavy saucepan, bring water to a boil. Add beef, onion, garlic and pepper. Simmer for 2 hours, stirring occasionally. Remove beef. Strain and chill broth. Skim and discard fat.

Thirty minutes before serving, combine beef, broth, carrots and potatoes. Simmer for 15 minutes.

Add mushrooms, green pepper, tomato, parsley and wine. Simmer another 10 to 15 minutes or until vegetables are tender.

Nutrient Analysis: 1 portion

Calories: 309	Fat: 9.1 g	Cholesterol: 55 mg
Sodium: 88 mg	Dietary Fiber: 2.1 g	
Calcium: 47 mg		

Diabetic Exchange: 3 lean meat, 1 starch,
2 vegetable

OLD-FASHIONED BEEF STEW

A hearty stew chock-full of meat and vegetables.

6 portions

½ cup all-purpose flour
½ teaspoon pepper
1½ pounds beef stew meat, cubed
2 tablespoons vegetable oil
1½ tablespoons low-sodium, beef-
   flavored bouillon granules
3½ cups water

In a paper or plastic bag, combine flour and pepper. Add meat and toss until well-coated.

In Dutch oven, heat oil over medium-high heat. Brown meat in several batches and set aside.

continued on next page

OLD-FASHIONED BEEF STEW (con't)

½ cup dry red wine
1 16-ounce can low-sodium tomatoes, drained (reserve juice) and chopped
½ teaspoon dried marjoram, crushed
½ teaspoon salt
4 carrots, sliced
1 pound pearl onions, peeled
1½ pounds potatoes, cubed
1 9-ounce package frozen cut green beans

Mix flour remaining in bag with bouillon and water and stir into pan drippings, scraping up brown bits from pan. Return meat to pot.

Add red wine, tomato liquid and marjoram and salt. Bring to a boil. Reduce heat, cover and simmer 1½ hours.

Add carrots, onions, potatoes and tomatoes. Cook, uncovered, 30 minutes, stirring occasionally.

Add green beans and cook 10 minutes longer, stirring to separate beans.

Nutrient Analysis: 1 portion

Calories: 400   Fat: 7.1 g   Cholesterol: 107 mg

Sodium: 285 mg   Dietary Fiber: 3 g

Calcium: 102 mg

Diabetic Exchange: 3 lean meat, 2 starch, 3 vegetable

BASIC STIR-FRY RECIPE

6 portions

¼ cup sodium-reduced soy sauce
1 tablespoon cornstarch
1 tablespoon grated fresh ginger
   (optional)
1-2 tablespoons vegetable oil
1 pound poultry, fish, or meat,
   cut in ¼" thick slices
   garlic clove (optional)
2 cups sliced vegetable or
   combination of vegetables
   such as carrots, broccoli, bok
   choy, celery, onion, green or
   red peppers
2-3 cups vegetable or combination
   of vegetables such as bean
   sprouts, sliced mushrooms,
   snow peas
½ cup bamboo shoots or water
   chestnuts

Mix soy sauce, cornstarch and ginger for marinade. Toss with meat and set aside while you prepare the vegetables.

When all ingredients are assembled beside wok, drain poultry, fish or meat, reserving marinade.

Heat wok over high heat for 30 seconds. Swirl in 1 tablespoon oil and count to 30. Add poultry, fish, or meat and stir-fry until blanched (about 2 minutes). Add vegetables, beginning with the first group which require longer cooking, and toss quickly. (You may have to add another tablespoon of oil with the vegetables.)

Push solid ingredients up side of wok. Cook only until vegetables are hot but still crisp-tender.

To reserved marinade, add water or sodium-reduced stock to equal one cup. Add mixture to wok and stir until sauce thickens and clears. Mix all ingredients together. Serve with steamed rice, or bean or rice thread noodles.

Nutrient Analysis: 1 portion (stir-fry with chicken)

Calories: 146	*Fat: 3.7 g*	*Cholesterol: 44 mg*
Sodium: 448 mg	*Dietary Fiber: 1.2 g*	
Calcium: 26 mg		

Diabetic Exchange: 2 lean meat, 2 vegetable

STIR-FRY BEEF WITH VEGETABLE

This recipe can be varied by using broccoli, cauliflower, snow peas, mushrooms or a combination of vegetables. Although the cooking time will vary depending on the vegetables used, the secret is to avoid overcooking.

6 portions

MARINADE
1 tablespoon cornstarch
1 tablespoon sodium-reduced soy
   sauce
  dash of pepper
1½ teaspoons sugar
1½ teaspoons sesame oil
1 tablespoon dry sherry

Combine cornstarch, soy sauce, pepper, sugar, sesame oil and sherry.

¾ pound round steak
1½ pounds bok choy
3 tablespoons peanut oil
¼ teaspoon salt
2 thin slices fresh ginger
¾ cup water
1½ teaspoons sodium-reduced soy
   sauce
1 teaspoon cornstarch
3 tablespoons water

Slice the beef across the grain in thin (¼") slices. Toss the beef with the marinade and allow it to marinate for an hour.

Slice the bok choy diagonally. Heat the wok over high heat. Add 1½ tablespoons of the oil, salt and ginger. Add the bok choy and stir-fry for 1 minute. Add water. Cover and cook for 1 minute. Remove the vegetable and set aside.

Heat the wok over high heat and add the remaining oil. Stir-fry the beef for 1 minute. Add the bok choy and soy sauce. Stir-fry for 2 minutes. Mix the cornstarch and water and add to wok. Cook until liquid is slightly thickened. Serve with steamed rice or Chinese noodles.

Nutrient Analysis: 1 portion without rice

Calories: 181	*Fat: 7 g*	*Cholesterol: 54 mg*
Sodium: 209 mg	*Dietary Fiber: 0.7 g*	
Calcium: 128 mg		

Diabetic Exchange: 2 lean meat, 3 vegetable

ONE-DISH MEAL

A quick and easy one-dish meal.

1 pound lean ground beef or
   sliced round steak
1 onion, chopped
6 medium potatoes, scrubbed and
   sliced
3 cups chopped fresh tomatoes
¼ teaspoon salt
4 cups sliced zucchini
   water
   Parmesan cheese (optional)

6 portions

In heavy teflon or non-stick sprayed skillet, brown meat and onion. Drain well.

Add potatoes, tomatoes and salt. Cook 15 minutes.

Add zucchini and simmer until potatoes and squash are tender. Add water if needed.

Serve sprinkled with Parmesan, if desired.

Nutrient Analysis: 1 portion

Calories: 320   Fat: 8.7 g   Cholesterol: 45 mg

Sodium: 153 mg   Dietary Fiber: 8.2 g

Calcium: 73 mg

*Diabetic Exchange: 2 medium-fat meat, 1½ starch,
                  2 vegetable*

EGGPLANT HAMBURGER CASSEROLE

1 eggplant (about ¾ pound)
½ pound lean ground beef
½ cup chopped onion
½ pound firm tofu (bean curd),
   cubed
1 large tomato, diced
½ pound part-skim farmer cheese,
   shredded
½ cup sodium-reduced tomato
   sauce
½ teaspoon dried oregano, crushed

8 x 8" baking pan; 4 portions

Peel eggplant and cut into ½" cubes.

In medium skillet over medium-high heat, sauté eggplant, ground beef and onion for 5 minutes.

Remove from heat and stir in tofu, tomato, half the cheese, tomato sauce and oregano.

Spoon into a non-stick sprayed 8 x 8" baking dish. Sprinkle remaining cheese on top. Bake.

Oven: 375°
Time: 25 to 30 minutes

Nutrient Analysis: 1 portion

Calories: 272   Fat: 14.2 g   Cholesterol: 37 mg

Sodium: 55 mg   Dietary Fiber: 2 g

Calcium: 182 mg

Diabetic Exchange: 3 medium-fat meat, 2 vegetable

VEGETABLE BEEF CASSEROLE

9 x 13" baking pan, 8 portions

1 pound lean ground beef
1 egg white
1 cup bread crumbs
½ teaspoon garlic powder
⅔ cup skim milk
½ 10-ounce package frozen
    spinach, thawed and drained
2-3 zucchini, thinly sliced
1 medium onion, sliced and
    separated into rings
1 medium green pepper, thinly
    sliced
1 6-ounce can no-salt-added
    tomato paste
1 8-ounce can no-salt-added
    tomato sauce
¼ cup water
½ teaspoon dried basil, crushed
½ teaspoon dried oregano,
    crushed
    freshly ground pepper
½ cup shredded part-skim
    mozzarella cheese
1 cup shredded part-skim farmer
    cheese

Mix together ground beef, egg white, bread crumbs, garlic powder and milk. Pat into a 9 x 13" baking dish. Bake at 350° for 15 minutes. Pour off any accumulated fat.

Spread spinach over meat. Layer zucchini over spinach and onion and green pepper over zucchini.

Mix together tomato paste, tomato sauce, water, basil, oregano and pepper. Pour over layered casserole. Cover with foil and return to oven. Bake until vegetables are tender, about 30 minutes. During last 10 minutes of baking time, remove foil and top with shredded cheeses.

Oven: 350°
Time: 15 minutes beef mixture
*   30 minutes casserole*

Nutrient Analysis: 1 portion

Calories: 285   Fat: 9.6 g   Cholesterol: 39 mg

Sodium: 168 mg   Dietary Fiber: 4 g

Calcium: 195 mg

Diabetic Exchange: 1 medium-fat meat,
*   1 skim milk, 3 vegetable, 1 fat*

SEASONING FOR VEAL

The following herbs add to the delicate flavor of veal: bay leaf, curry, dill, lemon, marjoram, and oregano.

The HERB BLEND FOR POULTRY, (page 267) is excellent with veal.

VEAL LOAVES

8 portions

¾ cup soft bread crumbs
½ cup skim milk
½ pound ground ham (light and lean)
1½ pounds ground veal
½ teaspoon pepper
½ teaspoon onion powder
1 egg white
¼ cup finely chopped parsley
¼ teaspoon poultry seasoning
2 tablespoons brown sugar
2 tablespoons prepared mustard

Pour milk over bread crumbs. Let stand 5 minutes.

In a large bowl, mix ham, veal, pepper, onion powder, egg white, parsley and poultry seasoning. Thoroughly combine bread and milk mixture with meat mixture.

Form into 8 loaves and place in shallow pan. Bake.

Mix brown sugar and mustard and baste loaves occasionally during last 15 minutes of baking.

Oven: 325°
Time: 45 to 60 minutes

Nutrient Analysis: 1 loaf

Calories: 275   Fat: 13.8 g   Cholesterol: 74 mg
Sodium: 484 mg

Diabetic Exchange: 3 medium-fat meat,
½ starch

SAUTÉ OF VEAL WITH MUSHROOMS

A great make-ahead dinner dish. Reheat just before serving. Pork tenderloin may be substituted for the veal.

6 portions

1½ pounds veal cut in ¾" slices
2 tablespoons margarine
1 tablespoon vegetable oil
1 8-ounce can of mushrooms, stems and pieces, or ½ pound fresh mushrooms
½ teaspoon dried tarragon, thyme, or mixed fine herbs, crushed
¼ teaspoon salt
   freshly ground pepper
1 or 2 garlic cloves, pressed (optional)
2-3 tablespoons finely minced green onions
¼ cup Madeira or dry white Vermouth

Dry the veal on paper towels.

In a heavy skillet, heat oil and margarine. Sauté the meat over high heat, browning lightly on all sides. Lower heat and continue cooking until meat has stiffened when pressed with finger (7 to 10 minutes).

Drain mushrooms, reserving liquid. Add mushrooms to veal along with herbs, salt and pepper. Add garlic and onions. Toss and cook for one minute.

Add mushroom liquid and wine. Cook uncovered until liquid is reduced by half.

Serve over rice or noodles.

Nutrient Analysis: 1 portion without rice

Calories: 230   Fat: 12.9 g   Cholesterol: 81 mg

Sodium: 389 mg   Dietary Fiber: 0.4 g

Calcium: 20 mg

Diabetic Exchange: 3 medium-fat meat

VEAL PARMESAN

8 portions

2 tablespoons flour
½ teaspoon paprika
⅛ teaspoon pepper
1 egg white
1 tablespoon water
½ cup dry bread crumbs
3 tablespoons Parmesan cheese
2 pounds veal rump roast cut in
   ⅓-½" slices
2 tablespoons olive oil
1 8-ounce can tomato sauce
¼ teaspoon dried basil, crushed
6 ounces part-skim mozzarella
   cheese, sliced

Mix flour, paprika and pepper. Beat egg white with water. Mix bread crumbs and Parmesan.

Dredge veal in flour mixture. Dip dredged veal into the egg white mixture and then into the bread crumb and cheese mixture. Chill in refrigerator for at least 1 hour.

In a large skillet, heat the olive oil. Sauté the breaded veal until nicely browned on both sides. Transfer meat to a shallow casserole or baking dish.

Mix tomato sauce with basil and drizzle around the veal slices. Top veal with thin slices of mozzarella. Bake.

Oven: 350°
Time: 25 to 30 minutes

Nutrient Analysis: 1 portion

Calories: 294   Fat: 14.4 g   Cholesterol: 95 mg

Sodium: 294 mg   Dietary Fiber: 0.1 g

Calcium: 185 mg

Diabetic Exchange: 3 medium-fat meat,
1 skim milk

VEAL SCALLOPINI

8 portions

2 tablespoons flour
½ teaspoon paprika
⅛ teaspoon pepper
2 pounds veal (rump roast or
   round steak) cut into scallops
   ⅓-½" thick
2 tablespoons vegetable oil
4 green onions with some of the
   tops, chopped
2 cups sliced fresh mushrooms
1 tablespoon chopped fresh
   parsley
¼ teaspoon dried tarragon,
   crushed
2 tablespoons lemon juice

Mix flour, paprika and pepper. Dredge veal in mixture.

In a large skillet, heat 1 tablespoon oil. Sauté veal until brown on both sides. Remove to a heated casserole or pan to keep warm.

Add the other tablespoon of oil to the skillet and sauté the onions and mushrooms until lightly browned.

Return the veal to the skillet and heat through. Sprinkle veal with tarragon and parsley. Pour lemon juice over all and serve.

Nutrient Analysis: 1 portion

Calories: 204   Fat: 10.3 g   Cholesterol: 81 mg

Sodium: 103 mg   Dietary Fiber: 0.4 g

Calcium: 19 mg

Diabetic Exchange: 3 lean meat, ½ starch

SEASONINGS FOR PORK

Reach for the spice rack instead of the salt shaker when preparing pork. You will find the following seasonings particularly good with pork: basil, lemon, marjoram, onion, paprika, parsley, poultry seasonings, sage, and summer savory.

HERB BLEND FOR PORK

1 tablespoon dried basil
1 tablespoon dried marjoram
1 tablespoon dried sage
1 tablespoon dried summer
  savory

Crush dried herbs and blend thoroughly. Sprinkle on steaks, chops or roasts during cooking or use in a shaker at the table. Store extra in tightly covered glass container.

See SEASONINGS for additional herb and spice blends.

PORK CHOPS WITH CARAWAY RICE

4 portions

1 cup sliced celery
½ cup thinly sliced onion
1 teaspoon vegetable oil
1¼ cups long grain rice
2½ cups water
2 teaspoons caraway seed
¼ teaspoon salt
4 pork rib or loin chops, cut
  1¼" thick (about 2 pounds)
1 teaspoon lemon juice

In a large skillet, cook celery and onion in oil until crisp-tender (about 2 minutes). Stir in rice, water, caraway seed and salt. Bring to a boil, reduce heat and cover. Simmer 20 minutes or until liquid is absorbed. Stir in lemon juice and fluff with a fork.

While the rice is cooking, trim fat from pork chops and place on broiler pan rack. Broil 4 to 5" from heat turning every 5 minutes until chops are done (about 20 minutes).

Arrange chops on top of rice mixture and serve.

Nutrient Analysis: 1 portion chop and rice

Calories: 485   Fat: 13 g   Cholesterol: 102 mg

Sodium: 285 mg   Dietary Fiber: 0.6 g

Calcium: 42 mg

Diabetic Exchange: 4 medium-fat meat, 2 starch,
1 vegetable

STIR-FRY PORK

4 portions

1 pound lean boneless pork cut
   in ¼" slices
1 tablespoon vegetable oil
1 small onion, sliced in rounds
1 garlic clove, minced
½ pound fresh broccoli, stems cut
   in ⅛" diagonal rounds, florets
   separated
½ pound carrots sliced in ⅛"
   diagonal rounds
1 tablespoon sodium-reduced soy
   sauce

In a wok or large skillet over high heat, quickly brown pork strips in hot oil.

Add onion, garlic, broccoli stems and carrots. Cook and stir constantly until vegetables are hot but crisp.

Add broccoli florets and soy sauce. Cook and stir 1 to 2 minutes.

Serve with steamed rice or bean or rice thread noodles.

Nutrient Analysis: 1 portion without rice

Calories: 240   Fat: 11.4 g   Cholesterol: 74 mg

Sodium: 254 mg   Dietary Fiber: 2.4 g

Calcium: 61 mg

Diabetic Exchange: 3 lean meat, 3 vegetable

MARINATED PORK CUBES

8 portions

MARINADE
- 8 brazil nuts, shelled
- ¼ cup sodium-reduced soy sauce
- 3 tablespoons lemon juice
- 2 tablespoons finely chopped onion
- 2 tablespoons ground coriander seed
- 1 tablespoon brown sugar
- 1 garlic clove, minced
- ¼ teaspoon black pepper
- ⅛ teaspoon red pepper

1½ pounds boneless pork, cut in 1½" cubes

Grind brazil nuts and mix with soy sauce, lemon juice, onion, coriander, sugar, garlic, black and red pepper.

Add pork cubes and mix well. Marinate pork 2 to 3 hours.

Skewer meat and grill slowly over low fire. Baste once or twice with marinade. Serve with rice.

Nutrient Analysis: 1 portion without rice

Calories: 168	Fat: 8.4 g	Cholesterol: 54 g
Sodium: 130 mg	Calcium: 13 mg	

Diabetic Exchange: 2 medium-fat meat

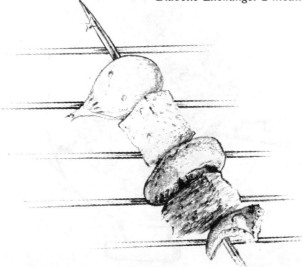

FRUITED PORK CHOPS

6 portions

6 loin pork chops, about 3
  pounds
⅔ cup apple juice
¼ teaspoon curry powder
¼ teaspoon pepper
1 large apple, unpeeled
¼ cup raisins

Trim the fat from chops. Brown in a non-stick pan. Remove chops to a large baking dish.

Pour the apple juice over the chops. Sprinkle with curry powder and pepper.

Core the apple and slice into 6 rings. Put one slice on each pork chop and fill the center hole of apple with raisins. Cover and bake until chops are tender.

Oven: 350°
Time: 60 minutes

Nutrient Analysis: 1 portion

Calories: 198   Fat: 7.1 g   Cholesterol: 55 mg

Sodium: 61 mg   Dietary Fiber: 1.4 g

Calcium: 15 mg

Diabetic Exchange: 3 lean meat, ½ fruit

CHOP AND SQUASH BAKE

4 portions

4 lean center-cut pork chops,
  about 2 pounds
½ teaspoon whole thyme
1 tablespoon vegetable oil
1 large onion, chopped
1 garlic clove, minced
1 small acorn squash
½ cup apple juice
1" slice of orange peel, 1" wide
1 teaspoon ground ginger
¼ teaspoon ground allspice
¼ teaspoon cayenne pepper

Trim fat from chops. Rub chops with thyme.

In a large skillet, brown pork chops lightly in oil adding onion and garlic when you turn meat to second side. Pour off any remaining oil.

Cut squash in half, seed, quarter, peel and slice thick. Add to skillet.

Combine apple juice, orange peel, ginger, allspice, cayenne and honey. Pour over chops and squash and bring to a boil.

continued on next page

CHOP AND SQUASH BAKE (con't)

1 tablespoon honey
1 large apple, peeled, cored and
    thickly sliced
4 orange slices

Cover and bake, turning chops after 30 minutes. Bake an additional 25 minutes, adding apples for last 10 minutes of cooking time.

Serve garnished with orange slices.

Oven: 375°
Time: 55 minutes

Nutrient Analysis: 1 portion

Calories: 444	*Fat: 16.6 g*	*Cholesterol: 102 mg*
Sodium: 116 mg	*Dietary Fiber: 4 g*	
Calcium: 87 mg		

Diabetic Exchange: 4 medium-fat meat, 1 starch, 1 fruit

PORK MEDALLIONS WITH PESTO

PESTO
¼ cup chopped fresh basil
2 tablespoons chopped fresh
    parsley
2 tablespoons grated Parmesan
    cheese
1 garlic clove, minced
1 tablespoon lemon juice
    freshly ground pepper
1 tablespoon sunflower or pine
    nuts

1 pound pork, tenderloin,
    trimmed
1 teaspoon olive oil

4 portions

In food processor, process basil, parsley, Parmesan, garlic, lemon juice, pepper and nuts until blended.

Cut tenderloin lengthwise; open and lay flat. Spread all but 1 tablespoon of pesto on cut side of pork.

Fold tenderloin together and tie with string at 1" intervals. Slice into eight medallions and place cut side up on rack in broiler pan. Spread with remaining tablespoon of pesto.

Broil 2 to 3" from heat for 6 to 7 minutes a side, brushing occasionally with olive oil.

Oven: Broil
Time: 12 to 14 minutes

Nutrient Analysis: 2 medallions

Calories: 222	*Fat: 11.7 g*	*Cholesterol: 70 mg*
Sodium: 121 mg	*Calcium: 119 mg*	

Diabetic Exchange: 3 medium-fat meat

PORK STEW

6 portions

1 pound lean boneless pork, cut into 1" cubes
4 carrots, diagonally sliced
2 celery ribs, diagonally sliced
1 onion, coarsely chopped
2 potatoes, cut into 1" cubes
1 6-ounce can tomato paste
2 cups water
¼ teaspoon pepper
½ teaspoon garlic powder
1 teaspoon sugar
½ teaspoon HERB BLEND for PORK, *(page 310)*.
2 tablespoons cold water
1 tablespoon flour

In a large, heavy saucepan, brown pork cubes over medium heat.

Add carrots, celery, onion, potatoes, tomato paste, water, pepper, garlic powder, sugar and spice blend. Bring to a boil. Cover and reduce heat. Simmer meat and vegetables until tender (about 30 minutes).

Blend cold water and flour and stir into stew. Cook and stir until thickened and bubbly. Serve.

Nutrient Analysis: 1 portion

Calories: 200   Fat: 6.5 g   Cholesterol: 47 mg

Sodium: 285 mg   Dietary Fiber: 4 g

Calcium: 44 mg

Diabetic Exchange: 2 lean meat, ½ starch, 2 vegetable

SEASONINGS FOR LAMB

Traditional seasonings for lamb range from spicy curries [HOMEMADE CURRY POWDER, (page 380)] to a subtle hint of mint. Try your choice of the following with lamb: basil, curry powder, garlic, marjoram, mint, parsley, rosemary, and savory.

HERB BLEND FOR LAMB*

1 tablespoon dried basil
1 tablespoon dried marjoram
1 tablespoon parsley flakes
1 teaspoon dried rosemary
1 teaspoon dried savory

Blend crushed herbs thoroughly. Sprinkle on lamb during cooking or use in a shaker at the table. Store extra in a tightly covered glass container.

See SEASONINGS for additional herb and spice blends.

LAMB SHISH KABOBS

Kabobs are probably of Turkish origin, but are served throughout the Middle East. Few peasants could afford meat more than perhaps once a week, or for special feast days. Their daily diet of soups, vegetable stew, black bread, cheese and fruit contributed to their low incidence of heart disease.

8 skewers

MARINADE
6 tablespoons olive oil
4 tablespoons sherry
½ cup vinegar or white wine
1-2 garlic cloves, minced
¼ large onion, minced
4 tablespoons finely chopped parsley
1 teaspoon oregano, crushed
½ teaspoon salt
   freshly ground pepper

2 pounds lamb, cut from leg
4 green peppers, seeded
4 medium onions
4 medium underripe tomatoes
8 ounces fresh mushrooms
1 tablespoon margarine

In a large bowl, combine olive oil, sherry, vinegar or wine, garlic, onion, parsley, oregano, salt and pepper.

Bone leg and cut meat in 1½" squares. Place meat in marinade making sure all pieces are covered. Cover bowl and refrigerate 12 to 24 hours. Turn meat several times.

When ready to cook, cut onion and green pepper into 1½" pieces. Cut tomatoes in half crosswise. Divide meat, onion and pepper into 8 portions and alternate on skewers beginning with tomato half.

Brush skewers with marinade and cook over medium-hot charcoal fire or under broiler, turning several times until desired degree of doneness (15 to 20 minutes for medium rare).

Shortly before kabobs are done, sauté mushrooms lightly in margarine.

Remove kabobs to large serving platter. Cover with mushrooms.

Serve with RICE PILAF, *(page 182)* and a green salad dressed with lemon juice and fresh mint.

Charcoal grill or broil, medium-hot.
Time: to desired doneness, about 8 to 10 minutes a side for medium rare.

Nutrient Analysis: 1 skewer

Calories: 275   Fat: 15 g   Cholesterol: 113 mg

Sodium: 175 mg   Dietary Fiber: 1.7 g

Calcium: 41 mg

Diabetic Exchange: 3 medium-fat meat, 2 vegetable

LAMB CURRY

Curry is better if made a day ahead and then reheated allowing the flavors to "marry". A traditional curry recipe has about 19 g of fat whereas this modified version has only 4.8 g.

8 portions

1½ pounds boned lamb
1 tablespoon vegetable oil
2 large onions, chopped
4 garlic cloves, chopped
2 tablespoons CURRY
      POWDER, *(page 380).*
¼ teaspoon salt
½ cup hot water
⅓ cup seedless raisins
2 large tomatoes, chopped
2 fresh green chilies

Cut lamb into ¾" cubes, removing visible fat. In heavy saucepan, heat oil and saute lamb cubes until well browned. Remove lamb.

In same pan, gently sauté onion and garlic until soft and transparent but not brown. Add curry powder and salt to the onion mixture making sure to "fry" the spices so their full flavor comes out. Return the lamb and stir until lamb is coated with spice mixture.

Add water, raisins, tomatoes and chilies. Cover and cook over low heat for 1¼ hours or until lamb is tender. Skim the fat from the curry and stir occasionally while it simmers.

Curry is traditionally served over steamed rice with some or all of the following condiments: chutney, chopped onion, diced pineapple, chopped banana, chopped apple, chopped peppers, chopped nuts, diced tomato.

Nutrient Analysis: 1 portion without condiments

Calories: 132	Fat: 4.8 g	Cholesterol: 40 mg
Sodium: 123 mg	Dietary Fiber: 0.8 g	
Calcium: 26 mg		

Diabetic Exchange: 2 lean meat, 1 vegetable

LAMB PIE (BOBOTIE)

10 x 10" baking pan, 8 portions

2 large onions, finely chopped
2 garlic cloves, crushed
2 tablespoons olive oil
1 tablespoon CURRY POWDER,
  (page 380).
1 slice day-old bread
1 cup skim milk
1 egg white
1 tablespoon sugar
½ teaspoon freshly ground pepper
½ teaspoon turmeric
  juice of 1 lemon
3 tablespoons hot mango chutney
5 tablespoons blanched almonds,
  chopped
½ cup raisins
4 strips lemon rind, ½ inch wide
2 pounds lean, coarsely ground
  lamb
1 egg

Sauté onion and garlic lightly in oil. Add curry powder.

Soak bread in the milk and squeeze dry, saving the milk.

In a large bowl combine the bread, onion mixture, egg white, sugar, pepper, turmeric, lemon juice, chutney, almonds, raisins, lemon rind and ground lamb. Mix well.

Pat meat mixture into a 10 x 10" non-stick sprayed baking pan. Bake 60 minutes and remove from oven. The mixture will have shrunk leaving lots of liquid. Skim off the fat leaving the other juices in pan.

Beat the whole egg with the reserved milk and pour over the meat. Bake an additional 15 to 20 minutes or until the custard is set and the top golden.

Serve with rice and a green salad.

Oven: 350°
Time: 60 minutes, meat mixture
      15 to 20 minutes, custard

Nutrient Analysis: 1 portion

Calories: 300   Fat: 14.7 g   Cholesterol: 110 mg

Sodium: 144 mg   Dietary Fiber: 1 g

Calcium: 84 mg

Diabetic Exchange: 4 medium-fat meat

STUFFED CABBAGE ROLLS*

A delicious Lebanese dish that is definitely worth the extra preparation time.

24 rolls

1 medium cabbage head

FILLING
1 pound ground lamb
1 cup raw rice
¼ teaspoon cinnamon
¼ teaspoon pepper
¼ teaspoon salt
2 tablespoons lemon juice

SAUCE
water to cover rolls
1 28-ounce can no-salt-added
    whole tomatoes or 4 cups
    peeled and seeded fresh
    tomatoes
4 large garlic cloves, peeled and
    cut in half

*SAUCE VARIATIONS FOR
CABBAGE ROLLS*
beef broth flavored with juice
    of one lemon
beef or chicken broth and ½
    cup tomato juice

Wash the cabbage and core it deeply enough that the outer leaves begin to separate from the head. In a pan large enough to hold the head of cabbage, bring water to a boil. Dip the head of cabbage in boiling water. As the leaves loosen, remove them. Continue removing leaves until you have at least 12. Blanch the 12 leaves in boiling water for 2 minutes. Cool. Cut the cooked leaves in half, removing the center ribs.

Knead together the lamb, rice, cinnamon, pepper, salt and lemon juice.

Place half a cabbage leaf with the cut side toward you. Place 1 or 2 tablespoons of filling on the center of the cabbage leaf. Fold the left and right sides of the cabbage over filling. Roll the leaf away from you starting with the cut side.

Arrange filled rolls tightly in a non-stick sprayed 9 x 13" baking pan. Break the tomatoes into small pieces and pour tomatoes with juice over the tops of rolls. Place the garlic over the tomatoes. Add water to the top of the rolls. Bake, uncovered.

Oven: 350°
Time: 45 minutes

*Nutrient Analysis follows the recipe for Spicy Rice Filling for Cabbage Rolls on the next page.

SPICY RICE FILLING FOR CABBAGE ROLLS

1 cup raw rice
½ cup chopped onion
2 tablespoons chopped fresh
   parsley
2 tablespoons olive oil
2 tablespoons sodium-reduced
   tomato sauce
1 teaspoon chopped fresh mint
½ teaspoon ground allspice
½ teaspoon pepper
¼ teaspoon salt

Mix together rice, onion, parsley, olive oil, tomato sauce, mint, allspice, pepper and salt. Stuff, roll, cover with sauce and bake as above.

Nutrient Analysis: 1 roll

	Lamb	Rice
Calories:	69	48
Fat:	1.2 g	1.2 g
Cholesterol:	13 mg	0
Sodium:	28 mg	32 mg
Dietary Fiber:	0.5 g	0.5 mg
Calcium:	6 mg	21 mg
Diabetic Exchange:	1 starch	½ starch

SOUPS, SANDWICHES, & PIZZA

Soup of the evening,
beautiful soup!

Lewis Carroll

SOUPS

Soup is nothing short of remarkable in its variety. Choices range from rich and tasty stocks to chunky vegetable, thick "cream" and chilled soups. Whether you choose a light or a hearty soup, it can provide protein, complex carbohydrates and fiber, vitamins A and C and essential minerals to your diet. Soups have an added bonus of making you feel full, thus helping curb your appetite and control calories.

Commercial soups, while tasty, are generally a source of fat and saturated fat with a considerable amount of sodium. Check the table below for a comparison of fat and sodium between commercial soups and the soups in *Cooking à la Heart.*

Table 27: Fat and Sodium Comparison of Soup

Commercial Soup (1 cup):	Fat grams	Sodium mg.	Fat grams	Sodium mg.	Cooking à la Heart Soup (1 cup):
Chicken Noodle soup	2	910	2	48	Chicken Noodle soup
Chicken Stock	<1	900	<1	15	Chicken or Turkey stock
Cup-a-Soup Chicken Vegetable	<1	910	<1	36	Chicken or Turkey Vegetable soup
Cream of Mushroom	7	820	5	200	Cream of Morel
New England Clam Chowder (with milk)	7	930	4	268	Hearty Chowder
Cup-a-Soup Virginia Pea	5	870	5	334	Hearty Pea

Source: Data from Manufacturer: Campbell's and Lipton soup labels.

*Soup is for
all seasons
and all ages.*

You'll enjoy the thick and robust soups on cool days; the savory light soups to serve as a first course; the hearty bean or pea soup to serve as a main dish and chilled soups to refresh your summer guests. You can further enhance your homemade specialty by serving soup in creative containers such as tureens, two-handled cups, mugs, soup plates, and, for chilled soups, frosted glasses. Soups are a good way to nourish children and they will be encouraged to eat soup if its served in an imaginative manner such as in a playware bowl, plastic construction hat or coffee mug.

SANDWICHES AND PIZZA

Pizza is a popular food evidenced by the fact that on the average, Americans eat an estimated 22.5 pounds of pizza each year. Pizza appears to be a national staple, more popular by far than any other food. With supermarket shelves and freezer cases providing us with an alluring array of options and the local pizzeria offering to deliver more quickly than you can say "cheese", you may wonder if all the pizza we're eating is healthy for us.

Pizza can be a good source of protein, calcium, iron, riboflavin and vitamin C. But it can also be a source of a great deal of fat, calories and sodium. In fact, pepperoni, a particular high-fat meat, is the favorite topping preferred by pizza lovers.

Sandwiches, like pizza, can offer much nutrition but can also be a source of hidden fat and contain high-sodium ingredients. Table 26 shows the amount of calories, fat and sodium contained in selected pizzas and sandwiches.

Table 26: Fat & Sodium Content of Selected Pizzas and Sandwiches

Item:	Calories:	Fat: (teaspoons)	Sodium: (milligrams)
Pizza:			
Cheese (2 slices of a 12" pizza)	340	1	660
Cheese (3 slices of a 10" thick crust pizza)	560	3	1040
Pepperoni (2 slices of a 12" pizza)	380	3	880
Pepperoni (3 slices of a 10" thick crust pizza	560	4	1220
Cooking à la Heart Heart Healthy Pizza Topping with Yeast Crust (2 servings)	292	3	266
Sandwiches:			
Fast Food			
McDonald's Quarter Pounder	427	5	718
Hardee's Fisherman's Filet	469	5	1013
Arby's Junior Roast Beef	218	2	345
Deli or Homemade:			
Bacon, Lettuce & Tomato (2 slices bread, 4 slices bacon, 1 T mayonnaise, lettuce and tomato)	445	7	621
Tuna Salad (2 slices bread, 2 ounces water-packed tuna, 1 T mayonnaise, lettuce)	330	3	805
Breaded Fish Sticks (2 slices bread, 4 fish sticks, 1 T margarine)	420	5	770
Cooking à la Heart Vegetable and Cheese Pockets	153	1	97
Cooking à la Heart Ham Healthwich	198	1	393

Sources: Michael Jacobson and Sarah Fritschner. *The Fast Food Guide.* New York: Workman Publishing, 1986. Marion Franz. *Fast Food Facts.* Minneapolis: Diabetes Center, Incorporated, 1987.

BOUQUET GARNI

For the well-seasoned soup or stew—a bouquet of fresh herbs. Bouquet garni also makes a fragrant package decoration or room freshener.

FRESH HERB BOUQUET GARNI

2 sprigs parsley
1 sprig marjoram
1 sprig basil
1 sprig thyme
1 bay leaf
1 branch tarragon
2 garlic cloves, sliced (**optional**)

Tie the fresh sprigs together with string or place in a cheesecloth bag and add to soup or stock.

Remove at the end of cooking time.

DRIED HERB BOUQUET GARNI

1 tablespoon parsley flakes
¼ teaspoon dried marjoram
¼ teaspoon dried basil
¼ teaspoon whole thyme
¼ teaspoon dried tarragon
1 bay leaf

Place dried herbs in a cheesecloth bag and use as above.

BEEF STOCK

Ready-to-use canned stocks contain approximately 1500 mg sodium a cup whereas this homemade stock contains only 14 mg sodium a cup. Stock freezes well. For convenience sake, freeze in pre-measured containers.

About 2 quarts

5-6 pounds soup bones
4 quarts water
2 large onions, quartered
1 medium carrot, halved
2 celery ribs with leaves, halved
1 cup drained or fresh tomatoes, diced
1 BOUQUET GARNI, *(see preceding page).*
8-10 whole peppercorns

In a large Dutch oven or stock pot, brown the bones.

Add water, onion, carrot, celery, tomatoes, bouquet garni and peppercorns. Bring to a boil, reduce heat and simmer, uncovered for about 3 hours.

Strain stock through cheesecloth or fine sieve into large pan or bowl. Let stand 15 minutes. Refrigerate until fat congeals on surface. Skim off and discard fat.

Storing: Stock can be stored in refrigerator for up to one week or frozen in ice cube trays or other containers up to 4 months. If you use ice cube trays, remove cubes once they are frozen and store in tightly closed freezer container.

Nutrient Analysis: 1 cup

Calories: 20	Fat: 0.2 g	Cholesterol: 0
Sodium: 14 mg	Calcium: 17 mg	

Diabetic Exchange: free

CHICKEN OR TURKEY STOCK

Ready-to-use canned stocks contain approximately 1500 mg sodium a cup whereas this homemade stock contains only 15 mg sodium a cup. Stock freezes well. For convenient use, freeze in small, pre-measured amounts.

About 2 quarts

3 quarts water
3 pounds uncooked chicken or turkey parts (backs, necks, wing tips) or cooked carcass with some meat left on bones
2 large onions, quartered
1 medium carrot, halved
2 celery ribs with leaves, halved
1 BOUQUET GARNI, *(page 327)*
8-10 whole peppercorns

In a large Dutch oven or stockpot, combine water, poultry parts, onions, carrot and celery. Bring to a boil; add bouquet garni and peppercorns. Reduce heat to low. Cover and simmer about 3 hours.

Strain stock through cheesecloth or fine sieve into large pan or bowl. Let stand 15 minutes. Refrigerate until fat congeals on surface. Skim off and discard fat.

Storing: Stock can be stored in refrigerator for up to one week or frozen in ice cube trays or other containers up to 4 months. If you use ice cube trays, remove cubes once they are frozen and store in tightly closed freezer container.

Nutrient Analysis: 1 cup

Calories: 28	*Fat: 0.1 g*	*Cholesterol: 0*
Sodium: 15 mg	*Calcium: 15 mg*	

Diabetic Exchange: 1 vegetable

A hot drink is as good as an overcoat.

Petronius

GRANDMA'S CHICKEN SOUP

About 2½ quarts; 8 portions

    3 quarts water
2½-3 pound chicken, cut up
    2 large onions, quartered
    1 medium carrot, halved
    2 celery ribs with leaves, halved
    1 BOUQUET GARNI,
        (page 327)
 8-10 whole peppercorns
    1 tablespoon margarine
    2 medium carrots, diced
    2 medium celery ribs, diced

In a large Dutch oven or stockpot, combine the water and the chicken. Bring to a boil; reduce heat and simmer, uncovered, 1 hour.

Add quartered onions, halved carrot and celery. Simmer, covered for 1 hour. Remove chicken pieces and cool.

Remove skin and bones from chicken and return them to stockpot. Cook broth for another hour. Shred meat and set aside.

Strain stock through cheesecloth or fine sieve into large pan or bowl. Let stand 15 minutes. Refrigerate until fat congeals on surface. Skim fat and discard.

Meanwhile, in small skillet, melt margarine. Add carrots and celery. Sauté until tender, 5 to 10 minutes. Add carrots, celery and shredded chicken to broth and heat thoroughly.

GRANDMA'S CHICKEN SOUP VARIATION

    1 tablespoon margarine
    2 medium carrots, diced
    2 medium celery ribs, diced
    2 quarts CHICKEN OR
        TURKEY STOCK, *(see
        preceding page)*.
    2 cups diced cooked chicken or
        turkey

In a small skillet, melt margarine. Add carrots and celery. Sauté until tender, 5 to 10 minutes.

In a large saucepan, combine sautéd vegetables, STOCK and diced chicken or turkey. Heat thoroughly.

Nutrient Analysis: 1 cup

Calories: 70	*Fat: 2.1 g*	*Cholesterol: 25 mg*
Sodium: 58 mg	*Dietary Fiber: 0.5 g*	
Calcium: 14 mg		

Diabetic Exchange: 1 lean meat, 1 vegetable

CHICKEN RICE SOUP

About 11 cups

2 quarts GRANDMA'S
    CHICKEN SOUP, *(see*
    preceding page).
3 cups cooked long grain rice
¼ cup chopped fresh parsley
¼ cup white wine (optional)

In a large saucepan, bring GRANDMA'S
CHICKEN SOUP to a boil.

Add rice, parsley and wine. Season to
taste with herbs.

Nutrient Analysis: 1 cup

Calories: 94   Fat: 1.6 g   Cholesterol: 18 mg

Sodium: 184 mg   Dietary Fiber: 0.5 g

Calcium: 19 mg

*Diabetic Exchange: 1 lean meat, ¼ starch,
                1 vegetable*

CHICKEN NOODLE SOUP

About 10 cups

2 quarts GRANDMA'S
    CHICKEN SOUP, *(see*
    preceding page).
2 cups uncooked wide noodles
¼ cup chopped fresh parsley

In a large saucepan bring GRANDMA'S
CHICKEN SOUP to a boil.

Add noodles and boil until tender, about
8 to 10 minutes. Stir in chopped parsley.
Season to taste with herbs.

Nutrient Analysis: 1 cup

Calories: 97   Fat: 2.2 g   Cholesterol: 30 mg
Sodium: 48 mg   Dietary Fiber: 0.6 g
Calcium: 16

*Diabetic Exchange: 1 lean meat, ¼ starch,
                1 vegetable*

CHICKEN OR TURKEY VEGETABLE SOUP

About 12 cups

2 quarts CHICKEN OR
   TURKEY STOCK,
   (page 329)
½-¾ cup of a starchy ingredient
   such as uncooked rice,
   barley, potatoes or pasta
   Up to 1 cup of a combination
   of highly flavored vegetables
   such as onion, celery, carrot,
   rutabaga
   Up to 3 cups of a combination
   of colorful vegetables such as
   peas, beans, corn, okra,
   tomato
   Up to 2 cups diced cooked
   chicken or turkey

Follow steps for CHICKEN OR
TURKEY STOCK. Bring stock to a boil.

Add other ingredients in order of
required cooking time (barley - 60
minutes; rice, potatoes and vegetables -
20 minutes; pasta and meat - 10
minutes).

Nutrient Analysis: 1 cup

Calories: 97	*Fat: 0.6 g*	*Cholesterol: 16 mg*
Sodium: 36 mg	*Dietary Fiber: 1 g*	
Calcium: 30 mg		

Diabetic Exchange: ½ starch, 2 vegetable

MULLIGATAWNY SOUP

A great use of left-over holiday turkey and it freezes well.

6 portions

¼ cup chopped onion
1½ teaspoons curry powder
   2 tablespoons vegetable oil
   1 tart apple, peeled, cored and
     chopped
¼ cup chopped carrots
¼ cup chopped celery
   2 tablespoons chopped green
     pepper

In a large saucepan, cook onion and
curry powder in oil until onion is tender.
Add apple, carrot, celery and green
pepper, stirring occasionally until
vegetables are crisp-tender (about 5
minutes).

continued on next page

MULLIGATAWNY SOUP (con't)

3 tablespoons flour
2 tablespoons low-sodium,
  chicken-flavored bouillon
  granules
4 cups water
1 16-ounce can tomatoes, cut up
1 tablespoon chopped fresh
  parsley
2 teaspoons fresh lemon juice
1 teaspoon sugar
2 whole cloves
¼ teaspoon salt
  dash of pepper
1 cup diced cooked turkey or
  chicken

Sprinkle flour over mixture, stirring to mix well.

Add bouillon granules, water, undrained tomatoes, parsley, lemon juice, sugar, cloves and pepper. Bring to a boil and add chicken or turkey. Simmer for 30 minutes, stirring occasionally.

Nutrient Analysis: 1 portion

Calories: 142   Fat: 4.1 g   Cholesterol: 25 mg

Sodium: 298 mg   Dietary Fiber: 1.2 g

Calcium: 39 mg

Diabetic Exchange: 1½ lean meat, 2 vegetable

TURKEY TOMATO VEGETABLE SOUP

1985 Heart's Delight Recipe Contest Grand Prize Winner—Junior Division.

About 16 cups

1 quart CHICKEN OR TURKEY
  STOCK, *(page 329).*
1 quart stewed, unsalted
  tomatoes
½ cup barley
4 teaspoons low-sodium, chicken-
  flavored bouillon granules
½ teaspoon garlic powder
¼ teaspoon black pepper
½ teaspoon dried oregano,
  crushed
1 tablespoon parsley flakes
½ teaspoon dried basil, crushed
2 cups diced cooked turkey
1½ cups sliced carrots
1½ cups sliced celery
1 cup chopped onions
1 cup chopped green pepper
1 10-ounce package frozen okra

In a large saucepan, simmer stock, tomatoes, barley, bouillon granules, garlic powder, pepper, oregano, parsley and basil for 1 hour.

Add turkey, carrots, celery, onions, green pepper, and okra. Simmer 30 minutes or until vegetables are tender.

Nutrient Analysis: 1 cup

Calories: 84   *Fat: 1.2 g*   *Cholesterol: 7 mg*

Sodium: 45 mg   *Dietary Fiber: 1.3 mg*

Calcium: 47 mg

Diabetic Exchange: ½ lean meat, 2 vegetable

MUSHROOM SOUP

The fresh, light flavor is a pleasant alternative to heavier, cream-style mushroom soup.

10 portions

1   **pound fresh mushrooms**
3   **tablespoons margarine**
2   **cups chopped carrots**
2   **cups chopped celery**
1   **cup chopped onion**
1   **garlic clove, minced**
6   **cups BEEF STOCK,** *(page 328)*
    or 4 tablespoons low-sodium,
    beef-flavored bouillon
    granules in 6 cups water
3   **tablespoons tomato paste**
    freshly ground pepper to taste
6   **sprigs parsley**
3   **celery rib tops with leaves**
1   **bay leaf**
¼   **cup dry sherry**
    lemon slices or parsley sprigs
    for garnish

Wipe the mushrooms. Chop half the mushrooms. Slice the other half and set aside.

In a large, heavy saucepan, melt 2 tablespoons of margarine. Add the chopped mushrooms and sauté 5 minutes. Add carrots, celery, onion and garlic and sauté 5 minutes longer. Stir in beef stock, tomato paste and pepper.

Form a bouquet garni by tying together with a string: parsley, celery tops and bay leaf. Add to soup. Bring to a boil, cover, reduce heat and simmer for 1 hour. Remove the bouquet garni.

In a blender or food processor, purée soup 1 cup at a time. Return puréed soup to pan. In a medium skillet, melt remaining tablespoon of margarine. Add reserved sliced mushrooms and sauté gently for 5 minutes. Add mushrooms and sherry to soup and heat thoroughly. Serve garnished with lemon slices or parsley sprigs.

Nutrient Analysis: 1 portion

Calories: 90   *Fat: 5 g*   *Cholesterol: 0*

Sodium: 176 mg   *Dietary Fiber: 1.4 g*

Calcium: 28 mg

Diabetic Exchange: 2 vegetable, 1 fat

SPICED TOMATO BOUILLON

Delicious served either hot or cold.

About 12 cups

¾ cup diced celery
¾ cup diced carrots
½ cup diced onion
3 tablespoons chopped fresh parsley
8 cups unsalted tomato juice
½-1 teaspoon white pepper
10 whole cloves
2 bay leaves
¼ teaspoon whole thyme
4 cups hot CHICKEN OR
   TURKEY STOCK, *(page 329).*

Simmer celery, carrots, onion, parsley, tomato juice, pepper, cloves, bay leaves and thyme about an hour, covered.

Strain and add broth. Heat to serving temperature.

Nutrient Analysis: 1 cup

Calories: 47	Fat: 0.4 g	Cholesterol: 0
Sodium: 29 mg	Dietary Fiber: 0.3 g	
Calcium: 8 mg		

Diabetic Exchange: 2 vegetable

TOMATO AND CLAM SOUP

About 11 cups

3 small onions, sliced
3 ribs celery, finely diced
1 sweet red pepper, finely diced
2 tablespoons margarine
6 cups no-salt-added canned
   tomatoes
4 cups water
2 bay leaves
½ tablespoon dried basil, crushed
½ teaspoon whole black peppers
¾ teaspoon curry powder
2 6½ ounce cans minced clams,
   undrained
⅓ cup plain low-fat yogurt for
   garnish

In a large saucepan, sauté onion, celery and pepper in the margarine until soft.

Add tomatoes, water, bay leaves, basil, pepper, curry and clams. Simmer 1 hour. Remove bay leaves.

Serve garnished with a dollop of yogurt.

Nutrient Analysis: 1 cup

Calories: 81	Fat: 2.9 g	Cholesterol: 11 mg
Sodium: 243 mg	Dietary Fiber: 0.5 g	
Calcium: 87 mg		

Diabetic Exchange: ½ lean meat, 2 vegetable

FRENCH ONION SOUP, GRATINÉE

8 portions

1½ pounds (5 cups) thinly sliced
    yellow onions
 2 tablespoons margarine
 1 teaspoon vegetable oil
 ¼ teaspoon sugar
 3 tablespoons flour
 2 quarts boiling BEEF STOCK,
    (page 328) or 5 tablespoons
    low-sodium, beef-flavored
    bouillon granules dissolved in
    2 quarts water
 ½ cup dry white wine
    pepper to taste
 8 slices hard toasted French
    bread
1½ cups shredded part-skim farmer
    or Swiss cheese

In a large, heavy, covered saucepan, cook onions slowly with the margarine and oil for 15 minutes. Uncover, raise heat to medium and add sugar. Cook 30 to 40 minutes, stirring frequently, until the onions have turned a deep golden brown.

Sprinkle the flour over the onions. Cook and stir for about 2 minutes. Remove from heat and stir in the beef stock, wine and pepper.

Return to heat. Simmer, partially covered, for 30 to 40 minutes, skimming occasionally.

Bring soup to a boil and pour into oven-proof tureen or individual bowls. Top with toasted French bread and cheese. Bake at 350° for 20 minutes, then set under broiler for 2 minutes or until the cheese is lightly browned. Serve immediately.

Nutrient Analysis: 1 portion

Calories: 201   Fat: 5.8 g   Cholesterol: 12 mg

Sodium: 257 mg   Dietary Fiber: 1 g

Calcium: 153 mg

Diabetic Exchange: 1 low-fat milk, 1 starch

SCOTCH BROTH

10 to 12 cups

3 pounds meaty lamb bones
12 cups water
1 onion, quartered
2 celery ribs with leaves, cut in
    thirds
½ teaspoon salt
½ cup barley
1 onion, chopped
2 ribs celery, sliced
2 carrots, sliced
    freshly ground pepper

In a heavy saucepan, brown the lamb bones. Add water, quartered onion, celery ribs with leaves and salt. Bring to a boil, reduce heat and simmer, covered, for 2 to 3 hours.

Strain the broth and cool until the fat congeals on the top. Skim and discard. Remove meat from the bones, dice and reserve.

Bring defatted broth to a boil. Add barley and simmer for 30 minutes. Add chopped onion, sliced celery, carrots, reserved meat and pepper. Simmer another 30 to 40 minutes.

Nutrient Analysis: 1 cup

Calories: 81   Fat: 1.5 g   Cholesterol: 20 mg

Sodium: 129 mg   Dietary Fiber: 1.4 g

Calcium: 12 mg

Diabetic Exchange: ½ lean meat, 2 vegetable

CONDENSED CREAM SOUP MIX

Use as a casserole sauce mix or as a base for cream soups such as mushroom, asparagus, broccoli, cauliflower, etc. A can of Campbell's Cream of Potato Soup contains 1860 mg sodium while our equivalent contains 152 mg sodium.

3 cups; equivalent to 9 cans of condensed cream soup

2 cups non-fat dry milk powder
¾ cup cornstarch
¼ cup sodium-reduced, chicken-flavored bouillon granules
2 tablespoons dried onion flakes
1 teaspoon dried basil, crushed
1 teaspoon whole thyme
½ teaspoon pepper

Mix dry milk, cornstarch, bouillon granules, onion flakes, basil, thyme and pepper. Store in an airtight container.

To substitute for one can condensed soup, combine ⅓ cup dry mix with 1¼ cup water. Heat to boiling and cook and stir until thickened.

Nutrient Analysis: equivalent to 1 can condensed soup

Calories: 156   Fat: 0.9 g   Cholesterol: 5 mg

Sodium: 152 mg   Calcium: 34 mg

Diabetic Exchange: 1 skim milk, 1 starch

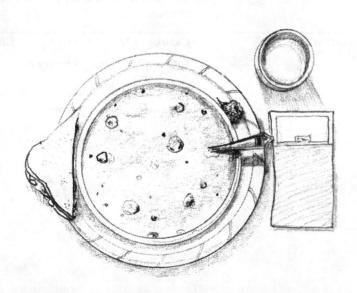

CREAM OF MOREL SOUP

Should you be fortunate enough to procure fresh or dried morels, there are none finer for mushroom soup.

4 portions

10 dried morels
1½ tablespoons margarine
  2 tablespoons finely chopped onion
  2 tablespoons finely chopped celery
  1 teaspoon dried parsley flakes or 1 tablespoon chopped fresh parsley
  1 tablespoon flour
1½ cups water (reserve water from soaking morels)
  4 teaspoons low-sodium, chicken-flavored bouillon granules
    freshly ground pepper to taste
1½ cups evaporated skim milk
1½ tablespoons sherry
    parsley or chives for garnish

Soak dried morels in tepid water until soft (about an hour). Drain, reserving liquid. Squeeze out remaining water and chop stems and caps.

In a medium saucepan, heat margarine and sauté onion, celery and parsley until limp. Add mushrooms to vegetable mixture and sauté a few more minutes. Stir in flour.

Add water, bouillon granules and pepper. Bring to a boil and simmer 15 to 20 minutes. Remove from heat and let stand several hours.

Just before serving, add the milk and sherry and heat. Serve steaming hot, garnished with chopped fresh parsley or chives.

Nutrient Analysis: 1 portion

Calories: 171   Fat: 4.9 g   Cholesterol: 4 mg

Sodium: 200 mg   Dietary Fiber: 1.1 g

Calcium: 282 mg

Diabetic Exchange: 1 low-fat milk, 2 vegetable

CREAM OF BROCCOLI SOUP

A good basic recipe for any cream of vegetable soup such as asparagus, cauliflower, carrot, etc.

8 portions

1 bunch fresh broccoli
1 tablespoon margarine
⅓ cup finely chopped onion
4 cups CHICKEN STOCK,
   (page 329).
1 bay leaf
⅛ teaspoon whole thyme
⅛ teaspoon dried tarragon,
   crushed
⅛ teaspoon dried rosemary,
   crushed
½ teaspoon salt
¼ teaspoon white pepper
1 large potato, peeled and thinly
   sliced
1 12-ounce can evaporated skim
   milk

Remove tips of broccoli florets and reserve. Peel broccoli stalks and slice very thinly into rounds.

In large saucepan, melt margarine. Sauté onions slowly until translucent.

Add chicken stock and herbs to saucepan and bring to a boil. Add potato and broccoli stalks to broth and simmer, covered, 20 minutes or until vegetables are tender.

Reserve ½ cup of florets. Add the remainder to the soup and simmer 5 minutes.

In a blender or processor, purée the soup mixture. Return to saucepan. Add skim milk and heat to simmering.

In a separate small pan, blanch reserved ½ cup of florets in boiling water for one minute. Plunge florets into cold water, drain and chop coarsely. Add to soup just before serving.

Nutrient Analysis: 1 portion

Calories: 103	Fat: 1.8 g	Cholesterol: 0
Sodium: 229 mg	Dietary Fiber: 1.1 g	
Calcium: 160 mg		

Diabetic Exchange: 1 skim milk, 1 vegetable

CREAMY ASPARAGUS SOUP

About 6 cups

1 cup chopped onion
½ cup chopped celery
1 tablespoon margarine
2 cups cooked fresh asparagus or
   1 10-ounce package frozen
   asparagus
1 cup cooked white rice
1 cup CHICKEN STOCK,
   (page 329).
3 cups evaporated skim milk
   nutmeg
   freshly ground pepper

In a heavy 3- to 4-quart saucepan, cook onion and celery in margarine until soft, about 5 minutes. Reserve ⅓ cup asparagus. Chop and set aside.

Add remaining asparagus, rice and stock. Cover and simmer 10 minutes. Purée in batches in food processor or blender. Return to saucepan. Add milk and reserved asparagus. Heat to boiling point. Season with nutmeg and pepper.

Nutrient Analysis: 1 cup

Calories: 182	Fat: 2.4 g	Cholesterol: 5 mg
Sodium: 181 mg	Dietary Fiber: 0.8 g	
Calcium: 387 mg		

Diabetic Exchange: ½ low-fat milk, 1 starch,
2 vegetable

LEEK AND POTATO SOUP (VICHYSSOISE)

About 7½ cups

3 medium leeks
1 medium onion, thinly sliced
1 tablespoon margarine
4 medium potatoes, peeled and
   thinly sliced
4 cups CHICKEN STOCK,
   (page 329) or 3 tablespoons
   low-sodium, chicken-flavored
   bouillon in 4 cups water
1½ cups evaporated skim milk
¼ teaspoon salt
¼ teaspoon white pepper
   chopped chives for garnish

Clean leeks (separate each piece, for leeks can be very sandy). Mince the white part.

In a medium saucepan, sauté leeks and onion in margarine until soft but not brown.

Add potatoes and chicken stock and simmer, covered, 15 minutes or until the vegetables are very tender.

Purée in small batches in blender or food processor. Return to saucepan. Add milk, salt and pepper.

Serve either hot or very cold garnished with chopped chives.

Nutrient Analysis: 1 cup

Calories: 138	Fat: 1.7 g	Cholesterol: 2 mg
Sodium: 161 mg	Dietary Fiber: 0.9 g	
Calcium: 160 mg		

Diabetic Exchange: ½ skim milk, 1 starch,
1 vegetable

CURRIED SQUASH AND APPLE BISQUE

4 portions

1 medium acorn squash
1½ tablespoons margarine
¾ cup chopped onion
1 large apple, diced
2 teaspoons CURRY POWDER,
   (page 380).
½ cup apple cider
4 teaspoons low-sodium, chicken-
   flavored bouillon granules
1½ cups water
1½ cups evaporated skim milk
   apple slices for garnish
   paprika or cayenne pepper

Preheat oven to 375°. Prick squash all over with fork and place in a baking pan. Bake 1 hour or until tender; cool. Cut in half and remove seeds. Scoop out flesh and set aside.

In medium saucepan, melt margarine. Stir in onion, apple and curry powder. Cook 5 minutes, stirring frequently.

Add squash, cider, bouillon granules and water. Heat to boiling. Reduce heat, cover and simmer 30 minutes or until vegetables and apples are tender.

In food processor or blender, purée in small batches until smooth. Return to saucepan and stir in milk. Cook over low heat until heated through.

Serve garnished with apple slices, paprika or cayenne pepper.

Nutrient Analysis: 1 portion

Calories: 200   Fat: 5.2 g   Cholesterol: 4 mg

Sodium: 163 mg   Dietary Fiber: 3.1 g

Calcium: 331 mg

Diabetic Exchange: ½ low-fat milk, 1 starch,
½ fruit

HEARTY CHOWDER

8 portions

4 ounces Canadian bacon, diced
1 tablespoon margarine
1 medium onion, chopped
2 cups water
1 cup diced celery (with leaves)
1 medium potato, diced
2 carrots, diced
3 sprigs parsley, chopped
2 tablespoons low-sodium,
   chicken-flavored bouillon
   granules
¼ teaspoon dried basil, crushed
2 dashes Tabasco sauce
  freshly ground pepper to taste
¼ cup flour
3 cups skim milk
1 7-ounce can clams, drained
1 15.5-ounce can corn, drained

In a heavy saucepan, lightly sauté the Canadian bacon in margarine.

Add the onions and cook until onions are wilted.

Add the water, celery, potato, carrots, parsley, bouillon granules, basil, Tabasco and pepper. Bring to a boil and simmer until the vegetables are tender (about 15 minutes).

Dissolve the flour in one cup of milk. Add to vegetable mixture and bring to a boil. Cook a minute or two until chowder is slightly thickened. Add the remaining milk, clams and corn. Heat thoroughly and serve.

Nutrient Analysis: 1 portion

Calories: 195	Fat: 4 g	Cholesterol: 17 mg
Sodium: 268 mg	Dietary Fiber: 1.3 g	
Calcium: 148 mg	Omega-3: 12 mg	

Diabetic Exchange: ½ skim milk, 1 lean meat,
*   1 starch, 1 vegetable*

ONE-OF-IT-SOUP

*An often-requested recipe shared by the food editor of **Tokyo Asahi Evening News**.*

About 6 cups

1 banana
1 apple, cored
1 potato
1 onion
1 large celery rib
2 cups CHICKEN STOCK,
   (page 329).
½ teaspoon curry powder
1½-2 cups evaporated skim milk
   shredded carrots
   chives, parsley or lemon thyme

Quarter the banana, apple, potato, onion and celery. Place in a medium saucepan with chicken stock. Bring to a boil. Reduce heat and simmer until the vegetables are soft.

Put vegetable mixture through food mill or blend in blender or food processor and return to saucepan. Add curry and milk (start with 1½ cup).

Serve hot or cold garnished with shredded carrots and chives, parsley or lemon thyme.

Nutrient Analysis: 1 cup

Calories: 132	Fat: 0.4 g	Cholesterol: 3 mg
Sodium: 108 mg	Calcium: 260 mg	

Diabetic Exchange: ½ skim milk, ½ starch,
1 vegetable, ½ fruit

BLACK BEAN SOUP

This soup is very black. The yogurt and green onion garnish provides a colorful contrast.

8 portions

1 pound dried black beans, navy beans or red beans
8 cups water
1 tablespoon vegetable oil
1 medium onion, diced
2 carrots, diced
1 teaspoon salt
¼ teaspoon ground nutmeg
2 tablespoons lemon juice
½ cup plain low-fat yogurt
2 green onions, sliced

Rinse beans and place in Dutch oven or large saucepan with water. Cover and let stand overnight. (Or heat to boiling and boil 2 minutes; cover and let stand 1 hour).

In small skillet, heat oil. Add onion and carrots; sauté until crisp-tender. Stir into beans with salt and nutmeg. Heat to boiling; reduce heat to low and simmer, covered, 1½ to 2 hours or until beans are very tender. Stir occasionally.

Spoon 2 cups of bean mixture into food processor or blender. Process or blend until finely chopped and almost smooth. Pour into large bowl and repeat with remaining beans. Stir in lemon juice.

To serve, spoon steaming soup into soup bowls and top each serving with 1 tablespoon yogurt and sliced green onions.

Nutrient Analysis: 1 portion

Calories: 231   *Fat: 2.7 g*   *Cholesterol: 0*

Sodium: 325 mg   *Dietary Fiber: 14.9 g*

Calcium: 118 mg

Diabetic Exchange: 2½ starch, ½ fat

CHICKEN LENTIL SOUP

First Prize Heart's Delight Recipe Contest - Junior Division

8 portions

2½ pounds chicken, skinned, and
    cut in pieces
1½ cups lentils
 ½ cup split peas
 3 quarts water
 1 cup chopped celery
 1 cup chopped carrots
 ½ cup chopped onion
 1 teaspoon parsley flakes
 ½ teaspoon whole thyme
 ½ teaspoon pepper
 ½ teaspoon ground turmeric
 ¼ teaspoon ground sage
 ¼ teaspoon poultry seasoning

The night before serving, bring skinned, defatted chicken, lentils and split peas to a boil in water. Reduce heat to low, cover and simmer 2 hours.

Remove chicken; bone, dice, and refrigerate. Cool soup and refrigerate.

The next day, remove and discard any congealed fat. Add celery, carrots, onion, parsley, thyme, pepper, turmeric, sage and poultry seasoning. Simmer 1¼ hours.

Just before serving, add diced chicken and heat thoroughly.

Nutrient Analysis: 1 portion

Calories: 212   Fat: 1.4 g   Cholesterol: 33 mg

Sodium: 69 mg   Dietary Fiber: 6.6 g

Calcium: 49 mg

Diabetic Exchange: 2 lean meat, 1 starch,
1 vegetable

LENTIL SOUP VARIATION
VEGETARIAN LENTIL OR SPLIT PEA SOUP

6 portions

Use LENTIL SOUP recipe omitting the chicken and decreasing the water to 2 quarts. Use either 2 cups lentils or 2 cups split peas and add 5 tablespoons low-sodium chicken- or beef-flavored bouillon granules if desired.

Nutrient Analysis: 1 portion

Calories: 231   Fat: 0.8 g   Cholesterol: 0

Sodium: 43 mg   Dietary Fiber: 11.4 g

Calcium: 67 mg

Diabetic Exchange: 2½ starch, 1 vegetable

BEEF LENTIL SOUP

1 pound lean beef stew meat,
   diced
2 tablespoons margarine
1 medium onion, chopped
2 celery ribs, chopped
2 quarts water
1 10-ounce package frozen leaf
   spinach
1 whole tomato
¾ cup lentils
½ teaspoon salt
   pepper to taste
3 tablespoons red wine vinegar

Nutrient Analysis: 1 portion

8 portions

In a Dutch oven, brown beef in margarine. Add onions and celery and sauté lightly.

Add water, spinach, tomato, lentils, salt and pepper. Simmer for 2 to 3 hours.

To serve, ladle soup into individual serving bowls. Stir a teaspoon of vinegar into each bowl just before serving.

Calories: 172   Fat: 5.7 g   Cholesterol: 41 mg

Sodium: 205 mg   Dietary Fiber: 3.6 g

Calcium: 58 mg

*Diabetic Exchange: 1 medium-fat meat, ½ starch,
              2 vegetable*

CREOLE-STYLE LENTIL STEW

8 portions

1	tablespoon vegetable oil
½	pound lean boneless pork, cut in ½" cubes
2	garlic cloves, minced
1	large onion, chopped
4	cups water
1	cup dry lentils, rinsed
1	6-ounce can no-salt-added tomato paste
2	bay leaves
1	10-ounce package frozen okra
2	medium tomatoes, peeled and chopped
2	teaspoons sodium-reduced Worcestershire sauce
1	teaspoon dried oregano, crushed
1	teaspoon sugar
½	teaspoon cayenne pepper
¼	teaspoon salt
2	cups cooked rice or bulgur wheat
4	teaspoons vinegar

In a Dutch oven or large saucepan, heat oil. Add pork cubes, garlic and onion and cook until meat is browned and onion is tender.

Stir in water, lentils, tomato paste and bay leaves. Bring to a boil; reduce heat, cover and simmer about an hour, stirring occasionally.

Add okra, tomatoes, Worcestershire sauce, oregano, sugar, pepper and salt. Simmer another 30 minutes or until lentils and okra are tender.

To serve, ladle mixture into individual soup bowls. Stir ½ teaspoon of vinegar into each serving. Top with a mound of rice or bulgur.

Nutrient Analysis: 1 portion

Calories: 238   Fat: 4.7 g   Cholesterol: 17 mg

Sodium: 115 mg   Dietary Fiber: 4.8 g

Calcium: 70 mg

Diabetic Exchange: 1 medium-fat meat, 2 starch

HEARTY PEA SOUP

8 portions

2 tablespoons vegetable oil
1 onion, diced
2 bay leaves
1 teaspoon celery seed
1 cup dry green split peas
¼ cup barley
¾ cup dry lima beans
10 cups water
6 ounces (¾ cup) diced lean ham
1 carrot, chopped
3 ribs celery, diced
1 potato, diced
½ cup chopped fresh parsley
    dash pepper
½ teaspoon dried basil, crushed
¼ teaspoon garlic powder
¼ teaspoon whole thyme

In Dutch oven or large saucepan, heat oil. Sauté onion, bay leaves and celery seed until onion is soft.

Add peas, barley, lima beans and water and bring to a boil. Reduce heat, cover and simmer for about 1½ hours.

Add ham, carrot, celery, potato, parsley, pepper, basil, garlic powder and thyme. Simmer for another 30 to 45 minutes. Remove bay leaf before serving.

Nutrient Analysis: 1 portion

Calories: 251   Fat: 5.2 g   Cholesterol: 10 mg

Sodium: 334 mg   Dietary Fiber: 4.9 g

Calcium: 41 mg

*Diabetic Exchange: 1 medium-fat meat, 2 starch,
                1 vegetable*

ORIENTAL HOT POT

The Oriental fondue (a tradition dating back to the 13th century) is an attractive, low-calorie, low-cholesterol choice for entertaining. You will need: a fondue pot or saucepan on a hot plate, wooden skewers, chopsticks or fondue forks, individual soup or rice bowls for each guest, platters for uncooked foods, spoons for broths, and dipping bowls for soy sauce, sherry or other sauces such as: ORIENTAL SWEET-SOUR, PLUM, SWEET-SOUR MUSTARD, all found in the Dressings & Sauces Section.

FONDUE

5 cups sodium-reduced chicken or beef broth

½ pound lean beef, cut into paper thin slices (partially frozen meat is easiest to slice)

½ pound boneless, skinless chicken, cut into thin slices

½ pound raw fish or seafood, cut into bite-sized pieces

12 whole small mushrooms

1 8-ounce cake of tofu cut into bite-sized pieces

6 green onions (green tops only) cut into 2" lengths (reserve the white part)

24 spinach or kale leaves, washed and trimmed of their stems

4 cups hot cooked rice

SOUP

¼ cup chopped cilantro or fresh parsley

1 teaspoon minced garlic

1 tablespoon grated fresh ginger

⅛ teaspoon cayenne pepper

1 cup shredded Chinese cabbage reserved white parts of green onions, diced

4 ounces bean threads or cellophane noodles, soaked for 30 minutes in warm water, drained and cut into 3 inch pieces

6 portions

Arrange raw beef, chicken, fish, mushrooms, tofu, onion tops and spinach or kale attractively on a platter.

Fill cooking pot two-thirds full of broth (have extra broth ready to add if necessary during cooking). Heat broth to boiling and place in center of table over heat source.

Using skewers, chopsticks or fondue forks, dip pieces of raw meat, beef, chicken, fish and vegetable into the boiling broth, cooking to the desired doneness. Serve with rice and dipping sauces.

When the meat and vegetables have been consumed, add to the broth: cilantro or parsley, garlic, ginger, pepper, cabbage, onion and noodles. Stir and cook for a minute or two. Serve the soup in individual bowls.

Nutrient Analysis: 1 portion

Calories: 388	Fat: 7.7 g	Cholesterol: 78 mg
Sodium: 99 mg	Dietary Fiber: 2.5 g	
Calcium: 128 mg	Omega-3: 190 mg	

Diabetic Exchange: 3 lean meat, 2 starch, 2 vegetable

PEACH AND CANTALOUPE SOUP

6 portions

1 medium ripe cantaloupe,
    peeled, seeded and cubed
1 medium ripe peach, peeled,
    pitted and cubed
½ cup dry white wine
¼ cup orange juice
1 tablespoon sugar
1½ cups buttermilk
    fresh peach slices

Place cantaloupe, peach, wine, orange juice and sugar in food processor or blender. Process or blend until almost smooth.

Add buttermilk and process until well blended. Refrigerate several hours or overnight to blend flavors.

To serve, pour into chilled bowls and garnish with sliced peaches.

Nutrient Analysis: 1 portion

Calories: 100   Fat: 0.8 g   Cholesterol: 2 mg

Sodium: 73 mg   Dietary Fiber: 1.6 g

Calcium: 88 mg

Diabetic Exchange: ½ skim milk, 1 fruit

MINTED PEA SOUP

The mint is a must! Good heated, also.

4 portions

2 tablespoons chopped onion
½ cup shredded Boston lettuce
1 10-ounce package frozen tiny
    baby peas
1 sprig fresh mint (18 leaves)
    dash nutmeg
1 tablespoon low-sodium,
    chicken-flavored bouillon
    granules
1½ cups water
½ cup buttermilk

In a medium saucepan, combine onion, lettuce, peas, mint, nutmeg, bouillon granules and water. Heat to boiling; reduce heat, cover and simmer 15 minutes or until vegetables are very tender.

Place soup in food processor or blender and purée until smooth. Strain, pressing out all the liquid.

Stir in buttermilk and refrigerate several hours or overnight

Nutrient Analysis: 1 portion

Calories: 81   Fat: 1.2 g   Cholesterol: 0

Sodium: 100 mg   Dietary Fiber: 3.3 g

Calcium: 56 mg

Diabetic Exchange: 1 starch

COOL SHRIMP SOUP

This is wonderful for lunch on a hot summer day.

8 portions

1 large cucumber, peeled and
   seeded
6 green onions, chopped, with
   some of the green tops
12 sprigs fresh dill, chopped, or ½
   teaspoon dried dill weed
   freshly ground pepper to taste
1 pound shrimp, fresh or frozen,
   cooked, cleaned and deveined
   juice of one lemon
1 quart buttermilk
   paprika
   parsley sprigs

Slice the cucumber into the bottom of a 4-quart, covered ceramic or glass casserole.

On top of cucumbers, layer onions, then dill and finally, shrimp. Grind on pepper to taste and sprinkle lemon juice over shrimp. Pour buttermilk over other ingredients and cover.

Refrigerate overnight or at least 6 hours. Just before serving, garnish with paprika and parsley sprigs.

Nutrient Analysis: 1 portion

Calories: 111   Fat: 1.6 g   Cholesterol: 90 mg

Sodium: 209 mg   Dietary Fiber: 0.5 g

Calcium: 189 mg   Omega-3: 285 mg

Diabetic Exchange: ½ skim milk, 1 lean meat,
*   1 vegetable*

GAZPACHO

This is the traditional Spanish gazpacho thickened with bread. Make "instant gazpacho" from left-over greens and vegetable salads. In food-processor or blender, process left-over salad with sodium-reduced tomato or V-8 juice.

6 portions

4 ripe tomatoes, peeled and chopped
½ cucumber, halved, seeded and chopped
1 rib celery, chopped
2 crosswise slices onion
½ green pepper, chopped
1 garlic clove
3 tablespoons white vinegar
2 tablespoons olive oil
3 slices French bread
1 cup water
1 cup tomato juice
⅛ teaspoon Tabasco sauce

GARNISH
½ green pepper, diced
½ cucumber, seeded and diced
1 small tomato, peeled and chopped
¼ cup diced celery
½ cup croutons

In a large bowl, mix tomatoes, cucumber, celery, onion, green pepper, garlic, vinegar, olive oil, French bread, water, tomato juice and Tabasco.

In a blender or food processor, purée half of the mixture and then the other half. Chill thoroughly.

Serve the soup in individual bowls and pass small dishes of diced green pepper, cucumber, tomato, celery and croutons for garnish.

Nutrient Analysis: 1 portion

Calories: 123	Fat: 5.5 g	Cholesterol: 0
Sodium: 279 mg	Dietary Fiber: 0.8 g	
Calcium: 30 mg		

Diabetic Exchange: 1 starch, 1 fat

CURRIED PEACH SOUP

6 portions

1 pound ripe fresh peaches (4 large), peeled and pitted
½ cup chopped onion
¾ teaspoon curry powder
1 bay leaf
2 tablespoons margarine
2 tablespoons whole-wheat flour
2 cups CHICKEN STOCK, (page 329). or 2 tablespoons low-sodium, chicken-flavored bouillon granules dissolved in 2 cups water
   dash of white pepper
¼ cup plain low-fat yogurt
   fresh mint leaves

Cut up peaches and purée in blender.

Sauté onion, curry powder and bay leaf in margarine for 3 minutes or until onions are tender.

Remove from heat and stir in flour until smooth. Return to heat. Gradually add chicken stock, pepper and peaches. Bring to a boil, reduce heat and simmer 3 minutes. Remove bay leaf and discard.

Chill soup.

Serve chilled with a dollop of yogurt and fresh mint leaf garnish.

Nutrient Analysis: 1 portion

Calories: 96	Fat: 4.4 g	Cholesterol: 0
Sodium: 51 mg	Dietary Fiber: 2.2 g	
Calcium: 31 mg		

Diabetic Exchange: 1 fruit, 1 fat

DATE SANDWICHES

For canapés, cut date sandwiches into small triangles and garnish with a slice of green pepper or sprig of parsley.

6 sandwiches

3 tablespoons margarine
3 tablespoons honey
3 cups shredded lettuce
1 cup sliced, pitted dates
½ cup thinly sliced celery
½ cup calorie-reduced mayonnaise
2 teaspoons lemon juice
12 slices whole-grain bread

In a small bowl, beat together margarine and honey until creamy.

In a medium bowl, toss shredded lettuce with dates, celery, mayonnaise and lemon juice.

Spread each slice of bread with honey mixture. Top with lettuce-date filling and another slice of bread. Press lightly and cut in half.

Nutrient Analysis: 1 sandwich

Calories: 401   Fat: 14.7 g   Cholesterol: 8 mg

Sodium: 319 mg   Dietary Fiber: 3.4 g

Calcium: 122 mg

Diabetic Exchange: 2 starch, 2 fruit, 3 fat

BETTER PEANUT BUTTER

Extra-good on plain or toasted 7-grain bread.

About 1¼ cups

2 cups roasted, unsalted peanuts
3 tablespoons vegetable oil
1 tablespoon honey

Place peanuts in food processor equipped with metal blade. Process on high until peanuts form a ball which will whirl briefly around bowl before breaking apart (about 2 minutes).

Remove cover and scrape down. Replace cover and continue processing, adding oil in a steady stream.

Add honey and blend until smooth and creamy.

Nutrient Analysis: 1 tablespoon

Calories: 103	*Fat: 9 g*	*Cholesterol: 0*
Sodium: 2 mg	*Dietary Fiber: 0.4 g*	
Calcium: 12 mg		

Diabetic Exchange: 1 high fat meat

CARROT AND CHEESE SANDWICHES #1

4 generous open-faced sandwiches

1 cup shredded part-skim
    mozzarella cheese
1 cup shredded carrots
¼ cup chopped nuts
2 tablespoons raisins
4 tablespoons calorie-reduced
    mayonnaise
4 slices whole-grain bread

In a bowl, combine cheese, carrots, nuts and raisins. Moisten with mayonnaise. Spread filling on bread.

Nutrient Analysis: 1 sandwich

Calories: 274	*Fat: 15 g*	*Cholesterol: 22 mg*
Sodium: 297 mg	*Dietary Fiber: 2.1 g*	
Calcium: 248 mg		

Diabetic Exchange: 1 starch, 1 vegetable, 1 fat

CARROT AND CHEESE SANDWICHES #2

4 open-faced sandwiches

1 large carrot, shredded
1 cup shredded part-skim farmer
   cheese
2 tablespoons finely diced green
   pepper
1 tablespoon diced onion
½ cucumber, diced
2 tablespoons calorie-reduced
   mayonnaise
2 tablespoons plain low-fat yogurt
1 tablespoon Italian dressing
4 slices whole-grain bread
   fresh sprouts

In a medium bowl, combine carrot, cheese, green pepper, onion and cucumber.

In a small bowl, stir together mayonnaise, yogurt and Italian dressing. Toss vegetable-cheese mixture with dressing and spread on bread. Top with sprouts.

Nutrient Analysis: 1 sandwich

Calories: 218   Fat: 10.6 g   Cholesterol: 6 mg

Sodium: 299 mg   Dietary Fiber: 1 g

Calcium: 254 mg

Diabetic Exchange: 2 medium-fat meat, 1 starch,
1 vegetable

GRILLED ZUCCHINI PARMESAN SANDWICHES

4 open-faced sandwiches

½ cup chopped onion
1 garlic clove, crushed
½ teaspoon dried basil, crushed
½ teaspoon dried oregano, crushed
¼ teaspoon salt
   freshly ground pepper to taste
2 tablespoons olive oil
2 cups grated fresh zucchini
4 slices whole-grain bread, toasted
1 tomato, thinly sliced
4 tablespoons Parmesan cheese

In a skillet, sauté onion, garlic, basil, oregano, salt and pepper in olive oil until onion is translucent.

Add zucchini and sauté until soft.

Spread vegetable mixture on toast. Top each sandwich with thin slices of tomato and a sprinkling of 1 tablespoon Parmesan. Broil until cheese turns golden.

Nutrient Analysis: 1 sandwich

Calories: 206   Fat: 10.2 g   Cholesterol: 7 mg

Sodium: 214 mg   Dietary Fiber: 1.6 g

Calcium: 168

Diabetic Exchange: 1 lean meat, 1 starch,
1 vegetable, 1 fat

HOT CHICKEN POCKETS

12 half pockets

¾ cup plain low-fat yogurt
½ cucumber, peeled and seeded
½ teaspoon dill weed
2 whole chicken breasts, boned and skinned
1½ tablespoons vegetable oil
¼ teaspoon garlic powder
6 pocket breads
6 radishes, thinly sliced
2 green onions, thinly sliced

In blender or food processor, combine yogurt, cucumber and dill weed. Blend until smooth. Set aside.

Slice chicken breasts across the muscle ¼" thick. Slice these into ¼"-wide matchsticks.

In a heavy skillet, heat the oil. Add the garlic powder and chicken strips. Cook and stir over high heat until no pink remains.

Cut pockets in half. Fill with chicken, radishes and onion. Top with sauce and serve immediately.

Nutrient Analysis: One-half pocket

Calories: 181   Fat: 6.9 g   Cholesterol: 32 mg

Sodium: 40 mg   Dietary Fiber: 2.8 g

Calcium: 58 mg

Diabetic Exchange: 2 lean meat, 1 starch

TOFU SALAD SANDWICHES

Described by one fan as "an egg salad sandwich only better." Tofu, once found only in Oriental food stores, is now available in the produce section of most grocery stores.

6 sandwiches

1 16-ounce package tofu	In a medium bowl, crumble tofu with a fork or pastry blender to small lumps.
¼ cup calorie-reduced mayonnaise	
1 tablespoon prepared mustard	
1 teaspoon sodium-reduced Worcestershire sauce	Stir in mayonnaise, mustard and Worcestershire sauce.
⅛ teaspoon ground cumin	
⅛ teaspoon ground turmeric	Sprinkle cumin, turmeric and paprika over salad mixture. Stir well.
¼ teaspoon paprika	
1 green onion, minced	Add green onion, carrot, celery and green pepper; stir.
¼ cup shredded carrot	
¼ cup minced celery	
2 tablespoons minced green pepper	
12 slices whole-wheat bread	Divide filling between six slices of bread and spread to edges. Top salad with generous layer of sprouts and another slice of bread. Cut in half to serve.
2 cups fresh sprouts (bean, lentil or alfalfa)	

Nutrient Analysis: 1 sandwich

Calories: 269	Fat: 7 g	Cholesterol: 5 mg
Sodium: 238 mg	Dietary Fiber: 2.1 g	
Calcium: 200 mg		

Diabetic Exchange: 1 medium-fat meat, 2 starch, 1 vegetable

VEGETABLE AND CHEESE POCKETS

12 half pockets

6 cups shredded lettuce or a combination of lettuce and fresh sprouts (alfalfa or bean)

1½ cups shredded part-skim farmer or mozzarella cheese

2 cups vegetables (⅓ cup each of 6 of the following or any proportion you choose)

continued on next page

VEGETABLE AND CHEESE POCKETS (con't)

⅓ cup diced green pepper
⅓ cup sliced green onion
⅓ cup sliced radishes
⅓ cup shredded carrots
⅓ cup diced cucumber
⅓ cup diced celery
⅓ cup seeded, chopped tomato
⅓ cup sliced fresh mushrooms
⅓ cup unsalted sunflower nuts

CREAMY YOGURT DRESSING

3 tablespoons calorie-reduced mayonnaise
2 tablespoons plain low-fat yogurt
1 teaspoon lemon juice
½ teaspoon mixed, crushed herbs (oregano, basil, marjoram, savory)
                 OR
6 tablespoons DILLED VINAIGRETTE DRESSING* (see page 158).
6 pocket breads

In a large bowl, combine shredded lettuce and sprouts, cheese, and your selection of vegetables.

Combine mayonnaise, yogurt, lemon juice and herbs. Toss with vegetables.

Cut pockets in half and fill.

*If using DILLED VINAIGRETTE fill pockets and then drizzle ½ tablespoon dressing over vegetables in pockets.

Nutrient Analysis: One-half pocket

	Creamy	Dilled
Calories:	153	173
Fat:	6 g	8.3 g
Cholesterol:	10 mg	8 mg
Sodium:	97 mg	73 mg
Dietary Fiber:	3.4 g	3.4 g
Calcium:	135 mg	130 mg
Diabetic Exchange:	1 lean meat	1 lean meat
	½ starch	½ starch
	2 vegetable	2 vegetable
		1 fat

MEAT OR SEAFOOD POCKETS

8 half pockets

2 cups diced cooked chicken,
   pork, beef or seafood
1½ cup shredded lettuce
1 cup alfalfa or bean sprouts
1 medium tomato, seeded and
   chopped
2 green onions with tops, thinly
   sliced
1 cup shredded part-skim farmer
   or mozzarella cheese
3 tablespoons olive oil
2 tablespoons red wine vinegar
1 teaspoon parsley flakes
¼ teaspoon dried basil, crushed
¼ teaspoon dried oregano,
   crushed
¼ teaspoon garlic powder
¼ teaspoon dry mustard
¼ teaspoon sugar
⅛ teaspoon pepper
4 whole-wheat pocket breads
   lemon wedges

In medium bowl, combine meat or seafood, lettuce, sprouts, tomato, green onion and cheese.

In a jar with a tight fitting lid, combine oil, vinegar, parsley, basil, oregano, garlic powder, mustard, sugar and pepper. Shake well and toss with meat and vegetables.

Cut pockets in half and spoon mixture into bread. Garnish each with a lemon wedge.

Nutrient Analysis: One-half pocket

Calories: 210   Fat: 9.5 g   Cholesterol: 38 mg

Sodium: 96 mg   Dietary Fiber: 2.6 g

Calcium: 123 mg

*Diabetic Exchange: 2 lean meat, ½ starch,
   2 vegetable*

TASTE O' THE SEA SANDWICHES

4 open-faced sandwiches

1 7-ounce can water-packed tuna
  fish (drained)
½ cup chopped roasted, unsalted
  peanuts
½ cup finely chopped tomato
¼ cup chopped green onion
¼ cup calorie-reduced mayonnaise
2 tablespoons lemon juice
2 tablespoons chopped fresh
  parsley
1 teaspoon dried basil, crushed
1 teaspoon dried marjoram,
  crushed
4 slices whole-grain bread

In a medium mixing bowl, combine tuna, peanuts, tomato, green onion, mayonnaise, lemon juice, parsley, basil and marjoram. Mix well.

Spread tuna mixture on bread slices.

Nutrient Analysis: 1 sandwich

Calories: 307	*Fat: 15 g*	*Cholesterol: 6 mg*
Sodium: 325 mg	*Dietary Fiber: 1.6 g*	
Calcium: 72 mg	*Omega-3: 180 mg*	

Diabetic Exchange: 2 medium-fat meat, 1 starch,
1 vegetable, 1 fat

HOT TUNA PINEAPPLE TOAST

4 open-faced sandwiches

1 6½-ounce can water-packed
  tuna, drained
1 8-ounce can unsweetened
  crushed pineapple, drained
¼ cup calorie-reduced mayonnaise
4 slices whole-wheat or rye bread

Combine tuna, pineapple and mayonnaise. Mix well.

Spread mixture over bread and place on baking sheet. Bake until hot. Serve immediately.

Oven: 450°
Time: 5 minutes

Nutrient Analysis: 1 sandwich

Calories: 225	*Fat: 6.2 g*	*Cholesterol: 6 mg*
Sodium: 320 mg	*Dietary Fiber: 1.2 g*	
Calcium: 57 mg	*Omega-3: 160 mg*	

Diabetic Exchange: 2 lean meat, 1 starch, ½ fruit

TOSTADAS

12 tostadas

FRIJOLES (REFRIED BEANS)
1½ cups dry pinto beans
5 cups water or unsalted stock
1 cup chopped onions
2 medium tomatoes, chopped
1 garlic clove, minced
1 teaspoon chili powder
   pinch cayenne pepper
2 tablespoons vegetable oil

SALSA
6 medium tomatoes, seeded and chopped
1 cup finely chopped onions
1 teaspoon dried oregano, crushed
½ teaspoon minced garlic
1 teaspoon honey
½ cup red wine vinegar

TOPPING
3 cups shredded lettuce
¾ cup chopped green onion
¾ cup shredded part-skim mozzarella cheese
¾ cup plain low-fat yogurt, optional

TORTILLAS
12 corn tortillas
   oil

FRIJOLES: Soak beans in 5 cups of water overnight. Cook in the water with half the onion, half of the tomato, half the garlic, the chili powder and the cayenne until tender, about 3 hours.

In a large frying pan, heat 2 tablespoons vegetable oil. Sauté the remaining onions and garlic.

Add the remaining tomatoes. Add beans gradually, mashing as they are added. Heat and stir until they have a nice consistency.

SALSA: In a medium bowl, combine tomatoes, onion, oregano, garlic, honey and vinegar.

TORTILLAS: Fry each tortilla in hot oil about 30 seconds on each side. Drain on paper towels.

To assemble tostadas: Spread a tortilla with about ⅓ cup frijoles. Top with ¼ cup shredded lettuce, a tablespoon of green onion, ¼ cup salsa, and a tablespoon of shredded cheese. Garnish with a tablespoon of yogurt and chopped chives if desired.

Nutrient Analysis: 1 tostada

Calories: 190   Fat: 2.7 g   Cholesterol: 4 mg

Sodium: 46 mg   Dietary Fiber: 7.4 g

Calcium: 178 mg

Diabetic Exchange: 1½ starch, 2 vegetable, ½ fat

TURKEY TACOS

12 tacos

3 tablespoons vegetable oil
1½ pounds ground turkey
¾ cup chopped onions
1 6-ounce can sodium-reduced
   tomato paste
1 6-ounce can water
¾ teaspoon ground cumin
1 tablespoon chili powder
1 teaspoon garlic powder
12 taco shells
4 ounces mozzarella cheese,
   shredded

In a large skillet, heat oil. Add turkey and chopped onion and sauté until meat loses its pink color.

Add tomato paste, water, cumin, chili powder and garlic powder. Simmer for 10 minutes.

Spoon into taco shells and garnish with cheese.

Nutrient Analysis: 1 taco

Calories: 172   Fat: 9.9 g   Cholesterol: 5 mg

Sodium: 97 mg   Dietary Fiber: 0.4 g

Calcium: 96 mg

Diabetic Exchange: 2 lean meat, ½ starch,
1 vegetable

CORN CRUST FOR PIZZA

12 x 15" crust; 20 pieces

1½ cups all-purpose flour
½ cup cornmeal
½ teaspoon baking powder
⅓ cup margarine
½ cup cold water

Sift flour, cornmeal, and baking powder into a bowl. Cut in margarine. With a fork, gradually stir in cold water adding only enough to bind the crumbly mixture together.

Turn dough onto a floured board and knead briefly. Roll out into a rectangle measuring 12 x 15". Place dough on ungreased baking sheet. Turn up edges and flute. Prick crust with tines of fork. Bake.

Add topping and return to oven to melt cheese.

Oven: 425°
Time: 12 minutes

Nutrient Analysis: 1 piece (crust only)

Calories: 76	Fat: 3.2 g	Cholesterol: 0
Sodium: 38 mg	Dietary Fiber: 0.2 g	
Calcium: 6 mg		

Diabetic Exchange: 1 starch

YEAST PIZZA CRUST #1

12" pizza crust; 8 slices

1 tablespoon or 1 package active
   dry yeast
1 cup warm water
2 tablespoons vegetable oil
¼ teaspoon salt
1 cup all-purpose flour
1 cup whole-wheat flour

In a large bowl, combine yeast and water. Add oil and salt.

Stir in the all-purpose flour. Add the whole-wheat flour gradually until the dough is no longer sticky. Knead lightly. Cover and put in a warm place to rise for 20 minutes.

Roll out crust on lightly floured surface. Place crust on pizza pan and press firmly to edges to get a good seal.

Add sauce and toppings and cheese of your choice. Bake.

Oven: 400°
Time: 20 minutes

Nutrient Analysis: 1 slice (crust only)

Calories: 146	Fat: 3.9 g	Cholesterol: 0
Sodium: 64 mg	Dietary Fiber: 1.7 g	
Calcium: 9 mg		

Diabetic Exchange: 1½ starch

YEAST PIZZA CRUST #2

VEGETABLE NUT PIZZA TOPPING, (see next page) is a winner.

Two 12" pizza crusts; 8 slices each

2 cups whole-wheat flour
2 cups all-purpose flour
1 package dry yeast
1¼ cups water
3 tablespoons margarine
2 tablespoons vegetable oil

In a large bowl, combine ¼ cup flour and yeast.

In a saucepan, heat water and margarine until very warm (120-130 degrees). Add to flour and yeast and beat 2 minutes. Stir in enough flour, alternating whole-wheat and all-purpose, to form a soft dough.

Turn out on floured board and knead 6 to 8 minutes. Place in oiled bowl. Turn dough so that it is completely coated with oil. Cover and let rise until doubled (about 50 minutes).

Punch dough down. Divide in half. On floured surface, roll out into two 12½" rounds. Press into pizza pans, forming dough over rims. Cover; let rise 30 minutes. Top with favorite pizza topping and bake.

Nutrient Analysis: 1 slice (crust only)

Calories: 148	*Fat: 4.2 g*	*Cholesterol: 0*
Sodium: 22 mg	*Dietary Fiber: 1.7 g*	
Calcium: 9 mg		

Diabetic Exchange: 1 starch, 1 fat

VEGETABLE NUT PIZZA TOPPING

2 cups shredded part-skim
   mozzarella cheese
1 teaspoon minced garlic
2 16-ounce cans sodium-reduced
   tomatoes, drained and coarsely
   chopped
1 cup chopped green pepper
½ cup chopped onion
1 teaspoon dried oregano, crushed
1 teaspoon dried basil, crushed
2 cups sliced fresh mushrooms
1 cup thinly sliced zucchini
⅔ cup unsalted cashews

Nutrient Analysis: 1 slice (topping only)

Two 12" pizzas; 16 slices

Sprinkle ¾ cup cheese over two 12" pizza crusts.

In a bowl, mix together garlic, tomatoes, green pepper, onion, oregano and basil. Spread the vegetable mixture evenly over the two pizzas.

Arrange the mushrooms and zucchini over the vegetable mixture and sprinkle with remaining cheese and cashews. Bake.

Oven: 400°
Time: 30 to 35 minutes

Calories: 86	Fat: 5.1 g	Cholesterol: 8 mg
Sodium: 76 mg	Dietary Fiber: 0.7 g	
Calcium: 112 mg		

Diabetic Exchange: 1 medium-fat meat, 1 vegetable

THREE CHEESE PIZZA TOPPING

1 15-ounce container part-skim
   ricotta cheese
1 egg, beaten
1 small zucchini, sliced
1 small red or green pepper, sliced
4 mushrooms, sliced
½ teaspoon dried oregano, crushed
8 ounces part-skim mozzarella
   cheese, shredded
¼ cup grated Parmesan cheese

Nutrient Analysis: 1 slice (topping only)

14" pizza, 16 slices

In a small bowl, combine ricotta and egg. Spoon onto a 14" pizza crust.

Arrange zucchini, pepper and mushroom slices over ricotta. Sprinkle with oregano. Bake 20 minutes.

Sprinkle pizza with mozzarella and Parmesan cheese. Bake 15 minutes more or until crust is lightly browned.

Oven: 400°
Time: 30 to 35 mintues

Calories: 181	Fat: 11.9 g	Cholesterol: 75 mg
Sodium: 228 mg	Dietary Fiber: 0.3 g	
Calcium: 332 mg		

Diabetic Exchange: 2 medium-fat meat, 1 vegetable

HEART-HEALTHY PIZZA TOPPING

12" pizza; 8 slices

1 6-ounce can sodium-reduced
   tomato paste
¼ cup water
½ teaspoon dried basil, crushed
½ teaspoon dried oregano,
   crushed
½ teaspoon garlic powder
½ teaspoon dried crushed red
   peppers
¾ cup chopped green pepper
¾ cup sliced fresh mushrooms
½ cup chopped or sliced onions
   other vegetables in season as
   desired
8 ounces shredded part-skim
   mozzarella cheese

In a bowl, mix thoroughly tomato paste, water, basil, oregano, garlic powder and red peppers. Spread evenly over an unbaked 12" pizza crust.

Layer green pepper, mushrooms, onions and other vegetables, if desired, evenly over sauce. Cover with shredded cheese. Bake.

Oven: 400°
Time: 20 minutes or until cheese is melted and crust lightly browned.

Nutrient Analysis: 1 slice (topping only)

Calories: 70   Fat: 3.6 g   Cholesterol: 13 mg

Sodium: 69 mg   Dietary Fiber: 0.3 g

Calcium: 92 mg

Diabetic Exchange: 1 lean meat, 1 vegetable

HAM HEALTHWICHES

An attractive, colorful choice for brunches or luncheons.

4 open-faced sandwiches

1 10-ounce package frozen
    chopped broccoli
½ cup chopped celery
¼ cup chopped green pepper
¼ cup chopped onion
1 hard-cooked egg, chopped
⅛ teaspoon pepper
½ package ranch-style dressing
    mix
1 cup plain low-fat yogurt
8 thin slices, sodium-reduced,
    97% fat-free ham (6 ounces)
1 tomato cut into 8 slices
4 slices thin-sliced whole-wheat
    bread

Combine broccoli, celery, green pepper, onion, egg and pepper. Combine dressing mix and yogurt.

Toss vegetables with ½ cup dressing. Chill remaining dressing.

Place 3 rounded tablespoons of vegetable mixture on each ham slice and roll up.

Arrange 2 tomato slices on each bread slice. Top with 2 ham rolls and 1 tablespoon chilled dressing. Pass remaining dressing.

Nutrient Analysis: 1 sandwich

Calories: 198   Fat: 5.3 g   Cholesterol: 92 mg

Sodium: 393 mg   Dietary Fiber: 2.7 g

Calcium: 170 mg

Diabetic Exchange: 2 lean meat, 1 starch,
*   1 vegetable*

SEASONINGS

Condiments are like old friends—
highly thought of, but often taken
for granted.

Marilyn Kaytor

SEASONINGS

We eat too much salt.

Our dependence on salt as a seasoning is not healthful. According to the guidelines for a more healthful eating pattern, we need to reduce our daily sodium intake. Fortunately, our taste for salt is acquired and it is possible to cut back on salt without feeling the pinch. In its place, the wonderful subtleties of spices and herbs remain to be discovered. The natural flavors of foods can often be masked by over-salting. These flavors can be enhanced by spices and herbs which add a whole new zest to food.

Reduce salt gradually while using more herbs and spices.

Since our appetite for salt is acquired, it is important to reduce the salt intake *gradually* allowing our taste buds to adapt to new, more subtle flavors. Here are some tips to help reduce our dependence on salt:

- Replace the salt shaker at the table with a spice shaker containing one of the many seasonings from this section. It is estimated that as much as a third of the salt we eat comes from adding salt to foods.

Tips to reduce salt intake.

- Begin to reduce foods that are noticeably salty, such as bacon, luncheon meats, hot dogs, sausage, potato chips, snack crackers, sauerkraut, olives and salted nuts. An extra bonus in reducing use of these foods is that you will also reduce the amount of fat in your diet.

- In preparing main dishes and vegetables, consider salt's actual contribution. Highly seasoned dishes generally do not need salt and the natural flavors of fresh, quickly cooked foods can stand alone or be enhanced with a little lemon juice. Be creative with spices, herbs and other flavorings.

- Become a sodium-wise food buyer. Nearly all processed foods are much higher in sodium than fresh foods. Learn to read package labels. Use Table 13 on page 44 to help you recognize sodium (and salt) contained in the foods you are purchasing. The sodium content of several foods are given in Table 14, pages 45-47 of *Cooking à la Heart*.

Due to the increased consumer demand for lower sodium products, many manufacturers are offering sodium-reduced alternatives in several types of packaged or canned foods, sauces, condiments and beverages.

Experiment with herbs and spices.

Various blends of herbs and spices complementing beef, pork, veal and other meats and certain vegetables are provided in the MEAT and VEGETABLE Sections. This section of *Cooking a la Heart* contains additional spice and herb blends. We encourage you to experiment with herbs and spices to determine which ones you like best. Begin using them in a few dishes and gradually increase, allowing your palate to be the best guide.

Fresh herbs add a particularly pleasing taste to foods and as a result their use has increased dramatically. They have become widely available in markets as well as in home gardens, where it has been found that they can be easily grown. Better yet, herbs will flourish in pots inside the home and provide attractive greenery in many a kitchen window. Either raised or purchased, herbs can be successfully dried for later use.

Rule of thumb for converting fresh herb to dried or powdered:

Use fresh herbs when they are available and dried or ground herbs when they're not. The rule of thumb for substituting one for another is:

> For every 1 Tablespoon of fresh herb, substitute 1 teaspoon dried herb or ⅓ teaspoon powdered herb.

Extended cooking diminishes the flavor of spices and herbs. They are generally added to meats, soups and stews about 45 minutes before serving and allowed to cook with the food. Spices and herbs should be added to vegetables during the last few minutes of cooking or just before serving.

The flavor in herbs and spices comes from their oils which will evaporate with time and exposure to light and/or heat. Store herbs and spices in tightly covered containers away from heat and light, keeping in mind they will not retain their freshness indefinitely. A few kernels of raw rice added to spice containers help to absorb moisture and prevent caking. It is wise to label and date your spice containers.

DESSERT SPICE BLEND

A spicy concoction to use in cakes and cookies or to sprinkle on toast.

About ⅓ cup

2 teaspoons ground cinnamon
2 teaspoons ground nutmeg
1 teaspoon ground ginger
½ teaspoon ground allspice
½ teaspoon ground cardamon
¼ teaspoon ground cloves

Mix ingredients together and store in shaker bottle for toast. Substitute mixture for spices in your favorite cookie or cake recipe.

SEASONING BLEND #1

A good "all-purpose" seasoning for meats and vegetables. Also try on broiled tomatoes.

½ cup

2 tablespoons dry mustard
2 tablespoons onion powder
2 tablespoons paprika
2 teaspoons garlic powder
2-3 teaspoons white pepper
2 teaspoons ground thyme
½ teaspoon ground basil

Blend thoroughly. Use in shaker on table. Store extra in tightly covered glass container.

SEASONING BLEND #2

An "all-purpose" seasoning guaranteed to pep up chicken, hamburger and tomato based dishes.

About ¾ cup

4 tablespoons onion powder
4 tablespoons parsley flakes, crushed
2 tablespoons garlic powder
2 tablespoons paprika
1 tablespoon ground basil

Blend thoroughly. Use in shaker on table. Store extra in tightly covered glass container.

SEASONING BLEND #3

A blend for meats, poultry and vegetables

About ½ cup

3 tablespoons onion powder
3 tablespoons dry mustard
3 tablespoons paprika
4 teaspoons white pepper

Blend thoroughly. Use in shaker on table. Store extra in tightly covered glass container.

SEASONING BLEND #4

Sprinkle this aromatic blend on grilled meats.

About ½ cup

2 tablespoons garlic powder
1 tablespoon ground basil
1 tablespoon ground anise seed
1 tablespoon ground oregano
1 tablespoon powdered lemon
   rind

Blend thoroughly. Store in tightly covered glass container.

SEASONING BLEND #5

The cumin in this blend gives a peppery hotness associated with Far Eastern and Mexican dishes.

About ½ cup

2 tablespoons dried basil
4 teaspoons dried savory
4 teaspoons celery seed
4 teaspoons ground cumin
4 teaspoons dried sage
4 teaspoons dried marjoram
2 teaspoons dried lemon thyme

Combine. Use mortar and pestle or blender to reduce to powder. Use in shaker on table. Store extra in tightly covered glass bottle.

SEASONING BLEND #6

An excellent seasoning for pork. Sprinkle on roasts or add to hamburger patties allowing time for the seasoning to permeate the meat.

About ¾ cup

4 tablespoons citric acid
2 tablespoons parsley flakes, crushed
2 tablespoons black pepper
2 tablespoons paprika
1 tablespoon garlic powder
1 tablespoon ginger powder
1 tablespoon onion powder

Mix together. Use in shaker on table. Store extra in tightly covered glass container.

SEASONING BLEND #7

About ¾ cup

1 teaspoon chili powder
2 teaspoons ground oregano
1 tablespoon garlic powder
2 teaspoons black pepper
6 tablespoons onion powder
3 tablespoons paprika
1 tablespoon poultry seasoning

Blend thoroughly. Use in shaker on table. Store extra in tightly covered glass container.

ITALIAN SEASONING BLEND

Try this in your favorite pasta sauce or in Italian meat balls.

½ cup

4 tablespoons dried parsley,
   crushed
4 teaspoons dried minced onion
1 teaspoon ground oregano
2 teaspoons dried basil, crushed
1 teaspoon ground thyme or
   marjoram
2 teaspoons celery seed
1 teaspoon garlic powder
¼ teaspoon black pepper

Blend thoroughly. Use in shaker on table. Store extra in tightly covered glass bottle.

HOMEMADE CURRY POWDER

Curry-lovers—it's worth the effort to make your own!

About 1 cup

1 tablespoon ground fenugreek
   seeds
3 tablespoons ground turmeric
4 tablespoons ground coriander
2 tablespoons ground cumin
1 tablespoon ground black
   pepper
1 tablespoon ground ginger
2 teaspoons ground cardamom
2 teaspoons ground nutmeg
2 teaspoons ground cinnamon
2 teaspoons cayenne or Spanish
   paprika
1 teaspoon ground cloves
1 teaspoon dry mustard

Mix all Seasonings together and put through a fine sieve. Store in an airtight container.

SHAKE AND MAKE

Use as a crispy coating for fish, poultry, meats and vegetables.

About ⅔ cup, enough for one chicken or several fish fillets.

⅔ cup non-fat dry milk powder
½ teaspoon pepper
½ teaspoon dry mustard
2 teaspoons paprika
2 teaspoons low-sodium, chicken-flavored bouillon granules
½ teaspoon poultry seasoning

Mix all ingredients thoroughly. Moisten meat slightly and shake in mixture. (If using chicken, remove the skin first.)

Bake according to recipe.

From
The
Heart

FRUIT DESSERTS & MORE

Winter or summer, I think the best dessert in the world, after no matter how plain or elaborate a meal, is what is at its peak of ripening from the fields and orchards.

M.F.K. Fisher

FRUITS AND FRUIT DESSERTS

Prepare desserts with less fat, sugar and calories.

Desserts are an American institution. To insist that we give up sweets to attain a healthy diet would be an unattainable goal. However, it is possible to cater to the sweet tooth without creating an upwardly mobile bathroom scale. It is also possible to prepare desserts that are delicious and nutritionally rich without excess fat, sugar, and calories.

Our guidelines in **Chapter 1** discuss maintaining desirable body weight, avoiding too much fat and limiting nutritionally-empty calories. The recipes in FRUITS AND FRUIT DESSERTS feature fruits which are low in fat and contain natural sugar. Cakes and pies are included in this section because fruits or vegetables are basic ingredients in the recipes.

Fruit Desserts

A little extra-special preparation (*Baked Pears or Berries 'n Cannoli Cream*) or an interesting, new combination, such as *Chestnut Fruit Pudding*, transforms ordinary fruit into extraordinary treats. Combinations of several different fruits make a simple and satisfying dessert.

Cakes

Cakes and pies contain fruits or vegetables as basic ingredients.

Classic cakes and crisps containing fruits or vegetables have the added bonus of supplying fiber. The two torten recipes are delicious when topped with your favorite fresh or frozen fruit.

Pies

Filling and crust recipes are printed separately to enable you to use these recipes in a variety of combinations. In matching crust and filling, take into account the fat and calorie content of both. A single pastry crust contains 140 to 160 calories and 7.5 grams of fat per slice. Adding a top crust adds another 80 to 100 calories and 6 grams of fat. Crumb crusts can be prepared with less fat than traditional pastry crusts and are somewhat lower in fat and calories. To reduce fat and calories still further, serve the fillings as crustless pies, chiffons and fruit desserts.

COOKIES, BARS, PUDDINGS & TOPPINGS

Curb the desire for sweetness by gradually reducing sugar intake.

We have modified traditional recipes for cookies, bars, puddings and toppings by reducing the sugar, limiting the fat and using unsaturated fat when needed. The desire for sweets can be curbed by gradually reducing sugar intake. You will find that reducing the sugar in most recipes by one-third to one-half and substituting unsaturated fat for shortening will affect neither the taste nor the texture of your product. (Follow the guidelines given in the *Recipe Modification Guidelines* in **Chapter 2.**) Gradually, you will find that you prefer less sugary sweets.

Cookies & Bars

Delicious and nutritionally sound treats will appeal to family and guests alike. Although our cookies and bars contain less fat, sugar and sodium than commercial or traditional home-baked varieties, cookie monsters should remember that bite for bite, even healthful cookies are relatively high in fat and sugar.

Puddings

The *Chocolate Mousse* will satisfy any chocoholic! The *Rice* and *Vanilla Puddings* are tasty, streamlined versions of old favorites and the *Cranberry Steamed Pudding* lacks none of the taste but a lot of the calories, fat and sodium of its ancestors.

Sauces

Rich sauces are often the culprits in turning an otherwise healthful dish into a nutritional disaster. Our *Caramel, Honey Fudge* and *Lemon Sauce* recipes fulfill that anticipated richness without the added fat, making them all low-calorie.

CITRUS FRUIT COMPOTE, HOT

Delightful for a special brunch. Notching the edges of the grapefruit shells adds a festive touch.

6 portions

3 medium grapefruit
2 medium oranges
⅓ cup honey
1 tablespoon margarine, melted
⅛ teaspoon curry powder
½ cup plumped raisins* or ½ cup chopped unsalted mixed nuts
fresh mint leaves (optional)

To plump raisins: bring raisins to a boil in 1 cup water. Let stand 2 minutes. Drain before using.

Cut grapefruit in half; remove sections and reserve. Remove and discard membrane from grapefruit shells; set shells aside. Peel and section oranges.

In a medium bowl, mix honey, margarine and curry powder. Fold in grapefruit, orange sections, and raisins or nuts. Spoon fruit mixture into grapefruit shells and place in shallow baking dish. Bake. Serve warm, garnished with fresh mint leaves if desired.

Oven: 450°
Time: 15 minutes or until hot

Nutrient Analysis: 1 portion

Calories: 180	Fat: 2.2 g	Cholesterol: 0
Sodium: 55 mg	Dietary Fiber: 2.2 g	
Calcium: 39 mg		

Diabetic Exchange: 2½ fruit, ½ fat

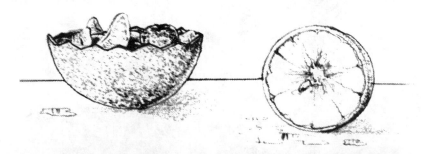

CURRIED FRUIT

Serve as a dessert, a brunch dish or as accompaniment with meat or poultry.

12 portions

½ **pound dried prunes (about 1 cup)**
½ **pound dried apricots (about 1½ cups)**
1 **29-ounce can water packed peaches**
1 **29-ounce can water packed pears**
1 **29-ounce can water packed pineapple**
1 **cup water packed sweet cherries**

SAUCE
½ **cup boiling water**
¼ **cup margarine**
¼ **cup brown sugar**
1-2 **teaspoons curry powder**

In a large bowl, combine fruits and their juices and soak overnight. Drain fruit and arrange in a large ovenproof glass baking dish.

In a small saucepan, heat water, margarine, sugar and curry powder until margarine is melted and sugar is dissolved. Pour over fruit. Bake. Serve hot.

Oven: 350°
Time: 60 minutes

Nutrient Analysis: 1 portion

Calories: 230	Fat: 3.9 g	Cholesterol: 0
Sodium: 34 mg	Dietary Fiber: 6 g	
Calcium: 51 mg		

Diabetic Exchange: 3 fruit, ½ fat

CHESTNUT FRUIT PUDDING

A tasty accompaniment with a pasta casserole or meat dish.

6 portions

1 cup dried apricots
1 cup water
1 15½-ounce can pineapple
    chunks in natural juices
1 cup liquid (reserved pineapple
    juice and apricot juice plus
    water to equal 1 cup)
1 teaspoon margarine
¼ cup sliced water chestnuts
4 teaspoons sugar
4 teaspoons cornstarch
¼ cup frozen orange juice
    concentrate
1 small cinnamon stick
    dash ginger
¾ teaspoon lemon rind
2 teaspoons lemon juice

Soak dried apricots in water until soft, about an hour. Drain the apricots and pineapple, reserving the juice. Place fruit in a bowl. Add water to reserved juice to equal 1 cup.

In a small skillet, heat margarine and sauté the drained water chestnuts.

In a small saucepan, combine the sugar and cornstarch and dissolve in ¼ cup of the juice and water. Add the remaining ¾ cup liquid, orange juice concentrate, cinnamon stick, ginger and lemon rind. Heat and stir over medium heat until clear and thickened, 5 to 10 minutes. Remove the cinnamon stick. Add the lemon juice and sautéd water chestnuts. Pour over fruit and stir gently. Chill before serving.

Nutrient Analysis: 1 portion

Calories: 120   Fat: 0.8 g   Cholesterol: 0
Sodium: 10 mg   Dietary Fiber: 0.7 g
Calcium: 25 mg

Diabetic Exchange: 2 fruit

PEAR AND GRAPEFRUIT TOSS WITH MINT

A hint of mint for a fresh taste

8 portions

2 grapefruit, peeled and sectioned
4 fresh pears, peeled and cut in
    wedges
1 8¾-ounce can apricot halves,
    drained
1 cup seedless grapes

GRAPEFRUIT MINT DRESSING
1 cup plain low-fat yogurt
2 tablespoons honey
1 tablespoon fresh grapefruit
    rind, grated
1 tablespoon grapefruit juice,
    reserved from sections
2 tablespoons chopped fresh mint
    leaves, or 1 teaspoon dried
    mint leaves, crushed

In medium bowl, combine grapefruit, pears, apricot halves and grapes. Cover and chill.

In small bowl combine yogurt, honey, grapefruit rind, grapefruit juice and mint. Mix well. Cover and chill.

To serve, arrange the fruit in individual serving bowls. Serve the mint dressing on the side.

Nutrient Analysis: 1 portion

Calories: 124   Fat: 0.6 g   Cholesterol: 1 mg

Sodium: 22 mg   Dietary Fiber: 2.5 mg

Calcium: 77 mg

Diabetic Exchange: 2 fruit

APPLESAUCE

About 4 cups

6-8 large Granny Smith apples (3½ pounds)
   juice and rind of 1 lemon
½ teaspoon cinnamon
½ cup sugar, sweeten to taste
½ teaspoon vanilla

Wash and quarter apples. Core and halve the quarters but do not peel. Place apples in heavy pan along with juice and rind of the lemon, cinnamon and sugar. Cover pan and set over moderately low heat. Apples will slowly soften and render their juices. Stir and mash frequently until tender throughout (about 30 minutes).

Purée through a vegetable mill or sieve. Return to pan: simmer, stirring for a few minutes, adding more sugar if necessary. The applesauce should be thick enough to hold its shape in spoon. Stir in vanilla.

Nutrient Analysis: ½ cup portion

Calories: 128	Fat: 0.5 g	Cholesterol: 0
Sodium: 1 mg	Dietary Fiber: 2.1 g	
Calcium: 17 mg		

Diabetic Exchange: 2 fruit

FRUIT TOPPING

A delicious topping for pancakes or waffles with only 8 calories a tablespoon as compared with 60 calories a tablespoon in commercial syrup.

About 2 cups

2 cups unsweetened fresh or frozen fruit: strawberries, raspberries, peaches, etc.
2 teaspoons frozen apple juice concentrate

In a blender or food-processor, process 1 cup of fruit and the apple juice concentrate until smooth. Cut remaining cup of fruit into small pieces. Pour the sauce over the cut fruit. Spoon over pancakes or waffles.

Nutrient Analysis: 1 tablespoon

Calories: 8	Fat: 0	Cholesterol: 0
Sodium: 0	Dietary Fiber: 0.4 - 1.3 g	

Diabetic Exchange: Up to 3 tablespoons: free

BAKED APPLES

4 medium-sized baking apples
½ teaspoon grated orange rind
¾ cup unsweetened orange juice
1 tablespoon raisins or currants
1 teaspoon cinnamon
½ teaspoon allspice

4 portions

Wash and core apples. Make several slits on upper portion of apples. Place in shallow baking dish.

In a small saucepan, mix orange rind, orange juice, raisins, cinnamon and allspice. Bring to a boil; reduce heat and simmer for 5 minutes. Pour sauce over apples and cover with aluminum foil. Bake until apples are tender, basting apples 3 times during baking. Serve warm or chilled.

Oven: 350°
Time: 45 minutes

Nutrient Analysis: 1 portion

Calories: 107	*Fat: 0.9 g*	*Cholesterol: 0*
Sodium: 29 mg	*Dietary Fiber: 3.2 g*	
Calcium: 17 mg		

Diabetic Exchange: 1½ fruit

BERRIES 'N CANNOLI CREAM

1 pint sliced fresh strawberries, blueberries, or raspberries
2 teaspoons sugar
1 12-ounce container low-fat cottage cheese
⅓ cup powdered sugar
1 teaspoon vanilla
1½ tablespoons grated orange rind
½ square (½ ounce) semisweet chocolate, grated

6 portions

In small bowl, toss berries with sugar; set aside.

Whip cottage cheese in blender until fluffy. Add powdered sugar and vanilla and whip until smooth and light. Stir in orange rind.

Divide berries among 6 dessert dishes. Top with cheese mixture and garnish with grated chocolate.

Nutrient Analysis: 1 portion

Calories: 112	*Fat: 2.2 g*	*Cholesterol: 5 mg*
Sodium: 231 mg	*Dietary Fiber: 0.9 g*	
Calcium: 50 mg		

Diabetic Exchange: 1 lean meat, 1 fruit

FRUIT FILLED ORANGE

The colorful and refreshing Grand Prize Winner: Heart's Delight (Elementary Division) Recipe Contest. For a salad, substitute CELERY SEED DRESSING, (page 156) for HONEYBERRY GLAZE.

6 portions

3 large oranges
1 medium banana, peeled and
   sliced
6 plums, pitted and sliced; or 1
   grapefruit, sectioned
1 cup seedless green grapes

HONEYBERRY GLAZE
½ cup jellied cranberry sauce
¼ cup honey
1 tablespoon orange juice
   fresh mint sprigs (optional)

Cut oranges in half. Remove orange sections and combine with banana, plums or grapefruit and grapes. Refill orange with the fruit mixture.

Beat cranberry sauce until smooth. Stir in honey and orange juice and pour over fruit. Garnish with fresh mint sprigs if desired.

Nutrient Analysis: 1 portion

Calories: 196	Fat: 1.2 g	Cholesterol: 0
Sodium: 12 mg	Dietary Fiber: 2.8 g	
Calcium: 48 mg		

Diabetic Exchange: 3 fruit

SPARKLING FRUIT

Grand Prize Winner (Elementary Division) Heart's Delight Recipe Contest

10 portions

3 medium peaches
2 cups sliced strawberries
2 cups blueberries
2 cups melon balls
3 medium bananas
1 25.6-ounce bottle pink sparkling
   catawba grape juice, chilled

Slice peaches into bowl. Top peach slices with strawberries, blueberries and melon balls. Cover and refrigerate. Just before serving, slice bananas into fruit mixture. Pour chilled catawba over fruit

Nutrient Analysis: 1 portion

Calories: 120	Fat: 0.6 g	Cholesterol: 0
Sodium: 16 mg	Dietary Fiber: 2.6 g	
Calcium: 24 mg		

Diabetic Exchange: 2 fruit

BAKED GLAZED PEARS

An elegant dessert.

8 portions

8	small or 4 large fresh pears, firm and slightly underripe
	juice of ½ lemon
	water to cover pears
1	cup sugar
1	stick cinnamon
2	whole cloves
2	strips lemon peel
1½	cups Port wine
⅔	cup WHIPPED TOPPING, (page 410).
1	tablespoon Kirsch (optional)

Peel pears, but leave on stems. Place them in a bowl containing the lemon juice, plus enough water to cover.

In a saucepan large enough to hold the pears upright, combine ⅔ cup lemon water in which pears are soaking, sugar, cinnamon, cloves and lemon peel. Bring to a boil, stirring to dissolve sugar.

Add pears and simmer, covered, for 15 minutes. Add all but ¼ cup of the wine and continue simmering, covered, until pears are tender. With a slotted spoon, carefully transfer pears to serving dishes.

At a rapid boil, reduce liquid to the consistency of a light syrup. Stir in remaining wine. Spoon syrup over pears several times to glaze them. Allow to cool, then chill thoroughly.

Serve with WHIPPED TOPPING flavored with Kirsch, if desired.

Nutrient Analysis: 1 portion (w/out topping)

Calories: 171	Fat: 0.3 g	Cholesterol: 0
Sodium: 1 mg	Dietary Fiber: 2 g	
Calcium: 10 mg		

Diabetic Exchange: 3 fruit

NORWEGIAN FRUIT SOUP

For a meat accompaniment resembling chutney, omit the raspberries.

10 portions

1 cup cut-up pitted prunes
1 cup raisins
1 cup peeled, chopped apple
1 tablespoon grated orange rind
1 orange, cut up
4 cups water
1 tablespoon lemon juice
¼ cup sugar
1 stick cinnamon
¼ teaspoon salt
2 tablespoons quick-cooking
   tapioca
1 10-ounce package frozen
   raspberries

In a large saucepan, combine prunes, raisins, apple, orange rind, orange, water, lemon juice, sugar, cinnamon and salt. Bring to a boil, reduce heat, cover and simmer for 1 hour.

Sprinkle tapioca over mixture stirring to avoid lumping. Cook another 15 minutes. Add frozen raspberries and stir occasionally until they are thawed. Serve either hot or cold in bowls.

Nutrient Analysis: 1 portion

Calories: 125   Fat: 0.1 g   Cholesterol: 0

Sodium: 66   Dietary Fiber: 2.1 g

Calcium: 30 mg

Diabetic Exchange: 2 fruit

STRAWBERRY PINEAPPLE FROZEN YOGURT

Use this recipe with any fresh fruit (except pineapple and kiwi fruit) as well as with all fruits canned in fruit juices. For a refreshing molded salad, serve squares on lettuce leaves.

8 portions

1 tablespoon unflavored gelatin (1 envelope)	In a small saucepan, sprinkle gelatin over water. Let stand 5 minutes. Heat gelatin over low heat until dissolved. Add sugar and stir until dissolved. Let cool.
¼ cup cold water	
½ cup sugar	
2 cups plain low-fat yogurt	
1 cup mashed fresh strawberries	Stir in yogurt. Refrigerate in shallow dish until thickened (about 45 minutes).
1 cup crushed pineapple, drained	

Add strawberries and pineapple and whip until light and fluffy (about 2 minutes with electric mixer). Pour into freezer tray (without dividers) or cupcake papers and freeze until firm (about 2 hours).

Let stand at room temperature about 10 minutes before serving.

Nutrient Analysis: 1 portion

Calories: 109	Fat: 0.2 g	Cholesterol: 1 mg
Sodium: 45 mg	Dietary Fiber: 0.6 g	
Calcium: 122 mg		

Diabetic Exchange: 1½ fruit

FROZEN FRUIT POPS

Fruit pops are a big favorite with kids.

BANANA POPS

2 pops

1 banana	Peel and cut banana if half crosswise. Insert stick into end of fruit. Roll in wheat germ. Stand in jar or muffin tin and freeze.
1 tablespoon toasted wheat germ	
1 tablespoon crunchy peanut butter (optional)	

For a nutty treat, freeze banana for about an hour, roll in melted peanut butter and then in wheat germ. Stand in jar and freeze.

continued on next page

PINEAPPLE POPS

1 pineapple wedge (⅛ pineapple)
1 tablespoon toasted wheat germ

Peel, core and cut pineapple wedge in half crosswise. Insert stick into end of fruit. Roll in wheat germ. Stand in jar and freeze.

Nutrient Analysis: 1 pop

	banana	w/peanut butter	pineapple
Calories:	62	110	97
Fat:	0.5 g	4.5 g	0.8 g
Cholesterol:	0	0	0
Sodium:	0.5 mg	48 mg	2 mg
Dietary Fiber:	1.9 g	2.5 g	3 g
Calcium:	7 mg	12 mg	27 mg
Diabetic Exchange:	1 fruit	1 fruit 1 fat	1½ fruit

ORANGE YOGURT POPS

Kids rate these "super".

6 pops

1 6-ounce can frozen orange juice concentrate
1 pint plain low-fat yogurt
2 teaspoons vanilla
    honey to sweeten, if desired

Beat orange juice concentrate, yogurt and vanilla together until well blended. Fill molds or paper cups and insert sticks.

Freeze 24 hours.

Nutrient Analysis: 1 pop

Calories: 92	Fat: 1.4 g	Cholesterol: 5 mg
Sodium: 54 mg	Calcium: 150 mg	

Diabetic Exchange: ½ skim milk, 1 fruit

RICE CRUST

A boon to pie lovers who can't eat wheat! Delicious filled with fresh sliced strawberries, peaches or raspberries and VANILLA PUDDING, (page 421) poured over all.

9" pie crust; 8 pieces

1 cup cooked white or brown
   rice
½ teaspoon vanilla
1 egg white
1 teaspoon margarine

In a medium bowl, beat together rice, vanilla, and egg white with a fork.

Coat 9" pie pan with margarine. Spread rice mixture evenly over bottom and halfway up the side of pan. Do not leave any holes! Bake. Cool and fill. Garnish with berries if desired.

Oven: 350°
Time: 5 minutes

Nutrient Analysis: 1 piece (crust only)

Calories: 34	Fat: 0.5 g	Cholesterol: 0
Sodium: 107 mg		

Diabetic Exchange: ½ starch

NUT CRUST

A light, crispy crust delicious filled with RASPBERRY CHIFFON, (page 402) or other fruit filling.

9" pie crust; 8 pieces

1 cup all-purpose flour
⅓ cup margarine, softened
¼ cup finely chopped pecans or
   walnuts
¼ cup powdered sugar

Mix flour, margarine, nuts and sugar into a soft dough.

Press firmly and evenly against the bottom and sides of a 9" pie pan. Bake. Cool and fill.

Oven: 400°
Time: 12 to 15 minutes

Nutrient Analysis: 1 piece (crust only)

Calories: 158	Fat: 10.1 g	Cholesterol: 0
Sodium: 75 mg	Dietary Fiber: 0.4 g	

Diabetic Exchange: 1 starch, 2 fat

GINGERSNAP CRUST

For an attractive, refreshing dessert, fill with a mixture of 1 pint each softened vanilla ice milk and your favorite sherbet. Freeze and top with fresh fruit.

9" pie crust; 8 pieces

¼ cup margarine, melted
¼ cup sugar
20 gingersnaps, crushed

In a medium bowl, mix margarine, sugar and gingersnaps.

Pat into a 9" pie pan. Bake. Cool and fill with favorite filling.

Oven: 350°
Time: 5 to 8 minutes

Nutrient Analysis: 1 piece (crust only)

Calories: 163	*Fat: 8.9 g*	*Cholesterol: 7 mg*
Sodium: 84 mg	*Calcium: 35 mg*	

Diabetic Exchange: 1 starch, 1½ fat

CRUMB CRUSTS (VANILLA, CHOCOLATE, GRAHAM CRACKER)

9" pie crust; 8 pieces

¼ cup margarine
1½ cups crushed vanilla or
   chocolate wafers or graham
   crackers

Melt margarine and mix thoroughly with crumbs.

Pat into a 9" pie pan. Bake, cool and fill.

Oven: 375°
Time: 6 to 8 minutes

Nutrient Analysis: 1 piece (crust only)

Calories: 145	*Fat: 10 g*	*Cholesterol: 0*
Sodium: 139 mg		

Diabetic Exchange: 1 starch, 2 fat

PIE FILLINGS

Over half the calories and most of the fat in many pies is in the crust. Try "crustless" pies for a delicious low-cal, low-fat dessert.

APPLE DESSERT OR PIE FILLING

As a pie filling, the APPLE DESSERT goes well in the VANILLA WAFER CRUST, (see preceding page).

9" pie pan or crust; 8 portions

1 6-ounce can frozen apple juice	In a saucepan, heat apple juice, cinnamon and nutmeg to simmering. Add apple slices and cook until crisp-tender (15 to 20 minutes). Remove the apple slices and arrange in pie pan or pre-baked crust.
¾ teaspoon cinnamon	
¼ teaspoon nutmeg	
3 cups fresh apple slices	
2 teaspoons cornstarch	
¼ cup cold water	

Dissolve cornstarch in cold water. Add cornstarch mixture to hot apple juice. Cook until thickened, stirring constantly. Pour thickened apple juice over apple slices in pan or crust. Bake. Serve warm.

Oven: 375°
Time: 7 minutes

Nutrient Analysis: 1 portion (filling only)

Calories: 32	*Fat: 0.1 g*	*Cholesterol: 0*
Sodium: 1 mg	*Dietary Fiber: 1 g*	

Diabetic Exchange: ½ fruit

PUMPKIN CUSTARD OR PIE FILLING

9" pie pan or crust; 8 portions

⅓ cup white sugar
⅓ cup brown sugar
¾ teaspoon cinnamon
½ teaspoon ginger
½ teaspoon nutmeg
   pinch of ground cloves
1½ cups canned pumpkin
1 teaspoon vanilla
1½ cups evaporated skim milk
½ teaspoon grated orange rind
3 egg whites, slightly beaten
¼ cup brandy, optional

In a mixing bowl, combine the sugars, cinnamon, ginger, nutmeg and cloves. Stir in the pumpkin.

Add the vanilla, evaporated milk, orange rind and egg whites. Beat with an electric mixer until smooth. Fold in brandy.

Pour into 9" glass pie pan or 1½-quart baking dish and bake.

For pie: Pour into 9" unbaked pie shell and bake.

Oven: 425° for 10 minutes. Reduce heat. 325° for 45 minues or until a knife inserted in the filling comes out clean.

Nutrient Analysis: 1 portion (filling only)

Calories: 129	Fat: 0.2 g	Cholesterol: 2
Sodium: 67 mg	Dietary Fiber: 0.7 g	
Calcium: 158 mg		

Diabetic Exchange: 1 starch, 1 fruit

RASPBERRY CHIFFON OR PIE FILLING

Light and airy. Spoon into stemmed glasses or fill NUT CRUST, (page 398) for a refreshing topper to any meal.

9" pie pan or crust; 8 portions

1¼ cups (10-ounce package) sweetened frozen raspberries
1 tablespoon unflavored gelatin
½ cup water, room temperature
6 tablespoons sugar
1 tablespoon all-purpose flour
3 tablespoons lemon juice
⅓ cup ice water
⅓ cup non-fat dry milk powder

Thaw raspberries and drain, reserving the juice and saving 8 firm berries for garnish. Soften gelatin in water.

In a saucepan, combine 4 tablespoons of the sugar with the flour. Add reserved raspberry juice and softened gelatin. Stir and heat slowly until sugar is dissolved. Remove from heat and add 2 tablespoons of the lemon juice and the berries. Cool until thick and syrupy, but not set.

Chill the beaters of an electric mixer. In a chilled bowl, combine ice water and non-fat dry milk powder. Beat until soft peaks are formed (about 3 to 4 minutes). Add the remaining tablespoon of lemon juice and beat another 3 or 4 minutes until stiff. Fold in the remaining 2 tablespoons of sugar, blending well on low speed. Fold mixture into raspberry gelatin mixture.

Spoon in stemmed glass or pour into pie shell and chill until firm.

Nutrient Analysis: 1 portion (filling only)

Calories: 97　　Fat: 0.1 g　　Cholesterol: 1 mg

Sodium: 28 mg　　Dietary Fiber: 0.8 g

Calcium: 67 mg

Diabetic Exchange: 1½ fruit

KEY LIME CHIFFON OR PIE FILLING

VANILLA or GRAHAM CRACKER CRUST, (page 399) is a good choice with KEY LIME.

9" pie pan or crust; 8 portions

1 tablespoon lime-flavored gelatin
¼ cup water
½ cup warm water
1 cup plus 2 tablespoons non-fat dry milk powder
½ cup sugar
½ cup fresh lime juice (about 4 large limes)
2 egg whites

Sprinkle the gelatin on the ¼ cup water to soften.

Mix the milk powder into the ½ cup warm water. Heat to steaming (40 to 50 seconds in microwave). Stir in gelatin and sugar to dissolve. Cool until thickened.

Add lime juice to milk mixture and stir well.

Beat egg whites until stiff and fold into lime mixture.

Pour into pie pan or cooled baked crust and refrigerate until ready to serve.

Nutrient Analysis: 1 portion (filling only)

Calories: 122	Fat: 0.1 g	Cholesterol: 3 mg
Sodium: 107 mg	Calcium: 215 mg	

Diabetic Exchange: 1 skim milk, 1 fruit

PEACH YOGURT DESSERT OR PIE FILLING

Delicious as a "crustless" tart but if you prefer, use to fill a crumb crust such as VANILLA WAFER, or GINGERSNAP, (both found on page 399).

9" pie pan or crust; 8 portions

1   16-ounce can sliced peaches,
    water or own juice packed
⅔   cup peach liquid
2   tablespoons sugar
1   envelope unflavored gelatin
⅓   cup frozen orange juice
    concentrate
⅛   teaspoon almond extract
¼   teaspoon vanilla
1   cup plain low-fat yogurt

Drain peaches, reserving juice. In a small saucepan, combine ⅔ cup peach juice and sugar. Sprinkle gelatin over top of liquid and allow to soften (about 5 minutes). Heat and stir until gelatin and sugar are thoroughly dissolved. Add orange juice concentrate, peaches, almond and vanilla.

Cool in refrigerator until slightly jelled, then fold in yogurt.

Pour into pie pan or cooled pie crust. Chill and serve.

Nutrient Analysis: 1 portion (filling only)

Calories: 65	Fat: 0.5 g	Cholesterol: 2 mg
Sodium: 27 mg		Calcium: 57 mg

Diabetic Exchange: 1 fruit

FRUIT PIZZA PIE

When using only one fruit such as strawberries, it is more attractive to mix glaze with fruit and then pour over filling.

11" pizza pan; 12 pieces

CRUST
1 cup granola
¼ cup margarine
1½ cups all-purpose flour
1 egg white

FILLING
1 8-ounce container light cream cheese
1 teaspoon vanilla
½ very ripe banana
¼ cup powdered sugar

FRUIT
Melon, berries, pineapple. Be creative! Or use one fruit such as strawberries.

GLAZE
1 cup fruit juice (orange, pineapple, apple)
2 tablespoons cornstarch
1 teaspoon lemon juice

In a food processor or bowl mix granola, margarine, flour and egg white. Spread on 11-inch pizza pan. Bake. Cool.

Beat together cream cheese, vanilla, banana and sugar. Spread over cooled shell.

Cut the fruit in bite-sized pieces and arrange in an attractive pattern over filling.

Heat fruit juice, cornstarch and lemon juice to boiling. When thickened, remove from heat and cool. Spoon cooled glaze over fruit. Chill and serve.

Oven: 375°
Time: 20 minutes

Nutrient Analysis: 1 piece

Calories: 212	Fat: 10 g	Cholesterol: 0
Sodium: 68 mg	Dietary Fiber: 1.4 g	
Calcium: 31 mg		

Diabetic Exchange: 2 fruit, 2 fat

APPLE CAKE

Warm and crumbly, this high fiber cake is the perfect finish for a light meal.

⅔ cup vegetable oil
½ cup sugar
1 egg
1 teaspoon vanilla
½ teaspoon baking soda
1 teaspoon baking powder
½ teaspoon cinnamon
1½ cups all-purpose flour
½ cup raisins
1½ cups diced apples
2 tablespoons chopped pecans

9 x 9" pan; 16 pieces

In a large bowl, mix oil, sugar, egg, vanilla, baking soda, baking powder, cinnamon, flour, raisins and apples.

Pour into a non-stick sprayed 9 x 9" pan. Sprinkle top with chopped pecans. Bake. Serve warm or cold.

Oven: 350°
Time: 30 minutes

Nutrient Analysis: 1 piece

Calories: 174	Fat: 10 g	Cholesterol: 16 mg
Sodium: 42 mg	Dietary Fiber: 2.4 g	
Calcium: 16 mg		

Diabetic Exchange: 1 starch, 2 fat

SPICY PUMPKIN BARS

1 cup brown sugar
3 egg whites or ¾ cup egg substitute
1 cup vegetable oil
1 16-ounce can pumpkin (2 cups)
1 cup all-purpose flour
1 cup whole-wheat flour
2 teaspoons baking powder
2 teaspoons cinnamon
1 teaspoon baking soda
½ cup chopped raisins
½ cup chopped nuts

15 x 10" jelly roll pan; 54 bars

In a mixing bowl, combine brown sugar, egg whites or substitute, oil and pumpkin. Beat until light and fluffy.

Combine flours, baking powder, cinnamon and soda. Stir chopped raisins and nuts into dry ingredients and add to pumpkin mixture. Stir thoroughly.

Spread batter in an ungreased 15 x 10" jellyroll pan. Bake. When cool, cut into bars.

Oven: 350°
Time: 25 to 30 minutes

Nutrient Analysis: 1 bar

Calories: 76	Fat: 4.8 g	Cholesterol: 0
Sodium: 31 mg	Dietary Fiber: 0.5 g	
Calcium: 18 mg		

Diabetic Exchange: ½ starch, 1 fat

RHUBARB CAKE

For an added attraction, top with a dollop of sweetened MOCK CREAM CHEESE, (page 82).

9 x 13" pan; 24 pieces

1¼ cups brown sugar
 ½ cup margarine
  2 egg whites or 1 egg
  1 teaspoon vanilla
1½ cups all-purpose flour
 ½ cup whole-wheat flour
  1 cup buttermilk or sour skim
      milk*
  1 teaspoon soda
2½ cups rhubarb, cut into ½"
      pieces

In mixing bowl, cream brown sugar and margarine.

Add egg whites or egg and beat. Add vanilla, flours, buttermilk or sour milk, and soda. Beat until smooth.

Fold in rhubarb. Spread in a non-stick sprayed 9x13" pan. Mix sugar, cinnamon and walnuts and sprinkle over the batter. Bake. Serve warm or cold.

Oven: 350°
Time: 35 to 40 minutes

TOPPING
 ¼ cup sugar
2½ teaspoons cinnamon
 ½ cup chopped walnuts (optional)

*To make sour milk, place 1 tablespoon lemon juice or vinegar in measuring cup and add milk to make 1 cup.

Nutrient Analysis: 1 piece

Calories: 187   Fat: 6.3 g   Cholesterol: 0 mg

Sodium: 56 mg   Dietary Fiber: 1.2 g

Calcium: 52 mg

Diabetic Exchange: 1 starch, 1 fruit, 1 fat

CARROT CAKE

Deliciously moist and spicy.

9 x 13" baking pan or bundt pan; 24 pieces

1 cup margarine
1½ cups sugar
4 egg whites
1 8-ounce can crushed pineapple
   with juice
1 teaspoon vanilla
1½ cups all-purpose flour
½ cup whole-wheat flour
2 teaspoons cinnamon
2 teaspoons soda
3 cups grated carrots
½ cup chopped walnuts

In a mixing bowl, cream margarine and sugar. Beat in egg whites. Stir in pineapple and vanilla.

Sift together flours, cinnamon and soda. Stir into liquid ingredients and beat well. Fold in carrots and nuts.

Pour into a non-stick sprayed 9 x 13" baking pan or bundt pan. Bake.

Oven: 325°
Time: 60 minutes

Nutrient Analysis: 1 piece

Calories: 154	Fat: 9.1 g	Cholesterol: 0
Sodium: 158 mg	Dietary Fiber: 0.6 g	
Calcium: 24 mg		

Diabetic Exchange: 1 starch, 2 fat

APPLE CRISP

Fragrant, bubbling, a fall delight!

9 x 13" baking pan, 15 pieces

8 cups unpeeled, thinly sliced
   apples
  juice of 1 lemon
1 teaspoon cinnamon
2 tablespoons whole-wheat flour
¾ cup raisins
  water or apple juice to cover
   bottom of pan, about ½ cup

TOPPING
1 cup rolled oats
⅓ cup toasted wheat germ
½ cup whole-wheat flour
2 teaspoons cinnamon
½ cup brown sugar
½ cup margarine

Mix apples, lemon juice, cinnamon, flour and raisins. Place apple mixture in a non-stick sprayed 9 x 13" baking pan. Add juice or water to cover bottom only of pan.

Mix rolled oats, wheat germ, flour, cinnamon, brown sugar and margarine until crumbly. Sprinkle on top of apple mixture. Bake. Serve warm or cold.

Oven: 375°
Time: 25 minutes

Nutrient Analysis: 1 piece

Calories: 175	Fat: 7.1 g	Cholesterol: 0
Sodium: 65 mg	Dietary Fiber: 3.9 g	
Calcium: 23 mg		

Diabetic Exchange: ½ starch, 1 fruit, 1½ fat

WHIPPED TOPPING

This polyunsaturated substitute has a taste and consistency similar to whipped cream; however, it has no saturated fat. Plan to use immediately as it does break down.

About 2 cups

⅔ cup evaporated skim milk
3 tablespoons sugar
½ teaspoon vanilla
¼ teaspoon cream of tartar

In an ice cube tray in freezer, chill milk until slushy. Scrape milk into a chilled bowl and with chilled beaters, beat milk on high until fluffy.

Add sugar, vanilla and cream of tartar and beat until stiff. Serve as a topping for desserts or fruit.

Nutrient Analysis: 1 tablespoon

Calories: 9	Fat: 0	Cholesterol: 0
Sodium: 8 mg	Calcium: 15 mg	

Diabetic Exchange: Up to 3 tablespoons: free

MERINGUE TORTE WITH FRUIT

9" round cake pan; 8 pieces

4 egg whites
¾ cup sugar
1 cup low-salt soda cracker crumbs
1 teaspoon baking powder
½ cup chopped nuts (walnuts, pecans or almonds)
½ teaspoon almond extract

Beat egg whites with electric mixer until they hold stiff peaks. Add sugar gradually while continuing to beat.

Stir in cracker crumbs, baking powder, nuts, and almond extract. Spread in non-stick sprayed 9" round cake pan (may double recipe and use 9 x 13" pan). Bake. Cool and top with fresh or frozen berries and WHIPPED TOPPING, *(see above).*

Oven: 325°
Time: 30 minutes

Nutrient Analysis: 1 piece (torte shell only)

Calories: 187	Fat: 6.9 g	Cholesterol: 10 mg
Sodium: 162 mg		

Diabetic Exchange: 1 starch, 1 fruit, 1 fat

NEW ZEALAND PAVLOVA

Melt-in-your mouth shell topped with your favorite fruit.

9" round; 8 pieces

3 egg whites
1 cup sugar
1 teaspoon cornstarch
1 teaspoon vinegar
1 teaspoon vanilla

In a large bowl, beat egg whites until very stiff.

Mix together sugar and cornstarch and fold into egg whites. Fold in vinegar and vanilla.

Spoon onto a baking sheet covered with brown paper to form a mounded 9" circle about 2" high. Bake. Turn off oven and allow to cool in oven.

Invert on plate and remove paper. Top with fresh or frozen fruit (kiwi fruit, strawberries, raspberries, peaches, etc.) and WHIPPED TOPPING, (*page 410*).

Oven: 300°
Time: 50 to 60 minutes

Nutrient Analysis: 1 piece (torte shell only)

Calories: 99   Fat: 0   Cholesterol: 0

Sodium: 19 mg

Diabetic Exchange: 1½ fruit

CHEWY OATMEAL COOKIES

A wheat-free recipe!

About 3 dozen

2 cups quick-cooking rolled oats	In a mixing bowl, stir together oats, sugar, and oil.

    2 cups quick-cooking rolled oats
    1 cup brown sugar
    ½ cup vegetable oil
    2 egg whites
    ½ teaspoon almond extract
    ½ cup chopped dates
    ½ cup chopped walnuts

In a mixing bowl, stir together oats, sugar, and oil.

Beat egg whites until frothy and add to oat mixture. Stir in almond extract. Stir in dates and walnuts.

Drop by teaspoonfuls onto non-stick sprayed baking sheet. Bake. Cool before removing from baking sheet.

Oven: 300°
Time: 12 minutes

Nutrient Analysis: 1 cookie

Calories: 75	Fat: 4.5 g	Cholesterol: 0
Sodium: 4 mg	Dietary Fiber: 0.8 g	
Calcium: 8 mg		

Diabetic Exchange: ½ fruit, 1 fat

HEARTY HEART OATMEAL COOKIES

About 4 dozen cookies

    ¾ cup margarine
    ½ cup brown sugar
    ½ cup granulated sugar
    2 egg whites
    ¼ cup water
    1 teaspoon vanilla
    ½ cup whole-wheat flour
    ½ cup all-purpose flour
    ½ teaspoon baking soda
    1 cup raisins
    3 cups rolled oats

Cream margarine and sugar.

Add egg whites, water and vanilla and beat mixture until creamy.

Mix flours and baking soda together and beat into liquid mixture. Stir in raisins and rolled oats.

Drop by teaspoonfuls onto ungreased baking sheet. Bake.

Oven: 350°
Time: 12 to 15 minutes

Nutrient Analysis: 1 cookie

Calories: 76	Fat: 3.2 g	Cholesterol: 0
Sodium: 40 mg	Dietary Fiber: 1 g	
Calcium: 8 mg		

Diabetic Exchange: 1 fruit, ½ fat

APPLESAUCE SPICE COOKIES

Deliciously soft, moist and chewy. Store in refrigerator to keep fresh.

About 6 dozen cookies

1 cup margarine
2 eggs, unbeaten
2 egg whites, unbeaten
2 cups unsweetened applesauce
1 tablespoon vanilla
1 cup whole-wheat flour
1½ cups all-purpose flour
2 teaspoons baking soda
1 teaspoon allspice
2 teaspoons nutmeg
1 teaspoon cloves
4 teaspoons cinnamon
2 cups quick-cooking rolled oats
2 cups raisins

In a large mixing bowl, mix together margarine, eggs and egg whites, applesauce and vanilla.

Mix together flours, soda, allspice, nutmeg, cloves and cinnamon. Beat into applesauce mixture.

Stir in oats and raisins.

Drop by teaspoonfuls onto non-stick sprayed baking sheet. Bake.

Oven: 350°
Time: 12 to 15 minutes

Nutrient Analysis: 1 cookie

Calories: 62	Fat: 2.9 g	Cholesterol: 8 mg
Sodium: 53 mg	Dietary Fiber: 0.8 g	
Calcium: 11 mg		

Diabetic Exchange: 1 fruit

PECAN MERINGUES

A delicate, melt-in-your-mouth cookie.

About 3 dozen cookies

1 egg white
1 cup sugar
1 teaspoon vanilla
1 teaspoon flour
1 cup finely chopped pecans

In medium mixing bowl, beat egg white until it forms soft peaks. Continue beating while gradually adding sugar.

Stir in vanilla. Sprinkle the teaspoon flour over mixture and stir in pecans.

Drop by small teaspoonfuls onto a baking sheet covered with brown paper. Bake and cool on sheet.

Oven: 275°
Time: 30 to 35 minutes

Nutrient Analysis: 1 cookie

Calories: 44	Fat: 2.2 g	Cholesterol: 0
Sodium: 1 mg		

Diabetic Exchange: ½ fruit, ½ fat

DATE-APPLE-NUT BARS

9 x 13" baking pan; 24 bars

1 8-ounce package pitted dates,
　 chopped (1¼ cups)
¾ cup water
½ cup unsweetened applesauce
1 cup sugar
½ teaspoon cinnamon
½ cup chopped, unsalted nuts
1½ cups all-purpose flour
1 cup quick-cooking rolled oats
¾ cup margarine

In a saucepan, combine dates, water, applesauce, ¼ cup of the sugar, and cinnamon. Cook over medium heat, stirring occasionally, until thickened. Cool. Stir in nuts and set aside.

In a large mixing bowl, combine flour, oats, and remaining sugar. Cut in margarine until mixture resembles coarse crumbs.

Press half the crumb mixture firmly into a non-stick sprayed 9 x 13" pan. Cover with date mixture, spreading evenly. Sprinkle remaining crumb mixture over date filling and press down firmly. Bake. Cool and cut into bars.

Oven: 350°
Time: 30 to 35 minutes

Nutrient Analysis: 1 bar

Calories: 165	Fat:7.5 g	Cholesterol: 0
Sodium: 58 mg	Dietary Fiber: 1.2 g	
Calcium: 11 mg		

Diabetic Exchange: 1 starch, 1 fruit, 1 fat

APRICOT SPICE BARS

9 x 13" baking pan; 24 bars

⅓ cup margarine
½ cup honey
1 egg
2 egg whites
½ teaspoon vanilla
½ cup all-purpose flour
½ cup whole-wheat flour
½ teaspoon baking powder
1 teaspoon cinnamon
½ teaspoon cloves
1 cup chopped, dried apricots
   (about 6 ounces)

LEMON GLAZE
½ cup powdered sugar
1 tablespoon lemon juice

In a mixing bowl, cream margarine. Mix in honey. Add egg, egg whites, and vanilla; beat well.

Mix together flours, baking powder, cinnamon and cloves and stir into egg mixture. Stir in chopped apricots.

Spread evenly in non-stick sprayed 9 x 13" baking pan. Bake. Cool slightly, then drizzle with lemon glaze. Cool and cut into bars.

Oven: 350°
Time: 20 to 25 minutes

Nutrient Analysis: 1 bar

Calories: 80	Fat: 2.8 g	Cholesterol: 11
Sodium: 43	Dietary Fiber: 0.8 g	
Calcium: 10		

Diabetic Exchange: 1 fruit, ½ fat

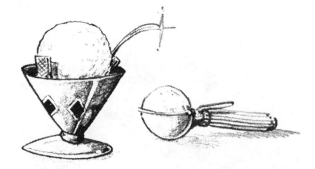

FRUIT BARS

9 x 13" baking pan; 24 bars

½ cup chopped dates
½ cup chopped prunes
¾ cup raisins
1 cup water
½ cup margarine
1 egg
2 egg whites
1 teaspoon vanilla
¾ cup all-purpose flour
¼ cup whole-wheat flour
1 teaspoon soda
1 teaspoon nutmeg
1 teaspoon cinnamon
½ cup broken walnuts

In a heavy saucepan, bring dates, prunes, raisins and water to a boil. Reduce heat and simmer 5 minutes. Add margarine to hot mixture and let mixture cool.

Beat egg, egg whites and vanilla into cooled fruit mixture.

Mix together flours, soda, nutmeg, cinnamon and walnuts and stir into fruit mixture thoroughly.

Spread in non-stick sprayed 9 x 13" pan. Bake.

Oven: 350°
Time: 30 to 35 minutes

Nutrient Analysis: 1 bar

Calories: 103   Fat: 5.6 g   Cholesterol: 11 mg

Sodium: 81 mg   Dietary Fiber: 0.8 g

Calcium: 19 mg

Diabetic Exchange: 1 fruit, 1 fat

DATE BARS

9 x 13" baking pan; 40 bars

1 pound pitted dates, cut up
1 cup water
2 cups all-purpose flour
2½ cups quick-cooking rolled oats
¾ cup brown sugar
1 cup margarine, melted
1 tablespoon hot water
1 teaspoon baking soda

In a medium saucepan, combine dates and water. Bring to a boil and simmer until thick, about 5 minutes. Cool.

In mixing bowl, combine flour, rolled oats and brown sugar. Add melted margarine and mix until crumbly. Dissolve soda in 1 tablespoon water and add to crumb mixture and mix well.

Pat two-thirds of crumb mixture into a non-stick sprayed 9 x 13" baking pan. Spread date mixture evenly over crust and sprinkle remaining third of crumb mixture on top of the date mixture. Bake. Cool and cut into bars.

Oven: 325°
Time: 45 minutes

Nutrient Analysis: 1 bar

Calories: 121	Fat: 4.9 g	Cholesterol: 0
Sodium: 67 mg	Dietary Fiber: 1.3 g	
Calcium: 17 mg		

Diabetic Exchange: 1 starch, 1 fat

RAISIN BARS

9 x 13" pan; 40 bars

1 teaspoon soda
1¾ cups rolled oats
¾ cup brown sugar
¾ cup all-purpose flour
1 cup whole-wheat flour
1 cup margarine

Mix together soda, rolled oats, brown sugar and flours. Cut in margarine until mixture is crumbly. Set aside a third of the mixture for topping and pat the remainder into a non-stick sprayed 9 x 13" baking pan.

continued on next page

RAISIN BARS (con't)

1 cup raisins
½ cup water
2 eggs
2 egg whites
½ cup sugar
3 tablespoons cornstarch
2 cups plain low-fat yogurt

In a small pan, bring raisins and water to a boil. Boil until almost all water is gone (5 to 10 minutes). Set aside.

Beat together eggs, egg whites, sugar, cornstarch and yogurt. Bring to a boil and boil, stirring constantly, until mixture thickens. Cool. Stir in raisins.

Spread filling mixture on crust. Sprinkle reserved crumb mixture over top. Bake.

Oven: 350°
Time: 25 minutes

Nutrient Analysis: 1 bar

Calories: 107	*Fat: 4.9 g*	*Cholesterol: 12 mg*
Sodium: 82 mg	*Dietary Fiber: 0.8 g*	
Calcium: 35 mg		

Diabetic Exchange: 1 fruit, 1 fat

BRAN BITES, UNBAKED

These nutty-flavored treats are a favorite with all kids...big and little! Flavor and texture are enhanced by aging 2 or 3 days in a refrigerated, tightly-covered container.

About 24 balls

3 cups bran flakes, crushed
½ cup toasted wheat germ
⅔ cup peanut butter
¼ cup orange juice
2 tablespoons honey
½ cup raisins, chopped

In a large bowl, combine bran flakes, wheat germ, peanut butter, orange juice, honey and raisins. Mix well.

Shape dough in palms to form balls. Chill. Store in refrigerator.

Nutrient Analysis: 1 ball

Calories: 80	*Fat: 3.8 g*	*Cholesterol: 0*
Sodium: 88 mg	*Dietary Fiber: 1.6 g*	
Calcium: 20.4 mg		

Diabetic Exchange: ½ fruit, 1 fat

HONEY MILK BALLS - UNBAKED

Quick, easy and inexpensive. Pre-schoolers enjoy making and eating these highly nutritious snacks. Roll in toasted sesame seeds or chopped nuts for an added taste treat.

2 dozen balls

½ cup honey
½ cup peanut butter
 1 cup low-fat dry milk powder
 1 cup rolled oats or 1½ cups
     graham cracker crumbs
 1 teaspoon vanilla
¼ cup toasted sesame seeds or
     chopped nuts (optional)

In a mixing bowl, combine honey, peanut butter, milk powder and oats or graham crumbs. Knead by hand until thoroughly blended.

Shape into small balls and roll in sesame seeds or nuts if desired.

Nutrient Analysis: 1 ball

Calories: 84   Fat: 3 g   Cholesterol: 1 mg

Sodium: 53 mg   Dietary Fiber: 0.6 g

Calcium: 67 mg

Diabetic Exchange: 1 fruit, ½ fat

CHOCOLATE MOUSSE

Delicious!

6 portions

1 egg
1 envelope unflavored gelatin
1 tablespoon cold water
1 cup boiling water
1 teaspoon instant coffee
½ cup part-skim ricotta cheese
½ cup cold skim milk
3 tablespoons unsweetened cocoa
   pinch salt
6 tablespoons sugar

In blender or food processor, combine egg, gelatin and cold water. Blend until combined (about 10 seconds). Scrape mixture down and blend 10 seconds longer. Let the mixture stand about a minute or until gelatin softens. Add boiling water and blend until gelatin is dissolved (about 10 seconds).

Add coffee, ricotta cheese, milk, cocoa, salt and sugar. Blend until smooth (about 1 minute). Pour into six dessert glasses and chill until set, at least 2 hours.

Nutrient Analysis: 1 portion

Calories: 112	*Fat: 2.8 g*	*Cholesterol: 46 mg*
Sodium: 61 mg	*Calcium: 89 mg*	

Diabetic Exchange: 1 skim milk, ½ fat

RICE PUDDING

Slow baking of the brown rice and brown sugar adds a fine carmelized quality.

8 portions

¾ cup raw brown rice
1 12-ounce can 2% evaporated
   milk plus water to equal 4
   cups
3 tablespoons brown sugar
½ teaspoon cinnamon
¼ teaspoon nutmeg
1 teaspoon vanilla, optional
½ cup raisins

In a 2-quart, non-stick sprayed, oven-proof dish, mix rice, milk, water, sugar, cinnamon, nutmeg, and vanilla, if desired.

Bake in a slow oven, stirring frequently. If skin forms on milk, skim off.

Stir in raisins during last half hour of baking time. Serve warm or cold.

Oven: 275°
Time: 2½ hours

Nutrient Analysis: 1 portion

Calories: 142	*Fat: 1.4 g*	*Cholesterol: 0*
Sodium: 51 mg	*Dietary Fiber: 0.9 g*	
Calcium: 121 mg		

Diabetic Exchange: 1 starch, 1 fruit

VANILLA PUDDING

This versatile pudding is tasty served plain, or in parfait glasses layered with fresh strawberries or other fruit, or as a pie filling.

8 portions

½ cup sugar
6 tablespoons cornstarch
4 cups skim milk
2 tablespoons margarine
1½ teaspoons vanilla

In a medium saucepan, combine sugar and cornstarch and mix well. Add ½ cup milk and stir until the sugar and cornstarch are dissolved. Stir in remaining milk.

Bring to a boil over medium heat, stirring constantly. Boil one minute. Remove from heat and stir in margarine and vanilla. Chill.

PUDDING VARIATIONS
CHOCOLATE PUDDING

Decrease sugar to ⅓ cup and add 1½ tablespoons of cocoa to sugar and cornstarch mixture.

BUTTERSCOTCH PUDDING

Substitute brown sugar for white sugar. Increase margarine to ¼ cup.

Nutrient Analysis: ½ cup

	Vanilla	Chocolate	Butterscotch
Calories:	138	138	165
Fat:	3 g	3 g	6 g
Cholesterol:	2 mg	2 mg	2 mg
Sodium:	92 mg	92 mg	120 mg
Calcium:	151 mg	151 mg	151 mg
Diabetic Exchange:	½ skim milk 1 fruit ½ fat	½ skim milk 1 fruit ½ fat	½ skim milk 1 fruit 1 fat

CRANBERRY STEAMED PUDDING

12 portions

2 cups fresh cranberries
1 cup all-purpose flour
3 tablespoons brown sugar
½ teaspoon baking powder
¼ teaspoon baking soda
½ teaspoon cinnamon
¼ teaspoon nutmeg
¼ teaspoon allspice
⅛ teaspoon ground ginger
dash ground cloves
3 tablespoons vegetable oil
½ cup skim milk
3 tablespoons molasses
½ cup raisins or chopped dates
½ cup chopped nuts

Wash, drain and cut cranberries in half.

In a bowl, mix flour, sugar, baking powder, baking soda, cinnamon, nutmeg, allspice, ginger and cloves.

Add oil, milk and molasses and mix until dry ingredients are moistened. Stir in cranberries, raisins or dates, and nuts.

Spoon into well-oiled, 1-quart mold or casserole or 6-cup fluted tube pan. Cover with lid or foil. Place on a rack in a large steamer or kettle. Pour boiling water into steamer to a depth of 2 inches. Cover. Steam on low heat 1½ to 2 hours or until pudding springs back when lightly touched in center. OVEN METHOD: Place mold in pan of water and bake at 150° for 1½ to 2 hours.

Serve warm with LEMON SAUCE, *(see next page)*.

Nutrient Analysis: 1 portion (without sauce)

Calories: 146	*Fat: 6.7 g*	*Cholesterol: 0*
Sodium: 40 mg	*Dietary Fiber: 1 g*	
Calcium: 52 mg		

Diabetic Exchange: 1 starch, ½ fruit, 1 fat

LEMON SAUCE

The crowning glory on CRANBERRY STEAMED PUDDING, (page 422).

About 1½ cups

⅓ cup sugar
2 tablespoons cornstarch
1 cup hot water
2 teaspoons grated lemon rind
2 teaspoons lemon juice
2 tablespoons margarine

In a saucepan, combine sugar and cornstarch. Blend in water. Cook over medium heat, stirring constantly until mixture boils. Boil 1 minute until it is clear and slightly thickened. Remove from heat.

Stir in lemon rind, juice and margarine. Serve warm or cool on steamed pudding.

LEMON SAUCE VARIATION
ORANGE SAUCE

Substitute orange juice for water and orange rind for lemon rind. Omit lemon juice.

Nutrient Analysis: 1 tablespoon

Calories: 22   Fat: 0.9 g   Cholesterol: 0

Sodium: 10 mg

Diabetic Exchange: ½ fruit

CARAMEL SAUCE

Delicious over fresh sliced apples, angel food cake or ice milk.

About 1½ cups

1 cup sugar
⅓ cup water
¾ cup evaporated skim milk,
    heated
½ teaspoon vanilla

In a heavy saucepan, bring sugar and water to a boil. Remove from heat and swirl pan by its handle (don't stir) until the sugar is completely dissolved and the liquid is clear. Cover the pan with a tightly fitting cover and boil over moderately high heat for several minutes. When bubbles are thick, remove cover and continue to boil, swirling pan until syrup turns a light caramel brown. Let cool to about the same temperature as the heated evaporated milk.

Pour caramel into milk: the caramel will lump. Simmer, stirring to melt caramel and blend it with the milk. Stir in the vanilla. Serve warm or cold. (If too thick, add a little more milk and simmer. If too thin, boil down, stirring.)

Nutrient Analysis: 1 tablespoon

Calories: 38	Fat: 0	Cholesterol: 0.3
Sodium: 9	Calcium: 23	

Diabetic Exchange: ½ fruit

HONEY FUDGE SAUCE

Great on ice milk or as topping for angel food cake.

About 1½ cups

4 tablespoons margarine
1 tablespoon cornstarch
2 tablespoons cocoa
½ cup honey
½ cup water
6 large marshmallows
1 teaspoon vanilla

In a saucepan, melt margarine. Add cornstarch and cocoa, blending well.

Add honey and water and cook over low heat until thick. Add marshmallows and stir until melted. Stir in vanilla. Serve warm or cold.

Nutrient Analysis: 1 tablespoon

Calories: 47	Fat: 2 g	Cholesterol: 0
Sodium: 26 mg		

Diabetic Exchange: ⅓ fruit, ½ fat

APPENDIX:

A GUIDE TO HEALTHIER EATING

Evidence strengthens the link between diet and chronic disease

Extensive research by the world's leading health investigators continues to document the relationship between health and lifestyle factors, especially diet. It's hardly surprising, therefore, that eating habits have been linked to a host of important health risks, ranging from heart disease to tooth decay. See Table 28 for a listing of major chronic illnesses and the dietary patterns associated with them.

Table 28: Risk Factors for Disease[11]

Disease	Lifestyle Factors
Heart Disease	Excess dietary fat, saturated fat, cholesterol and calories Obesity Smoking Inactivity
Cancer	Excess dietary fat and alcohol Low fiber intake Low vitamins A and C intake Obesity Smoking Smoking and alcohol combined Inactivity
High Blood Pressure (Hypertension)	Obesity Excess dietary fat and saturated fat Excess sodium Excess alcohol Low calcium Inactivity
Osteoporosis	Low calcium Excess fat, protein and alcohol Underweight Smoking Inactivity
Adult Onset Diabetes (Type II)	Obesity Inactivity
Obesity	Excess calories, dietary fat and alcohol Inactivity

[11]Minnesota Department of Health. **Healthy by Choice: The Minnesota Plan for Nutrition and Health.** Minneapolis, Minnesota Dept. of Health, December 1986.

Nearly a decade ago, the Senate Select Committee on Nutrition and Human Needs outlined the potential benefits that more healthful dietary practices would have on the incidence of our leading health problems. They estimated that improved national eating habits could result in an:

80% reduction in obesity
25% reduction in cardiovascular disease
25% reduction in cancer incidence and death
50% reduction in diabetes
15% reduction in digestive problems
50% reduction in dental diseases
1% annual increase in longevity[12]

Since then, leading health organizations, medical researchers and government agencies have translated the research findings linking lifestyle and health into specific recommendations—changes designed to greatly reduce the incidences of and mortality from certain diseases. As a result, we now have several widely recognized dietary recommendations to guide our food selection. The American Heart Association, the American Cancer Society, the National Cancer Institute, and the American Dietetic Association recommendations follow.

The American Heart Association
Dietary Guidelines to Prevent Heart Disease[13]

Cardiovascular disease remains the #1 killer of Americans.

At present, heart attacks and strokes remain the primary killers in the United States. The prevention of coronary heart disease (CHD) remains the foremost goal of the American Heart Association (AHA). The following recommendations appeared in the 1988 AHA position paper entitled "Dietary Guidelines for Healthy American Adults."

1. Total daily fat intake should be less than 30% of calories. Example: If you consume 2000 calories a day, then no more than 600 calories (66 grams or 13 teaspoons of fat) should come from dietary fat.

---

[12]U.S. Senate Select Committee on Nutrition and Human Needs. **Benefits of human research. Appendix A. Nutrition and Health II.** Washington, D.C.: U.S. Government Printing Office, 1976.

[13]American Heart Association. **"Dietary Guidelines for Healthy American Adults"** Position Paper, 1988.

Dietary Guidelines to Prevent Heart Disease, continued

Cardiovascular Disease includes heart disease and stroke

2. Saturated fat should be less than 10% of total daily calories. Example: If you consume 2000 calories a day, then 200 or fewer calories (22 grams or 5 teaspoons of fat) should come from saturated fat.

3. Polyunsaturated fat intake should not exceed 10% of calories.

4. Cholesterol intake should not exceed 300 milligrams of cholesterol a day.

5. Carbohydrate intake should constitute at least 50-55% of total daily calories, with an emphasis on increased complex carbohydrates. Example. Of 2000 calories a day, an intake of 1000-1100 calories should come from whole grains, legumes, vegetables and fruits.

6. Protein intake should be approximately 15% of total daily calories. Example: Of 2000 calories a day, 300 calories should come from high-quality protein sources, such as fish, poultry, legumes (dried peas and beans), lean red meat and low-fat dairy products.

7. Sodium intake should not exceed 3000 milligrams a day. Example: If your daily intake is 2000 calories, then you should consume no more than 3000 milligrams of sodium a day, which is the equivalent of one and a half teaspoons of salt.

8. Alcohol consumption should be moderate, at most: no more than 1½ ounces (the equivalent of 3 ounces of hard liquor, 100 proof; 14 ounces of regular beer or 5-10 ounces of wine a day.

9. Total calories should be sufficient to maintain the individual's recommended body weight.

10. A wide variety of foods should be consumed.

American Cancer Society and the
National Cancer Institute
Dietary Guidelines to Prevent Cancer[14-15]

Dietary Guidelines to Help Prevent Cancer

Growing evidence indicates that a diet low in fat and rich in fiber may reduce the risk of several common cancers. In 1983,

[14]American Cancer Society. Conference on Nutrition in Cancer Causation and Prevention. **Cancer Research** 43:5, 1983.

[15]National Cancer Institute, **Diet, Nutrition & Cancer Prevention: A Guide to Food Choices.** Bethesda, M.D.: U.S. Department of Health and Human Services; NIH Publication Number 85-2711, July 1985.

the American Cancer Society issued seven dietary guidelines which some experts believe could result in a 50 percent reduction of the cancer mortality rate by the year 2000.

1. Avoid obesity.
   Cancer Risk: Obesity, defined as 30% or more overweight, is associated with imbalances in hormone levels. This increases the risk of colon, breast, prostate, uterine, ovarian and gallbladder cancers.

2. Cut down on total fat intake.
   Cancer Risk: A high-fat diet changes hormone balances, increasing vulnerability to breast, colon and prostate cancers,

3. Eat more high-fiber foods such as whole-grain cereals, fruits and vegetables.
   Cancer Risk: A high-fiber diet may protect against colon cancer by speeding the passage of wastes through the colon. This decreases the time the colon is exposed to cancer-promoting chemicals (carcinogens). Research findings also suggest that the absorbing ability of fiber acts like a sponge to soak up the carcinogens.

Foods Rich in Vitamin A & C: Broccoli, spinach, papaya, tomatoes and cantaloupe.

4. Include foods rich in vitamins A and C in your daily diet.
   Cancer Risk: Foods rich in vitamin A (not vitamin A supplements) may diffuse carcinogens responsible for lung, esophageal and larynx cancers. Foods rich in vitamin C may prevent nitrites from combining with proteins to form cancer-promoting chemicals which increase the risk of stomach and esophageal cancers.

5. Include cruciferous vegetables in your diet.
   Cancer Risk: Vegetables in the cruciferous family such as cabbage, broccoli, brussels sprouts, kohlrabi and cauliflower, may reduce the risk of esophageal, stomach, colo-rectal, lung and bladder cancers.

6. Eat moderately of salt-cured, smoked and nitrite-cured foods.
   Cancer Risk: In areas of the world where salt-cured and smoked foods are eaten frequently, there is a higher incidence of esophageal and stomach cancers.

7. If you drink, keep alcohol consumption moderate.
   Cancer Risk: Heavy use of alcohol is directly linked with liver cancer. In addition, high alcohol consumption, especially when accompanied by cigarette smoking or smokeless tobacco usage, increases the risk of mouth, larynx, throat, esophageal and liver cancers.

Special nutritional needs of women

American Dietetic Association
Food Selections for Women[16]

As knowledge of nutritional science increases, so does awareness of the special nutritional needs of women. In 1986 the American Dietetic Association acknowledged these special needs and announced 14 nutrition recommendations for women.

A woman's awareness of healthy foods is particularly important for several reasons. Women are more prone than men to certain nutritional deficiencies—primarily calcium and iron. Women in general tend to take in fewer calories than men, and young women especially are more likely to engage in severe and possibly unhealthy weight-loss diets. During pregnancy and breastfeeding, a woman's nutrition requirements change, and a healthy diet becomes more important than ever. Furthermore, despite changes in family employment situations, in many households it is still primarily the woman who plans, purchases and controls food selection. These food choices help shape the eating habits of the children, and in this way are continued into the next generation.

These recommendations encompass and extend the revised 1985 Dietary Guidelines developed by the United States Departments of Agriculture and Health and Human Services.

1. Eat a daily variety of foods from all major food groups.
   Choose 3 to 4 low-fat servings of dairy foods; 2 low-fat servings of meat or meat alternatives; 4 servings of vegetables and fruits; and 4 servings of whole-grain breads and cereals.

2. Maintain healthy body weight.
   Use the 10-Calorie Rule: To lose weight safely and effectively, do not consume less than 10 calories a day for each pound *current* body weight and do not skip meals. Increase physical activity.

3. Exercise Regularly.
   Exercise at least three times a week for 30 or more minutes.

4. Limit total fat to no more than one-third of daily calories.
   Use a variety of fat sources but limit high-fat foods such as margarine, butter, cooking oils, salad dressings, cookies, cakes and cream. Choose low-fat selections of meat and milk.

5. Carbohydrates should supply at least one-half of daily calories. Select complex carbohydrates such as legumes, pasta, grains, vegetables and nuts and seeds.

[16]American Dietetic Association. "American Dietetic Association's Nutrition Recommendations for Women". **Journal of the American Dietetic Association.** Volume 86 Number 12, December 1986.

Food Selections For Women, continued

6. Eat a variety of fiber-rich foods.
   Make daily selections from fresh fruits with skin, such as apples and pears, citrus fruits, vegetables, legumes such as navy, pinto and kidney beans, and whole grains such as brown rice, oatmeal, wheat and oat bran.

7. Include 3 to 4 daily servings of calcium-rich foods. Include broccoli, collard greens, canned salmon or sardines with bones, and low-fat dairy products.

8. Include plenty of iron-rich foods.
   Make daily selections from lean meats, prunes, pinto and kidney beans, spinach, leafy green vegetables and enriched and whole-grain breads and cereals.

9. Limit intake of salt and sodium-containing foods.
   Use fewer processed foods, and limit the use of the salt-shaker.

10. Rely on foods for necessary nutrients, rather than relying on vitamin and mineral supplements.

11. If you drink, limit alcohol intake to 1 to 2 drinks daily.

12. Avoid smoking and smokeless tobacco usage.

13. Consult with your doctor about your risk of chronic disease (heart disease, cancer, diabetes) and adjust your lifestyle accordingly.

14. Consult a registered dietitian (R.D.) about the adequacy of your diet.

Adequate nutrition may prevent osteoporosis

The National Institutes of Health's Consensus Development Conference on Osteoporosis outlined three strategies for preventing osteoporosis which are of particular significance to women. They recommend adequate nutrition including 1000-1500 milligrams of calcium a day, modest weight-bearing exercise for all women, and possible estrogen replacement for women past menopause.[17]

---

[17]National Institute of Health. "Osteoporosis: Consensus Development Conference Statement". Bethesda, M.D.: National Institute of Health, 5:3, 1984.

*National
Cholesterol
Education
Program
Symbol*

*Recommendations
for the entire
population of
healthy Americans*

NCEP GUIDELINES

The National Cholesterol Education Program (NCEP), launched in the fall of 1985, is a focal point in the national effort to reduce high blood cholesterol levels in the American public. The goal of the NCEP is to reduce the prevalence of elevated blood cholesterol in the United States, thus contributing to a reduction in coronary heart disease.

The following recommendations are from the: NCEP Report of the Expert Panel on *Population Strategies for Blood Cholesterol Reduction* (NIH Publication No. 90-3046) published in November, 1990.

RECOMMENDATION A. 1: The panel recommends the following pattern of nutrient intake for all healthy Americans*:

- Less than 10 percent[6] of total calories from saturated fatty acids.
- An average of 30 percent of total calories or less from all fat.[6]
- Dietary energy (calorie) levels needed to reach or maintain a desirable body weight.
- Less than 300 mg of cholesterol per day.

RECOMMENDATION B. 1: The panel recommends that healthy Americans, both adults and children, select, prepare, and consume foods that contain lower amounts of saturated fatty acids, total fat, and cholesterol.

RECOMMENDATION B. 2: The panel urges the public to recognize that an elevated blood cholesterol level is one of the important modifiable CHD risk factors together with smoking, high blood pressure, excess body weight, and physical inactivity.

Recommendations for healthy children and adolescents

Healthy Children and Adolescents

The NCEP Panel recognizes that the caloric and nutrient needs of children are critical for supporting growth and development. Since eating habits developed during childhood can influence lifetime practices, the panel urges prudent movement to the recommended eating pattern.

> **RECOMMENDATION C. 1: The panel recommends that healthy children follow the recommended eating patterns that are lower in saturated fatty acids, total fat, and cholesterol as they begin to eat with the family, usually at 2 years of age or older.**

Infants and children under the age of 2 years have dietary requirements different from those of older people. Infants whose diet is primarily mother's milk or formula often appropriately consume 40 percent or more of the calories from fat. The NCEP Panel recommends that this well-established pattern of infant nutrition be encouraged. Care must be taken to ensure sufficient energy and nutrient intake to meet the needs of the growing child. A forthcoming report from the Expert Panel on Blood Cholesterol Levels in Children and Adolescents will deal with strategies for detection, evaluation and treatment of children and adolescents at high risk of coronary heart disease.

For more information, contact:

National Institutes of Health
National Cholesterol Education Program
National Heart, Lung and Blood Institute
C-200
Bethesda, MD 20892

(301) 951-3260

BIBLIOGRAPHY

Chapter 1

1. USDA and U.S. Department of Health and Human Services. *Nutrition and Your Health: Dietary Guidelines for Americans*. Home and Garden Bulletin Number 232. Washington, D.C.: U.S. Government Printing Office, November, 1990.

2. Franz, M.; Friedman, D.; Kerr-Hedding, B.; Siemers, D.; and Monk, A. *A Guide to Healthy Eating*. St. Louis Park, MN: International Diabetes Center, 1986.

3. U.S. Dept. of Health and Human Services. *Exercise and Your Health*. Washington, D.C.: NIH Publication #81-1677, May 1981.

4. Farquhar, J., M.D. *The American Way of Life Need Not Be Hazardous to Your Health*. New York: W.W. Norton & Co., 1978.

5. Stanford Heart Disease Prevention Program. *The Exercise Book: For People Who Don't Exercise*. California: Stanford University, 1981.

6. Anon. "Dieting-Induced Obesity: A Hidden Hazard of Weight Cycling." *Environmental Nutrition*. 10:2, February 1987.

7. Simopoulos, A. "The Health Implications of Overweight and Obesity." *Nutrition Reviews*. 43, 1985.

8. Bjorntorp, P. "Differences Between Male and Female Obesity." *Nutrition & the M.D.* 10:1, 1984.

9. National Institutes of Health. *National Institutes of Health Concensus Development Conference Statement on Health Implications of Obesity*. 5:9, 1985.

10. Brody, J. *Jane Brody's Good Food Book*. New York: W.W. Norton & Co., 1985.

11. Johnson, R. "Can You Alter Your Heart Disease Risk?" *Journal of the American Medical Association*. 245:19, 1981.

12. Minnesota Heart Health Program. *Heartbeat: Fat Facts*. Minneapolis: University of Minnesota, September 1987.

13. Glomset, J. "Fish, Fatty Acids and Human Health." *New England Journal of Medicine.* 312:19, 1985.

14. USDA. *Composition of Foods—Fats and Oils Raw, Processed, Prepared.* USDA Human Nutrition Information Service Agriculture Handbook 8-4, revised 1979.

15. Pennington, J. and Church, H. *Food Values of Portions Commonly Used.* 14th ed. New York: Harper & Row., 1985.

16. Franz, M. *Fast Food Facts.* Minneapolis: Diabetes Center, Incorporated. 1987.

17. Lipid Research Clinics Program. The Lipid Research Clinics Coronary Primary Prevention Trial Results. I: Reduction In Incidence of Coronary Heart Disease. *Journal of the American Medical Association.* 251:3, 1984.

18. Nettleton, J. *Seafood Nutrition.* Huntington, N.Y.: Osprey Books, 1985.

19. Nettleton, J. *Seafood and Health.* Huntington, N.Y.: Osprey Books, 1987.

20. Hepburn, F.; Exler, J. and Weihrauch, J.L. "Provisional Tables on the Content of Omega-3 Fatty Acids and Other Fat Components of Selected Foods." *Journal of the American Dietetic Association.* 86:6, June 1986.

21. US Dept. of Health and Human Services. *Eating to Lower Your High Blood Cholesterol.* Bethesda, M.D.: National Cholesterol Education Program. NIH Publication #87-2920, September 1987.

22. USDA, Human Nutrition Information Service. *Composition of Foods.* Agriculture Handbooks 8-1 through 8-14, revised 1976-1986.

23. Anon. "All Fiber is Not Created Equal; Colon Cancer Controversy." *Environmental Nutrition.* 9:10, October 1986.

24. DeBakey, M.; Goto, A.; Scott, L. and Foreyt, J. "Diet, Nutrition and Heart Disease." *The Journal of the American Dietetic Association.* 86:6, June 1986.

25. Lanza, E. and Butrum, R. "A Critical Review of Food Fiber Analysis and Data." *The Journal of the American Dietetic Association.* 86:6, June 1986.

26. Cumming, C. "A Review of the Impact of Nutrition on Health and Profits a Discussion of Successful Program Elements." *American Journal of Health Promotion*. 1:1, Summer 1986.

27. Franz, M.; Hedding, B. and Leitch, G. *Opening the Door to Good Nutrition*. Minneapolis: International Diabetes Center, 1985.

28. US Dept. of Agriculture, Economics Research Service. *Sugar and Sweetener: Outlook and Situation Report,* Washington, D.C., 1987.

29. Food and Drug Administration Sugars Task Force. *Evaluation of Health Aspects of Sugars Contained in Carbohydrate Sweeteners*. Washington, D.C., 1986.

30. Boyd, S. "Artificial Sweeteners: Doubts Linger Over Aspartame While New Products Await Approval." *Environmental Nutrition*. 10:12, December 1987.

31. Wynder, E., M.D. *Book of Health*. American Health Foundation. Franklin Watts, Inc., 1981.

32. National Cancer Institute. *Diet, Nutrition & Cancer Prevention: The Good News*. NIH Publication No. 87-2878, December 1986.

33. Whitney E. and Hamilton, M. *Understanding Nutrition*. St. Paul: West Publishing Co., 1977.

34. Korch, G. "Sodium Content of Potable Water: Dietary Significance." *The Journal of the American Dietetic Association*. 86:1, January 1986.

Chapter 2

1. Anon. "Dietary Fiber and Obesity." *Nutrition & the M.D.* 10:10, October 1984.

2. Longacre, D. *More-With-Less Cookbook*. Scottsdale, PA: Herald Press, 1976.

3. Minnesota Heart Health Program. *Eat to Your Heart's Content: A Guide to Healthier Eating*. Minneapolis: University of Minnesota, 1983.

4. Franz, M., et al. *A Guide to Healthy Eating*. St. Louis Park, MN: Diabetes Center, Incorporated, 1986.

Beverages

1. Pennington, J. and Church, H. *Food Values of Portions Commonly Used.* 14th edition, New York: Harper & Row Publishers, 1985.

Breads

1. Franz, M.; Hedding, B.; and Leitch, G. *Opening the Door to Good Nutrition.* St. Louis Park, MN: International Diabetes Center, 1985.

2. Yoder, E. *Allergy-Free Cooking.* Reading, MA: Addison-Wesley Publishing Co., Inc., 1987.

Salads

1. Anon: "Buying Guide: Greens" *University of California, Berkeley Wellness Letter.* 2:11, August 1986.

Dressings and Sauces

1. USDA, HNIS. *Composition of Foods: Dairy and Egg Products; Raw, Processed and Prepared.* Agriculture Handbook 8-1, revised 1976.

2. USDA, HNIS. *Composition of Foods: Fats and Oils; Raw, Processed, and Prepared.* Agriculture Handbook 8-4, revised 1979.

Grains, Pastas & Legumes

1. Lappe, F. *Diet For a Small Planet.* New York: Ballantine Books, Inc., 1971.

2. Brody, J. *Jane Brody's Good Food Book.* New York: W.W. Norton & Co., 1985.

3. Robertson, L., Flinders, C. and Godfrey, B. *Laurel's Kitchen.* New York: Bantam Books, 1982.

4. Longacre, D. *More-With-Less Cookbook.* Scottsdale, PA: Herald Press, 1976.

5. Minnesota Heart Health Program. *Eat To Your Heart's Content: A Guide to Healthier Eating.* Minneapolis: University of Minnesota, 1983.

Fish & Seafood

1. Hepburn, F.; Exler, J. and Weihrauch, J.L. "Provisional Tables on the Content of Omega-3 Fatty Acids and Other Fat Components of Selected Foods." *Journal of the American Dietetic Association.* 86:6, June 1986.

2. Nettleton, J. *Seafood Nutrition.* Huntington, N.Y.: Osprey Books, 1985.

3. Nettleton, J. *Seafood and Health.* Huntington, N.Y.: Osprey Books, 1987.

Poultry

1. USDA, HNIS. *Composition of Foods: Poultry Products, Raw, Processed and Prepared.* Agriculture Handbook 8-5, revised 1979.

Meats

1. Mullis, R. and Pirie, P. "Lean Meats Make the Grade—A Collaborative Nutrition Intervention Program." *Journal of the American Dietetic Association.* 88:2, February 1988.

2. Minnesota Heart Health Program. *Heartbeat: Fat Facts.* Minneapolis: University of Minnesota, 1987.

3. USDA, HNIS. *Composition of Foods: Beef Products, Raw, Processed, and Prepared.* Agriculture Handbook 8-13, revised 1986.

Sandwiches & Pizza

1. Anon. *Tufts University Diet & Nutrition Letter.* 6:2, April 1988.

2. Franz, Marion. *Fast Food Facts.* Minneapolis: Diabetes Center, Incorporated, 1987.

3. Jacobson, Michael and Fritschner, Sarah. *The Fast Food Guide.* New York: Workman Publishing, 1986.

Appendix

1. Minnesota Department of Health. *Healthy by Choice: The Minnesota Plan for Nutrition and Health*. Minneapolis: Minnesota Dept. of Health, December 1986.

2. U.S. Senate Select Committee on Nutrition and Human Needs. Benefits of human research. *Appendix: A Nutrition and Health II*. Washington, D.C.: U.S. Government Printing Office, 1976.

3 American Heart Association. "Dietary Guidelines for Healthy American Adults". Position Paper. *Circulation*. 77:3, 1988.

4. American Cancer Society. Conference on Nutrition in Cancer Causation and Prevention. *Cancer Research*. 43:5, 1983.

5. National Cancer Institute. *Diet, Nutrition & Cancer Prevention: A Guide to Food Choices*. Bethesda, M.D.: U.S. Department of Health and Human Services; NIH Publication Number 85-2711, July 1985.

6. American Dietetic Association. "American Dietetic Association's Nutrition Recommendations for Women". *Journal of the American Dietetic Association*. 86:12, December 1986.

7. National Institutes of Health. *"Osteoporosis: Consensus Development Conference Statement."* Bethesda, M.D.: National Institutes of Health. 5:3, 1984.

INDEX OF TABLES

COOKING À LA HEART AND ADDITIONAL APPLETREE PRESS PRODUCTS
REORDER PAGE

♥ **COOKING À LA HEART**
Second Edition, Revised and Updated with Diabetic Exchanges.

NEW! Hardcover Item #100 .... $24.95/book
        Softcover Item #125 ..... $19.95/book

♥ **GIFTS OF THE HEART**
Over three dozen new and original recipes with gift ideas.

Softcover Item #200 .... $7.50/book

♥ **TODAY'S SPECIALS**
Recipes from Florida's best restaurants and chefs. All recipes heart healthy.

Item #260 Softcover $14.95/book

♥ **Current Fruit and Vegetable Calendar**
Luscious, full-color photos for every month of the year.

Item #300 .... $9.95/ea.

♥ **From the Heart Aprons**
50/50 poly-cotton fabric. Adjustable strap, 26" x 32", Made in the U.S.A.

Blue Pinstripe w/red heart
Item #400 .... $21.00/each
Blue Pinstripe w/blue heart
Item #410 .... $18.00/each

♥ **Fruit and Vegetable Notecards**
NEW! Two each of four beautiful original pencil drawing, printed on recycled paper.

Item #600 .... $5.25/set
(8 notes and 8 envelopes to a set)

♥ **Heart Recipe Cards**
Two-tone blue heart logo on extra sturdy cards. 20 cards/set

Item #500 .... $3.75/set
3 sets or more $3.00/set

♥ **Heart Gift Tags**
With golden cord that stretches to give your gifts an elegant finishing touch.

Item #550 .... $1.75/set
(4 tags and 4 gold cords to a set)

✂ Cut on dotted line

ORDER FORM

Mail to: Appletree Press, Inc.
151 Good Counsel Drive
Suite 125
Mankato, MN 56001-3198

Ship to:
Name _____

Organization _____

Street Address _____

City _____

State _____ Zip _____

Daytime Phone Number ( ) _____

Make checks payable to: **Appletree Press, Inc.**

☐ Check   ☐ Money Order   ☐ VISA   ☐ Mastercard

VISA   **MasterCard**

Card No. _____

Signature _____

Expiration Date (month/year) _____

Qty.	Item #	Title	Unit Price	Total

Shipping and Handling
up to 20.00 add $4.00
$20.01 to $50 add $6.00
$50.01 to $80 add $7.00
$80.01 to $100 add $8.00
Over $100 add 10%

Subtotal	
Shipping and Handling	
MN state residents add 6.5% sales tax	
TOTAL	

*FAST SERVICE - your order should arrive in only 1-2 weeks
*RAISE FUNDS with select Appletree Press products. Call for details:

TOLL FREE 1-800-322-5679

We at Appletree Press are very pleased and flattered that COOKING À LA HEART was *the* book selected in the 1991 Universal Studios motion picture, Once Around. This funny and touching story is now available for rental (home purchase expected in 1992). We think you will enjoy this critically acclaimed tale of life, love and chance. And, oh, yes, watch for your favorite cookbook in its starring role!

"You have to see this picture."
Gene Siskel,
Siskel & Ebert

"Funny, flavorful and touching!"
David Sheenan,
KNBC-TV

"Out of the blue comes a remarkably fresh comedy! It's thrilling to see a film so honest and humane. Don't let it slip away."
Lawrence Frascella,
US Magazine

PREFACE BY JANE BRODY

Eating healthfully is neither difficult nor boring. Nor is it a life of deprivation and self denial. Rather, as diners who follow the guidelines, recipes and menu plans of Cooking à la Heart *are destined to discover, healthful eating is a stimulating trip into new and familiar taste sensations that can help to keep you enjoying good food for many more years than you otherwise might.*

Jane Brody, Personal Health Columnist
The New York Times

Cooking à la Heart *offers recipes your heart will love!*

Dr. Joyce Nettleton, RD
Nutrition Consultant and Lecturer,
Tufts University

This new and updated edition of Cooking à la Heart *includes the most recent national recommendations for healthy nutrition. It is an excellent resource for all Americans who want to learn and use healthy ways of preparing and serving food.*

Russell V. Luepker, M.D., Professor
Head of Division o...
University of Minn...
Population Panelist

One of the top twenty heart-healthy cookbooks in the country based on Originality, Up-to-Dateness and Scope!

Food & Wine Magazine

Practical and on target!

Runners World Magazine

ISBN 0-9620471-3-9

51995>

9 780962 047138